CliffsNotes® AP

U.S. Government and Politics

CliffsNotes® AP

U.S. Government and Politics

2ND EDITION

by
Paul Soifer

Houghton Mifflin Harcourt
Boston   New York

About the Author

Dr. Paul Soifer is chair of the History Department at Yeshiva University High Schools of Los Angeles, where he teaches both AP U.S. History and AP U.S. Government. He is co-author of *CliffsQuickReview American Government* (1997), *CliffsQuickReview U.S. History I & II* (1998), and *CliffsAP United States History,* 3rd Edition (2001).

Editorial

Acquisitions Editor: Greg Tubach

Project Editor: Elizabeth Kuball

Copy Editor: Elizabeth Kuball

Technical Editor: Nirmal Goswami

Composition

Proofreader: BIM indexing & Proofreading Services

Wiley Publishing, Inc., Composition Services

CliffsNotes® AP U.S. Government and Politics, 2nd Edition

Published by Houghton Mifflin Harcourt

www.hmhbooks.com

Copyright © 2010 Paul Soifer

Library of Congress Cataloging-in-Publication Data

Soifer, Paul.
  Cliffsnotes AP U.S. government and politics / Paul Soifer. -- 2nd ed.
    p. cm.
  ISBN 978-0-470-56214-7 (pbk)
  ISBN 978-0-470-63873-6 (ebk)
  1. United States--Politics and government--Examinations, questions, etc. 2. United States--Politics and government--Examinations--Study guides. I. Title. II. Title: U.S. government and politics. III. Title: United States government and politics.
  JK275.S65 2010b
  320.973'076--dc22

                    2010010324

DOH 10 9 8 7 6 5
4500485387

For information about permission to reproduce selections from this book, write to Permissions, Houghton Mifflin Harcourt Publishing Company, 215 Park Avenue South, New York, New York 10003.

Table of Contents

PART I: SUBJECT AREA REVIEWS WITH PRACTICE QUESTIONS AND ANSWERS

PART II: AP U.S. GOVERNMENT AND POLITICS PRACTICE TESTS

PART III: APPENDIXES

Study Guide Checklist

❑ 1. Become familiar with the format of the exam, particularly the weight given to each subject area in the multiple-choice section.

❑ 2. Review "The Multiple-Choice Section" in the introduction, making sure you understand the different types of multiple-choice questions you may encounter.

❑ 3. Review "The Free-Response Section" in the introduction, paying attention to the suggestions on reading and analyzing the questions. Read the sample essays. Would you have handled the questions differently?

❑ 4. Read over the "Frequently Asked Questions about the AP U.S. Government and Politics Exam" in the introduction.

❑ 5. Use the survey sections in Part I to prepare for taking the practice exams.

❑ 6. Strictly observing the time allotments, take Practice Test 1, section by section (take Section I, check your answers; take Section II, check your answers).

❑ 7. Review the answers and explanations in Section I and the sample essays and comments in Section II.

❑ 8. Analyze your strengths and weaknesses. Did you miss a specific type of multiple-choice questions or were you weak on a particular area—the courts or public policy, for example? Use the analysis for further preparation.

❑ 9. Strictly observing the time allotments, take Practice Test 2, section by section (take Section I, check your answers; take Section II, check your answers). Repeat steps 7 and 8 for Practice Test 2.

❑ 10. Strictly observing the time allotments, take Practice Test 3 straight through (take Section I and Section II, without checking your answers in between). Repeat steps 7 and 8 for Practice Test 3.

Introducing the Advanced Placement U.S. Government and Politics Exam

The Advanced Placement (AP) U.S. Government and Politics Exam is one of the increasingly popular subject exams that the College Board administers in cooperation with high schools and colleges across the country. Over 177,000 students took the exam recently. Although open to all students, most are high school seniors enrolled in a one-semester AP class that is similar both in terms of the depth of coverage and reading requirements to a university-level survey course in U.S. government and politics.

The exam, as well as the typical AP class, covers six broad areas:

- The Constitution, including such principles as the separation of powers and federalism
- Political beliefs and behaviors (how Americans learn about and participate in politics as well as the influence of public opinion)
- The role that political parties, interest groups, and the media play in politics
- The structure of U.S. government (Congress, the presidency, the bureaucracy, and the courts)
- Public policy and how it is formulated
- Civil rights and civil liberties

The successful student will have

- A sound knowledge of the key facts and concepts for each of these topics
- An understanding of the interrelationship between various elements of the political process, such as how interest groups influence the way members of Congress vote
- An ability to analyze and draw conclusions from data related to U.S. politics
- Strong writing skills

Format of the Exam

The AP exam is 2 hours and 25 minutes long and is divided into two sections. Section I consists of 60 multiple-choice questions and has a 45-minute time limit. Section II consists of four free-response or essay questions and has a 100-minute time limit; there is no choice of essays, and each essay carries the same weight—25 percent of your score for Section II. Sections I and II each count for 50 percent of your total score.

The multiple-choice questions are either a sentence stem or a question with five possible answers (A–E). Questions vary in the level of difficulty and become progressively more difficult. The test consists of several question types, and you can be sure there will be questions that ask you to evaluate data in the form of charts, graphs, or tables.

The subject matter of the multiple-choice section follows the six broad content areas outlined earlier, but each subject is not equally covered on the exam—some subjects have more questions than others, as the following table illustrates.

Subject	Percentage of Multiple-Choice Questions in Section I of the Exam
Constitutional basis of U.S. government	**5 to15**
Development and ratification of Constitution	
Separation of powers/checks and balances	
Federalism	
Theories of government	

(continued)

(continued)

Subject	Percentage of Multiple-Choice Questions in Section I of the Exam
Political beliefs and behaviors	**10 to 20**
Basic political beliefs	
Political socialization	
Public opinion	
Voting and other forms of political participation	
Factors shaping political attitudes	
Political parties, interest groups, mass media	**10 to 20**
Political parties and the election process	
Interest groups and political action committees	
Impact of mass media (print/electronic) on politics	
Structure of government	**35 to 45**
Congress	
The presidency	
The bureaucracy	
The federal courts	
Relationships between branches of government	
Impact of public opinion and interest groups	
Impact of political parties and the media	
Public policy	**5 to 15**
Policy formulation and implementation	
Role of Congress and the president	
Role of the bureaucracy and courts	
Impact of public opinion and interest groups	
Impact of political parties and the media	
Civil rights and civil liberties	**5 to 15**
Bill of Rights	
Key Supreme Court cases	
Important legislation	
Significance of the Fourteenth Amendment	

How the government works and how individuals, groups, and institutions participate in the political process can account for as much as 85 percent of the multiple-choice questions. When you are studying for the exam, do not ignore this emphasis.

The free-response section contains four mandatory essay questions. Multiple-part essays are common, and there is often some choice within a particular question. On a recent exam, for example, students selected one out of a list of four interest groups to answer a question on how interest groups influence policymaking by such national political institutions as Congress. It is likely that at least one of the essays in Section II will require you to interpret and draw conclusions from a graph, table, or chart. Students taking a recent exam were presented with a chart showing the reelection rates for incumbent members of the House of Representatives and the Senate, and were asked to explain the factors that contributed to the electoral success of incumbents and the consequences for U.S. politics. Multiple-part essay questions are common.

The subject matter that Section II covers is drawn from the same content areas as Section I. To get an idea of the topics that may come up, here is a summary of essay questions that appeared on recent exams:

- The changing role of majority rule in the U.S. political system
- The factors affecting voter turnout and analysis of an institution other than elections that connects people to the government
- The difficulty of enacting legislation given the rules in the House of Representatives and the Senate
- The role of the news media in setting the political agenda in light of the changing viewing patterns of network news programs
- The different goals of political parties and interest groups and how each can support the other
- Social Security as an entitlement program and the threats to its solvency in the future
- The policymaking functions of federal agencies and their relationship with Congress
- Congress as a bicameral legislature and the unique powers of the House of Representatives and the Senate
- The formal and informal powers of the president and Congress in conducting foreign policy
- The techniques used by interest groups to achieve their goals and an examination of why specific interest groups use the techniques they do
- The challenges faced by and the contributions of third political parties to the political system
- How divided government and the increasing cost of elections have affected trust and confidence in government
- The impact of divided government on presidential appointments
- The distribution of government benefits to children and the elderly and how they are affected by politics
- How political institutions help or hinder the achievement of political goals by racial minorities
- The factors affecting voter turnout in presidential and midterm elections

The exam may change in terms of emphasis of subject matter and structure. For example, the mandatory essay format of the free-response section was introduced in 1998, and that year's exam did not include a data question. Your AP U.S. Government and Politics teacher knows about any changes in the exam that the College Board may introduce, but it is always a good idea for you to visit the College Board's AP Web site (www.collegeboard.com/student/testing/ap/sub_usgov.html?usgolpol) on your own.

Scoring of the Exam

The College Board scores the exam on a five-point scale:

5 Extremely well qualified   2 Possibly qualified

4 Well qualified   1 No recommendation

3 Qualified

A score of 3 is considered passing. The breakdown of the scores on a recent exam was as follows:

Grade	Percentage of Students Earning Grade
5	13.1
4	17.0
3	25.4
2	24.2
1	20.3

Source: http://apcentral.collegeboard.com/apc/public/repository/ap09_USGoPo_GradeDistributions.pdf.

Students who do well on the AP exam—and this usually means receiving a score of 4 or 5—may get credit or placement from the college they attend. Colleges and universities establish their own policies regarding what scores qualify. The Web sites of the colleges you are applying to will explain their AP policy, or you can check with your college advisor.

Grading the Exam

A computer automatically scores the answer sheet for the multiple-choice questions. Your score on the multiple-choice section is based on the number of questions answered correctly. No points are taken off for incorrect answers and no points are awarded if you leave questions unanswered. This scoring method is intended to encourage you to answer all the multiple-choice questions. If you can eliminate two or three answers, select the best of the remaining answers.

A group of college professors and high school teachers grade the essay portion of the exam in June. AP readers follow scoring guidelines that indicate the criteria for awarding points for the various elements of a question. The four essays may have different point values depending on their complexity and the amount of information that the test asked for, but all the essays carry the same weight—each essay question counts for a quarter of your grade in Section II.

The Multiple-Choice Section

You have 45 minutes to answer 60 multiple-choice questions in Section I, which is worth 50 percent of your total score. The number of questions on a particular topic will generally follow the percentages presented in the "Format of the Exam" section, earlier in this introduction. If you concentrate on the Constitution in preparing for the exam, and just skim over how Congress works, the ability of the president to control the bureaucracy, and the way the Supreme Court reaches a decision, you may well find the multiple-choice questions more challenging than you expect.

The cardinal rule for the multiple-choice section is to read the entire question or sentence stem and all five choices before you mark your answer. If you think the answer is obvious just from skimming the question, read everything carefully anyway. After you've done this, the correct answer may, indeed, be crystal clear. There is a range of difficulty on the exam, and some questions are easier than others.

If you get stuck, the trick is to eliminate as many answers as possible. Although each question has one correct answer, the other choices may not be wrong. Several answers may be good answers, just not as good as the correct one. Put a line through the answers in the question booklet that you can eliminate.

A.
B.
C.
D.
E.

The process of elimination should make it easier to come up with the correct answer. If you still can't figure out the correct answer, you are faced with the guessing dilemma.

As noted earlier, you are encouraged to answer each multiple-choice question. But if you do skip a question, make sure that you fill in the correct space on the answer sheet for the next question. A mistake in filling in the answer sheet can be disastrous.

Time is a factor on the multiple-choice section. You have an average of 45 seconds for each question. You won't need that much time for some questions, but you may need a little more than 45 seconds for others. You can't afford to allow yourself to get stuck on any one question—move on! *Remember:* The questions get progressively more difficult as you go through the section, so do not let yourself get too cocky in the beginning. Also, keep in mind that there are typically three to five questions based on charts, graphs, and tables, which you have to analyze a bit more closely. In the following sections, you find examples of multiple-choice question types.

Direct Sentence Stem or Question

Most questions consist of a sentence stem where the possible answers complete the statement or a question where one of the possible choices is a correct statement. The latter often asks you which statement about something is true or is "most accurate."

Examples

1. The principal way that the president can influence the position that the Supreme Court takes on controversial issues is by

   A. cutting the budget for the Department of Justice
   B. asking for the resignation of a justice who consistently votes against the administration
   C. nominating justices to the Supreme Court who share the president's point of view
   D. proposing legislation to increase the number of justices
   E. meeting with members of the Supreme Court on a regular basis

The correct answer is **C**. The question is essentially about checks and balances, and the only power the president can exercise over the Supreme Court is to nominate justices when a vacancy arises. Justices serve for life specifically to free the Supreme Court from political interference (**B**), and President Franklin Roosevelt's attempt to "pack" the Court by adding new justices was flatly rejected by Congress (**D**).

2. The purpose of the Miranda warning is to protect the rights of individuals under the

   A. First Amendment
   B. Third Amendment
   C. Fourth Amendment
   D. Fifth Amendment
   E. Eighth Amendment

The correct answer is **D**. The Miranda warning, which the Supreme Court outlined in *Miranda v. Arizona* (1966) informs people in police custody and subject to interrogation that they have the right to remain silent because of the Fifth Amendment protection against self-incrimination.

---

3. Which of the following is an example of the revolving door?

    A. A company vice president is sent to Washington to meet with members of the state's congressional delegation.

    B. A staff member of the Senate Banking Committee is appointed to a post in the Department of the Treasury.

    C. An official in the Department of State resigns to take a job at a major university.

    D. A special assistant to the president resigns to run for Congress.

    E. A staff scientist leaves the Environmental Protection Agency to take a job with an environment lobby.

The correct answer is **E**. The term *revolving door* refers to a former official involved in lobbying the very people that he worked with while in government service. None of the other choices applies.

---

4. Which of the following statements best describes the role of the states in amending the Constitution?

    A. The states are responsible for ratifying amendments either through their legislatures or through state conventions.

    B. The states cannot reject an amendment proposed by two-thirds of both houses of Congress.

    C. State legislatures can propose and ratify amendments on their own, bypassing Congress.

    D. States have no role in proposing amendments.

    E. Ratifying an amendment requires a vote of two-thirds of the state legislatures.

The correct answer is **A**. It correctly explains the two methods of ratification under Article V. States can have a role in proposing amendments by recommending to Congress a national convention for that purpose, and you should know that three-fourths of the state legislatures are required for ratification.

Reverse Multiple-Choice

This type of multiple-choice includes the words NOT, EXCEPT, or LEAST in a sentence stem or question. These words, which always appear in capital letters, tell you that the correct answer is the one that isn't true or is the least likely choice. The reverse multiple-choice makes it very important to read each question completely and carefully; you never know when you may run into a NOT, EXCEPT, or LEAST that can turn around the question completely.

Examples

---

1. All the following Supreme Court decisions dealt with First Amendment issues EXCEPT:

    A. *Chaplinsky v. New Hampshire*

    B. *Engel v. Vitale*

    C. *Mapp v. Ohio*

    D. *The New York Times Co. v. Sullivan*

    E. *Texas v. Johnson*

The correct answer is **C**. *Mapp v. Ohio* (1961) is a search-and-seizure case (Fourth Amendment) that extended the exclusionary rule to the states. The other choices pertain to different parts of the First Amendment—freedom of speech (**A** and **E**), the Establishment Clause (**B**), and freedom of the press (**D**).

2. Which of the following is NOT a valid statement about voting behavior?

   A. African Americans show overwhelming support for Democratic candidates.
   B. College students are more likely to vote than older Americans are.
   C. The more ideologically committed members of a party vote in presidential primaries.
   D. The Democratic Party has an edge over Republicans among women voters.
   E. People who consider themselves very religious vote for conservative candidates.

The correct answer is **B**. Historically, young voters (ages 18 to 24) have the lowest voter turnout of any age group. Answer **D** refers to the so-called "gender gap."

3. A president is LEAST likely to appoint which of the following to the Supreme Court?

   A. a woman justice of a state supreme court
   B. a Court of Appeals judge from the president's home state
   C. a Hispanic who served as solicitor general
   D. a Court of Appeals judge from the other party
   E. a Harvard Law School professor

The correct answer is **D**. The issue the question addresses is what factors a president considers in making an appointment to the Supreme Court. Although you may like to think that politics isn't a consideration, the fact is that presidents rarely go outside their party in making judicial appointments. The Constitution does not specify any qualifications for a Supreme Court justice.

Multiple Multiple-Choice

This type of question presents you with three to five possible answers; more than one of which *may* be correct. I emphasize *may* because, on occasion, there may be only one right answer. Again, you need to read the questions carefully, eliminate the answers that do not apply, and realize that two or more answers are usually correct. A multiple multiple-choice may include a NOT or an EXCEPT.

Examples

1. Which of the following is part of the consideration of a bill in the House of Representatives?

   I. A hearing is held on the bill by a standing committee.
   II. The committee issues a report on the bill.
   III. A rule is issued setting a limit on the floor debate.
   IV. A cloture vote is taken on the House floor.

   A. I only
   B. I and II only
   C. I, II, and III only
   D. I, II, and IV only
   E. I, II, III, and IV

The correct answer is **C**. A cloture vote is used to end a filibuster, which is allowed only under the Senate rules. The Committee on Rules is unique to the House of Representatives.

2. All the following are arguments in favor of deregulation EXCEPT:

    I.   Deregulation reduces the size of the government by eliminating the need for federal agencies.

    II.   Deregulation increases federal revenue by raising corporate taxes.

    III.   Deregulation encourages competition and reduces the cost to consumers.

    IV.   Deregulation enhances worker safety and environmental protection.

    A.   I only

    B.   I and II only

    C.   I, II, and IV only

    D.   I and III only

    E.   II and IV only

The correct answer is **E**. The increased corporate tax rate is not specifically tied to deregulation; opponents of deregulation argue that worker safety and environmental protection suffer when we eliminate or relax federal rules governing an industry. A case can be made that, in the short run, deregulation increases competition by encouraging new companies to enter the market.

Data Questions

The multiple-choice section includes questions based on the interpretation of data presented in a map, table, chart, or graph, and, on occasion, a political cartoon. You need to be able to identify the trends shown by the data and draw conclusions from the information. The questions themselves often ask you to determine which statement the data best supports. Because there is usually at least one data question in Section II, it is a good idea to study the numerous graphic presentations in your AP course textbook a little more closely than you otherwise may. The more familiar you are with the various ways political scientists organize and present data, the more confident you'll be when you come across these questions.

Examples

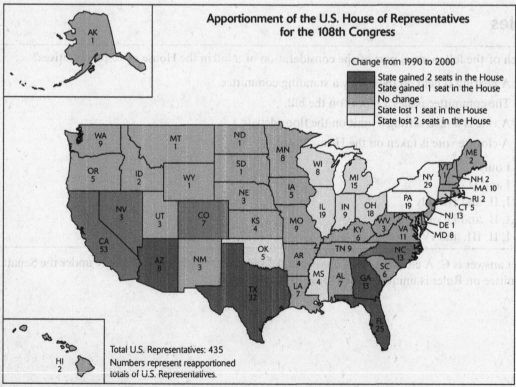

Apportionment of the U.S. House of Representatives for the 108th Congress

Change from 1990 to 2000

- State gained 2 seats in the House
- State gained 1 seat in the House
- No change
- State lost 1 seat in the House
- State lost 2 seats in the House

Total U.S. Representatives: 435
Numbers represent reapportioned totals of U.S. Representatives.

Source: U.S. Census Bureau.

1. What conclusions can be draw from the results of the 2000 census shown on the map?

    A. New York and Pennsylvania will not be battleground states in the 2004 presidential election.

    B. The political clout of the Sun Belt states continues to increase.

    C. The population decline in the Midwest has slowed.

    D. Support for Republicans is likely to remain unchanged in the Great Plains states.

    E. California will remain a Democratic state.

The answer is **B**. The shift in population from the Rust Belt (Northeast and Midwest) to the Sun Belt (South and West) is a long-term trend. As the Sun Belt states gain population and larger congressional delegations, the political influence of the region increases. Although New York and Pennsylvania lost representation, they remain large electoral vote states (29 and 19, respectively). The information that the map provides does not support choices **C**, **D**, and **E**.

2000 Democratic Party Identification for Select Demographic Groups

Group	Percentage
Education	
Grade school/some high school	58
High school diploma	53
Some college	48
College degree/post-graduate	44
Gender	
Males	46
Females	53
Occupation	
Professionals	46
White collar	50
Blue collar	55
Unskilled	50
Farmers	51
Race	
Whites	44
African Americans	83
Union/Nonunion	
Union	61
Nonunion	48
Region	
South	47
North	51

Source: The American National Election Studies (www.electionstudies.org). The ANES Guide to Public Opinion and Electoral Behavior. Ann Arbor, MI: University of Michigan, Center for Political Studies [producer and distributor].

2. Which of the following statements accurately reflects the character of Democratic voters in the 2000 presidential election based on the data in the table?

    A.   The New Deal coalition is still a factor in U.S. politics.
    B.   The gender gap between the two parties is narrowing.
    C.   Democrats draw their support from the less educated and less affluent.
    D.   Union members and blue-collar workers are identical.
    E.   Farmers are conservative Democrats.

The correct answer is **C**. The specific information on the educational level of the respondents as well as the data for occupation support this choice. Although African Americans and union members were important components of the New Deal coalition, so was the South. The data indicates stronger support for Democrats in the North, and you should know that Republicans have made significant gains in the South in congressional and presidential elections. You can't say anything about the gender gap because you have data from only one year. Farmers who identify with the Democratic Party may well be conservative, but the table gives no information on ideology.

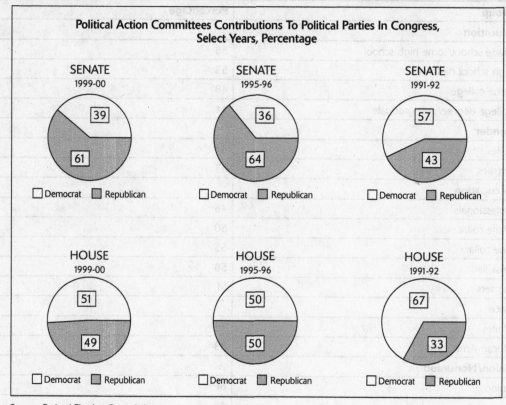

Source: Federal Election Commission.

3. What generalization can be made about political action committee contributions to Congress based on the above charts?

   A. Political action committees give more money to members of the House of Representatives than to members of the Senate.
   B. Political action committees give more money to incumbents than to challengers, irrespective of the party.
   C. Political action committees give more money to Republicans than to Democrats.
   D. Political action committees base their contributions on which party controls Congress.
   E. Political action committees give more money in a presidential election year.

The correct answer is **D**. Do not get fooled. Answers **A** and **B** are correct statements about how political action committees (PACs) operate, but they are not supported by the chart. Because the data does not give actual amounts of the contributions, you can't determine whether PACs give more money to Republicans than to Democrats or more money in a presidential election year. You can get the right answer by process of elimination. But you should also know that the Democrats controlled both houses of Congress in 1991 and 1992 and that the Republicans gained control of Congress in 1994, but with a small majority in the House.

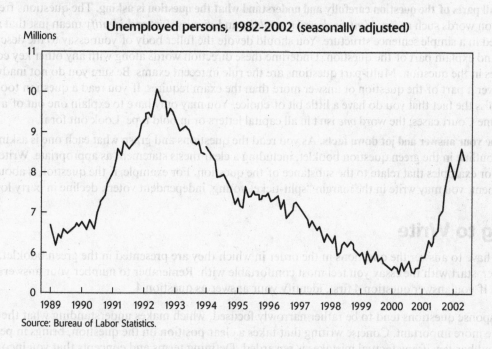

Unemployed persons, 1982-2002 (seasonally adjusted)

Source: Bureau of Labor Statistics.

4. What action was the Federal Reserve likely to take in response to the unemployment picture shown on the graph?

   A. Lower interest rates as unemployment rose.
   B. Raise interest rates in the aftermath of the events of September 11, 2001.
   C. Take no action because the overall economy was sound despite rising unemployment.
   D. Require member banks to keep more money in reserve to fight rising unemployment.
   E. Require the Federal Deposit Insurance Corporation (FDIC) to raise its insurance limit.

The correct answer is **A**. This question has less to do with unemployment per se than with how the Federal Reserve System operates. By lowering interest rates, the Federal Reserve System encourages business to borrow for expansion and new equipment, which can lead to a greater demand for workers. Answer **D** is a power that the Federal Reserve has, but it would have a negative impact on employment. Requiring higher reserves means there is less money for loans and interest rates go up. The Federal Reserve has no influence over the FDIC, and raising or lowering the maximum insured deposits would not affect employment. Taking no action is extremely unlikely given the sharp rise in unemployment in the early 1990s and 2001–2002.

The Free-Response Section

Section II consists of four, frequently multi-part, essay questions, and you must answer all four. You are given 100 minutes for this part of the exam, and the suggested writing time is 25 minutes for each essay. The essays have equal weight even though the scoring guidelines are different from one question to the next; your score on the free-response questions is 50 percent of your total grade.

Not having a choice is certainly a bit intimidating. What if you draw a complete blank on a question? Take confidence in the strong foundation that your AP U.S. Government class gave you and in your own preparation for the exam. Also, keep in mind that there is usually some flexibility in one or more of the essays, and the questions themselves do take into account the obvious time constraints. Keep the following points in mind before you actually tackle the essays:

- **Read the directions carefully and take them to heart.** Do not begin to write immediately. Take the time to review all four questions, and remember that readers are looking for factual information to prove points and good examples to illustrate the argument.

- **Read all parts of the question carefully and understand what the question is asking.** The questions frequently use direction words such as *list, identify, describe, explain,* and *discuss. List* and *identify* mean just that and can be handled in a simple sentence structure. You should devote the fuller body of your essay to the describe, discuss, and explain part of the question. Underline these direction words along with any other key concepts or phrases in the question. Multi-part questions are the rule in recent exams. Be sure you do not inadvertently skip over a part of the question or answer more than the exam requires. If you read a question too fast, you may miss the fact that you do have a little bit of choice. You may only have to explain one out of a list of four Supreme Court cases; the word *one* isn't in all capital letters or in bold type. Look out for it.

- **Outline your answer and jot down facts.** As you read the questions and grasp what each one is asking, prepare a short outline in the green question booklet, including a clear thesis statement as appropriate. Write down key terms or examples that relate to the substance of the question. For example, if the question is about party dealignment, you may write in the margin "split-ticket voting, independent voters, decline in party loyalty."

Starting to Write

You do not have to answer the questions in the order in which they are presented in the green booklet. As a confidence builder, start with the essay you feel most comfortable with. Remember to number your answers correctly if you do this. If you answer question 4 first, identify your answer as question 4.

The free-response questions tend to be rather narrowly focused, which makes understanding what the question wants all the more important. Concise writing that takes a clear position on the question, brings in pertinent examples, and has few if any factual mistakes is rewarded. Defining terms and concepts that you incorporate into your answer shows a command of the subject. Try to avoid just spouting verbiage even when you are stumped by a particular question; readers can spot that a mile away. When you see an essay that asks you, for example, to identify and discuss the role of the political leadership in the Congress, you may be tempted to write everything you know about the organization of Congress and how it functions, but such an answer may well earn no points. The readers expect you to stay on point, and the multi-part structure of the questions should help. Just be aware of going overboard.

Time management is a factor. Twenty-five minutes per question is a valid guide, but remember that it isn't an absolute rule; you won't be told by the proctor to move on to the next question when that time period is up. You'll find some questions easier to answer because of your mastery of the material or what the essay is asking; you may need a little more time to analyze the data questions than the others. The point is to know where you are at any point in the exam, and make sure you give yourself enough time to write on all four questions.

Tackling Data Questions

You can expect at least one question to include a chart, graph, table, map, or political cartoon. Here are a few examples from previous exams:

- Graph showing Social Security receipts, spending, and reserve estimates, 2001–2035
- Political cartoon of 2000 Green Party candidate Ralph Nader
- Graph showing federal civilian employees and state and local government employment, 1945–2000
- Table comparing ages and viewing frequency of network news over time
- Charts showing mandatory spending as a percentage of the federal budget
- Map showing voting patterns by state in select presidential elections

The data essay invariably has at least two parts:

- **The first part asks you to identify patterns or trends in the data or to summarize the data.** A recent exam asked students to identify two trends on a graph of reelection rates for incumbents in the House and the Senate. Possible answers include that reelection rates in both houses were high, House incumbents were reelected at a higher rate than Senators, or reelection rates fluctuated more dramatically in the Senate than in the House.
- **The second part of the question usually, but not always, requires you to explain or discuss points raised by what you found in the data.** In the preceding example, the other parts of the question asked about the factors that contribute to the incumbency effect and its political consequences. The essay often states that you need to use both the data and "your knowledge of U.S. politics."

Example 1

1. Since the ratification of the Bill of Rights, the Supreme Court has expanded and restricted its interpretation of the civil liberties protections that Americans enjoy.

   a. Identify one Supreme Court decision that has expanded and one decision that restricted rights in the following areas:

      - freedom of speech
      - unreasonable search and seizure

   b. For the cases selected, discuss the reasoning of the Court.

Scoring Guidelines

Part (a): 4 points (1 point for each case identified)

Part (b): 4 points (1 point for each case discussed)

- Freedom of speech—expansion
  - *Tinker v. Des Moines Independent Community School District* (1969)
  - *Texas v. Johnson* (1989)
- Freedom of speech—restriction
  - *Schenck v. United States* (1919)
  - *Chaplinsky v. New Hampshire* (1942)
  - *Red Lion Broadcasting Co. v. Federal Communications Commission* (1969)
- Unreasonable search and seizure—expansion
  - *Weeks v. United States* (1914)
  - *Mapp v. Ohio* (1962)

- Unreasonable search and seizure—restriction
  - *Nix v. Williams* (1984)
  - *United States v. Leon* (1984)
- Reasoning of the Court
  - *Tinker v. Des Moines Independent Community School District* (1969)—symbolic speech, rights of students
  - *Texas v. Johnson* (1989)—flag burning protected as symbolic speech
  - *Schenck v. United States* (1919)—clear and present danger test, wartime limitations
  - *Chaplinsky v. New Hampshire* (1942)—fighting words not protected
  - *Red Lion Broadcasting Co. v. Federal Communications Commission* (1969)—regulation of commercial speech
  - *Weeks v. United States* (1914)—evidence that is illegally obtained can't be used in court, exclusionary rule
  - *Mapp v. Ohio* (1962)—incorporation case, exclusionary rule applied to the states
  - *Nix v. Williams* (1984)—inevitable discovery exception to the exclusionary rule
  - *United States v. Leon* (1984)—good faith exception to the exclusionary rule

Sample Essay

Depending on its makeup and judicial philosophy, the Supreme Court has often expanded or restricted its understanding of the scope of the protections under the Bill of Rights. The decision in *Schenck v. United States* clearly put limits on freedom of speech, while these rights were broadened through its ruling in *Texas v. Johnson*. Through *Mapp v. Ohio*, the Court strengthened protection against unreasonable search and seizure, but, later, a more conservative Court weakened those protections. The Court's landmark decision in *Schenck v. United States* established the clear and present danger test. This meant that speech was not protected if it would likely lead to an illegal action. The circumstances in which the words are spoken is important. The illustration of the clear and present danger test is that you can't yell "Fire!" in a crowded theater. The Court also recognized that speech that may be legitimate in peacetime can be restricted in wartime. *Schenck* did not actually involve words per se; the issue was the distribution of flyers against the draft during World War I. Similarly, *Texas v. Johnson* involved an action—burning an American flag during a political protest. The Court had recognized that certain actions make a political statement that is protected under the First Amendment. These types of action are symbolic speech, and in *Texas v. Johnson* the Court ruled that flag burning was such an action. While Congress tried to get around the decision by legislation declaring burning an American flag a federal crime, the Court struck down that law as well.

The question under the Fourth Amendment is what makes a search "unreasonable." The Court long held in federal cases that evidence that was illegally obtained (for example, without a search warrant or through an invalid search warrant) was not admissible in court. This principle was extended to the states in *Mapp v. Ohio*, where the issue was pornographic materials seized by the police without a warrant. Courts have also recognized the "fruit of the poisonous tree" (additional evidence found as a direct result of illegally obtained evidence also can't be used at trial). The more conservative Supreme Court in the 1970s and 1980s saw blanket application of the exclusionary rule as an undue limitation on the police. In the need to balance the rights of the individual against the rights of society, the Court gave more leeway to the police in several decisions. In *United States v. Leon* (1984), the Court established the good faith exception to the exclusionary rule. If the police acted on what they believed was a valid search warrant, the evidence collected through that warrant was admissible in court even if it turned out the warrant was flawed in some way. The police had "acted in good faith."

Comments

This essay is well written and the student clearly demonstrates a knowledge of the information. Rather succinctly in an essay format, the student identifies the cases and gives an idea as to why the Court sometimes rules one way and then the other. The essay is to the point and shows an understanding of the issues. Pointing out that the Court also declared the Federal Flag Protection Act unconstitutional, noting the concept of the "fruit of the poisonous tree," and noting that the decision in Leon reflected the thinking of a more conservative court than the one that decided Mapp made the essay stronger. Score = 8.

Example 2

Federal Revenues and Outlays, 1962-2001, Billions of Dollars

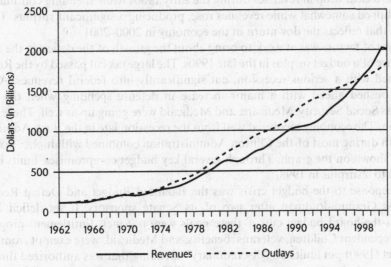

Source: Congressional Budget Office.

1. Based on the graph and your knowledge of U.S. economic policy between 1980 and 2000, perform the following tasks:

   a. Summarize the information presented on the graph, focusing on the period 1980 to 2000.

   b. Identify two factors that explain the data during the 1980s through mid-1990s and two factors that explain the data in the late 1990s.

   c. Discuss how Congress responded to the developments shown on the graph.

Scoring Guidelines

Part (a): 2 points maximum

Part (b): 4 points (1 point for each response/reaction discussed)

Part (c): 3 points maximum

- Summarize information on outlays exceeding revenues, the growth of the deficit, the surplus in the late 1990s, and recent declines in revenues
- Factors in the 1980s through mid-1990s and late 1990s
  - Factors in the 1980s through mid-1990s: recession in the early 1980s, the 1981 tax cut, increase in military spending, increase in mandatory spending
  - Factors in the late 1990s: strong economy, reductions in spending, tax increases, budget deficit reduction legislation
- Congressional response
  - Budget Reduction Act
  - Gramm–Rudman Act
  - Budget Enforcement Act
  - Omnibus Budget Reconciliation Act
  - Omnibus Reconciliation Act
  - Contract with America

Sample Essay

According to the data presented on the graph, federal outlays (expenditures) began to exceed revenues in the 1970s; the federal deficit (outlays minus revenues) grew dramatically, however, in the following two decades. There is a clear drop in revenues during the early 1980s while spending continued to rise. During the 1990s, outlays dipped somewhat while revenues rose, producing a significant surplus. The latest data show a drop in revenue that reflects the downturn in the economy in 2000–2001.

A combination of factors was at work to bring about the growth of the deficit in the 1980s and early 1990s and the emergence of a budget surplus in the late 1990s. The large tax cut passed by the Reagan Administration in 1981 combined with a serious recession, cut significantly into federal revenues. At the same time, the administration pushed ahead with a major increase in defense spending when the costs of entitlement programs such as Social Security, Medicare, and Medicaid were going up as well. These developments led the deficit to balloon. The economy recovered well from the recession late in the Bush Administration; the strong economic growth during most of the Clinton Administration combined with higher taxes brought about the rise in revenues shown on the graph. Through several key budget compromises, limits on spending were put in place that led to a surplus in 1998.

Congress's response to the budget crisis was the Balanced Budget and Deficit Reduction Act of 1985, better known as Gramm–Rudman after two of its Senate sponsors. It set deficit reduction goals, and instituted across-the-board budget cuts if these goals were not met. Entitlement programs such as Aid to Families with Dependent Children, veterans' benefits, and Medicaid, were exempt from the cuts. The Budget Enforcement Act (1990) put limits on "discretionary" spending that was authorized through appropriations, such as defense and domestic programs. In two difficult budget battles with Congress, the Clinton Administration put through tax increases on wealthier Americans and spending cuts (1993); the 1997 budget reduced both spending on entitlement programs as well as discretionary outlays. The cumulative effect of these legislative actions was to gradually reduce the deficit, but it was the strong economy that ultimately created the surplus.

Comment

The student does a good job in describing the information on the graph; the key points to make are, of course, the growth of the deficit and the shift to a budget surplus. The student succinctly explains the reason for the budget crisis in the 1980s; it may have been helpful to put Reagan's policies into context a bit regarding supply-side economics and intensification of the Cold War. The discussion of Congress's response to the budget issues isn't as strong: How effective was Gramm–Rudman and how serious was Congress about making cuts? The 1993 and 1997 budget compromises need to be expanded on, as does the Republican side of the issue. How did the Clinton Administration and the Republican-controlled Congress work out their differences? What did the Contract with America, the Republican legislative and policy agenda in 1994, have to say about the budget? Score = 7.

Frequently Asked Questions about the AP U.S. Government and Politics Exam

Q. What should I bring to the exam?

A. The essentials are at least two well-sharpened no. 2 pencils with good erasers and several blue or black ballpoint pens. You must fill in the answer sheet for the multiple-choice section with a no. 2 pencil and write the essays in pen. Make sure your pens write clearly and don't smudge. You should also have your high school code number, your Social Security number, and a watch with you. The proctor keeps you informed about the time, but it's always a good idea to be able to check the time yourself. If you must have a pager or cellphone with you, make sure to turn them off before you enter the exam. A much better idea is to leave them at home on exam day.

There is no reason to lug around books; notes; a pencil case filled with markers, highlighters, and corrective fluid; an iPod; a laptop; or any other equipment. Travel light. If you really don't know the material by the day of the exam, skimming over your notes or text in the minutes before you sit down isn't going to help you.

Q. What happens if I draw a complete blank on a multiple-choice question?

A. If you can't narrow down the possible choices at all, your best bet is to leave the answer blank and come back to it if you have time. The computer doesn't deduct points for a blank answer. You must make sure, however, that you answer the next question in the right place on the answer sheet, and never make any mark on the answer sheet indicating that you have to come back to that question. On the other hand, if you can eliminate two or, better yet, three choices, go ahead and make an educated guess. The odds are with you that you'll get the right answer.

Q. How long should my essays be in the free-response question?

A. How much you write isn't as important as what you write. Professors and teachers score the essays on content, and very often a reader is looking for rather specific information. You obviously need to write enough to answer the question in all its parts. The fact that the essays on the exam are usually multi-part should allow you to organize your response effectively. Also, remember that with four essays, you have to budget your time. If you find yourself writing page after page on one question, you're going to have trouble giving adequate attention to one or more of the other essays.

Q. Where should I outline my ideas for the essays?

A. Use the green booklet that has the questions for Section II. As you read each question, underline words that give you direction on how to approach the question—for example, *identify two* and *discuss*. Write down examples or facts relating to the subject of the essay in the margins. There is enough room in the green booklet to briefly outline your essay for each question.

Q. Do spelling and penmanship count?

A. The readers appreciate that you're taking the exam under pressure and that time can be a factor. The occasional misspelled word won't be a problem. If you know that your handwriting is poor, make the effort to write more clearly on the exam. If your essay is illegible, it won't receive the highest score possible regardless of the content. Readers can't spend a great deal of their time deciphering what you write. For the same reason, you also have to be wary about adding information to your essay after you finish it. Last-minute revisions scattered here and there can create the impression that you organized your essay poorly. Again, readers won't necessarily have the time to figure out just where these additions are supposed to go. Avoid this problem by planning your answers as fully as possible.

Q. How much reading should I do for the exam?

A. Your AP course determines the amount of reading that you need to do. Most likely, you'll be using a college-level textbook in U.S. government and politics and perhaps a reader that includes important Supreme Court decisions and articles on important topics by political scientists. You'll read the Constitution and very likely one or more articles from *The Federalist Papers*. Your teacher may assign you a research paper or a WebQuest on the Internet. The AP course should give you all the preparation you need for the exam, and you shouldn't have to do any special reading.

Q. What about reviewing for the exam?

A. See the following section for tips on how best to use this book to study for the exam. Many students take the AP U.S. Government and Politics class in the fall semester, and the test is in May. You certainly don't want to walk into the exam without having thought about the subject since January. Your teacher may hold review sessions in the spring, but you can be proactive and form your own study group, too. Don't bother trying to cram for the exam. Your best bet is to take a few weeks off after the AP class is over, and then set up a schedule that allows you to review the material in a systematic fashion in the months leading up to the exam.

Q. When are the scores sent and who receives them?

A. The exam is graded in June, and the scores are sent to the colleges that you indicate on your answer sheet, to your high school, and to you. You should receive your score no later than the end of July. If you want to get them earlier (the first few days in July), you can phone the AP Program at 888-308-0013 or 609-771-7366. There is an additional fee, payable by credit card only, to receive your scores early; you'll also need your AP number and Social Security number.

Q. What if I don't get a good grade on the exam?

A. A score of 3 is considered passing on the AP exam. If you score lower, there are a couple of things to keep in mind: If you take the exam during your senior year, as most AP U.S. Government and Politics students do, your score is not reported until July. If you've already been accepted to the college of your choice, then the only question is whether you'll qualify for credit or advance standing. If you take the exam as a junior or earlier, the simple fact that you took the test early says a good deal about you, despite your score; it says that you challenged yourself with a rigorous college-level course.

Q. Can I send my score to additional colleges?

A. Yes. You can arrange to have additional reports sent to colleges by contacting the AP Program at the phone numbers noted earlier. Again, there is an additional fee, and you'll need the four-digit college codes for the additional schools.

Q. Can I withhold or cancel my score?

A. The answer to both questions is yes. Requests for either grade withholding or grade cancellation must be made in writing to the AP Program by June 15; there is an additional fee for both services. For information on the fees and where to send the request, see www.collegeboard.com/student/testing/ap/exgrd_set.html.

How to Use This Book

1. **This book is not a substitute or a shortcut to reading the college-level text in U.S. government and politics and additional materials that are required as part of your AP course.** Nor is it a substitute or a shortcut for absorbing the information presented in that class, which is always enhanced by active participation.

2. **The purpose of the book is twofold:** to give you an understanding of what to expect on the AP U.S. Government and Politics Exam in terms of structure and types of questions, and to provide you with the helpful tools to review the subject matter of the exam.

3. **When you're taking the AP course, you can use the subject area review chapters to help you study for quizzes or exams.** The key terms in each chapter are in bold, and important Supreme Court decisions are in italics. Fuller information on both can be found in the relevant appendixes. Each chapter also includes 15 multiple-choice questions with answers and explanations. These are helpful at exam time, but don't mark the answers in the book; you want to go over these questions again when you review for the AP exam.

4. **When you begin preparing for the AP exam, the subject area review chapters give you a manageable synopsis on the topics that may come up.** You have the opportunity to test yourself on each topic by going over the practice multiple-choice questions again; if you find that you're weak on a particular subject, you can go back to your textbook for a more in-depth clarification, or use the Web sites listed for each topic to get more information. The appendixes of key terms and Supreme Court decisions give you the essential facts you need.

PART I

SUBJECT AREA REVIEWS WITH PRACTICE QUESTIONS AND ANSWERS

The Constitution

The U.S. Constitution is the starting point for the study of U.S. government and politics. It is a document that presents a republican form of government under which authority is divided among the legislative, executive, and judicial branches to ensure separation of powers; it also provides a system of checks and balances so that one branch doesn't dominate the others. The Constitution lays the framework for the relationship between the federal government and the states (known as federalism) and lays out the fundamental civil liberties and civil rights that Americans have strived for more than 200 years to expand and preserve.

The Historical Background to the Constitution

As the American colonies moved toward a formal break with Great Britain, early steps were taken to create a new political system. While the First Continental Congress (1774) limited itself to issuing statements of rights and principles, the Second Continental Congress (May 1775) assumed the functions of government. The Second Continental Congress created a postal system, established the Continental Army with George Washington at its head, and made decisions regarding foreign policy. Most important, the Second Continental Congress formally issued the Declaration of Independence on July 4, 1776.

Following an opening section that briefly states its purpose, the Declaration of Independence, written by Thomas Jefferson, is divided into three parts:

- **Theoretical Justification for Independence:** Here, Jefferson drew heavily from the English political philosopher John Locke's *Second Treatise on Civil Government* (1689), particularly the concept of natural rights—"life, liberty, and the pursuit of happiness"—and the social compact theory of government. The social compact theory of government holds that people create governments to protect their rights; when a government breaks that contract, the people have the right to create a new government.
- **Grievances against the King:** The bulk of the Declaration of Independence is a long list of specific charges against King George III. Jefferson's original draft of the grievances section held the king responsible for slavery and the slave trade in the colonies, as well as for encouraging American slaves to revolt against their masters. This provision was dropped from the Declaration of Independence that Congress approved.
- **Formal Declaration:** A statement that the colonies are "free and independent states" with no ties or allegiance to Great Britain.

The Second Continental Congress also urged the former colonies to draft new state constitutions. Two models emerged. In Pennsylvania (1776), there was a **unicameral** (one-house) **legislature**, whose members served for limited terms, and an executive council that had no real power. Massachusetts (1780) boasted a **bicameral** (two-house) **legislature** along with a governor, who could veto laws, and judges who served for life. A Bill of Rights that protected basic civil liberties such as freedom of the press was common in the states' constitutions.

The **Articles of Confederation** was the first written constitution of the United States. It was approved by Congress in 1777 but did not go into effect until March 1781 when it was finally ratified by all the states. The government created under the Articles was fundamentally weak for the following reasons:

- Congress was the only national institution; there was no executive or judiciary.
- Congress's power was limited; it didn't have direct authority to tax, to regulate interstate and foreign trade, or to raise an army.
- Each state had one vote in Congress, and a supermajority (9 out of 13) was needed to act on major issues such as the appropriation of funds.
- All powers not specifically granted to Congress belonged to the states.
- A unanimous vote of the states was required to amend the Articles.

Drafting the Constitution

The Constitution was written at the Federal Convention, better known as the Constitutional Convention, between May and September 1787. Many of the 55 delegates who met in Philadelphia that summer were seasoned politicians with experience in the Confederation Congress or the state legislatures. They were men who understood the art of compromise, and compromise was the key to such thorny matters as representation, slavery, and the presidency.

The Structure of the Legislative Branch

The early debates at the Convention focused on the proposal introduced by James Madison known as the Virginia Plan. It called for a bicameral national legislature with the lower house elected by the people in each state, and the upper house chosen by the lower house from candidates selected by the state legislatures. In both houses, representation was based on population; in other words, the large states would dominate. The legislature was empowered to veto state laws and to choose the national executive. Under the proposal, the national judiciary consisted of one or more "supreme tribunals" and "inferior tribunals" appointed by the legislature. Some members of the judiciary along with the national executive branches constituted the Council of Revision, which had the right to review and reject laws enacted by the national legislature and the states.

A less drastic departure from the Articles of Confederation was presented in the New Jersey Plan, which expanded the authority of Congress to include the power to tax and regulate interstate and foreign trade. While each state continued to have one vote in Congress, the plan envisioned a multi-person executive chosen by Congress, whose members could be removed from office through a petition to Congress from a majority of the state governors. The federal judiciary was appointed by the executive and had both original and appellate jurisdiction. The New Jersey Plan also recognized that laws enacted by Congress and treaties entered into by the United States were the "supreme law" of the land.

Differences between the Virginia and New Jersey plans were reconciled at the convention through the **Great Compromise** (also known as the **Connecticut Compromise**), which put legislative power in the hands of Congress—made up of the House of Representatives (lower house) and the Senate (upper house). Members of the House were elected directly by the people of each state, with the number of representatives determined by population. There was equal representation in the Senate: Each state had two senators, chosen by the state legislatures.

Dealing with the Slavery Issue

Although the Constitution never mentions the words *slave* or *slavery,* the delegates grappled with the problem. The first issue was whether slaves would be counted in the apportionment of seats in the House of Representatives. Under the **Three-Fifths Compromise**, five slaves would equal three free people in determining population for representation and taxation. While there was considerable sentiment to put an end to the slave trade, the Convention ultimately allowed it to continue for at least 20 years. Congress could not prohibit the "migration or importation of such persons any of the states now existing think proper to admit" until 1808 (the year Congress prohibited the importation of new slaves from overseas, thus ending the international slave trade to the United States). Furthermore, states were obligated to return runaway slaves to their rightful owners.

Deciding How Presidents Should Be Elected

There were several questions about the presidency. The delegates quickly settled on a one-person executive but hotly debated how the president should be elected and the term of office. Having Congress select the president was rejected because it violated the principle of the separation of powers; the popular election of the president was also problematic. The framers of the Constitution were not democrats; they equated the "people" with a mob that was too easily swayed.

The solution was a complex and indirect process known as the **Electoral College**. States would appoint electors equal to their total number of representatives in Congress; these electors would cast their ballots for two people. The person receiving the most votes—providing that is a majority of the votes cast—becomes the president, and the one who receives the second highest total becomes the vice president. In the event that no one receives a majority, the election is decided in the House of Representatives with each state having one vote.

In the first draft of the Constitution, the president served a single seven-year term and could not run for reelection. The language that the Convention finally adopted gave the president a four-year term and was silent on the subject of a second term.

Ratification of the Constitution

The Constitution provided for its own ratification procedures. Under Article VII, the Constitution went into effect when approved by conventions in 9 out of the 13 states. (New Hampshire became the ninth state to ratify the Constitution on June 21, 1788.) This ratification process was much easier to achieve than the unanimous consent required in order to change the Articles of Confederation, and it's significant that approval was left to state conventions rather than the state legislatures. State legislatures may well have voted against the Constitution that strengthened the federal government at the expense of the states.

Supporters of the Constitution were known as <u>Federalists</u>. Their most persuasive spokesmen were Alexander Hamilton, John Jay, and James Madison, who wrote a series of articles for the New York newspapers explaining and defending the strong central government created under the Constitution. The articles were collectively known as *The Federalist Papers* or simply *The Federalist,* and were widely disseminated throughout the country during the ratification debate. The opponents of ratification, including Virginia's Patrick Henry and Thomas Jefferson, went by the somewhat awkward and unfortunate name of **Antifederalists**. Their case against the Constitution rested on three points:

- A strong central government contained the seeds of tyranny and threatened the rights of the people.
- Too much authority was taken away from the states.
- The absence of a Bill of Rights left individual liberties unprotected.

With respect to the last point, certain civil liberties were guaranteed under the Constitution:

- Neither the Congress nor the states could suspend (except in time of war or rebellion) the **writ of habeas corpus** (authorities must show cause why a person under detention should not be released) nor enact an **ex post facto law** (a law that makes an action a crime after the fact) or a **bill of attainder** (a law that makes a person guilty of a crime without trial).
- The right of trial by jury was provided for in criminal cases.
- No religious test was required to hold public office.

The Federalists were quick to point out that state constitutions amply protected the individual. Further, they argued that the federal government can only do what is specifically permitted in the Constitution; anything not mentioned, cannot be done. Since the Constitution granted only limited powers to the federal government, there was no need to guard the people against actions against them that the government could not take. Still, the Federalists were willing to add a Bill of Rights as the price for ratification.

Basic Principles of the Constitution

The Constitution established a republican form of government, explained the organization of that government, and outlined the essential features of the federal system.

Republican Form of Government

The Constitution established the United States as a republic in which power is ultimately in the hands of the people and exercised through their elected representatives. The federal government guaranteed each state a republican form of government as well (Article IV, Section 4). The republic was not, however, a democracy. Participation in the political process was severely limited by state-imposed property qualifications for voting; even those who could vote were far removed from selecting members of the Senate and the president; moreover, slavery was accepted, albeit somewhat reluctantly.

Separation of Powers/Checks and Balances

The government is divided into three co-equal branches:

- The legislative branch, which makes the laws (Congress)
- The executive branch, which carries out the laws (president)
- The judicial branch, which interprets the laws (Supreme Court)

A system of **checks and balances** prevents any one branch from dominating the others. The easiest way to understand how checks and balances work is to review the powers each branch has, as well as how those powers are limited by the other branches.

The president has a broad appointment power: He or she nominates justices to the Supreme Court and judges to the lower federal courts, as well as appoints numerous officials in the executive branch. Under the Constitution, most presidential appointments must be confirmed by the Senate. The Senate can and has rejected a president's nominee to the Supreme Court and even to the cabinet. Congress (the House and the Senate) can impeach and remove a federal judge from office. It can also impeach and remove the president from office.

The Constitution requires the president to keep Congress informed about "the state of the union." This has become the annual State of the Union Address to a joint session of Congress, in which the president often outlines the administration's legislative agenda.

The president can ask Congress to pass legislation. As the lawmaking body, Congress can refuse to enact legislation that the president wants or can pass a law that the president opposes. In the latter case, the president can exercise the **veto**; in other words, the president can refuse to sign into law legislation approved by Congress. Congress can override a presidential veto with a two-thirds vote of both houses. If the vote passes, the legislation the president vetoed goes into effect.

The Supreme Court, of course, can declare a law passed by Congress or an action taken by the president unconstitutional. Congress can increase the number of justices on the Supreme Court and change the number and jurisdiction of the lower federal courts. The president usually nominates judges to the federal bench who support the administration's philosophy on the role of the courts.

The power of the Supreme Court to declare laws and executive actions unconstitutional is implied rather than specifically stated in the Constitution. Alexander Hamilton in *Federalist No. 78* argued that the Court did, in fact, have this authority, but the principle of **judicial review** was not firmly established by the Court itself until the landmark decision *Marbury v. Madison* (1803). In this case, Chief Justice John Marshall ruled that parts of the Judiciary Act of 1789 were unconstitutional.

Federal System

The federal system means that power is divided between the federal government and the states. Because the purpose of the framers was to strengthen the central government, it is not at all surprising that the Constitution is clearer on what the states can't do (Article I, Section 10) than on what they can do. The Constitution is also more specific in setting the parameters of interstate relations (Article IV, Sections 1 and 2) than on relations between the states and the federal government.

Summary of the Constitution

Article I

Article I grants legislative power to the Congress—the House of Representatives and the Senate. This article also covers the qualifications for holding office in each house, the organization of each house, and the impeachment and veto process. The officials of Congress mentioned in the Constitution are the Speaker of the House, the president of the Senate, and the president pro tempore of the Senate. The vice president serves as the president of the Senate, acts as the Senate's presiding officer when available, and casts a vote only when the Senate is tied. The longest section (Section 8) spells out the specific powers that Congress has, which are known as the **enumerated powers** or **delegated powers**. Section 8 includes the **Necessary and Proper Clause** (also known as the **Elastic Clause**), which expands the authority of Congress. This clause allows Congress to pass laws that it believes are "necessary and proper" to carry out its enumerated powers. The powers Congress assumes under the Necessary and Proper Clause are known as **implied powers**. Article I also states which actions both Congress and the states cannot undertake.

Article II

Article II pertains to the presidency. It covers the method of election (Electoral College), the qualifications for holding the office, the powers of the president—such as the president's role as commander-in-chief of the armed forces—and presidential authority to grant pardons, to negotiate treaties and make appointments (with concurrence of the Senate), and to propose legislation to Congress. Article II also makes clear that the president and vice president are subject to impeachment and removal from office.

Article III

The provisions on the judiciary are rather vague. Article III establishes the Supreme Court but does not describe its organization, such as how many judges sit on the high court.

Article III explains the jurisdiction of the Supreme Court—**original jurisdiction** and **appellate jurisdiction** (see "The Judiciary," later in this book). This article provides for trial by jury in all cases except impeachment and defines the crime of treason.

Article IV

Article IV deals with the relations between the states. The **Full Faith and Credit Clause** provides that the laws, records, and court decisions of one state are valid in every other state. In addition, Article IV states that citizens should be treated the same in all states and makes provision for extradition. This article also explains the creation of new states and the governance of territories, and the federal government commits to providing each state with a republican form of government and to protecting the states from invasion or domestic violence.

Article V

This article sets down the process by which the Constitution is amended (see "The Amendment Process and the Bill of Rights," later in this chapter).

Article VI

Under this article, the United States assumed all debts incurred by the government under the Articles of Confederation. The **Supremacy Clause** recognizes that the Constitution, laws passed by Congress, and treaties entered into by the United States are the supreme law of the land. This article also makes clear that no religious test for holding office is required.

Article VII

This article explains ratification of the Constitution by conventions of 9 of the 13 states. As noted earlier, this provision made it easier to ratify the Constitution, since all the states did not have to approve, as was the case under the Articles of Confederation.

The Amendment Process and the Bill of Rights

Amending the Constitution is a two-step process. First an amendment is proposed, and then it is ratified. There are two ways to propose an amendment:

- By a two-thirds vote of both houses of Congress
- By two-thirds of the state legislatures asking Congress to call a national convention for that purpose (though this method has never been used)

There are also two ways to ratify an amendment:

- Three-fourths of the state legislatures approve an amendment.
- Conventions in three-fourths of the states approve an amendment. (This method was used only to ratify the Twenty-first Amendment in 1933, which repealed Prohibition.)

The first Congress proposed 12 constitutional amendments to the states in September 1789; ratification was completed for 10 of these amendments by December 1791. The initial ten amendments are known as the **Bill of Rights**. One of the first two amendments that was not originally approved (which dealt with compensation for members of Congress) was ultimately ratified in 1992 and became the Twenty-seventh Amendment.

The Bill of Rights

The Antifederalists were concerned that basic individual liberties were not protected in the Constitution as ratified. The Bill of Rights was a response to this concern. Although the first ten amendments are referred to as the Bill of Rights, only the first eight pertain to specific rights that were often included in the state constitutions. The following is a summary of the Bill of Rights.

Amendment I: Prohibits the establishment of a state religion and guarantees freedom to practice religion; protects freedom of speech and the press, as well as the right to assemble and petition the government.

Amendment II: Protects the right to keep and bear arms, and mentions this right in the context of a "well-regulated militia."

Amendment III: Prohibits the stationing of troops in people's homes without their consent or as set down in law during wartime.

Amendment IV: Protects against unreasonable search and seizure; probable cause is required to get a warrant to conduct a search, and the warrant must describe the place to be searched and what is to be seized.

Amendment V: Provides for indictment by a grand jury for capital or serious crimes; protects against **double jeopardy** (a person cannot be tried for the same crime twice) and self-incrimination (a person cannot be forced to testify against himself or herself); guarantees due process and **eminent domain** (compensation must be paid for private property taken for public use).

Amendment VI: Guarantees the right to a speedy trial by an impartial jury in criminal cases, to be informed about charges, to confront witnesses and present witnesses in defense, and to have representation by an attorney.

Amendment VII: Provides for a trial by jury in most civil cases.

Amendment VIII: Prohibits excessive bail and fines as well as the infliction of cruel and unusual punishment.

Amendment IX: The people are not denied any rights not specifically mentioned in the Constitution. This amendment seems to refer to the rights covered in the first eight amendments, and recognizes that the people may be entitled to other rights. The Supreme Court, for example, based a constitutionally protected right of privacy in part on the Ninth Amendment (see "Civil Liberties," later in this book).

Amendment X: Powers not granted to the federal government or denied to the states in the Constitution, belong to the states or to the people. The powers referred to in this amendment are known as **reserved powers**. The authority that states have to determine their own marriage and divorce laws is an example of a reserved power.

Amendments to the Constitution, 1798–1992

The Constitution was amended only 17 times following the adoption of the Bill of Rights. Among these are amendments that significantly expanded democracy—the abolition of slavery, granting African Americans the right to vote, the direct election of senators, extending suffrage to women, and lowering the voting age to 18. Although many more amendment proposals were introduced, Congress and the states used the amendment process sparingly.

Indeed, the states refused to ratify six amendments that Congress passed, including one dealing with child labor and the **Equal Rights Amendment** (ERA), which provided that "equality of rights" cannot be denied on the basis of gender. The amendment was approved by Congress in 1972, and its original seven-year deadline for action by the states was extended to 1982. By that time, only 35 of the required 38 states had ratified the amendment.

Here are the 17 amendments that follow the Bill of Rights and their dates of ratification:

Amendments	What the Amendment Does	Ratification Date
Amendment XI	Sets limits on suits against states by citizens of another state or foreign country	1795
Amendment XII	Ensures that electors cast separate ballots for president and vice president in the Electoral College	1804
Amendment XIII	Prohibits slavery in the United States	1865
Amendment XIV	Defines a citizen as anyone born or naturalized in the United States; prohibits states from denying any person life, liberty, or property without due process, or denying any person equal protection under the law	1868
Amendment XV	Prohibits denying the right to vote on account of race, color, or previous condition of servitude	1870
Amendment XVI	Authorizes federal income tax	1913
Amendment XVII	Provides for direct election of senators	1913
Amendment XVIII	Prohibits the manufacture, sale, and distribution of intoxicating liquor; ushers in the era known as Prohibition	1919
Amendment XIX	Grants women the right to vote	1920
Amendment XX	Changes dates when president, vice president, and members of Congress take office and Congress convenes; covers presidential succession in an emergency	1933
Amendment XXI	Repeals the Eighteenth Amendment	1933
Amendment XXII	Effectively limits the president to two terms	1951
Amendment XXIII	Extends the right to vote in presidential elections to residents of Washington, D.C.	1961
Amendment XXIV	Prohibits payment of poll tax or other tax in order to vote in a federal election	1964
Amendment XXV	States that the vice president becomes the president if the president is removed from office, resigns, or dies; states that the new president nominates a new vice president to fill a vice president vacancy (the vice president is then confirmed by a majority of both houses of Congress); presents the procedures for dealing with presidential disability	1967
Amendment XXVI	Lowers voting age to 18 in state and federal elections	1971
Amendment XXVII	Changes law stating that the compensation of members of Congress does not go into effect until after an election to the House	1992

Informal Amendment Process

Although the language of the Constitution can be changed only by the formal process described earlier, other factors come into play that can change the meaning of the Constitution. Court decisions are obviously important. For example, *Marbury v. Madison* (1803) established as a matter of law that the Supreme Court had the power to declare a law passed by Congress as unconstitutional. In *McCulloch v. Maryland* (1819), the Court ruled that the Necessary and Proper Clause gave Congress the power to do things not specifically mentioned in the Constitution—in this case, create the Second Bank of the United States. Congress has tried to expand the powers of the president through legislation such as the Line-Item Veto Act (1996) and place limits on the president's actions like the **War Powers Act (1973)** (see "The Presidency," later in this book). Finally, political and social developments come into play. Even the most ardent Federalist would have found the unprecedented growth of the federal government since the Great Depression and World War II alarming; the maze of departments, bureaus, and agencies comprise a fourth branch of government—the bureaucracy—that the Constitution hardly contemplated (see "The Bureaucracy," later in this book).

Nor could the framers begin to grasp the multitude of issues that Congress, the president, and the courts have to deal with, ranging from abortion and stem-cell research to nuclear proliferation and the international space station.

Practice

1. Which of the following statements about the relationship between Congress and the Supreme Court is valid?

    A.   A decision can be overturned by a two-thirds vote of both houses.
    B.   Nominations to the Supreme Court must be approved by Congress.
    C.   A constitutional amendment is the only way Congress can overturn a Supreme Court decision.
    D.   Congress can expand the jurisdiction of the Supreme Court through legislation.
    E.   Congress can remove a Supreme Court justice.

2. A constitutional responsibility given to the vice president is

    A.   representing the president at official functions
    B.   serving as leader of the president's party in the Senate
    C.   recommending appointments to the cabinet
    D.   presiding over the Senate
    E.   heading special executive committees created by the president

3. All the following were weaknesses of the Articles of Confederation EXCEPT

    A.   Congress did not have the power to control interstate and foreign trade.
    B.   Congress had the power to make laws.
    C.   It was difficult to amend the Articles of Confederation.
    D.   There was no independent judiciary.
    E.   Few limits were imposed on the executive branch.

4. The arguments used by the Antifederalists against ratification of the Constitution included which of the following?

    I.   The Constitution gave too much power to the federal government.
    II.   The Constitution did not protect individual liberties.
    III. The Constitution protected the interests of small farmers against the country's wealthy elite.
    IV.   The Constitution took too many rights away from the states.

    A.   I only
    B.   I and II only
    C.   I, II, and III only
    D.   I, II, and IV only
    E.   II and III only

5. The authority that Congress has under the Necessary and Proper Clause is called

    A.   implied powers
    B.   enumerated powers
    C.   reserved powers
    D.   elastic powers
    E.   categorical powers

6. Limiting members of Congress to a specific number of terms can be imposed only by

    A.   a decision of the Supreme Court
    B.   laws enacted in all 50 states
    C.   an executive order of the president
    D.   a constitutional amendment
    E.   legislation passed by a two-thirds vote of both houses

7. All the following statements about the amendment process are true EXCEPT

    A.   Amendments are proposed by a vote of two-thirds of the state legislatures.
    B.   Conventions in three-fourths of the states can ratify an amendment.
    C.   A national convention can propose an amendment.
    D.   Amendments are proposed through a two-thirds vote of both houses of Congress.
    E.   Ratification requires approval of three-fourths of the state legislatures.

8. The Supremacy Clause in the Constitution states that

   A. Congress is the most important branch of government.
   B. The Constitution, federal laws, and treaties are the supreme law of the land.
   C. The federal government has more power than the states.
   D. The armed forces are under the control of civilian authority.
   E. The president has supreme power as commander-in-chief.

9. Evidence that the framers of the Constitution may have distrusted the common people is

   A. Senate approval of presidential appointments
   B. the introduction of money bills in the House of Representatives
   C. the method by which the president is elected
   D. the age and citizenship requirements for the Senate
   E. the apportionment of seats in the House of Representatives

10. The Virginia and New Jersey plans both provided for

    A. a bicameral legislature
    B. separation of powers
    C. a strong executive
    D. equal representation of states
    E. slavery

11. The purpose of the system of checks and balances in the Constitution is to ensure that

    A. The federal courts are independent.
    B. The president has the power to control Congress.
    C. The military is under civilian control.
    D. One branch does not dominate the others.
    E. Congress has a role in foreign policy.

12. Which of the following civil liberty protections is included in the Constitution as ratified?

    A. the prohibition of cruel and unusual punishment
    B. the protection of freedom of assembly
    C. the limitations imposed on the slave trade
    D. the power given the states over elections
    E. no religious test for holding office

13. Which of the following statements best characterizes the attitudes of the framers of the Constitution toward slavery?

    A. They were all slave owners and were determined to preserve slavery.
    B. They supported the expansion of slavery beyond the original 13 states.
    C. They wanted to limit slavery, but political considerations made that impossible.
    D. They believed that if slavery was not mentioned, ratification would be harder.
    E. They preferred the gradual emancipation of all slaves.

14. The Constitution prohibits the states from doing all the following EXCEPT

    A. granting titles of nobility
    B. giving sanctuary to runaway slaves
    C. determining qualifications for voting
    D. imposing tariffs on goods from foreign countries
    E. coining money

15. Which of the following statements about judicial review is NOT true?

    A. Judicial review gives the Supreme Court the power to declare an action by the president unconstitutional.
    B. The Supreme Court's decision in *Marbury v. Madison* was based on judicial review.
    C. Judicial review is specifically mentioned in the Constitution under the powers of the Supreme Court.
    D. Judicial review can significantly impact the meaning of the Constitution.
    E. The power of the Supreme Court to declare a law unconstitutional was recognized in *The Federalist Papers*.

Answers

1. **E** This question is essentially asking about the system of checks and balances. Congress's authority to impeach and remove from office certainly extends to Supreme Court justices. On the other hand, the only way that the jurisdiction of the Supreme Court, which Article III outlines, could be changed is through a constitutional amendment. Nominations to the Supreme Court must be approved by the Senate, not by both houses.

2. **D** The only power granted to the vice president in the Constitution is to serve as president of the Senate and to vote on matters if the Senate is tied. Although the vice president is certainly an important figure in the party, the party leader in the Senate will be either the majority leader or the minority leader, depending on whether the president's party is in control.

3. **B** The power to make laws remained in the hands of Congress under the Articles of Confederation, but it was the only branch of the national government. Neither a separate national court system nor any executive authority was in place. It was obviously difficult to amend the articles since all 13 states had to agree to any change.

4. **D** If anything, the Antifederalists believed that the Constitution reflected the interests of wealthy merchants, rich planters, and the professional classes. The other three choices were essential elements of the Antifederalist critique of the Constitution.

5. **A** This question focuses on the terminology used by political scientists to describe the Constitution. You should know immediately that the terms *elastic powers* and *categorical powers* have no meaning. The term *reserved powers* refers to the Tenth Amendment; these powers are effectively in the hands of the states. Enumerated powers are those powers specifically granted to Congress in Article I, Section 8. The powers that flow to the federal government or Congress under the Necessary and Proper Clause are implied powers.

6. **D** In *U.S. Term Limits, Inc. v. Thornton* (1995), the Supreme Court ruled that state laws could not impose term limits on members of Congress. The Court reasoned that term limits added another qualification to serve in either the House or the Senate and, therefore, required a constitutional amendment.

7. **A** The states do not have a direct role in proposing amendments. Two-thirds of the state legislatures may call for national convention for that purpose, but it is the convention that actually proposes the amendments (**C**).

8. **B** Although it is true that the armed forces are under civilian control, and a case could be made that Congress is the most important branch of government, neither of these choices relates to the Supremacy Clause. *Remember:* True statements are not necessarily correct answers. The Supremacy Clause just refers to defining the "supreme law of the land," which state courts are obliged to respect.

9. **C** The process by which the president is elected under the Constitution is quite indirect and, in original conception at least, removed the people as far as possible from the decision. A limited number of people (who had the necessary property qualifications for voting) elected members of the state legislatures, who, in turn, chose electors, who then cast their ballots for president and vice president.

10. **B** Although the details certainly differed significantly, both the Virginia and New Jersey plans envisioned a government that included legislative, executive, and judicial branches. The New Jersey Plan retained the unicameral Congress of the Articles of Confederation and equal representation of the states; in the Virginia Plan the executive was selected by the legislature, and the New Jersey Plan proposed a multi-person executive. The idea that slaves were three-fifths of a person is implied in the New Jersey Plan, but slavery is not alluded to in the Virginia Plan.

11. **D** The system of checks and balances goes together with the separation of powers. Its purpose is to make sure that one branch of the government does not dominate the other two. None of the answers provided is a clear example of the checks-and-balances system.

12. **E** The key in the question is "the Constitution as ratified." Cruel and unusual punishment (Eighth Amendment) and freedom of assembly (First Amendment) are in the Bill of Rights, not in the Constitution as ratified. The limitations on the slave trade and state control over elections are not civil liberties. You should be able to choose the right answer using process of elimination.

13. **C** Slavery was a hot-button issue, and not using the term made ratification easier. It is certainly true that many of the framers wanted to do something about slavery, but they were constrained by the need to get support from the Southern states, particularly South Carolina and Georgia, which had the highest percentage of slaves. On the question of the expansion of slavery, you should know that the Confederation Congress prohibited slavery in the Northwest Territory in the Northwest Ordinance (1787).

14. **C** The Constitution is very specific on the powers that the states do not have, and many of the limitations—such as coining money and imposing tariffs—were attempts to correct what were seen as shortcomings in the Articles of Confederation. The fugitive slave law in the Constitution makes it clear that states are responsible for returning runaway slaves. Establishing qualifications for voting falls under the states' power to determine the time, manner, and place of elections.

15. **C** Although judicial review may be *implied* in Article III, it is not mentioned. Alexander Hamilton, in *The Federalist Papers,* thought it was pretty clear that the Supreme Court had this power, but his opinion clearly had no force of law. The principle is established only through *Marbury v. Madison* (1803), perhaps the clearest example of how the Constitution can be changed outside of the formal amendment process.

Federalism

Federalism is a political system in which power is divided among the national government and other governmental units, such as states, counties, and municipalities in the United States. In a sense, it is the middle ground between a **unitary system**, in which all power is derived from the central government, and a **confederal system**, where the states are effectively sovereign and determine what authority the central government has. Several countries in Western Europe—France, Great Britain, Italy, and Sweden—have unitary governments. The United States under the Articles of Confederation is an example of the confederal system. As the articles clearly stated, "Each state retains its sovereignty, freedom, and independence, and every power, jurisdiction and right, which is not by this confederation expressly delegated to the United States, in Congress assembled."

Federalism in the Constitution

The Constitution is vague in the extreme on what the nature of the relationship is between the federal government and the states, and it does not make reference to any type of local government. James Madison stated the problem succinctly in *Federalist No. 45:* "The powers delegated by the proposed Constitution to the federal government are few and defined. Those that are to remain in the State governments are numerous and indefinite." As noted in the preceding chapter, what the states cannot do, the guidelines governing interstate relations, and the guarantees given the states by the federal government are rather obvious; the powers that states have are not.

There are provisions in the Constitution that specifically recognize the dominance of the federal government or allow for the expansion of its power:

- **Supremacy Clause:** Makes the Constitution, federal laws, and treaties the "supreme law of the land" by which state courts are bound.
- **Necessary and Proper Clause:** Enables Congress to pass laws needed to carry out its enumerated powers.
- **Commerce Clause:** Gives Congress the power to regulate interstate commerce.
- **General Welfare Clause:** Enables Congress's spending power to be used to promote the "general welfare."

The Supreme Court has defined federal-state relations based on the following elements:

- *McCulloch v. Maryland* **(1819):** Congress has broad implied powers under the Necessary and Proper Clause; states have no power to interfere with a law that Congress passes.
- *Gibbons v. Ogden* **(1824):** Under the Commerce Clause, *commerce* is defined as any "commercial intercourse" affecting two or more states. Congress used a broad interpretation of the Commerce Clause to prohibit discrimination in public accommodations in the **Civil Rights Act of 1964**. The law was upheld by the Supreme Court in *Heart of Atlanta Motel v. United States* (1964).
- *South Dakota v. Dole* **(1987):** The Supreme Court upheld a law that authorized the secretary of transportation to withhold a portion of federal highway funds from states that did not raise their minimum drinking age to 21 on the grounds that the legislation was pursuant to the General Welfare Clause.

Court decisions in the 1990s and early in the new century limited the power of the federal government in favor of the states. *United States v. Lopez* (1995) ruled that Congress cannot rely on the Commerce Clause to prohibit guns in the area around a public school. The Court upheld Oregon's "death with dignity" statute, which allows the terminally ill to end their lives, against a federal challenge in *Gonzales v. Oregon* (2006). In a case involving California's Compassionate Use Act (1996), however, the Court stated in *Gonzales v. Raich* (2005) that a federal law banning the possession of marijuana could be enforced even when states allowed its use for medical reasons.

The powers granted to the states are scattered throughout the Constitution. Here are some examples:

- States determine qualifications for voting (Article I, Section 2; limited thereafter by the Fourteenth, Fifteenth, Nineteenth, Twenty-fourth, and Twenty-sixth amendments).
- State governors call elections to fill vacancies in the House of Representatives (Article I, Section 2).
- Senators are chosen by state legislatures (Article I, Section 3; superseded by the Seventeenth Amendment).
- State governors fill vacancies in the Senate (Article I, Section 3).
- The time, place, and manner of elections determined by state legislatures (Article I, Section 4).
- State legislatures determine the method of appointing electors (Article II, Section 1).
- State legislatures can call a convention to propose amendments to the Constitution (Article V).
- State legislatures ratify amendments to the Constitution (Article V).

The Tenth Amendment sets out a large if undefined policy sphere for the states. Here are some examples of powers "reserved" for the states:

- Establishing public schools, including the curriculum and length of the school year
- Protecting the public health and safety (for example, police, fire, and paramedic services)
- Regulating businesses that operate in the state

The boundary between the powers of the states (those given in the Constitution and the reserved powers) and those of the federal government (enumerated powers and implied powers) is not fixed. The areas where the two overlap are called **concurrent powers**; they involve levying and collecting taxes, creating courts, borrowing money, and claiming private property for public use (eminent domain).

The relations between states are an important element of the federal system. Although states cannot enter into treaties or alliances with other countries, they can enter into agreements, Congress permitting, with each other. Such an agreement is known as an **interstate compact** and may involve all 50 states—for example, the Interstate Compact for the Placement of Children regarding adoption across state lines—or a group of states in a region. The Colorado River Compact (1922) was an agreement among Arizona, California, Colorado, Nevada, New Mexico, Utah, and Wyoming on the use of water from the Colorado River.

The Supreme Court has original jurisdiction, which means it is the first court to hear a case, in a suit involving two states. When Arizona and California, for example, could not reach a decision on their respective allotments of water from the Colorado River, the Supreme Court resolved the issue.

Three basic principles govern interstate relations under the Constitution:

- **Full Faith and Credit Clause:** Each state is obligated to recognize the laws, public records, and court decisions of every other state. An individual cannot avoid paying damages ordered by a court in California just by moving to Texas. The obligation imposed by the Full Faith and Credit Clause is not absolute, however. In *Williams v. North Carolina* (1945), the Supreme Court ruled against "quickie" divorces where parties did not establish residence in good faith. More recently, Congress passed the Defense of Marriage Act (1996) in response to action in the Hawaiian courts relating to same-sex marriage. Under the law, states are not required to recognize such marriages and marriage is defined as a legal union between one man and one woman for purposes of federal law. The Defense of Marriage Act does not prevent states from recognizing same-sex marriages, and several states have done so, either by legislation or state court action.
- **Extradition:** A fugitive from justice in one state must be returned to the state where he or she committed the crime. States can go to federal courts to enforce an extradition request according to the Supreme Court in *Puerto Rico v. Branstad* (1987).
- **Privileges and Immunities Clause:** Citizens of one state must be treated the same as citizens of every other state. However, the provision does not prevent states from imposing reasonable restrictions, such as establishing minimum residency requirements for voting or holding public office, or charging out-of-state residents higher tuition than in-state residents at state colleges and universities.

Types of Federalism

Federalism is a fluid concept. Over the course of U.S. history, the relationship between the federal government and the states has fluctuated depending on the issues of the times.

Dual federalism was the popular model throughout most of the 19th century and up to the Great Depression in the 1930s. It held that the authority of the federal government was limited to enumerated powers—those specifically granted in the Constitution to Congress, the president, and the courts. All other powers fall to the states. Proponents of dual federalism tended to ignore the Elastic Clause, which expanded the power of Congress to enact new laws and played up the Tenth Amendment, which focused on the authority of the states. They also maintained that the federal government and the states are each sovereign in their own sphere and that tension always characterizes federal-state relations. Political scientists often refer to dual federalism as **layer-cake federalism** to illustrate these points.

The emphasis on the Tenth Amendment in dual federalism when taken to its logical conclusion led to the theory of nullification. This extreme states' rights position held that the states—not the people—created the federal government, and the states had the power to declare a law passed by Congress null and void if it was contrary to a very strict interpretation of the Constitution. Dual federalism provided an important context for the events leading up to the Civil War.

As the power of the federal government expanded to meet the crisis of the Depression, a new model of federalism emerged: **cooperative federalism**. As the name implies, the tension and, indeed, antagonism between the states and federal government disappears in this model. Power is not concentrated in one level or the other, but both work together to carry out governmental functions. This is sometimes called **marble-cake federalism** because the responsibilities of the federal and state governments are "mixed and mingled." Backers of cooperative federalism take a much narrower view of the Tenth Amendment and broadly interpret the Elastic Clause.

Although many political scientists see cooperative federalism extending through the 1960s, others see a change during the Johnson Administration (1963–1969). During this period, **creative federalism** (also known as **centralized federalism**) emphasized that the federal government decided the needs of the country and pressed these needs on the states, which were either unwilling or unable to address issues relating to race, poverty, and urban development. Officials in Washington, D.C., were ready to withhold funds from the states and, indeed, sometimes bypassed the states completely. Johnson's Great Society, which included programs such as Head Start, the War on Poverty, and Model Cities, saw the federal government working directly with cities, counties, school districts, and even the nonprofit sector to provide a broad range of social services.

Beginning in the 1970s, the pendulum swung back toward the states. **New federalism**, introduced by the Nixon Administration (1969–1973), held that it was time that power flowed from the federal government back to states and localities, which understood better the needs of the people. It involved two key programs:

- **General revenue sharing:** Under this program, federal dollars were given to the states based on a complicated statistical formula, with few if any restrictions on how the money could be spent.
- **Special revenue sharing:** This program combined funding for various programs into a single block grant in such broad policy areas as healthcare, crime prevention, and community development and, again, allowed the states greater freedom as to how they could use the money.

Block grants were an important element of Ronald Reagan's effort to control the growth of the federal government. But the federal dollars available to the states declined in the 1980s and the promise of fewer restrictions didn't fully materialize. States responded by raising taxes, cutting programs, privatizing services, and looking for other revenue sources to make up general budget shortfalls.

Clearly, the flow of money is the key component to federal-state relations. This is sometimes called **fiscal federalism**. Revenue sharing (now defunct) and block grants are just two elements. Most federal funding that states and municipalities get continues to come through **categorical grants**. Categorical grants are given for a very specific purpose, typically require the state to "match" the spending, and do carry numerous limitations called *conditions of aid*. Conditions of aid can include nondiscriminatory hiring practices or affirmative action, environmental impact reports, and "prevailing" wage requirements. Conditions of aid can also be used to force a state to adopt a policy it might be reluctant to. During the energy crisis of the 1970s, a threat to reduce federal highway funds was used to get the states to lower the speed limit to 55 mph. Congress turned to essentially the same tactic to compel the states to raise their drinking age to 21 (in *South Dakota v. Dole* [1987]).

There are two types of categorical grants: **project grants** and **formula grants**. Project grants are made on the basis of a competitive application process. Grants for research to individual investigators, hospitals, or universities from the National Institutes of Health are project grants. As the name *formula grants* suggests, a calculation determines how the funds available through a formula grant are distributed. The formula may take into account a number of possible variables, including population, percentage of the population below the poverty line, and per-capita income.

Welfare reform during the Clinton Administration brought about an important shift in federal-state responsibilities. The Personal Responsibility and Work Opportunity Act (1996) used **block grants** to transfer control of assistance to the poor from the federal government to the states. A block grant is funding from the federal government to the states for a broad general purpose.

One of the most contentious federal-state issues of the 1990s concerned mandates. A **mandate** is a law, regulation, or court decision that compels a state or local government to take an action under the threat of legal action or loss or reduction of federal funding. In most instances, it is not the action that is troubling, but the fact that states and municipalities have to shoulder the financial burden. Under the Americans with Disabilities Act (1990), for example, states were required to make public facilities accessible to the handicapped, but Congress allocated no funds to the states for that purpose. (In other words, it was an unfunded mandate.) Many environmental laws include mandates as well. The problem remains controversial, even though Congress passed the Unfunded Mandates Reform Act in 1995, which requires both the House and the Senate to take a closer look at bills that impose at least $50 million in unfunded mandates and has the Congressional Budget Office report on the fiscal impact of nearly all bills.

Although education is traditionally left to state and local governments, President George W. Bush significantly expanded the federal role in elementary education through the No Child Left Behind Act (2002). The legislation imposed new demands on public school districts (such as annual standardized tests) with the aim of improving student performance. Although federal spending on education has increased since its enactment, critics charge that the law's numerous requirements came without adequate funding.

The deep recession that began in late 2007 led to increased federal help for the states. The American Recovery and Reinvestment Act (2009), better known as the stimulus package, earmarked around $150 billion for states and municipalities for healthcare, education, and transportation. Governors in several states, however, rejected part of the funding because of the restrictions attached or the obligation to continue expanded programs after the stimulus money ran out.

Local and state governments are not powerless in their dealings with Washington. In addition to congressional delegations that represent their concerns, cities and states have organized just like any other interest group to press their programs before both Congress and the executive branch. Groups such as the National Governors' Conference, the Council of State Governments, the National League of Cities, and the U.S. Conference of Mayors are known as intergovernmental lobbies and have a long history of influencing federal policy.

Advantages and Disadvantages of Federalism

It is clear that there is no perfect balance to be achieved in federal-state relations. Even with the attempts over the last quarter of a century to give states and localities a greater say in how federal money is used, the fact remains that it is still federal money and the federal government has a large say in how it should be used. Many Americans may complain about how big the federal government is, but it remains the dominant partner in the equation.

Advantages

Political scientists point to several advantages of a federal system. It promotes democracy by giving people and groups various levels of government to press their claims, allows for policy experimentation, and allows regional interests and diversity to be heard.

- **Federalism creates multiple layers of government, increases the possibility of political participation, and provides greater access to the political process.** Not only does a person have the opportunity to vote for local as well as national officials, but he or she can become more involved in grass-roots politics. During the 1950s and 1960s, for example, it was obvious to African Americans that Congress would be much more receptive to civil rights issues than state legislatures in the South were.

- **Federalism promotes innovation in handling complex policy questions.** States and even local governments are often the laboratories of change. When healthcare reform at the national level failed under Clinton, states pioneered the idea of health insurance pools that allowed small businesses to join together to buy insurance at lower rates with better coverage. Imposing work requirements on welfare recipients also began with the states.

- **The fact that there are both state and local centers of power gives regional interest groups a strong political voice on the national scene.** Ranchers in the Rocky Mountain West were able to press the federal government to open more public land to private use by influencing their congressional delegations to support the so-called "Sage Brush Rebellion," which began in the late 1970s.

- **Federalism encourages diversity on a broad range of policy questions.** States are free to develop their own positions on such questions as affirmative action, assisted suicide, and the death penalty. For example, the California Civil Rights Initiative, which voters approved in 1996, formally ended state and local affirmative-action programs, including those affecting admissions to the state's university system; Michigan, on the other hand, continues to take race into account at its institutions of higher learning. Texas law provides for the death penalty, while Illinois has suspended executions pending a review of the criminal justice system.

Disadvantages

Critics argue that federalism is counterproductive. They say that the structure of the political system turns people off to politics, produces inequality, and is often a barrier to important national policies.

- **Federalism leads to the fragmentation of U.S. politics.** Three levels of government and a myriad of government agencies can make the political process seem too complicated. Federalism provides so many outlets for political participation that voters become apathetic. Indeed, one of the explanations for declining voter turnout is that there are simply too many elections. The number of voters is often extremely small in school board or county commissioner elections.

- **There is a basic inequity in the federal system.** Some states and municipalities are wealthier than others, which creates a disparity in the level of public services that each provides. Per-pupil spending is much lower in Mississippi than it is in Massachusetts, and the same is true for welfare payments.

- **Strong state and local constituencies can obstruct and delay the implementation of national policy.** This was clearly the case with both court decisions and legislation affecting civil rights. The desegregation of public schools did not happen "with all deliberate speed" because of strong opposition in communities as varied as Little Rock, Arkansas; Boston, Massachusetts; and Los Angeles, California.

Practice

√1. Which of the following statements does NOT apply to dual federalism?

A. The federal government has no power beyond those specifically granted by the Constitution.

B. The states and the federal government are supreme in their own spheres.

C. The relationship between the states and the federal government is generally antagonistic.

✗D. There are numerous areas in which the states and federal government work together.

E. The constitutional basis of dual federalism is the Tenth Amendment.

√2. The theory behind the shift from categorical grants to block grants was to

A. give the federal government greater control over the money going to the states

B. let Congress impose new conditions on the grants

✗C. allow those most familiar with state and local needs to determine how to use available funds

D. eliminate funding for all welfare programs

E. make sure that anti-discrimination regulations were followed

Federal Civilian Employment, 1990, 1995, 2000–2005 (Employment in Thousands)						
Year	Total	Percent of U.S. Employed	Executive		Legislative	Judicial
			Total	Defense		
1990	3,233	2.72	3,173	1,060	38	23
1995	2,943	2.36	2,880	852	34	28
2000	2,879	2.10	2,816	681	31	32
2001	2,704	1.97	2,641	672	30	33
2002	2,699	1.98	2,635	671	31	34
2003	2,743	1.99	2,677	669	31	34
2004	2,714	1.95	2,649	668	30	34
2005	2,709	1.91	2,645	671	30	34

Source: U.S. Census Bureau. Statistical Abstract of the United States. Washington, D.C., U.S. Government Printing Office, 2006.

3. Based on the previous table, all the following statements are valid EXCEPT:

A. The size of the federal government has declined since 1990.

B. The most dramatic decline in government employment has been in the Department of Defense.

✗C. Employment in the judiciary has grown because of the hiring of more women and ethnic minorities in the Federal Bureau of Investigation.

D. Federal workers account for a small share of the labor force.

E. The numbers for the legislative branch probably reflect a decline in congressional staff.

4. The power of the federal government was expanded by the following Supreme Court decisions:

I. *McCulloch v. Maryland*

II. *Marbury v. Madison*

III. *Barron v. Mayor of Baltimore*

IV. *Gibbons v. Ogden*

A. I and II only

B. I, II, and III only

C. I, II, and IV only

D. III and IV only

E. I and IV only

5. A grant from the National Endowment for the Humanities to a historian researching the origins of the American Revolution is an example of a

    A. formula grant
    B. categorical grant
    C. grant-in-aid
    D. project grant
    E. scholarship

6. Which of the following is NOT a power specifically granted to the states under the Constitution?

    A. power to establish voting procedures
    B. power to appoint electors to choose the president
    C. power to ratify amendments to the Constitution
    D. power to impose state income taxes
    E. power to fill vacancies in the House of Representatives

7. The fact that out-of-state residents pay higher tuition at state universities than in-state students do is an exception to

    A. the Necessary and Proper Clause
    B. the Privileges and Immunities Clause
    C. the Commerce Clause
    D. the General Welfare Clause
    E. the separation of powers

8. The political system in which all the power is in the hands of the central government is known as a

    A. confederal system
    B. republican system
    C. unitary system
    D. federal system
    E. state system

9. The claim that federalism promotes democracy by increasing the opportunities for political participation is undermined by

    A. the low voter turnout in local elections
    B. the difficulty in finding candidates to run for local office
    C. the limited coverage the media gives to local races
    D. the role that interest groups play in U.S. politics
    E. the high turnover in the Congress

10. States and municipalities try to influence federal policy through all the following EXCEPT:

    A. National League of Cities
    B. U.S. Conference of Mayors
    C. Urban League
    D. Council of State Governments
    E. National Governors' Association

11. A concurrent power is shared by

    A. the president and Congress
    B. the governors and the president
    C. the House and the Senate
    D. the states and the federal government
    E. municipalities and the states

12. Education is a policy area that reflects the basic principles of

    A. dual federalism
    B. cooperative federalism
    C. supremacy of the federal government
    D. supremacy of the states
    E. intergovernmental relations

13. The constitutional right of the states to determine the qualifications for voting was limited by

    I. the Thirteenth Amendment
    II. *Brown v. Board of Education of Topeka*
    III. the Civil Rights Act of 1964
    IV. the Twenty-fourth Amendment

    A. I and II only
    B. III only
    C. III and IV only
    D. I, II, and III only
    E. I, III, and IV only

14. Congress exercised its power to determine the scope of the Full Faith and Credit Clause in which piece of legislation?

   A. Unfunded Mandates Reform Act
   B. Defense of Marriage Act
   C. Religious Freedom Restoration Act
   D. Voting Rights Act of 1965
   E. Title IX of the Education Act Amendments of 1972

15. The Clean Air Act of 1970 is an example of

   A. a decision of the federal courts that imposed a spending requirement on the states
   B. Congress attaching conditions of aid to federal funds
   C. Congress imposing a financial burden on the states but not providing funding
   D. a federal agency requiring the states to take action
   E. Congress assuming powers under the Elastic Clause

Answers

1. **D** The essence of dual federalism is that the areas in which the federal government and the states operate are distinct. The notion that there are areas of shared responsibility is identified with cooperative federalism.

2. **C** If you know the definitions of categorical grants and block grants, the question should not present any problems. The fundamental difference between the two types of federal funding is the matter of restrictions on spending. Block grants were intended to give the states discretion on how to use money allocated for such broad policy areas as community development or crime prevention. Money could be used, for example, to hire more police or buy new police vehicles.

3. **C** Although it is clear from the table that employment in the judicial branch has grown, there is no way to attribute the increase to the FBI's hiring of more women and ethnic minorities. It may well be true that the FBI has done this, but it is not supported by the data. All the other statements are valid based on the information you have.

4. **C** The three landmark decisions of Chief Justice John Marshall—*McCulloch v. Maryland, Marbury v. Madison,* and *Gibbons v. Ogden*—all enhanced the power of the federal government. By formally establishing the principle of judicial review, *Marbury v. Madison* certainly strengthened the Supreme Court, which is a part of the federal government, while the other two decisions gave Congress greater authority. *Barron v. Mayor of Baltimore* (1833) held that the Bill of Rights limited only the federal government, not the states.

5. **D** Project grants are awarded on the basis of a competitive application; states, municipalities, and individuals are eligible, depending on the source of the grant. Funding from an agency like the National Endowment for the Humanities often requires the submission of an application that describes the scope of the research planned and that goes through a peer review to evaluate its merits. Keep in mind that a project grant is a type of categorical grant, which, in turn, is a type of grant-in-aid.

6. **D** Although states obviously have the power to "lay and collect" state income taxes, the Constitution does not specifically mention this authority, whereas the Constitution does mention all the other authorities. The power to impose state income taxes is an example of a concurrent power—all levels within the federal system have the power to tax.

7. **B** The Privileges and Immunities Clause basically means that each state must treat the citizens of other states the same. States, however, can draw reasonable distinctions between their residents and residents of other states: In-state tuition versus out-of-state tuition is one example; residency requirements for voting and holding office is another.

8. **C** The question is the essential definition of a unitary government in which the states are the creation of the central government. It is pretty easy to distinguish between a confederal system and a federal system. You would speak about a republican form of government, but not a republican system; *state system,* although it is not a term that is common in political science, is the same as *confederal system.*

9. **A** The greatest opportunity for political participation in terms of voting, running for office, or becoming active in a campaign is at the local level. The most relevant fact here relating to federalism and democracy is that the vast majority of voters don't cast their ballots in many local elections, particularly for races for the school board, community college district, or county supervisor. There is no shortage of candidates for any elective office in the United States, and the fact of the matter is that turnover in Congress is very low. Limited media coverage of local elections may well be a factor, but voter turnout is the key.

10. **C** The Urban League is a civil rights organization that does actively lobby the federal government on issues affecting minority groups. All the other organizations are clearly examples of intergovernmental lobbies that press the case for states and municipalities.

11. **D** Concurrent power relates to authority held by both the federal government and the states (for example, the power to tax or to create courts).

12. **B** Educational policy is a good example of how the federal, state, and local governments work together. Although direct control over public schools is in the hands of local school boards, curriculum issues, the length of the school year, and teacher credentialing are state responsibilities. The federal government, through the Department of Education, provides funding for various school programs and imposes requirements for the teaching of students with disabilities, for example.

13. **C** The Thirteenth Amendment, which prohibits slavery, and *Brown v. Board of Education of Topeka* (1954), which deals with school desegregation, have nothing to do with voting. The Civil Rights Act of 1964 made it easier to file voting-rights lawsuits and banned arbitrary discrimination in voter registration, while the Twenty-fourth Amendment eliminated the poll tax that had often been used to deny African Americans the right to vote.

14. **B** The Full Faith and Credit Clause requires that each state recognize the public records, laws, and court decisions of every other state. When a Hawaiian court issued a ruling on same-sex marriages, Congress passed the Defense of Marriage Act, which effectively freed states from the obligation to recognize such unions approved in other states.

15. **C** The Clean Air Act is a good example of an unfunded mandate. National air pollution standards were set through the legislation, which the states were required to administer and assume the cost of implementation for.

Congress

The Constitution vests legislative power in a bicameral or two-house Congress made up of the House of Representatives and the Senate. The House of Representatives was always considered to be the body more responsive to the popular will of the people because its members were up for reelection every two years and were chosen by the people. The Senate, on the other hand, was seen by the Founding Fathers as the more deliberative body. Senators are older and have a longer residency requirement than representatives; they serve six-year terms and were originally selected by state legislatures. It wasn't until 1913 that the Seventeenth Amendment provided for the direct election of senators.

The Power of Congress in the Constitution

The specific powers that Congress can exert are spelled out in Article I, Section 8 of the Constitution. Included in the enumerated powers are the following:

- The right to impose and collect taxes
- The right to borrow and coin money
- The right to regulate foreign and interstate trade
- The right to declare war
- The right to create post offices and federal courts below the Supreme Court
- The right to raise and maintain the army and navy

Congress also has the power to admit new states to the union (Article IV, Section 3) and propose amendments to the Constitution (Article V). Amendments to the Constitution either gave the Congress additional power—for example, to collect federal income taxes (Sixteenth Amendment)—or new enforcement authority as civil rights, particularly the right to vote, and were extended after the Civil War (Thirteenth, Fourteenth, Fifteenth, Nineteenth, Twenty-third, Twenty-fourth, and Twenty-sixth amendments).

Under the Twenty-fifth Amendment (1967), the House of Representatives and the Senate must approve a president's nominee for vice president when a vacancy occurs; Congress also plays a key role in determining whether a president is disabled and can continue to perform his or her duties.

Congress is not limited to powers specifically mentioned in the Constitution. It has a broad range of implied powers that derives from the Necessary and Proper Clause, also known as the Elastic Clause. The Supreme Court, in *McCulloch v. Maryland* (1819), established the Necessary and Proper Clause, which gave Congress implied powers by recognizing its authority to create the Second Bank of the United States. It's possible to make a strong case that most of what Congress actually does falls under its implied powers.

Although both houses of Congress must approve bills to enact legislation, the Constitution gives each house certain exclusive powers. When no presidential candidate receives a majority of the electoral votes, the outcome of the election is determined by the House of Representatives (Article II, Section 1; Twelfth Amendment). All revenue bills must originate in the House (Article I, Section 7). The House also has the "sole power of impeachment." Again, impeachment means "charging" a federal official, president, vice president, judge, or other "civil officer" with "treason, bribery, or other high crimes and misdemeanors." The Senate, on the other hand, is responsible for *trying* cases of impeachment and can remove officials from office if found guilty. Quite importantly, the Senate's "advice and consent" authority, which effectively means approval, is an important check on the president. For example, a two-thirds majority vote of the Senate is necessary to ratify treaties negotiated by the president, and a majority of the Senate must approve most presidential appointments as well, including members of the cabinet, the Supreme Court, and other federal judges.

Who Serves in Congress

There are 100 senators (two from each state), and 435 representatives in the House. The latter number was set in the Reapportionment Act of 1929, which recognized that simply adding more seats as the population grew would make the House too unwieldy. Although the total number of members in the House is fixed, the representation from each state is not. States gain or lose seats depending on population changes between the federal census conducted every ten years. This process is known as **reapportionment**. After the 2000 census, for example, the Arizona House delegation increased by two while the New York delegation decreased by two. This reflected a continuation of a population shift away from the so-called Rust Belt in the Northeast to the Sun Belt states of the South, Southwest, and West. State legislatures are responsible for redrawing congressional district lines to account for population changes. In 1964, the Supreme Court ruled in *Westberry v. Sanders* that the districts have roughly the same number of people so that one person's vote in a congressional election is worth the same as another's. This is the "one person, one vote" principle.

The *Westberry v. Sanders* decision did not eliminate other potential problems with **redistricting**, however. The party in control of the state legislature may establish congressional and other legislative districts in such a way as to ensure that its candidates have safe seats. This process is called **gerrymandering**. In 2008, California voters approved creation of a 14-member commission made up of five Democrats, five Republicans, and four independents to handle redistricting. Although the state legislature is responsible for drawing congressional district boundaries, it follows the criteria established by the commission. The Court has also had to deal with racial gerrymandering (for example, the creation of districts intended to guarantee the election of minority candidates to office). In *Shaw v. Reno* (1993), the Supreme Court was extremely critical of oddly-shaped districts like North Carolina's 12th congressional district, and held that such districts could be challenged if race was the principal factor in their creation.

Racial gerrymandering is an attempt to deal with the fact that Congress does not reflect the demographic profile of the United States. Women and minorities have been elected in greater numbers over the last 30 years than previously, and the House is certainly more diverse than the Senate. But Congress as an institution remains predominately made up of white, middle-aged men. Members of Congress are much better off and more highly educated than the average American, and most have a business or law background.

Incumbency

Another key element of the makeup of Congress is incumbency. The percentage of incumbents (persons who hold office) reelected in the House historically ranges between 85 percent and 95 percent. Senate elections are somewhat riskier, but not that much; reelection rates for incumbent senators fluctuate more dramatically and are between 70 percent and 90 percent.

An incumbent has distinct advantages over a challenger, particularly for a House seat. The **franking privilege**, which gives members of Congress free use of the mail, allows the incumbent to communicate regularly with constituents through newsletters, reports, and surveys, as well as meetings and public forums back home. Representatives want to tell people about issues of consequence to them (for example, the federal highway, the additional construction on the army base, or the new water project from which the district will benefit). Bills that bring federal money directly into a member's district are called **pork-barrel legislation**. This term came into political usage after the Civil War; it refers to the practice of distributing salt-pork rations to slaves from wooden barrels. *Pork* in the political sense is often equated with wasteful spending; a project funded in this way may help a member of Congress get reelected, but taxpayers across the country are paying for it. An earmark is a type of pork-barrel spending; it is a specific project included in an appropriations bill that does not get a full hearing either in committee or on the floor. According to the Office of Management and Budget, there were over 11,000 earmarks totaling $16 billion in the 2008 fiscal year.

Incumbents also help voters through **casework**, providing a wide range of services to people in their district. Casework might involve resolving a dispute over the benefits due a Vietnam veteran or it might mean getting family tickets for a tour of the White House. Most important, those who already hold office get the lion's share of campaign contributions from political action committees (PACs) and other sources.

Concern over the power of incumbency led several states to pass laws or approve initiatives that limited the number of terms a member of Congress could serve. While term limits are in effect for elected officials at the local and state levels in many parts of the country, the Supreme Court ruled in 1995 that states cannot impose similar restrictions on representatives or senators (see *U.S. Term Limits, Inc. v. Thornton*). Opponents see term limits as a fundamental challenge to the right to vote. They argue that if a member of Congress is doing a good job, there is no reason to artificially limit how long he or she can serve; that is a decision that must be left to the electorate. Further, term limits mean a loss of valuable legislative experience.

Several factors help explain why Senate incumbents have a somewhat more difficult time winning reelection than members of the House do. A state is obviously much larger than a congressional district, and a senator's ability to satisfy all those diverse interests is limited. It's easier for opposition to develop. Senate races certainly attract better-known challengers than races in the House. An incumbent senator may find himself or herself in a battle with a popular governor whose name recognition is just as high. Also, because of the size of the constituency, senators are more remote from the voters and, thus, may not be able to communicate their positions as effectively as representatives can.

Organization of Congress

The Constitution is largely silent on the organization of Congress. It authorizes the House and the Senate to make their own rules, and names only three congressional officers. The vice president serves as president of the Senate but only casts a vote in the event of a tie. The president pro tempore presides over the Senate in the absence of the vice president; it is a ceremonial position usually given to the senior senator from the majority party. In contrast, the Speaker of the House does have real power. Traditionally elected from the majority party, the Speaker presides over the House, assigns bills to committees, influences committee assignments, appoints other party leaders, and controls debate on the floor. When the president is from one party and the House is controlled by the other, the Speaker is a national spokesperson for his or her party.

Political parties play an important role in Congress. Party whips assist the majority and minority leaders in both houses. In the House, the majority leader is second in command to the Speaker and is the party's chief legislative strategist. The minority leader represents the opposition but works with the majority leader and the Speaker to set the House agenda and schedule debate. Whips are the intermediaries between the leadership and the rank and file; whips are responsible for making sure party members vote with the leadership on important bills. Whips in the Senate have essentially the same tasks as they do in the House. The Senate majority leader has a role in assigning members to committees, schedules legislation together with the minority leader, and has the privilege of speaking first during debate. Both parties have a network of committees in each house that develop policy, make the final decision on who serves on what committee, and provide funds and advice for those who are up for reelection.

Much of the work that Congress does is through committees: Bills are introduced, hearings are held, and the first votes are taken on proposed laws. Committees also carry out Congress's oversight and investigative functions. There are four types of committees:

- **Standing committees:** Permanent committees that deal with legislation in their broad policy area—for example, the House Agriculture Committee or the Senate Foreign Relations Committee. Standing committees may also conduct investigations and/or oversight of federal agencies that come within their jurisdiction. The number and scope of standing committees can change from Congress to Congress. There were 20 standing committees in the House and 16 in the Senate in the 110th Congress (2007–2009); each standing committee has one or more subcommittees. The number of seats each party has on a standing committee reflects the party distribution in each house. Committee chairs, selected by the majority party (under rules established in 1995) are limited to six-year terms.

- **Joint committees:** Made up of members of both houses, joint committees are not concerned with legislation but look into and keep Congress informed on major policy concerns. An example would be the Joint Economic Committee.

- **Select or special committees:** These are temporary committees that are set up for a specific purpose outside the scope of standing committees; special committee functions can range from the Senate Special Committee on Aging to investigating scandals like Watergate (1973) and the Iran-Contra affair (1987).

- **Conference committees:** These committees reconcile differences between bills passed in the House and the Senate; standing committees that originally considered the legislation appoint the conference committee members.

Each committee has its own staff that prepares for hearings, does research, and assumes other administrative tasks. The staffs of senators and representatives have grown tremendously over the last half-century as the work of Congress has become more complex. Staff responsibilities can include helping constituents, drafting bills, helping with campaign matters, and negotiating with other congressional staff and the White House on legislation. Assistance is also available to Congress from specialized agencies:

- **Congressional Research Service:** Part of the Library of Congress, the Congressional Research Service answers questions and provides research at the request of members.

- **General Accountability Office:** This office audits federal spending by the executive branch, renders legal opinions, and conducts investigations at the request of Congress.

- **Congressional Budget Office:** Created in 1974, the Congressional Budget Office examines the economic impact of federal programs and evaluates the budget that the president prepares. It also offers a second opinion on budget matters.

Although the political parties are critical to the operation of Congress, informal groups exist that are increasingly important to the legislative process. A **caucus** is made up of members, who may or may not be from the same party, that share the same policy concerns and want to further legislation in their area of interest. Indeed, caucuses are seen as a rival to parties in shaping the policy agenda. Caucuses are organized by region, ethnicity, gender, and issue. The Congressional Black Caucus, the Bipartisan Disabilities Caucus, and the Oil and National Security Caucus are pertinent examples.

How a Bill Becomes a Law

The primary function of Congress is to enact legislation. Between 8,000 and 10,000 bills are introduced each term, but fewer than 10 percent actually become law. A **bill**, which is nothing more than a proposed law, usually has no single author. The executive branch develops much of the legislation that Congress considers. The president outlines the administration's legislative agenda in the State of the Union address.

Individual members working with their staffs, the party leadership in either the House or the Senate, a caucus, and interest groups may all have a hand in drafting a bill. The dance of legislation goes through a complicated process in the House and the Senate; the bill that finally becomes law rarely looks anything like the bill that was originally introduced.

Step 1: A bill is introduced

With the exception of revenue or tax bills that must originate in the House, legislation can be introduced in either house or in both simultaneously. Each bill is assigned a number (with the prefix *H.R.* for the House or *S.* for the Senate; H.R. 1 is the first bill introduced in that session of Congress) and is assigned to the appropriate committee.

Step 2: The bill in committee

The full committee refers the bill to one of its subcommittees, which may decide to hold hearings. Congressional hearings provide an opportunity for the administration, federal agencies impacted by the proposed legislation, and interest groups to provide their input. Testimony is taken and written materials are submitted and published. After the hearings, a markup session is held either in the subcommittee or the full committee, during which significant changes may be made to the bill. If the members then decide to "report the bill out," a **committee report** is prepared that contains the bill as amended, a summary of its main provisions, and the reasons for committee approval.

The committee may also table a bill, which means no further action is taken and the bill is effectively dead. If there are extensive amendments, the committee may decide to report the amended bill out as a new bill that is known as a clear bill. In rare instances, a bill can be reported out of committee with no recommendation or with a negative recommendation.

Committee reports are important to the courts. In trying to determine the meaning of language in a bill or the intent of Congress in enacting a statute, the courts often turn to the committee report as the most authoritative statement of what the bill was expected to accomplish. The reasoning is that the committee, which has sat through hearings and read submissions by a variety of interests, is the group most familiar with the legislation.

Step 3: A bill in the House Committee on Rules

In the House, most bills that are reported out go to Committee on Rules, which sets the scope of the debate on the floor. The Committee on Rules issues a rule that establishes the amount of time allocated for debate and whether amendments can be made. Under a **closed rule**, for example, there is a strict time limit and no amendments can be offered. The **open rule** allows for a general debate and provides that any member may offer an amendment. There are variations of both rules. Only germane amendments (amendments related to the substance of the bill) are allowed under the modified open rule. The modified closed rule (also called the structured rule) may limit amendments to a particular section of the bill as established by the Committee on Rules.

There is no equivalent to the Committee on Rules in the Senate; a bill goes from the committee directly to the Senate floor for action.

Step 4: A bill on the House and Senate floor

The Committee of the Whole debates most bills, which requires only 100 members to be present. Members of the sponsoring committee guide the debate with supporters and opponents given equal time to speak. If amendments are allowed under the rule, they must be related to the substance of the bill. Although the Committee of the Whole can get the bill into final shape, it cannot pass it; that requires a quorum of the House, or 218 members.

The debate in the Senate is much different. There is no time limit and no restrictions on the type of amendments that can be offered. A senator who wants to delay action on a bill or try to kill it completely may try to use a tactic called a **filibuster**; this is a marathon speech on any subject that may go on for hours, with the senator only yielding the floor to members who support his or her position. A filibuster can be cut off only through **cloture**. It takes 16 senators to ask for a cloture vote, and 60 senators must actually vote for cloture to end a filibuster. Even then, each senator still can speak on the bill for an hour.

Senators can introduce amendments completely unrelated to the bill. These amendments are known as **riders**, and they provide senators with the opportunity to enact pet projects. A senator may add an amendment to a defense appropriations bill for a water project to benefit his or her state, for example. A bill that has numerous riders is called a Christmas tree.

There are several ways in which Congress votes on a bill. For a voice vote, the members simply shout out "Aye" or "No," and the outcome is determined by the volume of each. If it's difficult to determine the outcome, a member can call for a *division,* or standing vote. First, those in favor of the bill stand and are counted; then those who are opposed do the same. The way an individual member votes is not recorded in a voice vote or a standing vote. Recorded votes are commonly done through electronic voting. Members insert their ID cards in machines located around the House and Senate chambers. Another type of recorded vote is the teller vote, in which members pass between two tellers—one for the yeas and one for the nays—and the clerks write down the names of those voting for or against the bill.

Step 5: A bill in the conference committee

In most instances, the House and the Senate pass different versions of the same bill. The **conference committee**, which is made up of majority and minority members of the committee that reported out the bill, is responsible for reconciling the differences. The compromise bill is sent to the House and Senate for approval, and no amendments are allowed.

Step 6: The bill goes to the president

A bill becomes law only when the president signs it. The president can *veto* (reject) a bill. If he does so, Congress can override the veto by a two-thirds vote of both houses. Most presidential vetoes are not overridden, however. If the president takes no action on the bill within ten days after he receives it, the bill becomes law without his signature. A **pocket veto** occurs when Congress adjourns within that ten-day period without the president signing the bill. The bill is, thus, effectively dead unless it is reintroduced in the next session of Congress.

A presidential signing statement is issued by the president when he or she signs a bill into law. It may simply comment on the value of the legislation or, more significantly, raise constitutional questions about the law and how the administration will implement it. Presidents of both parties have increasingly relied on signing statements in recent years.

Other Responsibilities of Congress

Congress has other responsibilities that are related to its lawmaking function: oversight and investigation.

Oversight

Oversight involves reviewing the operations of the executive branch to ensure that federal agencies implement laws the way Congress intends and that they use appropriated funds properly. Oversight is carried out by existing committees, often when agency heads or cabinet secretaries come to Capitol Hill to argue for their budgets. In the past, Congress could reject an executive action through a joint resolution; however, the Supreme Court declared the legislative veto unconstitutional in 1983. Today, Congress can accomplish the same goal by passing a law, and has the right to nullify a federal regulation within 60 days of issuance through a joint resolution. This is called **congressional review**.

Investigation

Whereas oversight is often routine, investigations usually focus on scandals or other crises. In addition to Watergate and the Iran-Contra affair, mentioned earlier, other examples of congressional investigations include the savings-and-loan industry scandal in the 1980s and allegations of illegal campaign contributions by the Clinton Administration.

How Congress Votes

Several factors explain how a member of Congress votes. Party considerations, constituent views, colleagues, interest groups, political action committees, and even the president may all play a role.

A clear sign of partisanship is when the majority of the Democrats vote one way and the majority of the Republicans vote the other way. Congress became increasingly partisan during the 1990s because we had a **divided government**—the president was a Democrat while the Republicans controlled both the House and the Senate for the first time in many years. Divided government returned following the 2006 midterm elections when the Democrats won majorities in both houses of Congress for the last two years of President George W. Bush's term. A member of Congress who consistently supports the party enjoys obvious advantages, such as choice committee assignments, increasing influence with the leadership, and perhaps even more assistance from the campaign committees. Obviously, a major reason for party voting in Congress is that Democrats and Republicans have basic ideological perspectives on legislation.

Political scientists often use the terms **trustee** and **delegate** to describe the relationship between a member of Congress and his or her constituents. Trustees believe in relying on their best judgment on the myriad of issues that come before them; delegates, on the other hand, closely follow how people in their district or state feel about a particular question and vote accordingly. The line between the two is blurred more often than not, and most senators and representatives try to adopt both roles as the situation warrants. One thing is clear, however: Elected officials cannot simply ignore the voters who sent them to Washington in the first place. Incumbents may be secure, but they are not invulnerable.

Despite the sometimes heated debates among representatives and senators, Congress is a collegial institution. Members develop strong bonds with one another, particularly if they serve on the same committee for a number of years. A personal appeal from a close friend can sometimes win over a vote on an important piece of legislation. There is also a long tradition in the Congress of **logrolling**; basically, one congressperson says to another, "I'll vote for your bill, if you vote for mine." Logrolling goes far in explaining why so much pork-barrel legislation passes.

Interest groups and political action committees don't buy votes; they buy access. With access comes the opportunity to explain a position on a bill to a member or his or her staff, and provide them with information that may be helpful in making a decision. Interest groups can, indeed, put pressure on a representative or senator by mobilizing constituent public opinion for or against legislation. The promise of campaign contributions may not fall on deaf ears on a minor bill that doesn't impact a member's state or district one way or the other.

The president can influence votes in Congress in several ways. On a close vote on a bill important to the administration, he or she can call up party members to ask for their support or even invite a few to the Oval Office for a chat. It isn't easy to refuse a request from the president. The president also can try to rally public opinion behind his or her legislative agenda much the same way an interest group might, with the idea of putting pressure on Congress to vote a certain way. Key administration officials can travel to different parts of the country to push the legislative program; they can also go on the Sunday morning talk shows. Finally, the president can publicly threaten to veto legislation.

Practice

1. The official who is an intermediary between the party leadership and the rank and file members of Congress is the

   A. Speaker of the House
   B. majority leader
   C. majority whip
   D. president pro tempore
   E. clerk of the House

2. Which of the following activities that members of Congress routinely perform is most important to their constituents?

   A. attending the meeting of the party caucus
   B. going to a fundraiser sponsored by a political action committee
   C. giving an interview on national defense issues
   D. drafting an amendment to the Department of Transportation appropriation bill
   E. contacting the Social Security Administration regarding a claim for benefits

3. Incumbent senators face greater competition when they run for reelection than members of the House do for all the following reasons EXCEPT

   A. A state is more diverse than a congressional district, providing a greater base for opposition.
   B. Senators have less contact with the constituents.
   C. Voters are less likely to know the issue positions of their senators.
   D. Senators tend to have better-known opponents.
   E. To overcome their advantage, Senate challengers outspend incumbents.

4. When courts examine the legislative history of a bill, they give the most weight to which type of evidence?

   A. committee hearings
   B. committee reports
   C. the markup bill
   D. floor debate in the *Congressional Record*
   E. the bill as introduced

5. Responsibility for reconciling the House and Senate versions of a bill falls to a

   A. conference committee
   B. standing committee
   C. select committee
   D. oversight committee
   E. joint committee

6. Which of the following provisions of a defense appropriations bill is considered a rider?

   A. funding for a new missile defense system
   B. increase in benefits for military dependents
   C. price support for dairy farmers in New England
   D. construction of family-housing units at an naval air station
   E. research and development funding on anti-terrorism tactics

7. Those who oppose term limits for members of Congress argue that

   I. A tremendous amount of legislative experience will be lost if term limits are imposed.
   II. The people have the right to vote for whomever they want.
   III. The Supreme Court will never allow term limits.
   IV. A less experienced Congress will lead the country into war.

   A. I only
   B. I and II only
   C. I, II, and III only
   D. III only
   E. II and IV only

8. All the following statements about the legislative process are true EXCEPT

    A. Only a small percentage of bills introduced become law.

    B. Anyone can write a bill, but only a member of Congress can introduce it.

    C. A majority of the House does not have to be present to debate a bill on the floor.

    D. A cloture vote cuts off debate on a bill immediately, and the Senate must vote.

    E. Identical bills can be introduced in both the House and the Senate.

9. Which of the following is a non-legislative function of the House of Representatives under the Constitution?

    A. to impeach federal officials

    B. to approve appointments to federal courts

    C. to advise and consent on treaties negotiated by the president

    D. to try cases of impeachment

    E. to debate all revenue bills

10. A bill or a provision of a bill that provides clear benefits to the district of a member of Congress is an example of

    A. logrolling

    B. a Christmas tree

    C. a public bill

    D. a private bill

    E. pork-barrel legislation

11. Political action committees make larger total contributions to House races than they do to Senate races because

    A. House members are more likely to vote the way the PAC wants.

    B. House members have more influence on legislation than the Senate.

    C. The entire house is up for election every two years.

    D. Senators are much wealthier than representatives.

    E. Senators cannot take PAC money under the Senate rules.

12. In the process of enacting legislation, the House Committee on Rules is responsible for

    A. establishing the procedures Congress follows

    B. appointing members of standing committees

    C. setting the limits of debate on the floor

    D. holding hearings on all revenue bills

    E. assigning bills to the proper committees

13. All the following are examples of Congress exercising its oversight function EXCEPT

    A. holding a floor debate on a bill to reduce eligibility requirements for Medicare

    B. hearing a Department of Defense official testify on B-1 bomber cost overruns

    C. submitting data to a committee on complaints against the Internal Revenue Service

    D. holding committee hearings on regulations issued by the Federal Communications Commission

    E. cutting the budget of a federal agency that consistently fails to meet its goals

14. A newly elected member of Congress who represents a district with a large number of aerospace companies would prefer to serve on which of the following committees?

    A. Banking and Financial Services

    B. Judiciary

    C. Ways and Means

    D. International Relations

    E. Armed Services

15. Which of the following statements about the Speaker of the House are valid?

    I. The Speaker is elected by only the members of the majority party.

    II. The Speaker is next in line for succession after the vice president.

    III. The Speaker presides over the House.

    IV. The Speaker assigns bills to committees.

    A. I, II, and III only

    B. I and II only

    C. II, III, and IV only

    D. III and IV only

    E. II and III only

Answers

1. **C** The question refers to members of Congress, so you should eliminate officials of one house or the other—Speaker of the House, clerk of the House, president pro tempore of the Senate. The major leader is obviously part of the leadership, which leaves you with the majority whip.

2. **E** Contacting the Social Security Administration is an example of casework, the type of services that constituents expect a member of Congress to perform for them and for which they reward him or her when election day comes. All the other choices are certainly part of the job description of a senator or representative. The interview on national defense issues might be significant to some voters, but helping out constituents would be more important.

3. **E** Although the cost of a statewide Senate race is considerably more than a House contest, the advantages of incumbency still hold. An incumbent in an election for a Senate seat almost always has more money to spend than his or her opponent.

4. **B** Those most familiar with the bill—the members of a committee or subcommittee who held hearings on the legislation, shifted through considerable testimony and other documentation, and amended the bill in a markup session—prepare the committee report. The report also gives a synopsis of the legislation and other elements that may help the court in determining the intent of Congress.

5. **A** This question requires you to know the functions of the four types of committees in Congress. Although there is no such thing as an oversight committee, the oversight function of Congress has nothing to do with working out the differences between House and Senate versions of a bill.

6. **C** By definition, a rider is a provision added to a bill, usually as an amendment, which has nothing to do with the substance of the legislation. It's a way for members to get pork-barrel legislation passed or to get support for a project that may not be able to get enough votes on its own. Support for dairy prices clearly is extraneous to the main purpose of a defense appropriations bill. All the other choices could certainly be funded by the legislation.

7. **B** The most often made argument against term limits—whether on the local, state, or federal level—is that it results in a loss of valuable experience. Opponents also claim that term limits deprive voters of electing the people they want to elect; they maintain that it isn't up to the government to determine when an elected official has served enough time—the voters are quite capable of making that decision. The Supreme Court struck down state-initiated term limits for the Senate and the House, but it did not say term limits per se were unconstitutional. In fact, the Court implied that term limits could be accomplished through a constitutional amendment. Congress failed to propose such an amendment in 1995 and again in 1997.

8. **D** Although a cloture vote ends a filibuster, each senator can still speak up to one hour on the bill on the floor; it does not immediately end debate. Don't be fooled by the opening phrase in **B**. Anyone can write a bill—interest groups, presidential aides, congressional staff, and even someone from the public. The legislative process does not begin until a representative or a senator introduces the bill in Congress.

9. **A** The purpose of this question is to see if you know the different responsibilities of the House and the Senate. You should realize that "advice and consent" on treaties and confirmation of presidential appointments is solely the function of the Senate. Debating revenue bills is a legislative function. The Constitution is very clear on the respective functions of the House and the Senate on impeachment. The House has the power to impeach, which is tantamount to an indictment; in other words, there is enough evidence to bring a federal official to trial for "treason, bribery, or other high crimes and misdemeanors." The trial takes place in the Senate.

10. **E** Pork-barrel legislation allows a member of Congress to "bring home the bacon" (for example, a federal program or project in the member's district or home state that translates into jobs or some other tangible benefit). You should recognize that pork-barrel legislation may be the product of logrolling or vote trading and can be an example of one of the ornaments on a Christmas tree. The term *Christmas tree* is used to describe a bill that has so many riders that extraneous provisions are just hung on it.

11. **C** The key word in the question is *total*. Every two years, all 435 members of the House are up for reelection while only a third of the Senate is running. Statewide contests are obviously more costly than contests in a congressional district, but there are simply many more congressional races for PACs to help fund. There are no rules prohibiting any elected official from taking PAC money; such a prohibition would be a major campaign finance reform.

12. **C** Although the House Committee on Rules does set the procedural rules of the House of Representatives, its key legislative function is to set the time limit of debate for most bills and whether and what type of amendments can be made from the floor. Some limits are necessary because of the size of the House—with unlimited debate and amendment and 435 members, nothing would ever get accomplished. It's important to remember that there is no counterpart to the Committee on Rules in the Senate.

13. **A** The oversight function of Congress largely takes place through the hearing process. A floor debate on a bill is an example of Congress engaged in lawmaking. All the other answers focus on committees examining budgets and/or on policy issues of federal agencies; the decision to cut the budget of an agency is made in committee.

14. **E** Members of Congress prefer to serve on committees that they believe will enhance their career or allow them to serve their district. Both the Judiciary and International Relations committees have a high profile, but the aerospace companies in this member's district rely heavily on defense contracts. Serving on the Armed Services Committee would certainly give him or her the opportunity to steer defense work to the district, which translates into jobs and economic development.

15. **C** Although the Speaker of the House is from the majority party, the entire House elects him or her. This is a pro forma exercise with members voting along strict party lines.

The Presidency

Because it was still fighting a war against King George III at the time the Articles of Confederation were drawn up, the Continental Congress was exceedingly wary of executive authority and didn't provide for it in the articles. The framers of the Constitution, on the other hand, appreciated the need for an executive but debated whether it should be in the hands of a multi-person board or a single individual. They eventually decided on a president to serve a four-year term and made sure, through the formation of the Electoral College, that presidential selection was as far removed from the people as possible. Since that time, the presidency has evolved considerably further than the delegates at the Federal Convention could have imagined.

Under many parliamentary systems, the head of state and the chief executive (or head of government) are different people. In Great Britain, the monarch is the head of state, but the prime minister is the chief executive (head of government). The president plays both roles. When accepting the credentials of a new ambassador to the United States or lighting the National Christmas Tree, the president is acting as the head of state. When meeting with the chancellor of Germany, the president is acting as the nation's chief diplomat.

Presidential Authority

In addition to seeing that all laws are faithfully executed and having the right to pardon individuals convicted of federal crimes (except impeachment), the authority granted to the president under the Constitution covers three broad areas: foreign policy/military powers, legislative authority, appointive powers. In addition, there are **inherent powers** implied in the Constitution.

Foreign Policy/Military Powers

Ever since George Washington announced American neutrality in the war between Great Britain and France, the president has been responsible for articulating and implementing the foreign policy of the United States. The president can employ numerous tools in U.S. relations with other countries, such as the threat or use of military force, or the promise of foreign aid. He or she also can work through intergovernmental organizations such as the United Nations, or use personal diplomacy and persuasion. The president's foreign policy and military powers are in Article II, Section 2 of the Constitution.

The president negotiates treaties with other nations, but such international agreements do not go into effect until the Senate approves them through a two-thirds vote. Although the Senate usually goes along with the administration, there have been notable exceptions. The Senate rejected the Treaty of Versailles, which ended World War I, because it included the Covenant of the League of Nations that, according to many in Congress, weakened U.S. freedom of action. As a result, the United States never became a member of the League of Nations and signed separate treaties with Germany and Austria in 1921.

An **executive agreement** is an understanding between the president and the chief executive of another country. It usually involves less important matters than a treaty, does not require approval by a two-thirds vote of the Senate, but has the same status of a treaty. Congress can vote to cancel an executive agreement or refuse to appropriate money to put it into effect. The president can also withdraw the United States from a treaty, as President George W. Bush did with the 1972 Ant-Ballistic Missile (ABM) Treaty with the Soviet Union.

The president isn't the only one who can make treaties. The secretary of state, which was the first cabinet position created in 1789, has responsibility here as well, along with the coordination and supervision of the diplomatic efforts of the United States. The president appoints ambassadors and other officials, in addition to the secretary of state, to carry out U.S. foreign policy.

The president's authority in foreign policy grew as the United States transformed itself from a minor player in world affairs to the only superpower after the collapse of the Soviet Union. The chief executive also receives ambassadors from other countries, confers diplomatic recognition, and is the commander-in-chief of the armed services. As the commander-in-chief, the president can commit U.S. troops overseas, confer commissions on military officers, and head the National Guard when called to serve the United States.

Under the Constitution, the president is the commander-in-chief of the armed services. This provision ensures civilian control of the military. The close link between the military and the conduct of foreign policy is clear. At the end of the Vietnam War, however, Congress became extremely wary of the president's ability to commit U.S. troops to hot spots around the world. With the presidency weakened by the Watergate scandal, Congress passed the **War Powers Act (1973)** to limit presidential power as commander-in-chief. Under the legislation, the use of combat forces is limited to 60 days without congressional approval. The War Powers Act was passed over President Nixon's veto, and the Supreme Court has never fully examined it. The history of U.S. military action since 1973 suggests that the War Powers Act has not unduly hampered U.S. foreign or military policy. Congress did authorize the use of force in the 1991 Persian Gulf War and in Iraq in 2002. As opposition to the war grew, however, Congress found it impossible to force President George W. Bush to change policy, short of cutting off funds for the war, which it refused to do.

The president is also the commander-in-chief of the state National Guard when called into federal service. National Guard units served in World War I, World War II, the Korean War, Vietnam, and most recently in Iraq and Afghanistan, as well as in numerous peacekeeping missions around the world. In 1957, President Eisenhower sent regular army troops and federalized the Arkansas National Guard to enforce a court order integrating Central High School in Little Rock, Arkansas.

Legislative Authority

Despite the separation of powers, the president has significant legislative authority under the Constitution. In fact, the president is often called the nation's chief legislator. Much, but by no means all, that Congress does during a term focuses on the legislation that the president wants to enact. The State of the Union address each January is an outline of the administration's legislative agenda for the coming session. In addition, the president can call the House and the Senate into special session and can adjourn both houses if they can't agree on an adjournment time.

In the past, presidential programs put before Congress defined administrations; Franklin Roosevelt's New Deal, John F. Kennedy's New Frontier, and Lyndon Johnson's Great Society are examples. The success a president has in moving legislation through Congress depends on several factors. It's an easier job if the same party controls both the White House and Congress; in recent years, however, divided government has been the rule. The president's own political skill is obviously important. Lyndon Johnson, who was Senate majority leader before becoming Kennedy's vice president, was a master at working Congress. Bill Clinton's relationship with Congress during his first term was miserable, but he learned from his mistakes. The president can use the prestige of the office to encourage members of Congress to support his or her policies or use the bully pulpit to mobilize public opinion behind a legislative initiative.

The most important legislative power the president has is the veto. A bill becomes law if it is signed by the president within ten days (Sundays excepted) after it passes both houses of Congress. Through the veto, the bill is sent back to Congress along with the reasons for its rejection. Congress can override the veto (meaning, the bill goes into effect despite the president's objections) by a two-thirds vote in the House and the Senate. Because Congress rarely can muster the necessary votes, the presidential veto or even the threat of a veto is a powerful tool for shaping national policy. Every president knows that only around 4 percent of vetoes are overridden. If the president neither signs nor vetoes a bill within the ten days, it becomes law. The president has another option: If the president takes no action on a bill and Congress adjourns during that ten-day period, the bill is dead; this is known as a **pocket veto**. Congress does not have the opportunity to override a pocket veto because it is no longer in session. Supporters of the bill have to reintroduce it in the next session, and start the legislative process all over again.

Appointive Powers

The president appoints a broad range of federal officials, including justices of the Supreme Court, subject to the approval of the Senate. The Constitution also provides a way around a recalcitrant Senate: The president can fill "all vacancies that may happen during the recess of the Senate, by granting commissions which shall expire at the end of their next session [of Congress]"; this is known as a **recess appointment**. It is an expedient that all recent presidents have used when the Senate balked at acting on nominees for high government positions.

The appointment power allows a president to have an administration that supports his or her policies and programs. All presidents appreciate that the selection of a Supreme Court justice is their most important appointment. Their selection can shape the direction of the Court for years to come.

Inherent Powers

Under the doctrine of **inherent powers**, the president can infer additional powers from the provisions of the Constitution. For example, Thomas Jefferson initially believed that a constitutional amendment was necessary to buy the Louisiana Territory from France, but he went ahead with the purchase after he was convinced it was justified under his ability to enter into treaties.

Many presidents claim **executive privilege**. This means that the president decides when information developed within the executive branch must be kept confidential and not released to either the Congress or the courts. The basis of an executive privilege claim is twofold: separation of powers and the need to protect diplomatic and military secrets. A somewhat broader concept holds that confidentiality of the advice given the president must be maintained, or else candid appraisals would not be rendered. Although recognizing the need for executive privilege in certain instances, the Supreme Court ruled in *United States v. Nixon* (1973) that the president did not have an absolute right to refuse to turn over evidence sought by the judiciary. The case involved tape recordings of White House conversations between the president and his aides that Nixon did not want to turn over to the special prosecutor during the Watergate scandal. More recently, President Clinton invoked executive privilege during the Monica Lewinsky scandal, as did President George W. Bush during the investigation into the firing of federal prosecutors.

There are also functions that the president performs that are not clearly spelled out in the Constitution or that the framers never envisioned. For example, one of the key functions of the president is to serve as the head of his or her party. In this capacity, the president helps raise money, campaigns for candidates for state and federal office, and appoints the chair of the national committee that runs the day-to-day operations of the party.

The Founding Fathers were opposed to political parties. James Madison criticized what he called "factions" in *Federalist No. 10,* and President George Washington warned against "the baneful effects of the spirit of party" in his farewell address to the nation in 1796. Today, a president can expect some but not unqualified support from members of his or her own party in Congress. Members are ultimately responsible to voters in their districts for political survival, and they must decide whether following the president is an advantage. Political scientists often refer to a president's "coattails"—the ability of the president or the party's candidate for president to get representatives and senators elected. Studies show, however, that the congressional gains of the party that takes the White House are rather modest. In **midterm elections** (those held between presidential elections), the president's party invariably loses seats; the Democrats lost control of both the House and the Senate under President Clinton in 1994, and the Republicans faced a similar reversal in 2006 under President George W. Bush. Along the same lines, every president enjoys a brief time after the inauguration when relations with Congress, the public, and the media are usually very good; this is known as the "honeymoon period" and reflects the sense of a new beginning after a hard-fought election campaign.

Congress, moreover, has given presidents additional power through legislation, which the Supreme Court has sometimes rejected and at other times endorsed. The Budget and Accounting Act of 1921, for example, gave the president the authority to establish the annual budgets for all federal agencies. It created the Bureau of the Budget, which became the Office of Management and Budget in 1970, to assist the White House with this new function. Congress also gave the president the power to negotiate trade agreements that reduce or modify tariff rates for a limited period of time. These are called **congressional-executive agreements**, and they require only a majority vote in both houses of Congress to go into effect, not a two-thirds vote of the Senate. The North American Free Trade Agreement (1993) is a good example.

The USA Patriot Act (2001), passed in the wake of the events of September 11, 2001, significantly expanded the power of the executive branch to deal with domestic and international terrorism. Often criticized for undermining civil liberties, protections were included when the law was reauthorized by Congress in 2006.

The Line-Item Veto Act (1996) allowed the president to selectively cancel portions of an appropriations bill without vetoing the entire bill. It provided a means to cut federal spending and reduce the deficit. The Supreme Court in *Clinton v. City of New York* (1998) found the law unconstitutional because the president was given the opportunity to "amend" legislation.

The Organization of the Executive Branch

The Constitution clearly envisioned that the executive branch would consist of more than just the president. It refers to "the principal officers in each of the executive departments," and holds out the possibility that the "Heads of Departments" may appoint other officials. In carrying out executive functions, the president relies on the following:

- The White House office
- The agencies that comprise the Executive Office of the President
- The cabinet

The White House Office

The closest advisors to the president comprise the White House office. As the president's personal staff, they do not require confirmation by the Senate and they serve at the pleasure of the president. Many have a long relationship with the president and/or play an important role during his election campaign. They include the following:

- The chief of staff, who is responsible for the overall operations of the White House office
- The national security advisor, who briefs the president on a daily basis on world situations
- The chief domestic policy advisor, who coordinates the administration's programs both within the executive branch and Congress
- The communications director/press secretary, who is the spokesperson for the president and the administration and meets with the White House press corps daily

In addition, there are numerous special assistants, counselors, and assistants to the president who deal with a broad range of political and legislative issues. The West Wing houses offices for key personnel on the White House staff, just a few steps away from the Oval Office. The vice president and his or her staff also have offices in the West Wing.

The Executive Office of the President

The Executive Office of the President (EOP) was created by Franklin Roosevelt in 1939 to help him oversee the myriad federal agencies and programs created as part of the New Deal. Today, the EOP is an umbrella organization for a variety of administrative agencies, the most important of which are the following:

- **Office of Management and Budget (OMB):** The OMB's primary responsibility is to prepare the administration's budget proposal. In addition, the OMB evaluates the operation of federal programs, reviews legislative proposals from the cabinet departments, and reviews the rules and regulations proposed by federal agencies.
- **National Security Council (NSC):** The statutory members of the NSC include the president, the vice president, and the secretaries of defense and state. The chairman of the Joint Chiefs of Staff and the director of the Central Intelligence Agency (CIA) are the statutory military and intelligence advisors, respectively. The

Secretary of the Treasury, the U.S. Representative to the United Nations, and the National Security Advisor are among those invited to all meetings. The NSC is the principal forum for discussing national security and foreign policy and is responsible for coordinating policies with various other federal agencies.

- **Council of Economic Advisers (CEA):** Provides assistance and advice to the president in preparing the annual economic report; it also collects and disseminates information on economic policy and trends and recommends policies to the president.

Unlike the White House staff, appointments to EOP agencies do require confirmation by the Senate.

The Office of National AIDS Policy, the Office of National Drug Control Policy, the Office of the U.S. Trade Representative, and the Office of Personnel Management are also part of the EOP. President George W. Bush added the Office of Faith-Based and Community Initiatives (2001), and President Obama added the President's Economic Recovery Advisory Board (2009).

The Cabinet

The cabinet has grown from 3 departments under George Washington—State, War (now Defense), and Treasury—to 15 today. That growth not only reflects the fact that the scope of the government's responsibilities has changed, but also reflects successful lobbying by interest groups—farmers in the case of the Department of Agriculture; workers and the early unions in the case of the Department of Labor. The creation of a new executive department says that an issue is important to the country.

The Cabinet		
Title	**Department**	**Comment**
Secretary of state	Department of State	The Department of State, established in 1789, is the main foreign affairs agency of the federal government. The secretary of state is the president's chief foreign policy advisor.
Secretary of the treasury	Department of the Treasury	The Department of the Treasury, established in 1789, is responsible for developing domestic and international financial, economic, and tax policy. The secretary of the treasury is a key economic advisor to the president.
Secretary of defense	Department of Defense	The Department of Defense maintains and directs the military and defense policy of the United States; originally, it was called the Department of War (which was established in 1789). The position of secretary of defense was created in 1947 for the National Military Establishment, and the Department of Defense was formally established in 1949.
Attorney general	Department of Justice	The Office of the Attorney General was established in 1789, but the Department of Justice, which the attorney general heads, was not established until 1870. The attorney general is the chief law enforcement officer of the United States. The Department of Justice is responsible for enforcing the law, preventing and controlling crime, administering justice, and protecting the public safety.
Secretary of the interior	Department of the Interior	The Department of the Interior, established in 1849, is responsible for the protection and management of the nation's natural and cultural resources, including the national parks and territories. Federal–Native American relations are also under the jurisdiction of the Department of the Interior.
Secretary of agriculture	Department of Agriculture	The Department of Agriculture, established in 1862, develops U.S. agricultural policy, including farm income maintenance programs and expanding markets for U.S. farm products. Food safety is also a responsibility of the Department of Agriculture.

(continued)

(continued)

Title	Department	Comment
Secretary of commerce	Department of Commerce	The Department of Commerce was established as the Department of Commerce and Labor in 1903, with separate departments established in 1913. It promotes international trade, economic development, and technological innovation. The Patent and Trademark Office and the Bureau of the Census are under its umbrella.
Secretary of labor	Department of Labor	The Department of Labor, established in 1913, enforces federal labor laws, improves working conditions, and promotes opportunities for workers through training and full employment.
Secretary of health and human services	Department of Health and Human Services	The Department of Health, Education, and Welfare (HEW) was created in 1953; when the education functions were transferred to the new Department of Education in 1979, the department was renamed the Department of Health and Human Services. The department is responsible for protecting the health of the nation and providing services to those who can least help themselves. Medicare and Head Start come under Health and Human Services.
Secretary of housing and urban development	Department of Housing and Urban Development	The Department of Housing and Urban Development, established in 1965, focuses on national housing needs and fair housing policies, insures mortgages, and provides federal housing subsidies.
Secretary of transportation	Department of Transportation	The Department of Transportation, established in 1966, oversees national transportation policy, including safety regarding airlines, railroads, federal highways, and maritime traffic.
Secretary of energy	Department of Energy	The Department of Energy, established in 1977, develops national energy policy, promotes energy source diversity, and is a source of information on energy technology.
Secretary of education	Department of Education	The Department of Education, established in 1979, establishes education policy and administers and coordinates federal aid to education at all levels.
Secretary of veterans affairs	Department of Veterans Affairs	Established in 1930 as the Veterans Administration, the Department of Veterans Affairs was created in 1989 and operates medical care, disability, and pension programs for veterans and their families.
Secretary of homeland security	Department of Homeland Security	The Department of Homeland Security, established in 2002, is responsible for the protection of the United States against terrorist attacks and responding to natural disasters. Immigration, customs enforcement, the U.S. Coast Guard, and the Transportation Security Administration fall under its jurisdiction as well.

In addition to the president, the vice president, and the cabinet members, other federal officials, including the following, are entitled to attend cabinet meetings at the president's discretion:

- Administrator of the Environmental Protection Agency
- Chair of the Council of Economic Advisers
- Director of the Office of Management and Budget
- U.S. ambassador to the United Nations
- U.S. trade representative
- White House chief of staff

With 15-plus members, the cabinet is too large to be an effective policymaking body. The cabinet members are, however, the link between the administration and their departments. They're expected to carry out the president's policies in their areas and manage their own bureaucracies in an efficient and effective manner. But they're also subject to other pressures—Congress determines their budgets and functions in the role of overseer, career civil servants within the departments have their own institutional culture, and interest groups are always trying to move policy in one direction or another.

Cabinet members are the most visible appointments that a president makes. Several factors are taken into account in selecting a nominee:

- The nominee's professional qualifications and experience for the job are obviously critical, as are the views of a candidate on the issues with which the department is concerned. A president who campaigned on a strong environmental platform is unlikely to consider someone for secretary of energy who advocates extensive off-shore drilling for oil or building a natural-gas pipeline through a wilderness preserve.

- The nominee's relationship with important constituent groups influences his or her chances as a cabinet choice. A nominee for secretary of labor or secretary of veterans affairs must have support from organized labor and veterans groups, respectively. Also, almost invariably, people whom the president names to the cabinet share the same party affiliation as the president.

- The cabinet candidate should reflect the diversity of the country. Recent presidents have appointed women and members of minority groups to key cabinet positions.

The White House office, the Executive Office of the President, and the cabinet do not exhaust the executive branch. Each executive department employs tens of thousands of workers in various agencies and bureaus. The Department of Justice, for example, includes the Federal Bureau of Investigation, the Immigration and Naturalization Service, and the Drug Enforcement Administration. In addition, there are **independent executive agencies** such as the Environmental Protection Agency and the National Aeronautics and Space Administration (NASA), as well as **independent regulatory agencies** such as the Federal Energy Regulatory Commission. Both independent executive and regulatory agencies are discussed in the next chapter.

The Vice President, Presidential Succession, and Impeachment

Under the Constitution, the vice president presides over the Senate and casts a vote in the event of a tie. Although John Adams called the vice presidency "the most insignificant office that ever the invention of man contrived or his imagination conceived," the fact remains that 14 vice presidents have become president through death (natural or otherwise), resignation, or winning the office in their own right. The election route to the White House is not an easy one. In the 20th century, only two vice presidents succeeded: Richard Nixon and George H. W. Bush, and Nixon lost to John Kennedy the first time around. As Al Gore learned in 2000, it's difficult for a vice president to escape the shadow of his predecessor.

All presidential candidates claim that their choice of a running mate is dictated by the ability of that person to assume the nation's highest office. Over the last quarter of a century, vice presidents have complemented the strengths of the top of the ticket. Jimmy Carter, a one-term governor from Georgia who ran as a Washington outsider, selected Senator Walter Mondale, who had considerable experience in Congress. Ronald Reagan's lack of expertise in foreign policy was balanced—to an extent—by George H. W. Bush, who had served as ambassador to China and as director of the CIA. To be sure, the president determines the responsibilities given to the vice president. Al Gore was a close advisor to President Clinton, and an important voice for the administration on environmental issues. Although there was much comment on the fact that Vice President Cheney became less visible after the events of September 11, 2001, there is little doubt that he was a major policymaker in the Bush Administration.

The Presidential Succession Act of 1947 established the order of succession after the vice president. If the vice president cannot serve, the office falls to the Speaker of the House, followed by the president pro tempore of the Senate, and then the cabinet members in the order in which their departments were created—for example, the secretary of state is first. There are several shortcomings with this system. The Speaker of the House and the president pro tempore may well be from a different party than the president in this era of divided government, and the president pro tempore may be elderly, given that the position is based on seniority. Moreover, the law did not address a vacancy in the vice presidency. The Twenty-fifth Amendment resolved the issue of a vice-presidential vacancy.

When a vacancy occurs, the president selects a nominee for the office whom a majority of both houses of Congress must confirm. This procedure has been used twice to date—the selection of Gerald Ford by President Nixon following the resignation of Spiro Agnew, and Ford's selection of Nelson Rockefeller when Nixon left office and Ford became president. The amendment also addresses the matter of presidential disability.

The vice president serves as acting president when the president declares that he cannot discharge the duties of the office. This section might be invoked, for example, if the president undergoes surgery. The vice president and a majority of the cabinet can also declare that a president is incapable of exercising his authority, and, in such an event, the vice president becomes acting president. If the president challenges this action, Congress must ultimately decide by a two-thirds vote if, indeed, the president is unable to serve.

The Constitution provides a means of removing a president from office by impeachment in the House of Representatives and conviction at trial in the Senate for "treason, bribery, or other high crimes and misdemeanors." Impeachment is the process used to determine whether there is enough evidence to bring the president to trial; it is very similar to an indictment. The investigation of the charges is the responsibility of the House Judiciary Committee, which issues Articles of Impeachment to the full House if warranted. Richard Nixon resigned in 1974 before the full House acted on the Articles of Impeachment. At the Senate trial, which is presided over by the chief justice of the Supreme Court, members of the House represent the "prosecution," while the president has his or her own lawyers. The Senate needs a two-thirds vote on any of the Articles of Impeachment to convict the president. At the 1999 trial of President Clinton, the Senate rejected the charge of perjury before the grand jury and split on the charge of obstruction of justice.

Practice

1. The period immediately after a new president is inaugurated is known as the honeymoon period because
   A. Other nations do not challenge the United States.
   B. The president's popularity is at its highest level.
   C. There is no infighting between members of the president's staff.
   D. The president has not vetoed any legislation.
   E. Partisanship in Congress is high.

2. All the following are powers granted to the president under the Constitution EXCEPT the power to
   A. negotiate treaties with other nations
   B. nominate justices to the Supreme Court
   C. present legislation to Congress
   D. serve as the leader of a political party
   E. call Congress into special session

3. Examples of Congress delegating additional powers to the president include the
   I. legislative veto
   II. line item veto
   III. War Powers Act
   IV. Budgeting and Accounting Act

   A. II only
   B. I and III only
   C. II and IV only
   D. IV only
   E. I and II only

4. The responsibilities of the vice president in an administration are determined by
   A. the provisions of the Constitution
   B. the relationship between the president and vice president
   C. polls indicating the popularity of the vice president
   D. the size of the election victory
   E. whether the president's party also controls Congress

5. Which of the following agencies is NOT part of the Executive Office of the President?
   A. Office of Management and Budget
   B. National Security Council
   C. Council of Economic Advisers
   D. Office of Personnel Management
   E. Environmental Protection Agency

6. The only presidential appointment on which the House of Representatives votes is
   A. chief justice of the Supreme Court
   B. U.S. ambassador to the United Nations
   C. chairman of the Joint Chiefs of Staff
   D. vice president, if the position is vacant
   E. director of the Central Intelligence Agency

7. What usually happens to the president's party in midterm elections?
   A. It loses seats in both houses of Congress.
   B. It loses seats in the Senate but increases its support in the House.
   C. It loses seats in the House but increases its support in the Senate.
   D. It gains seats in both houses of Congress.
   E. No pattern of gains or loses is discernible.

Presidential Vetoes, 1961–2008				
President	Term	Regular Vetoes	Pocket Vetoes	Vetoes Overridden
Kennedy	1961–1963	12	9	0
Johnson	1963–1969	16	14	0
Nixon	1969–1974	26	17	7
Ford	1974–1977	48	18	12
Carter	1977–1981	13	18	2
Reagan	1981–1989	39	39	9
Bush	1989–1993	29	15	1
Clinton	1993–2001	36	1	2
Bush	2001-2008	11	1	4

Source: The World Almanac and Book of Facts 2009. Pleasantville, NY: World Almanac Books, 2009.

8. According to the preceding table, which of the following statements about the use of the veto is valid?

   A. The use of the veto has become more common.

   B. A veto override is more likely when the president and Congress are from the same party.

   C. Pocket vetoes are less successful than regular vetoes.

   D. After a bill is vetoed, it is not likely to be passed.

   E. Democratic presidents used the veto more often than Republicans.

9. The strongest basis for withholding information from Congress under a claim of executive privilege is

   A. the need for secrecy in military planning and diplomacy

   B. to protect the president from embarrassment

   C. to ensure that the president does not turn over incriminating evidence

   D. the powers granted to the president under the Constitution

   E. legislation that recognizes that Congress cannot subpoena the president

10. The president can take action without the approval of Congress through

    I. executive orders
    II. recess appointments
    III. judicial appointments
    IV. executive agreements

    A. I only

    B. I and II only

    C. I, II, and III only

    D. I, II, and IV only

    E. III and IV only

11. An important function of the White House staff is to

    A. prepare the administration's budget for Congress

    B. assume responsibility for executive departments

    C. supervise campaign fundraising activities

    D. liaise with Congress on the bills of interest to the administration

    E. communicate the administration's views on matters before the Supreme Court

12. Which of the following statements about the cabinet is NOT valid?

   A. The cabinet is too large to be an effective policymaking body.
   B. The president can give officials other than the heads of departments cabinet rank.
   C. The cabinet is made up of close associates of the president who were involved with the campaign.
   D. Recent presidents have made cabinet appointments with an eye toward diversity.
   E. Cabinet members are primarily responsible for managing their own departments.

13. Which of the following would be affected if Congress invoked the War Powers Act?

   A. the closing of an army base in California
   B. a cost-of-living increase for enlisted navy personnel
   C. the commitment of U.S. ground forces to monitor a Middle East peace
   D. a defense treaty between the United States and the Russian Federation
   E. implementation of a missile defense system in Alaska

14. The term *presidential coattails* refers to

   A. the ability of a president to get legislation through Congress
   B. a president's success in getting nominees confirmed by the Senate
   C. the election of candidates from the president's party when the president is on the ticket
   D. the president's appointment of campaign workers to government jobs
   E. public support for a president's program

15. All the following are correct statements about a pocket veto EXCEPT

   A. It can be used only within ten days of the end of a Congress's term.
   B. It is not overridden by a two-thirds vote of both houses.
   C. The president does not sign a pocket veto.
   D. A bill that receives a pocket veto can be introduced in the next session.
   E. The bill automatically becomes law in the next session.

Answers

1. **B** The approval ratings of a president are always high immediately after the inauguration; the administration is brand-new and has not taken any action that might alienate a significant segment of the public. Congress is also willing to give a new president the benefit of the doubt, and the watchword is *bipartisanship,* even in a divided government.

2. **D** No provision is made for political parties in the Constitution. Indeed, the framers of the Constitution and George Washington in his farewell address as president warned about the dangers of political factions.

3. **C** The Line Item Veto Act (1996) and the Budgeting and Accounting Act (1921), the latter of which allowed the president to set the budgets for federal agencies, clearly enhanced the president's authority. In contrast, the War Powers Act (1973) and the Budget Impoundment and Control Act (1974) are examples of Congress trying to reassert its authority over the president. The latter limited the president's ability to impound or to refuse to spend money appropriated by Congress.

4. **B** The constitutional powers of the vice president are limited to presiding over the Senate and casting a vote in the event of a tie. He or she also has a role in evaluating presidential disability under the Twenty-fifth Amendment. The actual authority of the vice president depends on what responsibilities the president wants to give. Recent history indicates that vice presidents have become important presidential advisors and do more than just represent the United States at funerals of foreign leaders.

5. **E** The Environmental Protection Agency is an independent executive agency. Although the EPA administrator does have cabinet rank, the agency itself is not part of the Executive Office of the President.

6. **D** Under the Twenty-fifth Amendment, a majority of the House of Representatives and the Senate must approve a president's nominee to fill a vice-presidential vacancy; all other presidential appointments require only Senate confirmation. Because the vice president is an elected official, action by the Congress as a whole, in effect, substitutes for an electoral mandate.

7. **A** The historical trend is quite clear that the party that controls the White House invariably loses seats in both the House and the Senate in midterm elections.

8. **D** The table clearly shows that the veto is an effective, if negative, tool in the hands of a president; getting the two-thirds vote necessary to override a veto is rare. No trend is discernible to suggest that the use of the veto has become more common or that Democrats rely on the veto more than Republicans. If anything, veto overrides are more likely in a divided government.

9. **A** Executive privilege is not provided for in the Constitution, but it is a claim that goes back to Thomas Jefferson. Even though the Supreme Court in *United States v. Nixon* (1974) recognized that there is no absolute executive privilege, the Court did note that executive privilege may apply to issues of national security.

10. **D** The Senate must confirm all appointments to the federal courts. Executive orders and agreements have the force of law without congressional approval and are sometimes used to intentionally bypass Congress. President Truman used an executive order to desegregate the armed forces in 1947, knowing that such legislation could not get through Congress. President Clinton and President George W. Bush both used recess appointments because of the delays—procedural or intentional—in getting confirmation of appointment of judges and/or administrators.

11. **D** Part of the White House staff maintains a regular liaison with the leadership of Congress and key committees on the president's legislative program and other bills that interest the administration. Responsibility for the administration's budget falls largely to the Office of Management and Budget. Although the president's closest political advisors are usually members of the White House staff, fundraising activities are best left to the party leadership and the party's national committee.

12. **C** This answer applies much more to the White House staff than to the cabinet. Although the appointment of close political confidants is certainly not unknown—President Kennedy named his brother Robert as attorney general, for example—presidents usually nominate people who have expertise in the policy area of the department that they will head and strong management skills. Most appointments come from the same party as the president, but there are exceptions. President George W. Bush picked Norman Mineta, a Democrat, to serve as his secretary of transportation.

13. **C** This question is basically an identification one, and it's easy to answer if you know that the War Powers Act limits the president's authority to commit U.S. troops to combat. Although all the possible answers deal with the military in some way, only **C** mentions putting military personnel in a potentially hostile situation.

14. **C** The idea behind presidential coattails is that a strong presidential candidate or popular president at the top of the ticket will help the other members of the same party running for office to get elected. Examination of House and Senate races during presidential elections shows that the presidential candidate does not have that much influence, due to declining party loyalty and greater voter independence.

15. **E** Because of the timing of a pocket veto, there is no opportunity for Congress to vote to override. If the bill is to become law, it must be introduced in the next session of Congress, but there is no guarantee that the legislation will be passed.

The Bureaucracy

A bureaucracy is a complex organization in which employees have specific responsibilities and work within a hierarchical structure under formal rules. Americans come in contact with bureaucracies at all levels of government—getting a permit to add a room to your house from the municipal building department, registering a car at the Department of Motor Vehicles, and having your taxes audited by the Internal Revenue Service. There is a widespread perception that the federal bureaucracy is bloated and getting larger. The fact is, however, that most bureaucrats work for state and local government, whereas the number of civilian employees in the myriad of federal agencies has remained remarkably stable over the last half-century and has actually declined somewhat in recent years.

Growth and Structure of the Federal Bureaucracy

The federal bureaucracy began with the three executive departments—State, Treasury, and War (which became Defense in 1949)—that functioned under the Articles of Confederation and became the core of the cabinet under George Washington. Whereas the Office of the Attorney General was established in 1789, the Department of Justice was not created until 1870. Historically, the creation of new cabinet-level departments by Congress is the result of political pressure from constituent groups, for example farmers (Department of Agriculture, 1862), unions (Department of Labor, 1913), and teachers (Department of Education, 1979); their formation usually reflects new priorities in the national political agenda. The Department of Homeland Security (2002), for instance, was a response to the new challenges the country faced after September 11, 2001.

Sixty percent of all federal employees work in the executive departments. But the federal bureaucracy has not grown over the years by adding new agencies. Ambitious administrators are adept at convincing Congress or the administration to increase the size, scope, and personnel needed to carry out the duties of the organizations that they head. In addition to the executive departments, the federal bureaucracy consists of **independent regulatory agencies**, **independent executive agencies**, and **government corporations**. Independent regulatory agencies are independent in that they are not directed by an executive department or official, including the president. Independent executive agencies are independent because they are not part of a cabinet-level department, although they do report to the president. The Central Intelligence Agency is an example of the latter.

Regulatory agencies oversee a particular sector of the economy and/or economic activity. The first independent regulatory agency set up by Congress was the Interstate Commerce Commission (established in 1887, abolished in 1995) in response to abuses by the railroad industry. The number of such agencies has grown as the conception of the role and responsibilities of the federal government has expanded. A board or commission manages these agencies; board members are appointed by the president and confirmed by the Senate for a fixed term. Appointees to several independent regulatory agencies serve at the discretion of the president, but others can only be removed for cause. These agencies have quasi-legislative and quasi-judicial functions—they develop and implement rules and regulations relating to their policy areas and adjudicate disputes arising from them (see later in this chapter for a discussion of rule making). The Board of Governors of the Federal Reserve System, the Federal Communications Commission (FCC), the Federal Energy Regulatory Commission (FERC), and the Securities and Exchange Commission (SEC) are a few examples of independent regulatory agencies.

Independent executive agencies range from high-profile organizations such as the National Aeronautics and Space Administration (NASA) to little-known ones such as the American Battlefield Monuments Commission. They're run by a single administrator appointed by the president and confirmed by the Senate, but that person can be removed by the president at any time. Independent executive agencies administer programs for which they were established and may have rule-making authority, as the Environmental Protection Agency does. Executive agencies are independent in the sense that they're ideally above partisan politics, but clearly less so than regulatory agencies.

Government corporations are organized like private companies. Their workforce, however, consists of federal employees, and the corporations receive funding from Congress even though they may generate their own revenue. The Corporation for Public Broadcasting, which is responsible for public television and public radio, gets part of its operating budget from subscribers.

Creation of government corporations occurs for several reasons:

- **To assume responsibilities that the private sector is unwilling or unable to assume:** Examples include Amtrak, which runs passenger-rail service throughout the United States, and the Federal Deposit Insurance Corporation, which insures savings-account deposits.
- **To improve operating efficiency:** An example is the U.S. Postal Service.
- **To establish a standard that investor-owned companies would have to match:** This was one purpose behind the Tennessee Valley Authority (TVA); the rates charged for electricity by the TVA were envisioned as a "yardstick" for private utilities.

The Federal Civil Service

Until the late 19th century, most of those appointed to the federal bureaucracy got their positions based on who they knew. The so-called **spoils system** made federal jobs a way of rewarding political supporters. Corruption was a widely recognized problem, but it took the assassination of President James Garfield in 1881 by a disgruntled office seeker to bring about meaningful civil service reform. Under the Pendleton Act (1883), the Civil Service Commission was established and merit became the basis for hiring and promotion of federal employees. The Civil Service Commission was responsible for evaluating job applicants through competitive examinations, and establishing promotion guidelines that focused on performance reviews. In 1978, these functions were taken over by the **Office of Personnel Management**, which is part of the Executive Office of the President. Once a federal worker is hired through the merit system, it is extremely difficult to fire that worker. The rules in effect, which include the right to appeal to the Merit Systems Protection Board and to challenge its decision to the U.S. Court of Appeals, can drag out the process for a long time. The Civil Service System covered only 10 percent of all federal employees in the late 19th century, with the remainder appointed through patronage; today over 90 percent are covered.

The federal civil service is also expected to be politically neutral. Federal employees were barred from actively campaigning for candidates; for example, they could not distribute political literature and could not run for office themselves under the **Hatch Act (1939)**. These restrictions were eased somewhat in 1993. Today, federal bureaucrats can hold positions in political parties and/or political organizations and can run for office in nonpartisan elections. Many local elections for the school board, city council, and even mayor are nonpartisan, meaning that candidates are effectively independents, without party affiliation.

What the Federal Bureaucracy Does

The routine of a bureaucracy—collecting fees, issuing permits or licenses, giving tests—is the administration of its defined purpose. The bureaucrat typically performs these tasks by following **standard operating procedures** (SOPs), which are rules and practices intended to enhance efficiency. To the person dealing with the bureaucracy, on the other hand, SOPs often seem to have the opposite effect, creating delay, confusion, and excessive paperwork. Bureaucrats also do not have the luxury of interpreting policy goals. The job of U.S. Immigration and Customs Enforcement agents is to arrest narcotics smugglers, not to ask whether the nation's drug policy is wise.

When Congress passes a law, it often sets down guidelines to carry out the new policies. Putting these policies into practice typically falls to one or more federal agencies and is known as implementation. After the Eighteenth Amendment outlawing the sale, transport, and manufacture of liquor was ratified, Congress passed the Volstead

Act to create the bureaucratic machinery necessary to enforce the amendment. Policy directives from Congress are not always clear. Although the legislation may direct a federal agency to develop rules and regulations to implement the statute, bureaucrats have some flexibility in what these rules and regulations actually say. This flexibility is known as **administrative discretion**.

The rules and regulations that govern how a federal program operates are developed through a complicated and often lengthy process called **rule making**.

Under the Administrative Procedures Act (1946), a federal agency must provide public notice as to the time, place, and nature of the rule making and give interested parties the opportunity to submit written comments or provide testimony through formal hearings.

At a minimum, the process is likely to include the following:

1. Issuance of a notice of proposed rule making
2. Publication of the proposed rules
3. A 30- to 60-day public comment period
4. Publication of the final rules

The public notice, the proposed and final rules, and occasionally the comments will be published in the *Federal Register*. The final rule can be challenged in the federal courts and will not go into effect until all legal issues are resolved.

The federal bureaucracy directly affects our lives every day by making regulations. Law-created agencies determine and set such regulations as the quality standards of our drinking water, the amount of particulate matter a local power plant can emit, the requirement that the label on a can of food lists its contents and nutritional values, the safety guidelines for using a piece of farm machinery, and the content of the television programs children watch in the evening. The process of creating these regulations is the same as rule making. Hundreds of volumes make up the *Code of Federal Regulations*.

An often-heard criticism is that federal regulations significantly increase the cost of doing business for U.S. companies, which is passed on to consumers in the form of higher prices. **Deregulation** (reducing or eliminating altogether the federal government's role and allowing industry greater freedom in how it operates) became a political watchword in the late 1970s. The domestic airline industry was effectively deregulated through the Airline Deregulation Act (1978), which spelled out the gradual demise of the Civil Aeronautics Board, which set rates and controlled routes. Although the legislation did bring new carriers into the industry that increased competition in the short run, today there are fewer major airlines providing service and rates are high. Deregulation was also the goal of the Telecommunications Act of 1996, which covers radio, television, telephone, and cable services. Critics charge that deregulation led to greater media concentration and higher prices for consumers. Many argue that deregulation and lax regulation contributed to the financial collapse in 2007–2008. Clearly, deregulation does not always achieve the goals its supporters hope and is not a very effective way of controlling the bureaucracy.

Criticism of Bureaucracy

Almost everyone who has contact with a bureaucracy comes away dissatisfied—it may be the long lines to get a passport or the complexity of the federal tax forms. The word *bureaucracy* itself conjures up negative images. The following are common criticisms of bureaucracy:

- **Red tape:** Bureaucracies operate under complex rules and procedures that often cause delays in providing services or implementing policy; calls to eliminate an agency's "red tape" often mean reducing the number of forms the agency uses or the number of pages a form has.

- **Waste:** The best-known example of waste is the scandal in the 1980s that revealed that the Department of Defense spent hundreds of dollars on routine hardware items such as screws and hammers. The fact is that clear-cut rewards for cutting costs in a federal agency are less obvious compared to a private company. Money saved by the agency simply goes back to the U.S. Treasury.

- **Fragmentation/duplication:** Two or more federal agencies often have jurisdiction over the same policy area. The U.S. Customs Service and the Drug Enforcement Administration both have responsibility for preventing illegal drugs from getting into the United States. Another aspect of fragmentation and duplication occurs when two or more federal agencies operate at cross purposes. The departments of Commerce and Agriculture both help tobacco growers to market their products, but the Food and Drug Administration wants to define cigarettes as a drug-delivery system.

Controlling the Federal Bureaucracy

Although the federal bureaucracy was certainly anticipated by the framers of the Constitution, they probably did not envision it becoming the "fourth branch" of government. Unlike the Congress, the president, and the courts, there are no formal checks and balances written into the Constitution that specifically limit the power of the bureaucracy. This does not mean, however, that the federal bureaucracy is beyond control.

Though the president names only a small fraction of all federal employees, he or she does appoint all the policy-makers and decision makers in the cabinet departments, independent executive and regulatory agencies, and the highest level of the civil service who qualify for the Senior Executive Service (SES). Established in 1978, the SES is comprised of about 8,000 high-level managers who can be hired and fired more easily than other federal bureaucrats and receive incentive bonuses based on job performance. A chief executive committed to reducing the size of the federal government, improving services to the public while cutting red tape, and eliminating frivolous rules can have an impact by the people appointed to key posts. Through the Office of Management and Budget, the president can influence the bureaucracy in two ways: by adding or reducing an agency's budget request and by approving or killing new regulations through its rule-making oversight function. Finally, the president can issue an executive order, directing a federal agency to take some action or initiate a new policy. During the Reagan Administration, there was talk of reorganizing the federal bureaucracy by eliminating entire executive departments, such as the Department of Education. Reagan and subsequent presidents learned, however, that the bureaucracy has well-placed friends in Congress and powerful interest groups represent them.

The Senate must give its "advice and consent" on the president's high-level federal appointments. Although it is doubtful that a presidential nominee would be rejected based on his or her views on the bureaucracy, confirmation hearings are a good place to impress upon the future secretary of the interior how important Congress thinks controlling the size of government is. Whatever amount is earmarked in the administration's budget for a particular agency, it is Congress who authorizes and appropriates the money. The power of the purse is just one way in which Congress can influence the federal bureaucracy. Congress can also limit the scope of a federal agency's responsibilities and, more rarely, eliminate the agency itself. In the latter case, some or all of the agency's functions are assumed by another part of the bureaucracy. Another way is through its oversight function, usually carried out through public hearings, which can give Congress a considerable say on the status of federal programs and how an agency is operating. Congress has also enacted laws to ensure that the federal bureaucracy operates in the most open manner possible. The Freedom of Information Act (1966), for example, provides that all government records, except those dealing with military, intelligence, or trade secrets, or those that reveal personal private actions, must be made available to the public. If Congress is serious about reducing the number of federal regulations, it is always free to write laws with more specificity. If statutes clearly state how the law is to be implemented, there would be less need for agency rule making.

The federal bureaucracy is also limited by judicial review and the actions of whistleblowers. All rules and decisions of federal agencies can be challenged through the federal courts up to the Supreme Court. A **whistleblower** is a employee who reports improper and perhaps illegal activities by a federal agency. Congress passed the Whistleblower Protection Act (1989) to provide such employees with a means to challenge dismissal or similar reprisals for the actions.

The federal bureaucracy is not without resources to defend its interests. Its sheer size and the fact that it provides critical services to the American people make the bureaucracy difficult to control. The bureaucracy is also the repository of expertise that the Congress and the president rely on. Political scientists refer to the close relationship that develops between interest groups, federal agencies, and congressional committees and subcommittees that have authorization and/or oversight authority as **iron triangles**. A good example would be the Social Security Administration, AARP (which in theory represents all Americans over the age of 50), and the House Subcommittee on Social Security. The relationship among the elements of an iron triangle brings benefits to each, but not necessarily to the nation as a whole. Interest groups can provide information as well as campaign contributions to members of the subcommittee; the subcommittee can push for a higher level of appropriations for the agency; the agency and the subcommittee can work together to promote legislation or policies that the interest group supports.

As the number of interest groups have grown in recent years and the scope of committee responsibilities have changed, **issue networks** have come to replace iron triangles. Issue networks are much looser relationships and involve a broader range of participants. In addition to members of Congress, agency officials, and lobbyists, issue networks are likely to include academics, attorneys, and journalists who share an interest in broad policy areas like healthcare, the environment, or deregulation.

Practice

1. Which of the following statements best describes the federal civilian workforce?

    A. Political factors play no role in making civil service appointments.

    B. Employees must pass competitive examinations for promotion.

    C. Half of the employees in the executive branch are appointed by the president.

    D. Federal employees face no limitations on their participation in the political process.

    E. Once hired, a federal employee can never lose his or her job.

2. The growth of the federal bureaucracy can be attributed to all the following EXCEPT

    A. the need to regulate business

    B. responsibility of the government for the welfare of the people

    C. administrators who push for larger budgets and staff

    D. Supreme Court decisions on federal-state relations

    E. the creation of new agencies to give policy issues a high profile

3. An important difference between an independent executive agency and an independent regulatory agency is that

    A. Executive agencies are funded through executive departments.

    B. The head of an executive agency holds cabinet rank.

    C. Presidential appointments to a regulatory agency serve for a fixed term.

    D. Executive agencies do not engage in rule making.

    E. Actions by regulatory agencies must be approved by Congress.

4. An iron triangle refers to the close relationship between

    A. the White House press corps, the press secretary, and major networks

    B. congressional committees, interest groups, and federal agencies

    C. the National Security Advisor, the secretary of defense, and the secretary of state

    D. congressional campaign committees, political action committees, and party national committees

    E. defense contractors, the Department of Defense, and the Joint Chiefs of Staff

5. A common criticism of the federal bureaucracy is that

    A. Too many civil servants are political appointees.

    B. There are no controls over federal agencies.

    C. The public is unaware of how federal agencies make decisions.

    D. Overlapping jurisdiction contributes to wasteful spending.

    E. It is constantly growing in responsibilities and labor force.

6. Which of the following is NOT a government corporation?

    A. Corporation for Public Broadcasting

    B. Tennessee Valley Authority

    C. Amtrak

    D. U.S. Postal Service

    E. National Endowment for the Arts

Executive Branch Employment
By Gender & Race/National Origin, 1986-2000

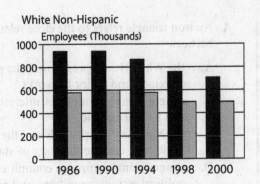

White Non-Hispanic

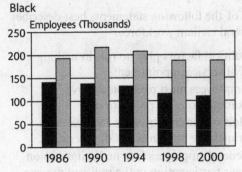

Black

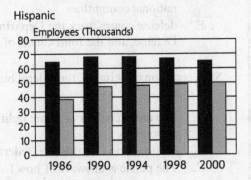

Hispanic

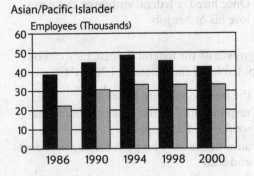

Asian/Pacific Islander

American Indian/Alaska Native

Men
Women

Source: U.S. Office of Personnel Management. *The Fact Book: Federal Civilian Workforce Statistics, 2001 Edition.* *www.opm.gov/feddata/factbook.*

7. What conclusions can be drawn about the labor force in the executive branch from the preceding chart?

   A. The executive branch staff declined after 1994.

   B. Affirmative-action programs targeted African American women.

   C. Hispanic men were the largest minority group employed in the executive branch.

   D. Male, white, non-Hispanic employees remained a minority in the executive branch throughout the period.

   E. Most minority employees held low-level positions.

8. Which of the following is NOT part of the rule-making process?

   A. publication of proposed rules in the *Federal Register*

   B. review of proposed rules by the Office of Management and Budget

   C. the comment period on proposed rules

   D. publication of final rules in the *Federal Register*

   E. review of final rules by congressional oversight committees

9. Critics of government regulation of business argue that

    I.   Regulation leads to higher prices for consumers.

    II.   Regulation adds to corporate profits.

    III. Regulation ultimately harms the environment.

    IV. Regulation makes the United States less competitive in world markets.

    A.   I only

    B.   I and II only

    C.   II and III only

    D.   I and IV only

    E.   I, II, and IV only

10. With regard to the federal bureaucracy, recent presidents have tried to

    A.   reduce the size of the workforce and reorganize the structure

    B.   increase spending for all federal agencies

    C.   get Congress to approve additional staffing levels for executive departments

    D.   eliminate the Department of Labor

    E.   limit congressional oversight of independent regulatory agencies

11. A regulatory agency that selects from a range of policy options is said to exercise its

    A.   rule-making authority

    B.   administrative discretion

    C.   oversight responsibility

    D.   mandate power

    E.   administrative routine

12. All the following are included in the standard definition of *bureaucracy* EXCEPT

    A.   hierarchical organization

    B.   standard operating procedures

    C.   patronage

    D.   specialized tasks

    E.   formal rules

13. Which of the following tools at the disposal of a president is LEAST likely to impact the bureaucracy?

    A.   the appointment of people to government positions that are committed to the president's policy goals

    B.   the use of executive orders to direct bureaucracy to take a particular action

    C.   the appointment of federal judges who support the principle of judicial activism

    D.   either reducing or increasing funding for an agency in the administration's budget

    E.   the ability of the president to speak directly to agency heads about the administration's priorities

14. The purpose of the Pendleton Act was to

    A.   ensure that federal workers were paid the same as workers in the private sector

    B.   give federal workers the right to form labor unions

    C.   develop a professional civil service based on merit

    D.   reduce corruption by substantially increasing the salaries of federal employees

    E.   allow the president to appoint the higher levels of the federal civil service

15. The means Congress has at its disposal to control the bureaucracy include all the following EXCEPT

    A.   issue networks

    B.   power of the purse

    C.   confirmation presidential appointments

    D.   agency/program authorization

    E.   oversight hearings

Answers

1. **B** If the answer isn't immediately clear, it should become clear through the process of elimination. Political factors certainly play a key role; remember that the federal civilian workforce includes members of the cabinet. Even with the creation of the Senior Executive Service, the president still appoints only a small fraction of the federal bureaucracy, which is almost synonymous with the executive branch. The Hatch Act and subsequent amendments put some limitations on how politically active a federal worker can be. Federal workers can be fired; firing a federal worker isn't easy, but it can be done.

2. **D** The Supreme Court's decision in *Wabash, St. Louis & Pacific Railway Company v. Illinois* (1886) that only Congress could regulate railroads engaged in interstate commerce led to the creation of the Interstate Commerce Commission in 1887. With that exception, the Supreme Court has had no role in expanding the federal bureaucracy.

3. **C** Appointments to an independent regulatory agency—either a commission or a board—is for a fixed number of years. Although the head of the Environmental Protection Agency does have cabinet rank, this is not automatically extended to all independent executive agency heads. The EPA head's appointment to cabinet rank reflected the high priority that various administrations give to environmental issues.

4. **B** This is a straightforward definition question. If you know what an iron triangle is, the answer is obvious; if you don't, you're in trouble. There is nothing in the question that gives you a hint to the right answer, and several of the possible answers seem logical.

5. **D** This question tests whether you can distinguish between valid criticisms of bureaucracy and popular misconceptions. Three of the answers are simply wrong—the federal bureaucracy is not growing, there are controls over the federal bureaucracy, and the overwhelming majority of civil servants are not political appointees. Although the public may be unaware of how decisions are reached, legislation requires that the decision-making process be as open as possible. It may take a little research, but anyone can find out the information.

6. **E** The National Endowment for the Arts is part of the National Foundation for the Arts and Humanities, an independent executive agency. Its chair is appointed by the president.

7. **A** This question will take a little bit of time because several of the possible answers require you to do quick calculations. Your first step is to eliminate the answers that the data doesn't address. There is no way of knowing from the graphs whether affirmative-action programs explain the difference between black men and black women workers or what positions minorities held. Keeping in mind that each graph uses a different scale, it should be pretty obvious that African-American men were the largest minority group. Through the quick calculations, it should become clear that white, non-Hispanic men were never a minority of the labor force and that the only correct answer is **A**.

8. **E** Final rules go into effect shortly after they're published in the *Federal Register*. There is no requirement under administrative procedures that allows Congress to review final rules either before or after they are published.

9. **D** There is no doubt that regulation costs. Stricter emission standards for cars adds to car sticker prices, and a requirement that only U.S.-made steel be used in a federal construction project adds to the construction project's cost. Price increases due to regulation tend to make U.S. products more expensive and, therefore, less competitive in world trade.

10. **A** A good example is the performance review conducted by Vice President Gore for the Clinton Administration, which called for reducing the size of several federal agencies, reorganizing others, and simplifying procedures. The report was entitled *From Red Tape to Results: Creating a Government that Works Better and Costs Less*.

11. **B** In this question, you're given the definition and asked to identify the appropriate term—administrative discretion. Rule making is often the way in which administrative discretion is exercised.

12. **C** A bureaucracy is not defined by the way its labor force is selected. An organization that has a hierarchical structure, follows formal rules, and relies on standard operating procedures, and assigns its workers specialized tasks is considered a bureaucracy irrespective of whether those workers are political appointees or successful exam takers.

13. **C** Although the federal courts may rule on the validity of a federal agency's action, who sits on the bench is clearly not as important as the other things a president can do to influence the direction of the bureaucracy. If the president supports a strong deregulation effort, judges who adhere to judicial restraint and have a more conservative legal approach might be helpful.

14. **C** Don't confuse the Pendleton Act with the Civil Service Reform Act of 1978, which created the Senior Executive Service and gave the president more control over the highest level of the civil service.

15. **A** Issue networks, the successor to the iron triangles, would be considered an obstacle to Congress exercising control over federal agencies.

The judicial system in the United States functions at all three levels of government—there are local, state, and federal courts. The overwhelming majority of cases are heard in local and state courts. These include criminal cases that involve fraud and bribery, as well as violent crimes such as murder and armed robbery, and civil cases that usually involve disputes over property, money, contracts, and personal injury. State courts, like the federal system, are organized hierarchically. At the lowest level are trial courts where a jury or a judge decides a case. A defendant who loses at trial may ask that the state court of appeals—the next level—review the case if there are matters of legal procedure or law at issue. The side that loses an appeal may opt to take the case to the state supreme court, or what is sometimes called the state court of last resort. In contrast to federal judges, whom the president appoints, most local and state judges run for election.

The Judiciary in the Constitution

Article III of the Constitution gives the barest outline of the organization and responsibilities of the judicial branch. It mentions the Supreme Court but does not indicate how many justices shall sit on the court or, in contrast to members of Congress and the president, state any required qualifications. It was left up to Congress to establish federal courts below the Supreme Court. The Constitution outlines jurisdiction of the federal judiciary—the Supreme Court—in particular. Under the Constitution, the Supreme Court has **original jurisdiction**; for example, it is the first court to hear cases that involve a state, two or more states, the United States and a state, a state and the citizens of another state that are parties to a suit, or ambassadors or other foreign diplomats. The Supreme Court also has **appellate jurisdiction** to hear cases that come from lower federal courts, state supreme courts, and the military court system.

The Constitution does not specifically state that the Supreme Court has the power to declare a law enacted by Congress unconstitutional—a power called **judicial review**. Such authority may be implied by Article III, which clearly gives the Court the right to hear cases arising out of the "laws of the United States." The debates during the Constitutional Convention strongly suggest that at least some of the delegates believed that the Supreme Court would have such power, and Alexander Hamilton argued the point effectively in *The Federalist Papers*. It was the Supreme Court itself, however, that clearly stated the principle of judicial review by declaring parts of the Judiciary Act of 1789 unconstitutional in its landmark decision in *Marbury v. Madison* (1803).

The Structure of the Federal Court System

Under the Judiciary Act of 1789 and subsequent legislation, Congress created **constitutional courts**, which derive their judicial authority from Article III, and whose judges serve for life. In addition to the Supreme Court, constitutional courts include the U.S. district courts, the U.S. courts of appeals (including the Court of Appeals for the Federal Circuit), and the U.S. Court of International Trade. Congress has created **legislative courts** over the years pursuant to its power under Article I that have much narrower jurisdiction and deal with specialized cases; legislative court judges serve for a fixed term. The Court of Appeals for the Armed Services, the Court of Federal Claims, the Courts of the District of Columbia, the territorial courts, the Court of Veterans Appeals, and the U.S. Tax Court fall into this category. The Foreign Intelligence Surveillance Court (created by the Foreign Intelligence Surveillance Act [FISA]) reviews warrant requests from the government for investigations involving national security. The Bush Administration was criticized for bypassing the court in its domestic wiretapping program implemented in the wake of the events of September 11, 2001. I'll focus here on the district courts, the courts of appeals, and the Supreme Court.

There are 94 federal district courts. Each state has at least one district court, and large states like California, New York, and Texas can have as many as four. District courts are courts of original jurisdiction, and the vast majority of their cases deal with civil matters that a judge may hear alone or that both a judge and a jury may hear. District courts are the only courts in the federal system that have jury trials. They hear around 270,000 cases a year involving the federal government, federal law, or civil actions between citizens of two states where the value at issue is more than $50,000.

The courts of appeals are intermediate appellate courts and do not have original jurisdiction. There are a total of 13—one for each of 11 circuits plus the U.S. Court of Appeals for the D.C. Circuit (which primarily handles cases involving federal regulatory agencies) and the U.S. Court of Appeals for the Federal Circuit (which specializes in cases involving patent law, claims against the United States, and matters decided by the Court of International Trade). These courts hear over 50,000 cases a year on appeal from district courts within their circuits, from federal agencies, and the legislative courts. A three-judge panel hands down decisions, but all judges in a circuit can hear a case and rule by majority vote. A decision of one of the courts of appeals is only binding within that circuit. For example, the U.S. Court of Appeals for the Fifth Circuit encompasses Texas, Louisiana, and Mississippi, and its rulings only apply in those states.

The Supreme Court is the highest court in the land. Nine justices, eight associate justices, and the chief justice, all of whom are appointed by the president and confirmed by the Senate, make up the Supreme Court. The process of selecting a justice is examined later in this chapter.

The Court exercises great discretion on which cases it decides to take. Thousands of cases may appear on the document, but only a small number (fewer than 100) written opinions are issued in a term. As noted earlier, the Supreme Court has both original and appellate jurisdiction. The overwhelming majority of its cases, however, are on appeal from the lower federal courts, the highest state courts (provided there is a federal, meaning a constitutional, issue), and such legislative courts as the Court of Appeals for the Armed Services. How the Supreme Court reaches a decision is discussed in detail later in this chapter.

Who Serves on the Federal Courts

The president appoints and the Senate confirms all federal judges. The fact that they serve for life is intended to insulate them from partisan politics, but the selection of federal judges is highly political. First, partisanship is obvious—Democratic presidents put Democratic judges on the federal bench and Republican presidents put Republican judges on the federal bench. Partisanship also expresses itself in the confirmation process. In an era of divided government, where one party controls the White House and the other party controls the Senate, confirmation of a judicial nominee is not an easy task. The Senate does not often reject a president's candidate, but it can delay action on the nomination. There is also the long tradition of **senatorial courtesy**; the Senate will not approve a nominee for the federal district court if the senior senator from the nominee's state is a member of the president's party and objects.

Although presidents are not above naming someone to a vacancy on a district court who played a key role in the election campaign, the most important qualification for a federal judge is certainly competence. Since 1946, the American Bar Association (ABA), which represents attorneys throughout the country, has rated judicial nominees as "well qualified," "qualified," or "not qualified." It is next to impossible for a candidate who the ABA deems "not qualified" to receive a confirmation. In March 2001, the Bush Administration informed the ABA that it would no longer provide names of candidates for federal judgeships prior to their formal nomination; the ABA continues, however, to rate judicial nominees. The Obama Administration has gone back to the rating system. The federal judiciary looks very much like Congress—the overwhelming majority of judges are white men. In recent years, Democratic presidents, in particular, have appointed more women and minorities.

Many consider the appointment of a justice to the Supreme Court to be the most important responsibility of a president. Justices invariably outlive an administration, and their decisions can affect public policy for generations. Numerous factors go into the selection of a Supreme Court nominee. First and foremost is competence and experience. Although there is no requirement in the Constitution, the overwhelming majority of those who have served on the Court in the last half-century had been judges on state or federal courts. Judicial experience is important for trying to determine where a potential nominee stands on key issues that are likely to come before the Court (for example, abortion or federal-state relations). Before a president selects a person, his or her previous decisions, law-review articles, and speeches are scrutinized for clues. Political considerations come into play as well. Just as with the lower federal courts, presidents invariably make nominations from within their own parties. Presidential candidates are routinely asked what type of person they would appoint to the Court.

With one or two appointments, no president can create a high court that looks like the United States, but ethnicity, religion, and gender are taken into account to some degree. The replacement of Justice Thurgood Marshall with Clarence Thomas preserved the African-American seat on the Court, even though the judicial philosophy of the two men could not be farther apart. President Ronald Reagan was true to his campaign promise and appointed Sandra Day O'Connor, the first female justice, in 1981. Ruth Bader Ginsburg became the second woman on the Court in 1993, when she was named by President Clinton. President Obama put forward the name of a Hispanic woman, Sonia Sotomayor, to fill the vacancy left by the retirement of Associate Justice David Souter; she was confirmed in 2009.

In addition to whatever advice the president is getting from his political advisors, the Federal Bureau of Investigation does a thorough background check on the short list of potential nominees, and—as is the case with all federal judges—they are rated by the ABA. After the nomination is announced, the Senate Judiciary Committee, which is responsible for overseeing the confirmation process, continues the investigation. It goes over much the same ground as the White House, examining the published record by and about the nominee. The nominee is asked to complete a detailed questionnaire and, of course, is invited to testify before the Senate Judiciary Committee. Although the senators are likely to ask about hot-button legal questions such as abortion and the death penalty, nominees usually refuse to take firm positions on matters that may come before them on the Court. Other parties, as well, may testify for or against the nomination. If a candidate for the Court has made pro-life decisions, for example, women's groups and other organizations that are pro-choice will urge the committee not to confirm; the opposite is equally true. The Judiciary Committee votes for or against confirmation, and its recommendation is invariably followed by the full Senate. It is rare for the Senate to reject a president's choice; in fact, it only happened four times in the 20th century.

The Supreme Court in Action

The work of the Supreme Court can be divided into two phases: selection and decision. *Selection* means determining which among the thousands of cases that come to the Court each term the justices will actually hear. Law clerks assist the justices in reviewing the cases; those that are considered significant are put on a "discuss list" by the chief justice, and are examined further at the Court's weekly conference. About a third of cases may make it to the "discuss list"; the remainder are on the "dead list" and cannot be brought up at conference unless one of the justices insists. At conference, in what is known as the **rule of four**, if four justices vote to hear a case, a **writ of certiorari** (a formal document sent to a lower court indicating that the Supreme Court will hear the case) is issued and the matter is put on the docket. For all the other cases that were "denied *cert*," the decision of the lower court stands.

The justices do not explain why they decided to hear some cases and not others. Analysis has shown, however, that several factors come into play. The Court is likely to grant cert when

- The federal government, typically through the solicitor general, is the party asking for review.
- Lower federal courts have taken different positions on the issue.
- The case involves a constitutional question of civil liberties or civil rights.
- There is high public interest in the case as demonstrated by the number of **amicus curiae** briefs submitted. *Amicus curiae* literally means "friend of the court" and is usually an organization that is not a party to the lawsuit but is interested in its outcome.

After a writ of certiorari is granted, the parties submit **briefs** to the Court. Briefs are written documents that summarize the main points of the legal argument, citing statutes and previous court decisions. Third parties, interest groups, or advocacy groups like the American Civil Liberties Union and the federal government through the solicitor general, have the opportunity to submit amicus curiae briefs at this time. Oral argument is scheduled for when the Court is "sitting," a two-week period that is followed by a two-week recess. An attorney for each party has 30 minutes to present the case. The attorneys are almost never allowed to speak for the full time without interruption by questions from the justices. The only other person allowed to address the Court on the matter at hand is the solicitor general.

The justices meet in conference—which the chief justice presides over—on Wednesdays and Fridays to discuss the argued cases. Most of the time, justices come to the conference knowing how they'll vote on a particular case. There must be a majority vote. In the event of a tie, which can happen if one of the justices is ill or has not participated in the case because of previous involvement with one of the parties, the decision of the lower court stands. Although the vote at conference is not final, it is the basis for assigning the writing of the opinion (the written version of the decision). When the chief justice is in the majority, he assigns the opinion or may opt to write it himself. This responsibility falls to the senior associate justice if the chief justice is in the minority.

Writing the opinion can take weeks or months. The justice writing the opinion circulates drafts for comment to the other justices and makes changes. Votes may also change as the legal arguments in the decision are fleshed out, but that is rare. The decision is final when it is announced in open court and a majority opinion is issued. A majority opinion sets out the legal reasoning behind the Court's decision, and both the decision and the argument become precedent for future cases. A **plurality opinion** has the backing of only three or four justices, but it is controlling because the decision, not the legal argument, is supported by one or two additional justices; it doesn't have the same weight as a majority opinion. The Court may also issue an unsigned opinion (called a per curiam opinion) reflecting the decision of all the justices or a majority. **Concurring opinions** are written by justices in the majority who agree with the decision but not necessarily with the reasoning. Justices in the minority are free to issue **dissenting opinions** that reflect their positions.

Judicial Decision Making

Beyond the mechanics, what are the factors that go into judicial decision making? A key legal principle is **stare decisis**, which literally means "let the decision stand." The Court gives precedents (previous decisions on the same issue), considerable weight. This does not mean, however, that the Supreme Court never overturns a ruling it has made.

In *Plessy v. Ferguson* (1896), the Court found that "separate but equal" facilities for African Americans and whites were constitutional. A subsequent Court, in the landmark *Brown v. Board of Education of Topeka* (1954) case, stated that "separate but equal" schools were inherently unequal, and its decision paved the way for desegregation. A less dramatic way around precedent is to "distinguish cases." Here, the Court claims that the facts and or legal issues of a previous case are different from the case under review, when, in fact, they are essentially the same.

Courts are often called on to interpret or determine the intent of federal and state laws. Statutory construction refers to the rules and techniques used to do this. Under the **plain meaning rule**, for example, a statute means exactly what the words of the statute say it means. When the "plain meaning" is not clear, courts turn to the legislative history of the statute, which for federal laws includes the bill as introduced, hearings before congressional committees, the committee report, and statements in the *Congressional Record*. Most weight is given to the committee report as a statement of what the bill was expected to accomplish by the members of Congress most familiar with it.

Judicial restraint and **judicial activism** are two ways of viewing the role of the courts. Judicial restraint emphasizes that the function of the court is to say what the law means, not to make new law. It gives great deference to the other branches of government, particularly the legislature. Judges who support judicial restraint tend to take a strict constructionist view of the Constitution; in other words, what is important to determine is the original intent of the framers. Judicial activists, on the other hand, see the power of the court as much more expansive and believe that they have a part to play in shaping public policy. They aren't bound by the specific provisions of the Constitution, which is seen as a flexible document that can respond to contemporary concerns (loose construction). The reliance on a constitutionally protected right to privacy in *Griswold v. Connecticut* (1965) and *Roe v. Wade* (1973) is a good example.

Judges, even those who sit on the Supreme Court, have political views and are not immune to the influence of public opinion. There is a good reason why presidents appoint federal judges from within their own party: Common party affiliation means that they share, to some extent, the same political ideology. Supreme Court watchers classify the justices as liberals, conservatives, and moderates; moderates are often swing votes, and these justices side with the liberals or conservatives depending on the issue. Judges read newspapers and magazines, watch television, have conversations with friends, and bring all this input with them into the courtroom. Studies have shown that Supreme Court decisions on most controversial questions track with public opinion a majority of the time; a notable exception is school prayer. (The Court has rather consistently held that prayer in the public schools violated the Establishment Clause of the First Amendment; polls, on the other hand, show rather broad support for allowing some type of prayer in the school setting.) A final factor that comes into play at the Court is the personal relationships between the justices and the politicking that goes on behind the scenes. As the draft of an opinion circulates, changes are suggested and negotiations takes place among the justices over language and tone.

The Court, the President, the Congress

The Supreme Court has no enforcement authority; it relies on the president, Congress, and the lower federal and state courts to implement its decisions. *Brown v. Board of Education* is a good example of both sides of this issue. The Court's decision was extremely vague both on how desegregation was to be accomplished and on the timetable. It called for desegregation "with all deliberate speed," a phrase that allowed for foot-dragging in many communities. On the other hand, when the Little Rock, Arkansas, school district balked at a desegregation order in 1957, President Eisenhower sent in federal troops to see that it was carried out.

Through appointments, presidents can affect how the Court rules; there is no doubt that the Court today is much more conservative and more committed to judicial restraint than the Court of the 1960s, a trend largely due to the justices named by presidents Nixon, Reagan, and George W. Bush. Assumptions about nominees can be wrong, however, as President Eisenhower found out after he named Earl Warren chief justice. The Warren Court (1953–1969) was the most activist of the 20th century, much to the chagrin of the conservative Eisenhower. More recently, Justice David Souter has voted with the liberal wing of the Court more often than President George H. W. Bush would have thought when he appointed Souter in 1990.

Congress's role in the judicial appointment process is limited; it rarely rejects a president's candidate for the high court. But under the Constitution, Congress can change the scope of the jurisdiction of the lower federal courts and the appellate jurisdiction of the Supreme Court. Congress also can change the number of justices that make up the Supreme Court, and it has done so on several occasions. If the Court declares a law unconstitutional, Congress has options: It can enact the legislation again with modifications to meet the justices' objections or it can pass a constitutional amendment.

The Sixteenth Amendment (1913) got around a Supreme Court decision in 1895 that found the income tax unconstitutional. In *Texas v. Johnson* (1989), the Court declared that burning an American flag was protected speech under the First Amendment. Congress responded with the Federal Flag Protection Act of 1989, which was promptly found unconstitutional as well. Attempts to ban flag burning through a constitutional amendment have not been successful to date.

Practice

1. The tradition of senatorial courtesy is criticized because

   A. It effectively allows a senator to nominate a federal judge.
   B. It gives too much power to the Senate to investigate judicial nominees.
   C. It gives the president pro tempore responsibilities not provided for in the Constitution.
   D. It allows the Senate Judiciary Committee to delay hearings on a judicial appointment.
   E. It gives the Senate Judiciary Committee alone, rather than the full Senate, the power to reject a nominee to the federal bench.

2. Which of the following courts has only original jurisdiction?

   A. U.S. Court of Appeals for the Ninth Circuit
   B. California Supreme Court
   C. U.S. District Court of the Southern District of New York
   D. New York State Court of Appeals
   E. U.S. Supreme Court

3. In making nominations to the federal courts, recent Democratic presidents have

   A. selected more women and minorities than Republican presidents have
   B. not taken party affiliation into account
   C. required that candidates have previous judicial experience
   D. relied heavily on recommendations from large corporations
   E. looked for candidates who were pro-life

4. The Supreme Court will agree to hear a case when

   A. The chief justice orders it.
   B. A majority of the justices agree.
   C. A single justice insists a case be put on the docket.
   D. There is unanimous agreement among the justices.
   E. Four justices agree.

5. The authority to determine how many justices sit on the Supreme Court is in the hands of

   A. the Supreme Court itself
   B. Congress
   C. the president
   D. the Judicial Conference of the United States
   E. the House Judiciary Committee

6. A Supreme Court justice who agrees with the decision but not with the legal reasoning is likely to write a

   A. majority opinion
   B. per curiam opinion
   C. concurring opinion
   D. dissenting opinion
   E. plurality opinion

7. Which of the following cases is LEAST likely to reach the Supreme Court?

   A. a dispute between Oregon and Washington over coastal fishing
   B. a case on the rights of students to publish a newspaper without supervision by the administration
   C. a case involving the constitutionality of a state law limiting abortion
   D. a case that challenges the president's right to establish military tribunals to try suspected terrorists
   E. a case involving the murder of a police officer during a drug arrest

8. All the following statements about the judicial branch are true EXCEPT

   A. The overwhelming majority of criminal cases are handled by state courts.
   B. Only judges hear cases in the federal courts.
   C. The only court specifically established in the Constitution is the Supreme Court.
   D. Most judges who sit on state or municipal courts are elected.
   E. Most cases come to the Supreme Court on appeal from the lower federal courts.

9. An important difference between constitutional courts and legislative courts is

   A. Judges in legislative courts serve for a fixed term.
   B. Only legislative courts are established by Congress.
   C. Constitutional courts do not have jury trials.
   D. The jurisdiction of legislative courts is broader.
   E. The Constitution only mentions constitutional courts.

10. Prerogatives of the chief justice of the Supreme Court include

   I. determining the cases on the "discuss list"
   II. nominating the next chief justice
   III. assigning the opinion when in the majority
   IV. determining the order of seating when the Court is in session

   A. I only
   B. I and II only
   C. I, II, and III only
   D. III only
   E. I and III only

11. Supreme Court Justice William O. Douglas said, "I don't follow precedents. I make 'em." This statement reflects

   A. judicial conservatism
   B. judicial activism
   C. strict constructionism
   D. judicial restraint
   E. stare decisis

12. Which of the following statements about amicus curiae briefs is NOT valid?

   A. Amicus briefs are an opportunity for third parties to provide information to the Court.
   B. Most amicus briefs are filed by individuals who want the Court to consider their cases.
   C. Amicus briefs are filed in connection with petitions for a writ of certiorari.
   D. With the exception of the solicitor general, attorneys who submit amicus briefs cannot participate in oral arguments.
   E. Amicus briefs are a factor in the decision of the Court to hear a case.

13. A ruling made by a court of appeals is

   A. valid only within the states that make up the circuit of that court
   B. automatically brought to the Supreme Court
   C. most likely the result of a decision of all the judges in the circuit
   D. based on the factual evidence introduced at trial
   E. made on the basis of oral argument alone

14. When President Andrew Jackson heard about the Supreme Court's decision in *Worcester v. Georgia* (1832), he is said to have remarked, "[Chief Justice] John Marshall has made his decision. Now let him enforce it!" This raises the issue of

   A. judicial nationalism
   B. judicial federalism
   C. judicial implementation
   D. judicial review
   E. judicial jurisdiction

15. In establishing the judicial branch, Article III of the Constitution provided for all the following EXCEPT

   A. original jurisdiction of the Supreme Court
   B. the scope of appellate jurisdiction
   C. the definition of treason
   D. trial by jury
   E. Office of the Attorney General

Answers

1. **A** The tradition of senatorial courtesy gives the senior senator from the president's party and the home state of a nominee for the federal district court veto power over a presidential appointment. If there is opposition, the Senate Judiciary Committee, which is responsible for holding confirmation hearings, will simply table the nomination.

2. **C** U.S. district courts are courts of original jurisdiction; they hear cases involving federal statutes or federal crimes first. Relatively few original jurisdiction cases come to the Supreme Court, which mainly hears cases on appeal. Although you may not know specifically the jurisdiction of the California Supreme Court or the New York State Court of Appeals, you should realize from their names that they are appellate courts.

3. **A** Although President Reagan nominated the first woman to the Supreme Court, presidents Carter and Clinton appointed more women and minorities to the federal bench. Democratic presidents are very unlikely to support pro-life candidates or turn to large corporations for advice. Requiring the candidates to have judicial experience would severely restrict the pool of potential candidates.

4. **E** As the possible answers make clear, this question is about how the Supreme Court decides which cases it will hear. The answer is the rule of four. An individual justice can have a case moved from the "dead list" to the "discuss list," but this is no guarantee that the case will be heard.

5. **B** Under Article III, Congress is given considerable authority to shape the structure of the federal courts. The Judiciary Act of 1789 originally fixed the number of justices at six. The number was changed several times by Congress until it was set at nine by the Judiciary Act of 1869. The Judicial Conference of the United States is the judicial branch's administrative policymaking body that is chaired by the chief justice of the Supreme Court.

6. **C** A concurring opinion is written by a justice who is in the majority but disagrees with the argument put forward in the majority opinion. Concurring opinions can be cited as precedent. You should be aware that the other answers are types of opinions the Court does render and know the definition of each.

7. **E** On its face, a case involving the murder of a police officer would not involve any federal questions that would allow the case to make it to the Supreme Court. The other choices, however, are either original jurisdiction cases (**A**) or raise clear constitutional issues—freedom of expression (**B**), right of privacy (**C**), and presidential power (**D**). The murder case might be appealed to the Supreme Court if matters like illegal searches or a forced confession came up on appeal. Remember, however, that the question asks which case is *least* likely.

8. **B** This question focuses on the differences between municipal/state courts and federal courts. If you know that many cases in U.S. district courts are handled as jury trials, the answer should be clear enough. All the other answers are obviously true.

9. **A** Constitutional courts are established under the power granted to Congress under Article III, while legislative courts derive from the enumerated powers in Article I, specifically that Congress can "constitute tribunals inferior to the Supreme Court." Article III makes it clear that both Supreme Court justices and judges in the lower federal courts hold office "during good behavior"—in other words, for life. A typical term for judges in the legislative courts is 15 years.

10. **E** The president nominates the chief justice. Chief Justice William Rehnquist served as an associate justice before his appointment to chief justice, and John Roberts was initially nominated as an associate justice and was then nominated for chief justice when Rehnquist died before his confirmation hearings. The order of seating is established by tradition and is determined by seniority; the chief justice always sits in the middle, and the most junior justice sits farthest to the left of the chief justice.

11. **B** All the other answers would strongly respect precedent; remember that stare decisis means "let the decision stand." Douglas is the longest serving justice to date (1939–1979) and is credited with "discovering" the right of privacy in the "penumbras" (shadows) of the First, Third, Fourth, Fifth, and Ninth amendments to the Constitution in *Griswold v. Connecticut* (1965).

12. **B** The overwhelming majority of amicus briefs are filed by organizations that have a political and/or ideological interest in the outcome of the case. In *Harris v. Forklift Systems, Inc.* (1993), a workplace sexual harassment case, amicus briefs were submitted by the National Women's Law Center, the Federation of Organizations for Professional Women, the American Civil Liberties Union, and the AFL-CIO.

13. **A** Cases before a court of appeals are most often heard by a three-judge panel that deals only with claims of errors in legal procedure or errors in law. These cases are argued by brief and oral argument just as in the Supreme Court. There is no automatic appeal; a petition for a writ of certiorari can be filed with the Supreme Court, but there is certainly no guarantee that it can be heard. The fact that the ruling is only valid within the circuit sets up the possibility that there may be a conflict between circuits on an issue; such cases are invariably heard by the Supreme Court.

14. **C** The statement attributed to Jackson is the clearest statement of the dilemma of judicial implementation. Again, the Court relies on others to enforce its decisions. Direct confrontation between the president and the Court, as in the Jackson case, is rare. Congress alone or the president and Congress working together have less dramatic means of expressing their displeasure with the direction of the Court.

15. **E** The Office of the Attorney General is not provided for or mentioned anywhere in the Constitution. The attorney general was one of the executive officers established by President Washington; the position is part of the executive branch, not the judiciary. All the other answers are mentioned in Article III, even though trial by jury and the definition of treason do not deal with the establishment of the federal court system.

Public Opinion

Public opinion refers to the views of the American people on the issues facing the nation. It can reflect deep divisions in U.S. society on such emotional questions as healthcare reform or homosexual rights, or demonstrate the broad consensus that exists on the war against terrorism. People's attitudes may change quickly, however. A president's approval ratings, for example, are very sensitive to the cycles of the economy and world events; the president takes the blame for a recession, but the country rallies around the president in time of war. Certain issues, moreover, take center stage because of demographics. For example, Social Security and prescription drugs were important issues during the 2000 campaign because baby boomers were approaching retirement age and they vote.

Measuring Public Opinion

A television station flashes a question on the screen and gives viewers two toll-free numbers to call: one if you agree with the statement and the other if you disagree. A Web site asks, "Do you think the president is doing a good job handling the economy?", and asks you to click Yes or No. These are attempts to gauge public opinion by polls. But these two examples tell us very little about what the people who called in or clicked online think. They are straw polls and are highly unreliable because they emphasize quantity (the more people who respond, the better) rather than the quality of the sample. Also, keep in mind that in phone-in or Internet polls, people who feel strongly about an issue can call in or log on as many times as they like.

Random sampling, a statistical technique that ensures that everyone has an equal opportunity to participate in the poll, produces valid results. A sample of between 1,200 and 1,500 persons can represent all Americans in terms of such key variables as gender, ethnicity/race, income, and education. The same approach is used for smaller target groups such as all eligible voters or all women. A poll is still an estimate, and no poll is completely accurate. A **margin of error** of plus or minus 3 percentage points is common. If a presidential preference poll shows candidate A getting 53 percent of the vote and candidate B getting 47 percent, the difference might actually be as great as 12 percentage points (56 percent to 44 percent) or the election might be too close to call (50 percent to 50 percent).

In the fall of 1936, *The Literary Digest* polled over 2 million Americans on whether they planned to vote for President Franklin Roosevelt or his Republican challenger, Governor Alf Landon of Kansas. The magazine predicted an overwhelming Landon victory, but Roosevelt went on to win in a landslide. The error was the result of a sample bias: The people included in the poll were drawn from automobile registration lists and telephone directories. Those who owned cars and had phones in the midst of the Depression were the more affluent, and they were much more likely to vote Republican than the population as a whole.

In addition to sample bias, the questions asked and how the poll is conducted can skew results. For example, "Do you believe that convicted serial killers should be put to death?" will get a much different answer than "Do you believe in capital punishment?" Pollsters need to avoid loaded questions or phrases that might prompt a particular response. Most polls today are conducted over the telephone through computer-assisted **random digit dialing**. Numbers are called until the target sample is reached; wrong numbers, unanswered calls, and hang-ups are not a factor. Factors such as the physical appearance, dress, and demeanor of the interviewer don't come into play in a telephone poll as they might during an in-person poll.

One type of poll that is particularly controversial is the **exit poll**. On election day, every tenth voter in selected precincts is asked how he or she voted when leaving the polling place. The purpose of an exit poll is to predict the outcome of an election as soon after the polls close as possible. The news media uses such polls. In the 2000 election, exit-poll data from Florida was misinterpreted and the state was first awarded to Al Gore and then to George W. Bush. Most Americans consider voting a very private matter and will often not answer exit-poll questions candidly.

Polling is pervasive in U.S. politics. Pollsters are key members of a campaign staff; candidates want to know what issues the voters care about and whether their message is getting across. Presidents beginning with Franklin Roosevelt commissioned polls to take the public pulse on a broad range of policy and political questions; President Clinton was often criticized for allowing polls to determine policy options. News organizations— including the major networks and cable outlets, along with national newspapers such as *The New York Times* and *The Wall Street Journal*—routinely conduct polls and publish or air the results. The poll often becomes the story. During presidential primaries and the general election, the media focuses on polls to determine which candidate is ahead; coverage becomes less about issues and more like a horse race.

Political Socialization

Political socialization refers to the way in which individuals learn about the political process and develop their political views. It is, to a large degree, an informal process, with families, schools, and the media as key factors in shaping people's political outlook.

Although teenagers may shudder to think that they have anything in common with their parents, political values are passed down from generation to generation. Things said around the dinner table and offhand comments made during an election campaign have an impact. Studies have shown that people tend to share their parents' politics, particularly when it comes to party affiliation. If the parents are Republicans, the likelihood is that their children will vote Republican as well.

Schools inculcate political values in direct and indirect ways. Basic facts about the U.S. political system are introduced in the elementary grades. Typically, high school students take a U.S. government course that covers how the Congress, the president, and the courts function and interact. But school is also the first laboratory of politics. Children learn about voting, campaigning for office, and candidate speeches when they run for class monitor or student-body president or when they participate in school elections.

Newspapers, magazines, television, the Internet, and social networking mediums like Facebook and Twitter are essential sources of political information. The media plays a role in setting the nation's political agenda—the issues that people consider important for the government to tackle—simply by the amount of print space or airtime they give to a particular story. The importance of the media in political socialization, particularly compared to families and schools, is open to debate. Americans do watch a great deal of television, but they aren't necessarily tuned into local or national news programs, the explosion of 24-hour all-news cable stations notwithstanding. Adults have different viewing and reading habits than young people.

Political socialization is a lifelong process; it doesn't stop when a person moves out of the family home or finishes high school. Another group of variables comes into play that helps explain the political attitudes of different groups within U.S. society. These include religion, race/ethnicity, gender, region, and age. Income and class are involved as well. Wealthy Americans are much more likely to consider themselves conservatives.

As a rule of thumb, the more religious a person is in terms of beliefs and practices, the more politically conservative he or she tends to be. The "religious right," associated with fundamentalist Protestant groups affiliated with Reverend Pat Robertson and the late Reverend Jerry Falwell, has been an important constituency of the Republican Party since the 1980s. But the principle is valid across denominational lines. Both an evangelical Protestant and a religiously observant Jew are likely to support vouchers for students attending private schools. When level of observance is taken out of the equation, a different picture emerges. As a general rule, Protestants are more conservative than either Jews or Catholics, both of whom have traditionally supported the Democratic Party. Jews remain the most liberal of any religious group. There is little data on American Muslims, but one would expect that they would be strong social conservatives on issues such as abortion, school prayer, and family, but have more liberal opinions on economic questions such as the minimum wage. You should be aware that other factors come into play as well. Well-to-do Catholics may support Republicans, while a party's or candidate's position on the Middle East may affect both Jewish and Muslim voters.

There are sharp differences between racial/ethnic groups on a variety of political questions. In contrast to whites, African Americans oppose the death penalty, support affirmative action, and favor less spending on defense. To the extent that they could vote, African Americans identified with the Republicans, the "party of Lincoln," until the 1930s. Since the New Deal, African Americans have voted in overwhelming numbers for Democratic candidates; Bill Clinton was a beneficiary of that support in 1992 and 1996.

Large segments of Hispanic Americans also traditionally back Democrats, but not to the same extent as blacks. Nor is there necessarily an association of interests among racial/ethnic groups. Data collected in the late 1990s, for example, showed that a higher percentage of Hispanics favored capital punishment than did whites. There are also significant differences within the Hispanic community: Cuban Americans tend to be more affluent, and more politically conservative, but they are largely confined to Florida. On the other hand, Mexican Americans, the largest Hispanic group and the fastest-growing population group in the United States, are heavily concentrated throughout the southwestern states and have political opinions very different from Cuban Americans or immigrants from Central America.

We will have to see if the election of Barack Obama in 2008 marks the beginning of a "post-racial" era in U.S. politics as some commentators claim.

The **gender gap** refers to the fact that women and men have significantly different positions on a range of political issues and the relative strengths of the major parties among women voters. Women are less supportive of defense spending and the commitment of U.S. troops than men; they give priority to assistance to the poor and unemployed, education, and gun control. A popular bumper sticker that asks the question "What if schools had all the money they ever needed and the Pentagon had to hold a bake sale to buy a B-1 bomber?" summarizes the differences. The issues that concern women are traditionally associated with the Democratic Party, and women are more likely to vote for Democrats. Ronald Reagan was so concerned about the gender gap in 1980 that he pledged to appoint the first woman to the Supreme Court in an attempt to narrow that gap.

Although the mobility of Americans has, to an extent, reduced regional differences, these differences still remain. The South remains more socially conservative than the rest of the country. It also went through a political transformation in the last quarter of the 20th century. From the end of Reconstruction to the 1960s, the "solid South" meant that the Democratic Party dominated politics in the states of the Confederacy. The Republicans began to make inroads with Richard Nixon's Southern strategy, which aimed at bringing conservative Democrats into the Republican Party; today, Republicans control not only many of the Southern congressional delegations but the state legislatures as well. Certain issues are more important in one part of the country than another; water resources and access to public lands are vital questions to people in the Southwest and Mountain West, but they probably wouldn't even register in public opinion polls in the Northeast.

The population of the United States is getting older; the fastest-growing age group are those over 65. The "graying of America" has influenced, and will continue to influence, the issues that elected officials need to pay attention to (for example, the solvency of Social Security and Medicare benefits). Younger Americans, whatever their political concerns may be, lack the clout to put those concerns on the national agenda; not only do they not have the numbers, but they have the lowest voter turnout. The case of older Americans illustrates an important point: Public opinion is often explained by personal interest, particularly when it comes to things like cutting the capital gains tax, increasing deductions for childcare, making more loans available for college, or raising the minimum wage.

Political Ideology

Political ideology is a coherent set of beliefs about politics and the role of government. Consistency over a wide range of issues is considered a vital element of a political ideology. The lack of consistency in the positions taken by elected officials and voter behavior suggest that U.S. politics is non-ideological. George W. Bush called himself a "compassionate conservative"—he favored returning power to the states but was prepared to enhance the role of the federal government in education. Many Americans have no problem supporting more spending on defense (conservative) while agreeing with limits on prayer in the public schools (liberal). Even if non-ideological, most people recognize that U.S. politics operates within a narrow range in the middle of the political spectrum, and the terms *liberal* and *conservative* are useful in defining the limits of that range.

The meanings of *liberal* and *conservative* have changed over time. Nineteenth-century liberalism was associated with the principles of laissez faire—government should keep its hands off business. Conservatives opposed change and put their trust in traditional institutions such as the monarchy and the church. In the 21st century in the United States, liberals have called on the federal government, in particular, to regulate the economy in the public interest and help those who can't help themselves; they strongly oppose any government attempt to restrict personal freedom. Conservatives, on the other hand, favor less intrusion from Washington, and want power to flow back to states and local governments; they believe that the government does have a role to play, however, in promoting certain types of social behavior (for example, programs that encourage abstinence). Libertarians, usually considered to be on the political right, believe in maximizing individual freedom and severely curtailing the power of the state; they reject both the liberal government as regulator and the conservative government as moral arbiter. The following chart summarizes liberal and conservative positions on several important policy areas.

Liberal and Conservative Positions on Key Issues		
Issue	**Likely Liberal Position**	**Likely Conservative Position**
Abortion	Pro-choice	Pro-life
School prayer	Oppose	Favor
Defense spending	Spend less	Spend more
Crime	Focus on underlying social causes	Focus on law enforcement; longer sentences
United Nations	Positive; force for world peace	Somewhat negative; promotes world government
Affirmative action	Favor	Oppose
Regulation of business	Favor	Oppose
Civil liberties	Favor	Oppose if perceived to compromise law enforcement

The table reflects views typically held by people who considered themselves liberal or conservative before September 11, 2001. In the immediate aftermath of the terrorist attacks, the attitudes of Americans on a range of foreign policy and national defense questions quickly changed. There was broad agreement on the need to intervene militarily in Afghanistan and to bolster defense (including homeland defense) spending, which suggests how events can affect public opinion and blur political labels. Although there was initial support for the Iraq War, that quickly faded as assumptions about the war proved incorrect and the length of the commitment grew.

Practice

1. A poll conducted over the Internet is of questionable accuracy because

   A. The participants were not randomly selected.
   B. The margin of error is over plus or minus 3 percentage points.
   C. The sample is biased in favor of the more affluent.
   D. The sample is too large.
   E. Questions typically are not worded clearly.

2. In light of the "graying of America," which issues are likely to get attention from elected officials?

   A. deregulation of the energy industry
   B. missile defense programs
   C. term limits for members of Congress
   D. patients' bill of rights
   E. gun control

3. Which of the following statements about political ideology in the United States are accurate?

   I.   Political movements on the extreme right and the extreme left have had little support.
   II. People who identify themselves as conservatives always oppose laws restricting abortions.
   III. Most Americans consider themselves moderates.
   IV. Consistency is not essential to political ideology.

   A. I only
   B. II only
   C. I and III only
   D. II and IV only
   E. IV only

4. Political socialization refers to

   A. why a person identifies with a political party
   B. how an individual's political views are developed
   C. the measure of the public's attitude on national issues
   D. a person's position on social questions such as abortion
   E. the role of government in promoting national identity

5. Data collected on the political attitudes of ethnic/racial groups shows that

   A. All minorities tend to take liberal positions on major policy questions.
   B. African Americans are shifting back to the Republican Party.
   C. The views of African Americans are not significantly affected by income.
   D. Asian-American support for the Democratic Party is strong.
   E. Hispanic Americans are the most consistently liberal group.

6. A month before a primary election, a poll shows the following breakdown in a three-candidate race:

   Candidate A: 45 percent
   Candidate B: 32 percent
   Candidate C: 23 percent

   The margin of error is plus or minus 3 percentage points. What conclusions can we draw from the data about the outcome of the election?

   A. Candidate A will get a majority of the votes cast.
   B. Candidate C will drop out of the race because of limited support.
   C. The election is too close to call because of the margin of error.
   D. No conclusion can be drawn because the election is still a month away.
   E. There will be a runoff between candidate A and candidate B.

7. Women are more likely than men to favor

   A. capital punishment
   B. gun-control legislation
   C. no increases in the federal minimum wage
   D. less spending on public housing
   E. abortion

8. Libertarians support all the following EXCEPT

   A. an end to tax breaks for large corporations
   B. a prescription-drug plan for seniors paid for by the federal government
   C. the repeal of laws restricting gun ownership
   D. the legalization of marijuana and similar drugs
   E. full exercise of freedom of speech, including materials considered "obscene"

9. Which of the following statements best describes the relationship between an individual's income and attitudes toward federal spending?

   A. Lower-income groups support spending for social programs.
   B. There is no correlation between income and views on federal spending.
   C. Economic self-interest requires wealthy Americans to back more government spending for jobs.
   D. Minorities approve of higher defense spending.
   E. Higher-income Americans tend to support the Democratic Party.

10. Despite migration from the Rust Belt to the Sun Belt, the South

    I.   is a more conservative region than the Northeast
    II. is a stronghold for the religious right
    III. remains committed to the Democratic Party

    A. I only
    B. II only
    C. I and II only
    D. III only
    E. II and III only

11. The political party that an individual identifies with is largely determined by

    A. mass media
    B. peers
    C. teachers
    D. parents
    E. employers

12. A politician who advocates raising the federal minimum wage, cutting spending on new weapons systems, and increasing the budget for the Environmental Protection Agency is considered a

    A. populist
    B. liberal
    C. conservative
    D. radical
    E. libertarian

13. Polls taken during an election campaign focus on

    A. which candidate is ahead
    B. the views of the candidates on the issues
    C. the amount of money each candidate has raised
    D. the character of the candidates
    E. the candidates' position on foreign policy

14. In recent years, occupation has become less significant in determining political attitudes because

    A. Few Americans are blue-collar workers.
    B. Americans are more mobile than they were in the past.
    C. Education is a more important factor.
    D. Political parties don't frame issues in terms of class.
    E. Workers adopt the views of their unions.

15. Which of the following is NOT a conservative position?

    A. support for prayer in the public schools
    B. support for voucher plans for private schools
    C. support for increases in corporate and income taxes
    D. support for deregulation of business
    E. support for limits on affirmative-action programs

Answers

1. **A** Anyone who sees the poll on the Internet can participate, which is little more than a straw poll. There is no random sampling, an essential feature of a scientific poll. Although those who participate in the poll may be more affluent than the majority of the country's citizens as a whole (because they have access to a computer and the Internet), the fact remains that there is no sample. The margin of error given, if it can be determined with a straw poll, is common with a much smaller sample.

2. **D** The "graying of America" is a reference to the fact that the population of the United States is getting older. Patients' bill of rights, which relates to coverage by health insurance and/or health maintenance organizations (HMOs), is the only answer that is clearly an issue with which older Americans are concerned.

3. **C** U.S. political activity has traditionally maintained a place in the middle of the political spectrum; groups like the Communist Party and the American Nazi Party have never garnered much political support. Reflecting this, most Americans consider themselves moderates. Conservatives are generally in favor of controls on abortion (such as parental permission for teenage girls to get an abortion), and consistency of belief is a key element of the definition of *ideology*. Political scientists argue that Americans are not ideological because of this lack of consistency.

4. **B** This question is looking for the definition of political socialization. Three of the possible answers are actually aspects of political socialization—party identification, views on abortion, and education promoting national identity. Answer **C** would be correct for a question about polls or polling.

5. **C** This question is probably best handled by the process of elimination. You should be aware that ethnic/racial minorities are not monolithic; Hispanic Americans are less liberal than African Americans but more liberal than Asian Americans. African Americans vote overwhelmingly for the Democratic Party, as shown in the 2000 election results. Asian-American party identification more closely resembles that of whites, and the Hispanic demographic includes Cuban Americans who are conservative and support Republican candidates.

6. **D** The key fact about the poll is that it was taken a month before the election. It is effectively a tracking poll that tells you where the candidates are at this point in the campaign, but you can't predict the outcome based on this poll. Candidate A may make a major mistake or may run out of money; candidate B's message may finally reach the voters.

7. **B** The gender gap indicates that women take a stronger position than men on "compassion issues" like gun control. They more often oppose the death penalty and support more spending on social programs. Interestingly enough, men and women do not hold significantly different positions on abortion.

8. **B** Libertarians believe in a weak central government and maximum freedom for the individual. They maintain that the only solution to the spiraling costs of medical treatment is to completely restructure how services are provided. The Libertarian Party's 2008 platform called for a "free market" in healthcare. Among other things, Libertarians support replacing Social Security with a voluntary system.

9. **A** Government support for social programs—whether the federal minimum wage, funding for Head Start in the public schools, or more money for public housing—benefits lower-income Americans. Just as wealthy Americans support cuts in personal income taxes or the capital gains rate, lower-income Americans back actions that are in their economic self-interest.

10. **C** The South remains more conservative than other parts of the country, and part of the explanation for that is the strength of fundamentalist religion in the region. Although the South consistently voted Democratic from the end of Reconstruction into the 1960s, the Republican Party has shown increasing strength in presidential, congressional, and state elections. The "solid South," which was a key element of the New Deal coalition for the Democrats, no longer exists.

11. **D** Studies on political socialization show a strong correlation between the party affiliation of parents and the party with which their children identify.

12. **B** The positions outlined in the question are all typically liberal positions. Liberals believe that government has a major role to play in protecting the country's economic well-being and ensuring that business operates in the public good through regulation. At the same time, liberals have been less willing, particularly since the Vietnam War, to spend money on the military. Monies earmarked for defense are seen as reducing the ability of the government to provide assistance to groups that cannot help themselves.

13. **A** One of the criticisms of polls during either a primary or general election campaign is that they emphasize how much support each candidate has. Instead of highlighting the issues voters are concerned with, polls turn the election into a horse race. There may be a serious downside to this type of poll: Political scientists have noted the "bandwagon effect"—the candidate who is ahead in the polls stays ahead because voters want to go with a winner.

14. **C** Greater educational opportunity—most Americans finish high school and a ever-increasing number go on to college—seems to have a leveling effect on the relative importance of occupation/class as a factor shaping political attitudes.

15. **C** As the legislative agenda of recent Republican presidents has made clear, tax cuts are a fundamental conservative position. Conservatives believe that individuals know best how to spend their own money; they see tax cuts both as a means of stimulating the economy by encouraging spending and as a means of limiting the size of the federal government.

The president holds a televised press conference. Members of the administration, as well as congressional leaders, go on the Sunday morning news shows to present their respective positions on the budget. A reporter writes a series of articles on cost overruns in the Department of Defense. An important Senate race is covered heavily by both the national press and the major networks. A State Department official holds a daily briefing with journalists on the latest developments in the Middle East. A candidate uses the Internet to raise donations. And a blogger comments on foreign policy. These are just a few examples of the relationship between the mass media and U.S. politics.

Evolution of the Mass Media

The mass media is composed of two parts: print media and the electronic media. The print media is primarily made up of newspapers and magazines, but it can include books, such as an instant campaign biography or a reporter's lengthy analysis of a campaign. Radio, television, and the Internet constitute the electronic media. The number of daily newspapers in the United States has declined somewhat over the past 20 years, but access to cable television and the Internet has grown tremendously. Today, Americans get most of their news and information from the electronic media.

The earliest newspapers in the country were little more than mouthpieces for partisan politics—Alexander Hamilton and the Federalists published the *Gazette of the United States,* while Thomas Jefferson and the Democratic-Republicans put out the *National Gazette.* By the 1840s, improvements in technology and rising literacy rates had led to mass-circulation newspapers (known as the penny press). Late 19th-century newspaper publishers like William Randolph Hearst often turned to sensational reporting, known as **yellow journalism**, to boost readership and shape public opinion. Yellow-journalist stories about alleged Spanish atrocities against Cubans trying to win their independence were a factor in President William McKinley's decision to declare war on Spain in 1898. The Progressive Era (1900–1920) saw the rise of the **muckrakers**, reporters committed to bringing political corruption and unsavory business practices to the public's attention through articles in national magazines and books.

Today, most newspapers focus on local coverage. Only a handful cover national issues in depth and include editorials that can influence national policy; these influential papers are *The New York Times, The Washington Post,* and *The Wall Street Journal,* followed closely by the *Chicago Tribune,* the *Los Angeles Times, The Christian Science Monitor,* and *USA Today.* The most widely-read national magazines are *Newsweek, Time,* and *U.S. News & World Report.* In addition, some weekly public-affairs periodicals reflect different points on the political spectrum; these publications include *The Nation* (liberal), *National Review* (conservative), and *The New Republic* (liberal).

How important the print media is to the average American is subject to debate, however. The number of Americans reading newspapers and magazines is down, and polls indicate that the public has more confidence in the accuracy of stories aired on television than in stories printed in the papers. On the other hand, those who get their news from the print media are better informed.

Commercial radio first began to broadcast in 1920 and got into politics very quickly, carrying the results of that year's presidential election. President Franklin Roosevelt effectively used radio to communicate directly with the American people through his "fireside chats" during the worst days of the Depression. Radio's importance as a news and information source declined however with the introduction of television in the late 1940s.

The new media changed the nature of running for office. The first campaign ads for a presidential candidate appeared on television in 1952 and the first presidential debate was aired in 1960 between Senator John Kennedy and Vice President Richard Nixon.

Television also provided Americans with insights into the political process at work by covering party conventions, as well as such momentous national events as the Watergate hearings and the impeachment and trial of President Clinton. A glimpse into the work of Congress became available in 1979 when the Cable-Satellite Public Affairs Network (C-SPAN) began to cover the proceedings of the House.

Today, news and public-affairs programming through the broadcast media is expanding. The major networks (ABC, CBS, and NBC) have supplemented their half-hour national news coverage with shows like *60 Minutes, Dateline,* and *20/20.* Whether the latter are less hard news and more "infotainment" is a matter of debate. Cable stations such as CNN, MSNBC, and Fox News created the 24-hour news format. The need of cable stations to fill time, however, often leads to redundancy and a reliance on "talking heads" or pundits to explain the most minute details of a story.

The Internet plays a key role in U.S. politics. Candidates for political office use the Internet to raise campaign funds and to explain their positions to voters. Essentially, all print media have online editions, and some newspapers are considering only publishing on the Internet. There are Web sites that cover politics from the left (Daily Kos; www.dailykos.com), right (Drudge Report; www.drudgereport.com), and center (Politico; www.politico.com). The same is true for political blogs, personal online journals that provide analysis and commentary on current events. Even social-networking sites, such as Facebook and Twitter, can become sources of fast-breaking news.

Organization of the Mass Media

The media in the United States is privately owned. Public radio and television, which receive part of their funding from the federal government, have a comparatively small audience. Although it provides coverage of the House and the Senate, C-SPAN is a private, nonprofit public service of the cable television industry. Private ownership, however, particularly for the electronic media, does not mean freedom from government oversight. Many newspapers in the United States are not individually owned; indeed, chains such as the Gannett Company and the McClatchy Company, which control newspapers across the country, account for close to 60 percent of the daily circulation.

A clear trend is the limited competition among newspapers in many of the nation's largest cities. For example, whereas there were once five or six dailies in Los Angeles, offering readers a range of editorial opinions, today there are just two. The availability of a national newspaper such as *USA Today* or the national edition of *The New York Times* alleviates the problem somewhat. Competition has also been restricted by fewer companies owning more newspaper outlets.

Although the First Amendment protects newspapers from direct government interference, this doesn't mean that they're free from political pressure. It isn't unusual for a reporter, an editor, or even the publisher to get a call from a White House official. In the wake of the events of September 11, 2001, newspapers such as *The Washington Post* left out details in some stories dealing with terrorism so as not to divulge intelligence-gathering techniques at the request of the Bush Administration.

News and public affairs are not the major business of network television, which is concerned with maximizing advertising revenues from programming. ABC, CBS, and NBC have proven to be quite willing to reduce staff and make programming changes in their news departments to enhance profits; in contrast, some cable stations, such as CNN, C-SPAN, Fox News, and MSNBC, are completely devoted to news; the latter two are affiliated with networks.

Both network and cable stations are subject to regulation by the Federal Communications Commission (FCC). Regulation of the electronic media began in 1927 when the Federal Radio Act declared that the public owned the airwaves, and broadcasters were required to obtain a license to operate from the federal government.

The licensing requirements continued with the creation of the FCC in 1934, and the scope of regulation was expanded to include ownership and content. The FCC limits the number of radio and television stations owned by a single company. These limits were relaxed in the 1980s during the Reagan Administration and again under the Telecommunications Act of 1996. The FCC recently relaxed **cross-ownership** rules regarding ownership of a broadcast outlet and a newspaper in the same market. Other FCC rules include the following:

- With respect to content, broadcast stations must include educational and information programming for children.
- Although obscene material is banned, the FCC prohibits the airing of "indecent material" at times when children may be able to watch it.
- If a station provides airtime, either free of charge or on a fee basis, to a candidate for political office, all candidates for that office must be given the same opportunity to be heard. This is known as the **equal-access rule**.
- Under the equal-time rule, broadcasters are required to give candidates for political office access to airtime on the same terms.
- A person who is attacked verbally on a radio or television station must be given a "reasonable opportunity" to respond. The station is required under the **right-of-rebuttal rule** to identify the broadcast in which the attack was made and provide the individual involved with a tape or accurate transcript.

In 1985, the FCC abolished the **fairness doctrine**, which obliges broadcasters to present opposing sides of controversial issues. Congress tried to control the content of the Internet through the Communications Decency Act, which was part of the Telecommunications Act of 1996. It made it a crime to transmit "indecent" materials over the Internet to individuals under 18, but the act was struck down by the Supreme Court in 1997 as a violation of freedom of speech under the First Amendment.

Reporting and Presenting the News

In covering the national news, there is often a close, informal relationship between individual journalists, administration officials, members of Congress, and their respective staffs. Reporters rely on sources within the government for a good deal of the information they use in their stories. A press release issued by a federal agency, the daily briefing by the White House press secretary, an interview with a member of Congress, sitting in on a congressional committee hearing or oral argument before the Supreme Court—all these can be part of a journalist's typical day.

One type of contact that has become less common over the years is the presidential press conference. When a president goes before reporters nowadays, the give and take is not as spontaneous as it appears. The White House staff doesn't know the actual questions journalists will ask, but they're very familiar with the key issues and the administration's position. A president rehearses his or her responses on important topics before the news conference, often taping and reviewing these sessions.

Reporters are bound by the rules of their profession in collecting news. If an interview is **on the record**, the name of the interviewee can be mentioned and anything he or she says can be quoted in the story. Information provided **off the record**, on the other hand, can't be printed at all, but it may lead to other sources. A government official may agree to talk with a journalist **on background**, which means that the substance of the interview can be published and even quoted, but the official can't be specifically named—for example, a news report might attribute a statement to "a senior White House aide." Even an indirect reference to the source is not used in a story obtained **on deep background**, however. Reporters who violate any of these rules soon find that no one in the government will talk to them, the result of which is that it eventually becomes impossible for them to do their jobs; perhaps for this reason, they insist on protecting the confidentiality of their sources. The Supreme Court has generally upheld the right of the government to force news organizations to reveal their sources when a crime is involved, but several states have passed **shield laws** to protect journalists.

Government officials use the media to promote their own interests. All administrations are skilled at staging **media events**, which are opportunities for reporters from the print and electronic media to see the president in action, pushing an important policy or program. These media events can range from a president's trip to a foreign country to a visit to a public school to push an education agenda. Politicians also aren't averse to giving a story to the press just to gauge the public's reaction; this is known as a **trial balloon**. If the reaction is favorable, Congress may push for the legislation or the executive branch might proceed with a new foreign policy initiative.

A **leak**, on the other hand, is the unauthorized release of information to the press that is mutually beneficial; the reporter gets an exclusive while the individual providing the story makes points with the media. Administration officials may intentionally give a friendly reporter a tip to advance the president's agenda, blurring the distinction between a leak and a trial balloon. Not all leaks are orchestrated by the administration. Indeed, government officials, as well as members of Congress or their staff, have provided confidential information to reporters, resulting in embarrassment to the president. Every administration wants to prevent politically damaging stories from getting out to the public. President Nixon created a group known as the "Plumbers" to stop leaks in the White House.

The government doesn't always share information with the press, particularly in time of war. During the Vietnam War, reporters and television crews went along with troops into combat. Vietnam was the first television war, and the media coverage was certainly a factor in turning Americans against our continued involvement. Perhaps because of the Vietnam experience, the press's access to the front lines during the Persian Gulf War was much more limited. A good deal of the reporting was through briefings given by the military. During the Iraq War, however, reporters were embedded with troops during the invasion.

Time and space are factors in determining how the news is presented. The major networks have only a half-hour (minus commercial time) to cover the international and national news of the day; frequently the depth of news coverage suffers. Television news is often little more than headlines. In covering a presidential campaign, for example, stations are satisfied with giving just a brief excerpt from candidates' speeches. The so-called **sound bite** has become shorter and shorter over the years. To get the full flavor of what the candidates are saying takes a little effort. The full text of major speeches by presidential candidates is available on the Internet or may be carried by one of the national newspapers, and may be shown live or by tape delay on C-SPAN. All-news cable stations obviously have more time, but as discussed earlier, they're often forced to repeat stories in the 24-hour format and rely on pundits to provide analysis. Newspapers have a finite amount of space, and editors must decide where to place a story and how many column inches to give it. A front-page story that is "above the fold" is more important than one that is "below the fold." In *The New York Times,* the story that is in the far-right column is the lead story for the day.

The charge is often made that the media has a liberal bias. Numerous studies have shown that journalists, both print and broadcast, are more liberal in their personal views than the general public and usually vote for the Democratic Party. It, therefore, would be surprising if strongly held beliefs did not affect coverage to some degree. But there are other factors that come into play. Reporters are trained to be objective, which means keeping their biases in check by presenting both sides of an argument. As a group, publishers, network executives, and the heads of corporations that control many media outlets are more conservative than their news staff. Moreover, the media is a business; news and political coverage is less about ideology and more about increasing readership and audience share.

Media and Politics

As noted in the preceding chapter, the media has a role in political socialization; it helps shape our views on politics and our understanding of how the political system operates. In addition, newspapers, magazines, television, and, increasingly, the Internet help set the political agenda, play a key part in electing a president, and expose government wrongdoing.

The **political agenda** is made up of the issues that the American people think are important for the government to handle. The extent to which the public thinks the economy, crime, immigration, foreign policy, and military spending have a high priority depends on the amount of coverage these topics get in the print and broadcast media. Coverage can also affect attitudes on particular subjects. There is no doubt that during the late 1960s and early 1970s, the war in Vietnam was a critical issue facing the nation; it was also a televised war, and every evening brought words and pictures about the conflict into American homes that contributed to the growing opposition to the war. Sometimes the media gets it wrong; for example, the Monica Lewinsky scandal and the subsequent impeachment and trial of President Clinton received extensive media coverage, even though polls showed that Americans were not interested in the story because the economy was strong.

Presidential elections have become media events. The hordes of reporters and television crews who follow candidates through the primaries and the general-election campaign focus more on who is ahead than on policy questions. The major networks and cable stations join together to issue tracking polls that show the candidates' relative support. Candidate debates are covered in terms of who won or lost, not the issues raised. Network broadcasters give considerably less time to the party conventions because the race for the nomination is already over and there are no surprises. Candidates have media consultants whose job is to present them in the best possible light; they're masters of the media event and the sound bite. A good part of the money raised by presidential hopefuls goes to television advertising. More often than not, the purpose of the television spots is not to state the candidate's views but to attack his or her opponents. Although the press and the public often complain about negative advertising, the fact is that it works—votes shift according to what people see on television.

New broadcast formats give candidates free airtime. In recent elections, radio and television talk shows have become regular stops during presidential campaigns. A candidate can expect to field relatively easy questions on a show like *Larry King Live*—easier questions than he or she might face in an interview with a network news anchor. H. Ross Perot, a wealthy businessman who ran surprisingly well in the 1992 election, created the political infomercial (a paid for half-hour block of airtime) to speak at length to the American people.

Muckraking, or investigative reporting as it's called today, has been a tradition in American journalism since the early 20th century. The most classic recent example is the series of stories on the 1972 Watergate break-in by Carl Bernstein and Bob Woodward of *The Washington Post,* which ultimately led to the resignation of Richard Nixon. National leaders are far from the only targets. Reports about abuses in the treatment of the mentally ill in public hospitals and the residents of nursing homes have forced state legislatures to make meaningful reforms. Print and television news coverage of the civil rights movement in the South during the 1960s contributed to changing attitudes toward race. Journalists have also raised awareness about corporate wrongdoing on matters ranging from product liability to environmental hazards. In sum, a key function of the media is to serve as a watchdog on government and business, thereby exposing corruption, misconduct, and the abuse of power.

Practice

1. In covering a political campaign, the media is best described as a

    A. watchdog
    B. scorekeeper
    C. muckraker
    D. gatekeeper
    E. cheerleader

2. Under the FCC's equal-access rule, broadcasters must

    A. give free airtime to all candidates for public office
    B. assure that both sides on a controversial subject like abortion get equal time
    C. air debates for candidates running for office in their market
    D. provide the same opportunity for all political candidates to present their views
    E. take the diversity of their market into account in deciding news coverage

Audiences for Select Mass Media by Age Group (in Percentages)			
Age Group	Television Viewing	Newspaper Reading	Internet Access
18 to 24	92.0	73.1	74.4
25 to 34	93.1	72.1	76.1
35 to 44	93.4	78.0	73.5
45 to 54	94.4	79.1	69.8
55 to 64	95.6	81.0	58.9
65 and older	97.3	79.1	27.1

Source: U.S. Census Bureau. Statistical Abstract of the United States. Washington, D.C.: U.S. Government Printing Office, 2006.

3. Which of the following statements is NOT valid based on the table above?

    A. Elderly Americans are least likely to check out a candidate's Web site.
    B. Political ads on television reach the voting-age population.
    C. Younger voters get more of their news from newspapers than older voters do.
    D. The high rate of Internet use for 45- to 54-year-olds probably reflects the fact that they have access to the Internet at work.
    E. The older a person is, the more likely he or she is to watch television.

4. Which of the following contemporary news outlets is similar to the yellow journalism of the late 19th century?

    A. network news programs
    B. radio talk shows
    C. newspapers like USA Today
    D. all-news cable stations
    E. the tabloid press

5. In a wide-ranging examination of U.S. policy, the secretary of defense stated, "American troops are well-trained and prepared to meet our nation's commitments." The reporter who wrote these lines may have gotten the information from

   I. the secretary of defense's press conference at the Pentagon
   II. a deep-background interview with the assistant secretary of defense
   III. an off-the-record interview with the secretary of defense
   IV. a press briefing book prepared by the Pentagon's public-affairs staff

   A. I only
   B. I and III only
   C. IV only
   D. I and IV only
   E. I, II, and IV only

6. The fact that election campaigns are often reduced to sound bites suggests that

   A. Television provides superficial coverage of politics.
   B. Politicians are not very dynamic speakers.
   C. Voters turn to newspapers and magazines to understand the issues.
   D. Network news shows are too long.
   E. Editors need to take more responsibility for programming.

7. *Cross-ownership* refers to

   A. a company owning radio and television stations in different parts of the country
   B. companies like Gannett, which owns numerous newspapers
   C. a company owning a newspaper and television station in the same market
   D. entertainment giants like Walt Disney, which owns television networks
   E. cable companies that are the sole service providers in a community

8. The purpose of the Communications Decency Act, which was declared unconstitutional by the Supreme Court, was to

   A. require the FCC to limit indecent material on television
   B. restrict minors' access to indecent material over the Internet
   C. make indecent phone calls a federal crime
   D. ban the use of certain language on radio
   E. establish a rating system for network and cable television

9. All the following work against a liberal bias in the media EXCEPT:

   A. Most news about government and politics comes from official sources.
   B. Journalists are trained to be objective and present both sides of a story.
   C. Editors and publishers are more conservative than reporters.
   D. Broadcast and print journalists as a group tend to support the Democratic Party.
   E. Major media outlets are owned by larger corporations whose primary business is not news.

10. The Supreme Court made it more difficult for public officials falsely attacked in the media to sue for libel in

    A. *The New York Times Co. v. Sullivan*
    B. *The New York Times Co. v. United States*
    C. *Red Lion Broadcasting Co. v. Federal Communications Commission*
    D. *Engel v. Vitale*
    E. *Buckley v. Valeo*

11. News coverage of Congress

    A. is devoted to scandals like the impeachment of President Clinton
    B. is primarily the responsibility of C-SPAN
    C. focuses on the leadership in the House and the Senate
    D. is influenced by the White House press secretary
    E. is more thorough on network television than in the print media

12. Which of the following newspaper headlines suggests investigative reporting?

    A. "Abuse of Patients in Nursing Homes in the State Uncovered"

    B. "Fire Guts Office Structure; Arson Suspected"

    C. "President to Hold Summit with Chinese Leaders"

    D. "Stock Prices Drop as Corporate Bankruptcies Rise"

    E. "Attorney General to Rule on Special Prosecutor"

13. The media plays a key role in politics by

    A. determining who gets elected to state and federal offices

    B. helping to set the issues that political leaders need to address

    C. presenting elected officials in the best possible light to the public

    D. reinforcing values such as patriotism and family

    E. paying candidates for exclusive stories

14. In covering which of the following stories would a reporter rely primarily on news releases and press briefings?

    A. 2002 congressional elections

    B. Senate hearings on the bankruptcy of a major corporation

    C. U.S. troops in combat in Afghanistan

    D. death-penalty case before the Supreme Court

    E. a major earthquake in California

15. Which of the following is NOT a difference between local and network news coverage?

    A. Network news is limited to a half-hour program.

    B. Local news programs rely on multiple anchors.

    C. The networks devote more time to "hard news," such as politics, world events, and the economy.

    D. The networks have reporters based around the country and the world.

    E. Unless of national importance, the networks do not regularly cover sports.

Answers

1. **B** The coverage of political campaigns, particularly presidential elections, concentrates on which candidate is ahead. The media tends to pay more attention to reporting the results of daily tracking polls, very often commissioned by newspapers and/or networks, than the issues facing the electorate. This is often called horse-race journalism.

2. **D** The principal obligation of broadcasters under FCC rules is to provide candidates for office "equal opportunities" to utilize the station. If one candidate is given free access to the airwaves, all candidates must have free access—in other words, the same rate must apply to all candidates. The equal-access rule does not apply to coverage of a candidate in a newscast, interview program, or documentary or "on-the-spot coverage" at a political convention, for example. Stations can't censor material that candidates broadcast.

3. **C** Although they spend the least amount of time watching television, 18- to 24-year-olds clearly spend more of their time watching television than reading a newspaper. The extremely high rate of television viewing for all groups underscores the importance of the electronic media. The drop-off in Internet access for the oldest Americans is also a significant statistic.

4. **E** With their sensational headlines and stories and extensive use of photographs, today's tabloid press continues the late 19th-century yellow-journalism tradition, with the exception that it doesn't have the same power to influence public opinion and national policy.

5. **D** Since the text of the newspaper article quotes the secretary of defense directly, the only two possible sources are a press conference—which by definition is on the record—and an official record provided by the Department of Defense, such as the press briefing book. In either a deep-background or off-the-record interview, the statement could not be directly attributed to the secretary of defense.

6. **A** Sound bites are a symptom of the lack of depth in television's coverage of politics. The amount of time that speeches by candidates are given on the air has, in fact, shrunk over the last 20 years. A strong case can be made that too much power is given to television news editors because, in distilling what part of a speech gets on the air, they're using their judgment of what the audience needs to know.

7. **C** Under the FCC, *cross-ownership* refers to a company owning a newspaper and broadcast media in the same market. The issue with cross-ownership is the monopolization of the news and information outlets in a community that might undermine the diversity of opinion.

8. **B** The Communications Decency Act prohibited "knowing transmission of obscene or indecent messages to any recipient under 18 years of age" or "knowingly sending or displaying patently offensive messages" that are available to people under 18. The constitutionality of the law was challenged on First Amendment grounds. In *Reno v. ACLU* (1997), the Supreme Court ruled that the Internet is not subject to government regulation except under the highest standards. It found the statute's use of "indecent messages" and "patently offensive messages" too broad.

9. **D** This answer is the best of the available choices. The fact that political reporters depend heavily on the people and institutions they're writing about for their information supports news treatment that presents official positions. The simple fact that decisions need to be made about how much time or space to give a particular story doesn't necessarily mean that the story will have a liberal slant. There are numerous examples of the corporate owners of media outlets interfering with news departments when a story affects their interests.

10. **A** In *The New York Times Co. v. Sullivan* (1964), the Supreme Court set a higher standard for libel when a public official is involved. Instead of just showing that the statements made were false, they had to be made with malice—in other words, with knowledge that they were false or with disregard as to whether they were false. You should be aware that two of the other choices—*The New York Times Co. v. United States* (1971) and *Red Lion Broadcasting Co. v. Federal Communications Commission* (1969)—deal with prior restraint (censorship) of the press and the FCC's right-of-rebuttal rule.

11. **C** Because Congress is such a large institution, reporting focuses on the House and Senate leadership—the Speaker of the House, the House minority leader, and the Senate majority and minority leaders. These individuals are invariably interviewed by the press and appear on television talk shows.

12. **A** Investigative reporting, which received a tremendous boost from Carl Bernstein and Bob Woodward's work on Watergate, is required for in-depth stories on political corruption, abuse of power, and corporate wrongdoing that require the journalist to go beyond official sources. With the exception of the nursing-home case, which uses the word *uncovered* in the headline (suggesting an investigation), the stories are rather routine.

13. **B** An important function of the media is to set the political agenda. The more coverage that newspapers and television give to a particular issue, the more significant that issue becomes to the public. The media traditionally takes a very skeptical attitude toward elected officials, particularly since the Watergate era and the scandals that followed, and is often criticized by conservatives for not promoting patriotism and family values.

14. **C** Since the Vietnam War, American reporters have been given considerably less access to troops in the field than in the past; in fact, the media strongly criticized the limits on coverage during the Persian Gulf War.

15. **D** Although cut back significantly in recent years, local stations in major markets like Chicago, Los Angeles, and New York maintain bureaus in Washington, D.C., and key spots around the world.

Political Parties

There is no provision for political parties in the Constitution; indeed, the framers were extremely wary of what they called "factions," and George Washington in his farewell address warned the American people "in the most solemn manner against the baneful effects of the spirit of party. . . ." The divisions that surfaced over the ratification of the Constitution, however, quickly led to the creation of parties. The presidential election of 1796 pitted Federalist John Adams against Democratic-Republican Thomas Jefferson. From that point on, U.S. politics has been a battleground between two political parties in contrast to the multiparty systems common in Europe and other parliamentary democracies.

The Development of Political Parties

In the early days of the country, the Federalist Party was identified with the ideas and programs of Alexander Hamilton, Washington's secretary of the treasury. These ideas included a strong central government, economic development based on commerce and manufacturing, and loose construction of the Constitution. Jefferson's Democratic-Republicans, on the other hand, wanted to give more power to the states, keep the central government in check by strict construction of the Constitution, and view the United States as a nation of small farmers. The Democratic-Republicans controlled the White House for a quarter of a century (1800–1824), but the Federalist Party faded from the scene so quickly that it didn't even put up a presidential candidate in 1820 or 1824. (In contrast, there were four Democratic-Republican candidates in 1824.) Although Andrew Jackson received the most electoral votes, he didn't have the majority needed to win and the election was thrown in the House of Representatives. In what became known as the "corrupt bargain," Henry Clay, the Speaker of the House and one of the candidates, used his influence with the members to ensure that John Quincy Adams was elected. In return, Clay became secretary of state, a position he wanted.

Although usually associated with the election of Jackson in 1828, the so-called Era of the Common Man began somewhat earlier with the significant expansion of suffrage. From as early as the 1790s and through the 1820s, the states dropped property qualifications for voting. Jacksonian Democrats drew support from the West and the South, from small farmers and the working class, as well as from recent immigrants. Opposition to Jackson came together around the Whig Party, which, much like the old Federalists, backed business, the national bank, and a strong federal government. The years before the Civil War also saw important changes in how presidential candidates were chosen. The national party convention made up of delegates from each state replaced the caucus of congressional members; presidential candidates ran on a **platform** that outlined the party's goals and positions on issues facing the country. Each issue became a plank of the platform.

When the Whigs faded as a political force in the 1850s, they were replaced by the Republican Party; the election of Republican Abraham Lincoln in 1860 was the proximate cause of the Civil War. In the aftermath of war and Reconstruction, the Republicans emerged as the majority party. Only two Democratic presidents—Grover Cleveland (1885–1889 and 1893–1987) and Woodrow Wilson (1913–1921)—were elected up until 1932, even though the two parties vied for control of Congress. The South remained a stronghold for the Democrats even longer. With a few notable exceptions, the states of the old Confederacy remained solidly Democratic well into the 1960s.

Party realignment occurs when voter loyalties dramatically shift in response to critical events. The onset of the Depression ushered in a period of Democratic ascendancy with Franklin Roosevelt's election in 1932. Roosevelt was able to put together the **New Deal Coalition**, which included the South, labor, urban voters, immigrants, and ethnic minorities; this coalition remained a factor in national politics for more than three decades. African Americans, who had previously found a home in the party of Lincoln, turned to the Democrats after 1932, because the New Deal programs seemed to offer a way out of poverty. The Republican Party was able to make inroads into Democratic support by appealing to traditionally conservative voters in the South. Richard Nixon's **Southern strategy** paid off for Ronald Reagan and George H. W. Bush.

During the last quarter of the 20th century, divided government became increasingly common. Divided government occurs when one party controls the White House and the other controls one or both houses of Congress. Under Nixon, Ford, Reagan, and George H. W. Bush, Congress was in the hands of the Democrats, while Clinton faced a Republican-controlled House and Senate after 1994. George W. Bush was faced with a Democratic Congress in his last two years in office.

From time to time in U.S. politics, third parties have played a key role in presidential elections. Those who impact the election results or garner the most support in the popular and electoral vote are splinter parties that break off from the Democrats or Republicans. When Theodore Roosevelt ran as the Progressive Party candidate in 1912, he split the Republican vote and allowed the Democrat, Woodrow Wilson, to win. Southern Democrats, upset with the civil rights program adopted by the party's national convention in 1948, ran Strom Thurmond of South Carolina as the States' Rights Party candidate. Thurmond won 39 electoral votes in the deep South and polled over a million votes. Similar concerns led Governor George Wallace of Alabama to run for president in 1968 under the banner of the American Independent Party. Wallace took Alabama, Arkansas, Georgia, Louisiana, and Mississippi, but he also showed strength outside the South by receiving almost ten million votes. Ralph Nader and the Green Party were spoilers in the 2000 election, given the closeness of the vote in Florida and the likelihood that Nader votes would have gone to the Democrat, Al Gore.

Other types of third parties include single-issue parties like the Prohibition Party, whose platform is clear from the name, and the Free Soil Party, which campaigned against the expansion of slavery into the western territories in 1848 and 1852. The Socialist Party, which won about 3 percent of the popular vote in presidential elections between 1904 and 1920, and today's Libertarian Party are examples of ideological parties on the left and right. Third parties face significant obstacles in getting on the ballot. Requirements vary from state to state but may include getting a certain number of signatures or having a percentage of eligible voters register in the name of that party.

Political Parties: Functions, Organization, and Responsibilities

A party is a group that shares the same political beliefs or common interests and works to achieve political goals through the electoral process. Political scientists examine parties in several ways:

- **Party-as-organization:** This designation refers to the party professionals and activists, as well as the infrastructure—precinct committee, county committee, state central committee, national committee—through which they function. Party professionals tend to be pragmatic, focused on winning elections. Ideology and specific issues are less of a concern for them than they are for the volunteer activists whom the party attracts.

- **Party-in-government:** Politicians who hold local, state, or federal office and are members of a party make up this category. The president, as the party leader, is at the apex of this pyramid. The success of the party in translating its goals into policies depends on these officials, who have their own organizations (such as the Democratic Governors' Association) to formulate election strategy and develop issues.

- **Party-in-the-electorate:** Voters who identify with one party or the other and who usually support the candidates of that party make up this category.

The first task of a party is to find people to run for office and get as many of them elected as possible. Except for **nonpartisan elections,** in which candidates are effectively independents without party affiliation, anyone running for office needs to get the endorsement of a political party. The party's county committee might choose a prominent businesswoman for an open seat in the state assembly, but it's more likely that she'd have to win a primary election to get the nomination. Those who want to become the party's candidate for governor also have to battle it out in the primary, but they can't ignore speaking to the state party convention or the state central committee. Once the nomination is secure, candidates can expect help from the local, state, or national party organizations. Political parties serve as fundraisers for candidates.

Political parties also provide the American people with choices—both broad policy positions and narrower party platforms. Perhaps because the Republican and Democratic parties try to appeal to the broadest cross-section of the American public, some people argue that there is essentially no difference between the two major parties, but each party has right and left wings. Essentially, however, Republicans are pro-business, conservative on social issues, and concerned with the growth of the federal government, whereas Democrats support the regulation of business, are liberal on social issues, and see government as the solution to many of the problems facing the nation. Outside these broad policy positions, Republican and Democratic platforms adopted at their respective national conventions are likely to take opposing stands on issues ranging from abortion to defense spending to school vouchers. The nominee has a major role in shaping the platform, which becomes an important part of the political agenda of the administration if the nominee is elected. Most Americans never take the time to read the party platform before they vote, but they should; the programs and policies put into effect by a president follow the platform quite closely.

Political parties are organized at the local, state, and national levels. This doesn't mean, however, that there is a strict hierarchy within the party; indeed, local and state party organizations often function quite independently from the national organization. Because of different state laws, parties operate differently from state to state.

The importance of political parties at the local level is much different today than it was in the past. Many local elections are nonpartisan. Moreover, the days of the **party machine** and the political boss whose power was rooted in the neighborhood are long passed. From the late 19th century through a good part of the 20th century, the promise of jobs on the city payroll as a reward for party service and loyalty (patronage) allowed the system to flourish. Changes in the civil service and particularly primary elections, which provided an opportunity to reformers to compete for the party's nomination, undermined the strength of the political machine. Today, depending on their strength in a particular community, political parties may either select or identify candidates for local office, as well as provide organizational and financial assistance to candidates and stake out positions on issues of importance to voters.

States regulate political parties, and state law provides how they operate. Political parties are responsible for finding candidates, strengthening party unity, and organizing elections; the state central committee and its chair generally oversee and direct these functions. Each party in the state legislature may have a campaign committee (similar to those in Congress) that channels money to candidates for office. Both the Democratic and Republican national committees provide money to state parties as well. Party activists may be recognized by their appointment as electors in a presidential election; electors for a particular party cast their votes in the Electoral College only if their candidate wins the popular vote in the state.

The most important responsibility of a political party is the nomination of a candidate for president. This nomination is done at the national convention, which also determines what the party stands for through the adoption of the platform and establishes the rules the party will follow. Traditionally, most of the delegates to national conventions have been chosen by the party leadership. This was certainly the case at the 1968 Democratic National Convention, where party activists and elected officials were well represented. The violent clashes with antiwar protesters outside the convention hall and the heated debates inside prompted the party to appoint a commission to review the party structure and delegate the selection process. The McGovern-Fraser Commission brought about significant changes. To ensure a more open selection of delegates, the number of states holding presidential primaries doubled from 15 in 1968 to 30 in 1972. Quotas were imposed to ensure a broader representation of women and minorities. Although the quotas were ultimately replaced by guidelines, the makeup of each state delegation to the convention must still be half-male and half-female. The commission's reforms, however, went too far in removing party activists from the process; after 1982, a portion of the delegates were reserved for party leaders and officeholders known as **superdelegates**, who are not necessarily bound by the primary results.

The national committee runs each party between nominating conventions. Each state elects its own members who are typically apportioned on the basis of population or party strength in the last election. But the national committee chair and his or her staff do the hardest work of the committee. He or she is responsible for day-to-day operations, including staffing, fundraising, and scheduling. The chair also is a spokesperson for the party, particularly for the party out of power. The party's presidential nominee selects the chair, and, if the nominee does not win, the national committee replaces the chair. As party leader, the president can replace the chair at any time. Although Robert Dole and George H. W. Bush both served as chair of the Republican National Committee, the position is not usually a stepping-stone to high elected office.

Each party has numerous groups affiliated with the national committee. The National Federation of Democratic Women, for example, encourages Democratic women to run for office and provides fundraising help for them and helps to write the party platform. It has three seats on the Democratic National Committee and one seat on the Executive Committee. The Young Republicans is a group for members of the party between the ages of 18 and 40; it has chapters in each state. There are also organizations of party members that work from outside the party; for example, the Democratic Leadership Council, which was formed in 1985, represents the moderate to conservative wing of the party.

Political Parties Today

In recent years, U.S. politics has become increasingly candidate centered. Parties, for example, have no control over who or even how many candidates enter a primary; the winner is the nominee irrespective of what the party leadership thinks about the individual or his or her chances in the general election. When, for example, David Duke, a former grand wizard of the Ku Klux Klan, ran for governor of Louisiana as a Republican in 1990, both the state party organization and the Republican National Committee were opposed. Although parties remain sources of funding, provide help in getting out the vote, and share political expertise, candidates today raise most of their own money and manage their campaign through their own staff.

Party identification develops early in the political socialization process; if your parents are Republicans, the likelihood is that you'll be a Republican. Recent studies indicate, however, that party loyalty is weakening. Voters increasingly identify themselves as independents not aligned with either major party rather than Democrats or Republicans; ballots are cast for the candidate rather than the party label. When party loyalty is strong, people vote a **straight ticket**; for example, if they're Democrats, they'll vote for all Democrats on the ballot regardless of what they know about a candidate for a particular office. Today, **split-ticket voting** is more common; you may vote for the Democrat for Congress, but vote for the Republican for governor and president. The weakening of the bonds between voters and the two major parties is known as **party de-alignment**.

Although the electorate as a whole may become more independent, there are exceptions to the general trend. African Americans remain strongly committed to the Democratic Party, as the results of elections over the last 20 years clearly show. Voter independence is not the only factor that seems to undermine the role that parties have traditionally played in U.S. politics. Candidates are increasingly independent as well; they do their own fundraising and hire their own pollsters or media specialists, and rely less on the party organization for assistance. The rise of single-issue politics has also had an impact: Some Americans seem genuinely uninterested in the broad vision that a party or a candidate has for the country; their only focus is the candidate's stand on the single issue they care about—abortion, tax reduction or restructuring, defense spending, or gay rights, for example.

Practice

1. Voting a straight ticket reflects

   A. voter apathy
   B. party loyalty
   C. weak party structure
   D. influence of campaign advertising
   E. support for the Democratic Party

2. When the Republican Party emerged in the 1850s, it replaced which of the following?

   A. Federalist Party
   B. Know-Nothing Party
   C. Whig Party
   D. Populist Party
   E. Labor Reform Party

3. The party platform is developed

   A. by the nominee's campaign staff
   B. by the chair of the national committee
   C. at the national convention by the platform committee
   D. through questionnaires sent to registered members of the party
   E. by members of the party's Senate and House campaign committees

4. The Democrats' New Deal Coalition relied on support from all the following groups EXCEPT:

   A. Southerners
   B. labor union members
   C. Catholics and Jews
   D. African Americans
   E. business leaders

5. The boss, who was a fixture in local party politics in many U.S. cities, kept power through

   I. election rigging
   II. support for primary elections
   III. patronage
   IV. constituent services

   A. I only
   B. I and II only
   C. II, III, and IV only
   D. I, III, and IV only
   E. II and III only

6. Party realignment occurs when

   A. A majority of the voters register as independents.
   B. There is a shift in voter support from one party to another.
   C. There is a change in which party controls one or both houses of Congress.
   D. The president is from one party, but the Congress is in the hands of another.
   E. A third party determines the outcome of the election.

7. The Democratic Congressional Campaign Committee and the Republican Mayors and Local Officials are examples of

   A. the party-as-organization
   B. affiliate party organizations
   C. the party-in-government
   D. the party-in-the-electorate
   E. the party-as-fundraiser

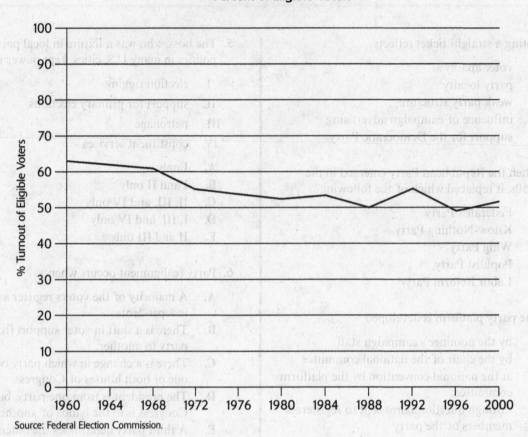

Voter Turnout In Presidential Elections, 1960-2000
Percent of Eligible Voters

Source: Federal Election Commission.

8. What conclusion can be drawn from the above chart?

   A. Voter turnout steadily declined from 1960 to 1992.
   B. The number of registered voters has decreased over the last 40 years.
   C. More Americans vote when third-party candidates are on the ballot.
   D. There is a correlation between voter turnout and the health of the economy.
   E. Voter turnout increases when the pool of eligible voters increases.

9. Which of the following is NOT a function of a political party?

   A. to select candidates for office
   B. to inform voters about issues
   C. to run political campaigns
   D. to raise money for candidates
   E. to determine qualifications for office holders

10. The most successful third parties

   A. represent a particular region of the country
   B. have strong ties to an ideological position
   C. break off from one of the two major parties
   D. focus on a single issue
   E. support a particular group

11. Which statement best characterizes the relative strengths of the Democratic and Republican parties in the period between 1968 and 2000?

   A. Republican presidents always faced a Congress controlled by Democrats.
   B. The Democrats controlled the House of Representatives from 1968 to 1994.
   C. Democrats were more successful than Republicans in presidential elections.
   D. Divided government was the rule under Democratic presidents.
   E. The Republicans had a majority of the seats in the Senate as a result of the 2000 election.

12. Reforms in the Democratic Party after the 1968 election resulted in

   A. more power given to party professionals and activists
   B. the creation of the Democratic Leadership Council
   C. a substantial increase in the amount of money raised for presidential campaigns
   D. greater participation of historically underrepresented groups at the convention
   E. a decline in the number of presidential primaries

Composition of House Delegation by Party, Select Southern States, 1991–1999								
State	1991		1993		1997		1999	
	D	R	D	R	D	R	D	R
Alabama	5	2	4	3	2	5	2	5
Florida	9	10	10	13	8	15	8	15
Georgia	9	1	7	4	3	8	3	8
Louisiana	4	4	4	3	2	5	2	5
Mississippi	5	N/A	5	N/A	2	3	3	2
South Carolina	4	2	3	3	2	4	2	4

Source: U.S. Census Bureau. Statistical Abstract of the United States. Washington, D.C.: U.S. Government Printing Office, 2000.

13. The above chart strongly suggests that, in the Southern states,

   A. Democrats remain in control of state government.
   B. The two-party system is not viable.
   C. The Republicans increased their voter support after the 1994 midterm election.
   D. The Democratic Party is weakest in Mississippi.
   E. Black voters are moving back to the Republican Party.

14. Those who argue that political parties are declining in importance point to

   I. a decline in voter turnout
   II. candidate-run campaigns
   III. an increase in ticket splitting
   IV. an increase in the cost of running for office

   A. I only
   B. I and II only
   C. I, II, and III only
   D. II and III only
   E. II, III, and IV only

15. During the campaign and during his first term, Republican George W. Bush adopted which issue that was usually considered Democratic?

   A. tax cuts
   B. missile defense system
   C. campaign finance reform
   D. support for gays in the military
   E. greater federal support for education

Answers

1. **B** Voting for all the party's candidates on the ballot is a reflection of strong party loyalty. Straight-ticket voting is not exclusive to one party or the other. Commitment to the party is much more a factor influencing voting than campaign advertising, but you should be aware that the literature sent to voters by a party's local or state organization during the campaign urges them to vote for all its candidates.

2. **C** The Whig Party developed around opposition to Andrew Jackson and found its support among industrialists in the North and planters in the South. It was successful in the 1840s and 1850s—William Henry Harrison, Zachary Taylor, and Millard Fillmore were all Whig Party members—but the party split over the issue of slavery. Anti-slavery Whigs found their way into the Republican Party, which was established in 1854. The Federalist Party had long since collapsed by the 1850s, and the Populist Party was not formed until 1892. Although the Know-Nothing Party was active in the 1850s, it was a small, single-issue party opposed to immigration.

3. **C** The platform committee drafts the party platform at the national convention. If determined by the time the convention meets, supporters of the party's nominee will have a strong say as the committee deliberates. If the nominee is still in doubt, representatives of the leading candidates will likely serve on the committee.

4. **E** Business leaders were, by and large, Republicans who strongly opposed Roosevelt's policies. Roosevelt was able to build the coalition despite the apparent contradiction between the support from the South, where segregation was in full swing, and support of African-American voters. The latter began to vote for the Democratic Party in significant numbers in the 1930s.

5. **D** Urban political machines were certainly not above rigging elections by having people vote twice or including the deceased on voter rolls. They also maintained their power by providing jobs on the public payroll as a reward for party loyalty and providing a broad range of social services and assistance to constituents. Primary elections became a means to undermine the political machines by giving reformers the ability to challenge the bosses' handpicked candidates for office.

6. **B** Party realignment refers to a change in which party is the dominant one in U.S. politics. Although voters are becoming more independent, the overwhelming majority of voters register either as Democrats or as Republicans. Answer **D** describes a divided government, which became a fact of U.S. politics in the late 20th century but is not related to party realignment.

7. **C** Both groups are made up of elected officials from the respective parties. The Democratic Congressional Campaign Committee supports Democratic candidates for the House. The Republican mayors and city council members that join the Republican Mayors and Local Officials are committed to promoting the policies of the Republican Party in their communities. Affiliate party organizations such as the Young Republicans do not involve elected officials.

8. **A** The decline in voter turnout is rather obvious, and it should be clear that several of the other answers are wrong. The chart does not provide you with information on the number of registered voters, but logic should tell you that the numbers have gone up. Although the presence of Ross Perot in the race in 1992 seems to have generated voter interest, the decline was not affected by George Wallace's candidacy in 1968. No correlation between voter turnout and the economy is evident; the voting-age population increased significantly when 18-year-olds were given the right to vote, but voter turnout was not impacted.

9. **E** State legislation determines qualifications for holding office (for example, age and residency requirements), and the Constitution determines qualifications for members of Congress and the president.

10. **C** Splinter parties that break off from either the Democrats or Republicans have been the most successful third parties. Pertinent examples include the Progressive Party in 1912, the States Rights Party in 1948, and the American Party in 1968. The strength of both the States Rights Party and the American Party was in the South, but other parties that had a regional base quickly faded.

11. **B** Between 1968 and 2000, the Democrats controlled the White House; they lost their majority in the House of Representatives only in 1994. During Ronald Reagan's first term, the Republicans had a majority in the Senate.

12. **D** The McGovern-Fraser Commission reached out to women and minorities and made sure they were well represented as convention delegates. After the defeats in 1980 and 1984, this trend was reversed, and professional politicians and elected officials were given a greater voice at the convention.

13. **C** Although the table does not include data for 1994 through 1996, it clearly shows that the makeup of six of the congressional delegations in the South had Republican majorities in 1997 and that this was a change from 1993. An argument could be made, based on the chart, that the Democrats are strongest in Mississippi.

14. **D** Ticket splitting (which is symptomatic of a decline in party loyalty) and candidate-run campaigns (which suggest a greater independence from the party) suggest that the party is declining in importance.

15. **E** Greater federal support for education has historically been an issue for the Democratic Party, but George W. Bush supported it. He opposed campaign finance reform. Gays in the military was an issue identified with Clinton. Tax cuts and missile defense are strong Republican issues.

Voting and Elections

Today, every U.S. citizen 18 years of age or older has the right to vote. However, to exercise this right, voters must be registered under the electoral laws of each state. Meeting the most fundamental requirements of U.S. citizenship and age are not sufficient to actually be able to vote. Though each state has its own electoral laws, no state can have laws that contradict federal laws and the U.S. Constitution. Many eligible voters cannot or do not vote because they are not registered. The number of eligible voters who actually cast ballots in the 1996 presidential election was less than 50 percent, but that number has grown over the last three presidential elections. Voter turnout does vary significantly based on age, education, and race/ethnicity. Voter turnout in presidential elections is high, however, compared to turnout in midterm elections (elections between presidential elections) and voting in many state or local races. As the level of voter participation changes, so does the process of electing public officials, particularly the president. Elections are more media-, money-, and candidate-driven today than ever before.

The Expansion of Suffrage

Suffrage is the right to vote, and, in a sense, the history of the United States is the story of the expansion of that right. The founders were extremely wary of democracy as they understood it; they believed that only men of substance should have a say in who ran the government. Voting rights in the early republic were limited to white male property owners. Beginning in the 1790s and continuing through the 1820s, the states adopted new constitutions that eliminated these property qualifications. The results were seen quickly: While less than 400,000 Americans voted in 1824, the number jumped to over a million just four years later.

African Americans were excluded from the franchise; even free blacks in the North were not allowed to vote before the Civil War. The Fifteenth Amendment (1870) prohibited the federal government and the states from denying the right to vote on the basis of "race, color, or previous condition of servitude." In the South, however, literacy tests, the poll tax (a tax imposed by local or state governments as a perquisite for voting), and the grandfather clause (which exempted individuals from the poll tax or literacy test if they or their ancestors could vote before the adoption of the Fifteenth Amendment) were all used to keep African Americans largely disenfranchised. The struggle for the vote in the South lasted well into the 20th century and involved the Supreme Court, Congress (Voting Rights Act of 1965), and a constitutional amendment that finally outlawed the poll tax (Twenty-fourth Amendment [1964]). The vote was also at the top of the agenda for the women's rights movement. (Civil rights for African Americans is discussed later, in the "Civil Rights" chapter.)

Although the women's rights movement was unsuccessful in getting the word *gender* added to the Fifteenth Amendment, women's suffrage was the rule in the West by 1910 through state legislation. Despite this trend in the West, on the eve of the passage of the Nineteenth Amendment (1920), 20 states denied women full participation in the electoral process. Black women in the South were largely denied the right to vote.

Two other amendments are important to the expansion of suffrage:

- In 1913, the Seventeenth Amendment gave eligible voters (rather than the state legislatures) the right to elect senators; the direct election of senators removed one of the last anti-democratic vestiges from the Constitution.
- In 1971, the Twenty-sixth Amendment lowered the voting age from 21 to 18. Section 2 of the Fourteenth Amendment recognized the age of 21 as the legal voting age. But in the early 1970s, with the war in Vietnam generating protests by young people, the argument grew that if 18-year-olds were old enough to fight for their country, they were old enough to vote.

Voter Turnout and Who Votes

As defined by the Federal Election Commission, **voter turnout** is the total number of votes cast for the highest office on the ballot. When we say that voter turnout is low in the United States, it means that the number of people who actually vote is considerably less than the nation's total voting age population (*Note:* The voter turnout number is not the same as the number of eligible voters because it includes noncitizens.) Voter turnout is lower in midterm elections, when all the seats in the House of Representatives and a third of the Senate are contested, and lower still in many local and state races. In 2008, over 131 million Americans cast their vote for president.

There are several possible explanations for low voter turnout. Voter apathy is one. Some Americans believe that the government is unresponsive to their concerns and conclude that voting does no good. Others may be turned off by the sheer number of elections in which they're expected to participate; Americans go to the polls more than any other country. Moreover, political parties are less effective today in organizing registration drives and get-out-the-vote campaigns. Most observers agree, as well, that the process of voting itself is a key factor in low voter turnout.

Voting in the United States involves two steps:

1. You have to register.
2. You have to go to the polls on election day to cast your vote or get an absentee ballot. (Many states allow early voting.)

Studies have shown that registration is the major hurdle to voter turnout. If you've moved from one state to another or from one county to another since the last election, you have to register again. This involves filling out an application and submitting it before the deadline, which varies from ten days to a month before the election. Only a handful of states allow you to register and vote on the same day. Because the overwhelming majority of those who register actually vote, the focus in improving turnout has been on making it easier to register. The National Voter Registration Act, which Congress passed in 1993 and became effective in 1995:

- Allowed eligible voters to register when they applied for or renewed their driver's licenses (hence, the popular name, Motor Voter Act)
- Directed the states to make registration services available at various government offices
- Provided for registration by mail
- Resulted in the creation of the National Mail Voter Registration Form, which allows a person to register from anywhere in the country

Turnout might also improve if other voting changes were made. Streamlining absentee balloting, which often requires a witness and a notary, is one suggestion. Oregon's voting-by-mail system, which allows individuals to become "permanent absentee" voters, has shown encouraging results. Because many people claim they're too busy to vote, making election day a state or federal holiday would also encourage participation. Many states have also established early voting procedures. Individuals are encouraged to vote in person during a designated early voting period before the formal election day at conveniently located polling places. In Texas, you do not even have to get out of your car; "curbside voting" is available to make early voting as convenient as possible.

States across the country use different types of voting systems—paper ballots, mechanical lever machines, mark sense (optical scanning where voters fill in circles, ovals, or rectangles, or complete an arrow), and direct recording electronics (touch screens or push buttons). Punch cards are widely used and were the source of tremendous controversy during the recount of the Florida vote in 2000; the problem with punch cards is that the perforations are not always punched out completely, leaving the infamous "hanging chads." States reexamined their voting technologies in light of the problem with the punch card system in the 2000 presidential election. There is still no national consensus on which of the many systems available is best.

A closer look at who actually votes indicates that a number of socioeconomic factors affect turnout, among them:

- **Income:** Individuals with higher incomes are more likely to vote than the poor. The well off feel that the system works for them, while the poor are more alienated. There is also a correlation between income and education: More-affluent people tend to have more education, and the more education a person has, the more likely he or she is to vote.

- **Age:** The lowest voter turnout historically is with 18- to 24-year-olds, which has been the case since the voting age was lowered in 1971. (Factors other than apathy probably come into play; this age group is very mobile and often must vote by absentee ballot at college.) Americans 65 years of age and older, on the other hand, have the highest voter turnout.

- **Gender:** Since 1980, women have consistently outvoted men in presidential elections, but just by a slight margin. The more significant fact is that women tend to be Democrats and men tend to be Republicans. The so-called "gender gap" is a factor in presidential politics.

- **Race/ethnicity:** African Americans are less likely to vote than whites, but they're more likely to vote than Hispanics or Asian Americans. The lower voter turnout among minorities generally is certainly impacted by income and education. Middle-class African Americans vote at a slightly higher rate than whites. The candidacy of Barack Obama clearly was a positive factor in African-American turnout in 2008.

Types of Elections

Like voting, elections in the United States are more often than not a two-stage process. The nominee of a party is elected through a primary election, and the general election decides who wins the office. Only declared members of the party can vote in a **closed primary**. In an **open primary**, you may either take the ballots of the parties into the voting booth and vote for one of them, or ask for a particular party ballot at the polling place. You don't have to be a party member to vote in an open primary; for example, a Democrat can vote in the Republican primary and vice versa. A variant is the **blanket primary**, in which candidates from all parties are on the same ballot; you could vote Republican for governor but choose the Democratic candidate running for the Senate. The Supreme Court declared California's blanket primary unconstitutional; the Court ruled in *California Democratic Party v. Jones* (2000) that the blanket primary violated a political party's First Amendment right of association.

Not all elections pit a candidate from one party against a candidate from another. Many local elections are nonpartisan, which means candidates run as independents without party affiliation. Elections for the school board, county offices, and even mayor can be nonpartisan. Even in an election where the Democratic and Republican candidates have won their place on the general election ballot through the primary process, there is nothing to prevent an independent or a third-party candidate from running.

Although the forms may be the same, the purpose of a **presidential primary** is not to nominate a candidate, but to select delegates to the party's national convention that support a particular contender in the race. The nominee is then formally chosen at the convention. In some races, the primary is the most important election. This is because voter registration so heavily favors the Republicans or Democrats that winning the nomination is tantamount to election. On rare occasions, the other party might decide not even to run a candidate in the general election.

In addition to candidates for public office, propositions might be on the ballot. A **proposition** is a proposed law submitted to the electorate for approval either by citizens themselves (initiative) or by the state legislature (**referendum**). Over the years, California has used this process to lower property taxes and end municipal and state affirmative-action programs. Initiative and referendum propositions were introduced in the early 20th century to give the people a greater say in politics. Another reform during this time was **recall**, which allows voters to remove an elected official from office; recall elections are held separately from the primary and general elections.

Running for President

A presidential campaign is a long one. Candidates announce their intent to run as early as two years before the general election. They have to put together a campaign organization; raise a considerable amount of money for staff, travel, and advertising to get their names known to the voters (particularly those in the early primary states); develop a theme or focus for their campaign; and devise a strategy for winning. Candidates for the presidency must have a strong political base; this usually means holding or having held elected office. Over the last quarter-century or so, voters have often turned to former governors to lead the nation. The 2008 election of Barack Obama was the first time a sitting senator was elected president since John Kennedy in 1960.

Running for president, like running for almost any other elective office today, involves winning the party's nomination and then going on to win the general election. To win the nomination, a candidate must receive a majority of the votes of the delegates at the party's national convention. Delegates are won largely through the presidential primaries and caucuses.

There have been significant changes in the way the parties select their presidential candidates. In 1960, there were only a handful of primaries and party leaders played a key role in selecting candidates. Today, every state, either through a primary or a caucus, selects the delegates to the nominating conventions of the party. The primary season has become much shorter; many states have moved their causes or primaries up early in the year so that their voters have greater say in who gets the nomination. In 2008, the process began with the Iowa caucuses on January 3, and 24 states held primaries on February 5. The bunching of primaries early in an election year is known as **front-loading**. It gives candidates with name recognition and money a distinct advantage, because the candidates need to get their messages across in so many states so early, which is expensive. Former Secretary of Transportation Elizabeth Dole dropped out of the race for the Republican nomination in 2000 before the first primary because her campaign ran out of money. If a candidate is less successful in a primary than the pundits expect, his or her sources of money will likely dry up and support will fade. But the opposite is also true: A candidate who does surprisingly well can very quickly move from dark horse to front-runner in the eyes of the public.

How many delegates a candidate receives from a primary or caucus depends on the rules established by the state party organizations. Republican primaries may be **winner-take-all** contests in which the candidate with the most votes gets all the state's delegates. The Democrats, on the other hand, favor dividing the delegates based on the number of votes received as long as a minimum percentage—such as 15 percent—is reached; this is known as **proportional representation**. Studies show that voters who come out for a presidential primary are more ideologically committed to the party than the electorate as a whole is. Democratic primary voters take more liberal positions and Republicans take more conservative positions than the country as a whole. It follows that the delegates to the respective national conventions also represent the more extreme wings of both parties.

At one time, each party's national convention was the best show in U.S. political theater. This was because the nomination was decided at the convention. With so few primaries, candidates came to the convention with some delegate support but far from the majority needed to win the nomination. At such an **open convention**, there were often heated debates over the platform and even over which delegates to seat, and the party's pick for vice president was chosen as well. Today, the nominee is determined by the spring or even earlier; he or she announces a running mate before the convention, which becomes little more than a coronation. If there is any controversy over the platform, the nominee's supporters try to keep it as quiet as possible. The **closed convention** is stage managed and receives considerably less media coverage than in the past.

The Role of the Media

The Democratic and Republican nominees both get a bump in the polls following the conventions because of the media attention given the nomination. As the general election campaign gets underway, candidates often find it necessary to adjust their strategies and positions to a degree. To win their respective nominations, they were forced to appeal to the extremes in their parties because the extremes vote in the primaries. Because the electorate on the whole is more moderate, however, candidates must move back to the center in the final months of the campaign. This is a tricky maneuver: A candidate who appears to change position too drastically can be accused of doing a "flip-flop" on an issue (and lack of consistency is a problem for voters); a candidate who moves too far away from the views of his or her core supporters runs the risk of alienating them.

The key vehicle for getting a presidential candidate's message across is the electronic media, either through paid campaign advertisements or sound bites on the nightly news, just as it is during the primaries. In recent years, the Internet emerged as a major vehicle for organizing supporters. Although voters claim to abhor negative campaigning, the fact is that negative ads work. Also known as "attack ads," these ads criticize the opponent's position or actions without directly saying what the candidate is for.

The media plays a role in other ways as well. The networks, cable stations, and radio carry debates between presidential candidates that can have an impact on the election. The Kennedy-Nixon debate in 1960, which television viewers (rather than radio listeners) believed that Kennedy won, probably did not swing many votes, even though the election was extremely close. It's interesting to note here, however, that Nixon refused to debate in either 1968 or 1972. During Gerald Ford's 1976 debate with Jimmy Carter, Ford's mistake about whether Poland was under the control of the Soviet Union was significant, however.

The Electoral College

Winning the general election means winning electoral votes, not the popular vote. The intricacies of the Electoral College might have been little understood by most Americans in the past, but the 2000 election changed all that. Democrat Al Gore won the popular vote handily, but he lost to George W. Bush when the Supreme Court effectively put Florida's 25 electoral votes in the Republican column. The Constitution sets up an indirect system of selecting the president: When you cast your vote in a presidential election, you're actually choosing a slate of electors in your state who make up the Electoral College.

There are 538 votes in the Electoral College. The number of electoral votes for each state is equal to its senators (two) plus the size of its House delegation. The total number is 538, which includes the three votes given to the District of Columbia under the Twenty-third Amendment (1961). The candidate with the most popular votes in a state wins all of that state's electoral votes, and the one who receives a majority (270) of the votes in the Electoral College is elected president. In Maine and Nebraska, however, two electors are chosen by statewide popular vote and the remainder by popular vote within each congressional district. In 2008, Barack Obama received one electoral vote from Nebraska for taking the popular vote in one congressional district. If no candidate wins a majority, the House of Representatives decides the election, with each state having one vote. The 2000 election—in which Al Gore received the majority of the popular vote but lost in the Electoral College to George W. Bush—sparked new calls for the abolition of the Electoral College, which requires a constitutional amendment to effect.

Financing Presidential Campaigns

Prior to 1971, presidential candidates could raise as much money as they could to win the White House. There were no limits on the size of individual contributions, and most of the money came from wealthy individuals, corporations, and labor unions. The Federal Election Campaign Act of 1971 established spending limits on all federal campaigns and strict disclosure requirements. Amendments added in 1974 in the wake of Watergate (Federal Election Campaign Act Amendments of 1974) broadened the limits on contributions and set up a system of federal matching funds in presidential primaries and public funding of presidential general elections. The Federal Election Commission (FEC) was also established to administer and monitor the process. Subsequent legislation, court rulings, and FEC decisions, however, created loopholes that created demands for even further reform. Spending on presidential campaigns has skyrocketed over the last three decades; the same is true in congressional races.

Under the rules in effect through the 2009–2010 election cycle, an individual is allowed to contribute a maximum of $2,400 to a candidate in each election (for example, the primary and general election) and $30,400 a year to the national party. The limits for a **political action committee** (PAC) is $5,000 per election for candidates, and $15,000 per year to the national committee. The Supreme Court ruled in *Buckley v. Valeo* (1976) that restrictions on how much an individual can contribute to his or her own campaign from family resources is a violation of the First Amendment guarantee of free speech; the decision at least partially explains the candidacies of Ross Perot and Steve Forbes, both of whom are extremely wealthy. In the primaries, candidates who are able to raise $5,000 in contributions of $250 or less in each of 20 states qualify for federal matching funds; for example, the federal government will match each contribution of $250 or less on a dollar-to-dollar basis. Pre-convention spending limits are in effect, and matching funds are cut off if a candidate fails to get 10 percent of the vote in successive primaries. The Democratic and Republican parties receive payments from the FEC to cover all general election expenses; a much smaller amount of money is available after the election for third parties that receive at least 5 percent of the vote.

Money raised under the federal campaign laws that is subject to FEC scrutiny and is used directly by the candidates during the campaign is known as **hard money**. On the other hand, national, state, and local parties use **soft money**, which is not subject to regulation. There are effectively no limits on the amount of money that individuals, corporations, or unions can contribute to political parties for such grass-roots activities as voter education, voter registration, and get-out-the-vote efforts. Funds can also be spent on issue advocacy advertisements that do not endorse a particular candidate. The tremendous amount of soft money raised by both Democrats and Republicans in recent elections was used for these purposes and was the source of calls for an overhaul of the campaign finance system. This reform was accomplished through the Bipartisan Campaign Finance Reform Act (2002); the law banned all soft-money contributions to political parties, while individual contributions to candidates and to national party committees increased. PAC limits remain unchanged. The most controversial feature of the legislation is a restriction on media advertising by corporations, trade associations, and unions that refer to a specific candidate in the months before an election. Supreme Court decisions have watered down this provision; the controversial Supreme Court ruling in *Citizens United v. Federal Election Commission* (2010) struck down the ban on ads paid for by corporations and unions late in a campaign on First Amendment grounds.

Practice

1. The National Voter Registration Act encouraged voting by

    A. requiring states to allow election day registration
    B. declaring election day a federal holiday
    C. allowing voter registration at Department of Motor Vehicles offices
    D. eliminating residency requirements for voting
    E. imposing fines on eligible voters who do not register

2. Which of the following statements about voter turnout is valid?

    I. Income and education levels have no effect on minority voting.
    II. The gender gap refers to the fact that women are more likely to vote than men.
    III. The lowest voter turnout is among college-age Americans.
    IV. The most common reason given by Americans for not voting is that they were too busy.

    A. I only
    B. I and II only
    C. I, II, and III only
    D. I and III only
    E. III and IV only

3. One of the effects of winner-take-all primaries is that

    A. Candidates can get a majority of the delegates quickly.
    B. The cost of the campaign is higher.
    C. The media focuses on who is ahead.
    D. Candidates stay in the race longer.
    E. More candidates decide to enter the primaries.

4. Today, the most important function of a party's national convention is to

    A. select the electors for the Electoral College
    B. develop the strategy for the general election
    C. formally nominate the president and vice president
    D. choose the party's leaders for the House and the Senate
    E. name a new chair for the national committee

5. An amendment to the Constitution that did NOT extend the right to vote to a particular group was the

    A. Fifteenth Amendment
    B. Nineteenth Amendment
    C. Twenty-sixth Amendment
    D. Twenty-fourth Amendment
    E. Twenty-third Amendment

6. A primary election in which a registered Democrat can ask for a Republican ballot is a

    A. presidential primary
    B. open primary
    C. closed primary
    D. blanket primary
    E. proportional representation primary

7. The Supreme Court in *Buckley v. Valeo* (1976) ruled that

    A. Limits on a candidate's use of personal money was unconstitutional.
    B. Limits on individual contributions violated the First Amendment.
    C. Labor union contributions were protected under the right of association.
    D. Federal matching funds had to be made available for state races.
    E. Contributions to political parties for voter registration drives were valid.

8. Lower voter turnout in the United States can be explained by all the following EXCEPT:

   A. weak political parties
   B. an aging electorate
   C. difficulty in registering
   D. difficulty in voting
   E. frequency of voting

9. In recent years, campaign finance reform efforts have focused on

   A. reducing the influence of political action committees
   B. curbing spending on negative advertising
   C. decreasing the cost of presidential elections
   D. prohibiting the use of union dues for political campaigns
   E. eliminating soft money available to political parties

10. Over the last 30 years, most successful candidates for the presidency have served

    A. in the Cabinet
    B. in the Senate
    C. as business executives
    D. as governors
    E. in the House of Representatives

11. During the general election, a candidate is likely to do which of the following?

    I. Moderate positions taken during the primaries to appeal to the electorate as a whole.
    II. Campaign vigorously in all 50 states.
    III. Participate in a series of televised debates with the other major party candidate.
    IV. Continue to actively raise money.

    A. I only
    B. I and II only
    C. I and III only
    D. II and IV only
    E. I, III, and IV only

12. Above all else, the results of the 2000 presidential election showed that

    A. The "solid South" remains a fact of U.S. politics.
    B. The winner of the popular vote always wins the electoral vote.
    C. The vote of every person is important.
    D. A balanced ticket is the key to victory.
    E. The party that spends the most will win the presidency.

13. A candidate who qualifies for federal matching funds

    A. loses the money if contributions over $250 are accepted
    B. must accept spending limits during the primaries
    C. needs to finish in the top four in each primary that he or she has entered
    D. does not have to report contributions less than $250 to the FEC
    E. receives a check from the United States Treasury for the total amount raised during the campaign

14. The campaign staff that a presidential candidate puts together includes all the following EXCEPT:

    A. a pollster
    B. a media specialist
    C. a foreign policy consultant
    D. a domestic policy advisor
    E. a political action committee chair

15. In comparing congressional and presidential elections, which of the following statements is/are NOT valid?

    I. The power of incumbency is stronger in congressional races.
    II. Congressional candidates get no federal matching funds.
    III. Presidential campaigns are considerably longer than congressional campaigns.
    IV. The money spent on congressional and presidential campaigns has remained stable.

    A. I only
    B. I and II only
    C. I, II, and III only
    D. IV only
    E. II and IV only

Answers

1. **C** The National Voter Registration Act is popularly known as the "Motor Voter Act" precisely because it allows for registration when a person obtains or renews his or her driver's license or visits the Department of Motor Vehicles for another purpose. Because the Constitution gives the states power over elections, a federal law that eliminated state residency requirements would be challenged in the courts. The other answers are other ways that have been suggested to increase voter turnout.

2. **E** Since they were given the right to vote in 1971, the 18-to-24 age group has consistently had the lowest voter turnout. Time seems to be the reason people give for not voting, and because of this, there has been an interest in voting by mail and Internet voting. Minorities with higher income and education levels have a higher turnout than members of the same minority group who are poor and have less education. The term *gender gap* refers to the fact that women vote Democratic significantly more than men.

3. **A** This is the obvious answer just based on the numbers. In primaries with proportional representation, several candidates are likely to get delegations. If most of the primaries are winner-take-all, a successful candidate will be able to reach the number needed to get a majority much faster.

4. **C** The function of the convention remains the same today even though it's quite likely that the nominee is determined early in the primary season. A candidate and his or her campaign staff develop the strategy for the general election; a change in the chair of the national committee is made after the election, certainly not at the convention.

5. **D** The Twenty-fourth Amendment abolished the poll tax. The other amendments listed granted African Americans, women, citizens 18 years of age or older, and residents of the District of Columbia the right to vote.

6. **B** In the open primary, a registered voter can ask for the ballot of any party. The blanket primary has one ballot with candidates from various parties listed, and you can vote for one candidate for any office.

7. **A** Federal Election Campaign Act Amendments of 1974 put limits on the amount of money individuals could personally contribute from family resources to his or her own campaign. The Court found this a violation of the First Amendment. Candidates such as Ross Perot in 1992 and 1996 and Steven Forbes in 1996 and 2000 benefited from this ruling.

8. **B** Studies show that older Americans, particularly those 65 and over, are the most likely to vote. If the population is aging, we would expect to see a higher voter turnout.

9. **E** The efforts at campaign finance reform, which became a significant political issue after the irregularities in fundraising in the 1996 election, have focused on the tremendous amounts of soft money donated to the Democratic and Republican parties that is not regulated under the rules in effect. The Bipartisan Campaign Finance Reform Act of 2002 addressed this issue directly.

10. **D** Jimmy Carter, Ronald Reagan, Bill Clinton, and George W. Bush all served as governors of their states before making successful runs for the White House. Barack Obama was the first sitting senator in almost 50 years elected president.

11. **C** Democrats tend to take more liberal positions and Republicans tend to take more conservative positions to win over the more ideologically committed voters who participate in primaries; both move to the center in the general election. Televised presidential debates, which have become important even in the primaries, are an accepted part of the fall election campaign. The two major candidates get federal money to run their election campaigns; they don't have the time for fundraising during the short general election campaign.

12. **C** The outcome of the election in Florida depended on a few hundred votes, and because of the count in the Electoral College, those few hundred votes determined the presidency.

13. **B** If a candidate in the primary accepts federal matching funds, he or she must accept spending limits established by law and regulation. The federal government matches contributions of only $250 or less, but candidates can accept larger donations as long as they're within the guidelines of the law. Contributions of $100 or more must be reported by all candidates to the FEC. Matching funds are lost only if the candidate fails to win 10 percent of the vote in consecutive primaries.

14. **E** A chair of a political action committee may have contact with the candidate and the campaign fundraiser but is not part of the campaign staff.

15. **D** The costs of both congressional and presidential campaigns based on data maintained by the Federal Election Commission have increased significantly over the last 30 years.

Interest Groups

An **interest group** is an organization whose members share common concerns and try to influence government policies that impact those concerns. Elected officials frequently complain about the influence of "special interests" on U.S. politics. The fact is, however, that interest groups work closely with members of Congress and the administration to draft legislation and policy initiatives, provide information both to government and the public on a broad range of topical issues, and contribute significantly to political campaigns. The number of interest groups has grown dramatically in recent years, and it's difficult to think of a segment of U.S. society that isn't represented by one.

Types of Interest Groups

Interest groups can be classified according to the groups that they represent.

Economic interest groups represent

- Big business (for example, the National Association of Manufacturers)
- Big unions (for example, the AFL-CIO)
- Trade associations concerned with a particular industry or segment of the economy (such as the American Petroleum Institute)
- Organizations of professionals (such as the American Medical Association)

The goal of economic interest groups is to protect the economic well-being of their clients or members. The American Medical Association, for example, long opposed Medicare and the development of health maintenance organizations (HMOs) as "socialized medicine" in favor of traditional fee-for-service.

Public interest groups support policies that benefit most Americans or the country as a whole, regardless of whether the people who join these organizations are helped. Examples of such groups are Ralph Nader's Public Citizen and the League of Women Voters. Public Citizen is broadly concerned with consumer advocacy, including such issues as automobile safety (see Nader's book *Unsafe At Any Speed*), the environment, healthcare, world trade, and globalization. The League of Women Voters promotes voter education by making information available on how to vote and candidates running for office; it's also involved in such political areas as election and campaign finance reform. Environmental organizations such as the Sierra Club and the Environmental Defense Fund are other examples of public interest groups.

A third large category of interest groups is composed of equity interest groups, which focus on protecting the rights and interests of people who have historically faced discrimination on the basis of race/ethnicity, gender, or sexual orientation. This category includes the National Association for the Advancement of Colored People (NAACP), the Mexican American Legal Defense and Educational Fund (MALDEF), the National Organization for Women (NOW), the Anti-Defamation League (ADL), the Arab-American Anti-Discrimination Committee, and the National Gay and Lesbian Task Force. These groups are not narrowly concerned with civil rights. The NAACP and other African-American organizations actively supported efforts to end apartheid in South Africa, while both the ADL and the Arab-American Anti-Discrimination Committee take positions on the Middle East conflict.

This does not exhaust the list of interest groups by any means. Because of the nature of the federal system, there are government interest groups such as the National Governors' Association and the U.S. Conference of Mayors, which bring state and municipal issues to decision-makers in Washington. The National Rifle Association (NRA) and organizations on both sides of the abortion debate—such as NARAL Pro-Choice America and the National Right to Life Committee—are single-issue interest groups. Political organizations on the left and the right—for example, Americans for Democratic Action (ADA) and the American Conservative Union (ACU)—are considered ideological interest groups. Interest groups also represent different religions on a range of issues; the American Jewish Committee, the Christian Coalition, the Council on American Islamic Relations, and the U.S. Catholic Conference are examples.

Interest Groups and Their Members

Interest groups are composed of institutional/corporate members or individuals. Although there is probably nothing to prevent you from joining the American Public Power Association (APPA), its true dues-paying constituents are municipally owned electric utilities, rural electric cooperatives, and state power authorities. AARP, on the other hand, is primarily made up of men and women over the age of 50. It's clear why the Sacramento Municipal Utility District is a member of APPA; it needs a voice in Washington on such issues as competition with private utilities in a deregulated market, oil and natural gas prices, and a range of environmental problems. But who joins an interest group like AARP and why?

Research confirms that membership in an interest group parallels voting patterns; the higher the income and education level, the more likely a person is to join. The most obvious reason for becoming involved is that you support the purpose and the goals of the organization, and appreciate that protecting the environment or improving the healthcare system requires the strength of numbers. Also, there are often very tangible and immediate benefits of membership in an interest group. The National Education Association (NEA), for example, offers its more than 3 million members health- and life-insurance programs, access to special money-market funds and home financing, and discounts on rental cars and vacation packages. Interest groups certainly recognize the need to maintain and increase membership, which is an important source of their funding and their political clout. In addition to enhancing the benefits package, they keep members informed about how they're doing in Washington or the state capital through newsletters, direct mailing, and the Internet. Those 3 million members make a difference when a lobbyist for the NEA meets with a member of Congress on an education bill.

The function of an interest group is to represent its members, but membership never comes close to all the people that could join; for example, less than half of Americans over 50 are active in AARP and a relatively small percentage of African Americans are in the NAACP. Let's say AARP plays a key role in getting Congress to pass and the president to sign legislation providing federal funding of certain prescription drugs. The law helps out all Americans on Social Security, not all of whom are actually AARP members. This is an example of the **free-rider problem**—there is little incentive to join the organization or become an active participant if you'll reap the benefits anyway. If enough people think this way and become free riders, membership in the interest group will decline and it will become less effective.

What Interest Groups Do

Interest groups educate their members, the public at large, legislators, and bureaucrats about the issues of concern to them. They have expertise in a policy area, and disseminate information through newsletters, press releases, magazines, books, conferences, reports, and Web sites. In addition to publishing its own magazine and its annual report, for instance, AARP conducts or sponsors research on a broad range of age-related topics such as healthcare, long-term-care insurance, and Social Security. Other interest groups rate legislators on how well their voting record conforms to their policy goals. A high or low rating from the American Civil Liberties Union (ACLU) or the Consumer Federation of America is information that a voter might find helpful.

Lobbying is the way in which interest groups try to influence public policy. An interest group may have lobbyists on staff or may hire a law firm or public relations firm to do the job. Although they operate wherever public policy is made, lobbyists do most of their work within the state and federal government.

A distinction can be made between "inside" and "outside" lobbying. The key to the former is personal contact with elected officials and their staffs. Inside lobbyists testify before congressional committees on bills, as well as before federal agencies considering a change in regulations; indeed, they may propose or even draft the legislation and the new rule. Mothers Against Drunk Driving (MADD) was the driving force behind a 1986 law that withheld a portion of the federal highway funds from states who did not raise their minimum drinking age to 21. Inside lobbyists meet with officials to present their perspective on issues. Representatives of the energy industry provided input to Vice President Dick Cheney on the formulation of energy policy early in the administration of George W. Bush. Inside lobbyists representing various interest groups certainly make their views known at the confirmation of cabinet members and federal judges. Not surprisingly, women's organizations supported President Obama's nomination of Sonia Sotomayor to the Supreme Court.

Lobbying is not always one on one, nor is it always directed at the government. Outside lobbying, more accurately described as **grass-roots lobbying**, is an effort to mobilize public opinion and put pressure on public officials. It may involve organizing a letter-writing or e-mail campaign or taking out ads in the print and electronic media in support of an issue. Organized labor's attack against the North American Free Trade Agreement (NAFTA) is a good example of grass-roots lobbying. Labor's ads on billboards and in newspapers, as well as its television/radio spots, emphasized that NAFTA would export U.S. jobs to other countries.

Another way interest groups try to affect policy is through the courts. Public interest law firms can bring suits challenging a law or federal regulation on behalf of an individual or a group of individuals. The NAACP Legal Defense and Education Fund initiated the case that culminated in the Supreme Court's landmark *Brown v. Board of Education of Topeka* (1954) decision against school segregation. The ACLU not only monitors the courts but is often a party to litigation on First Amendment issues. It raised the challenge to the Communications Decency Act, which the Supreme Court found unconstitutional in *Reno v. American Civil Liberties Union* (1997). A more common practice is for interest groups to file amicus curiae (friend of the court) briefs in cases that deal with issues of concern. This strategy is effective because the Supreme Court is more likely to hear a case that generates a high level of public comment than one that doesn't.

Interest groups participate directly in electoral politics. They openly endorse candidates who support their goals, and encourage their members to vote for those candidates. This approach is somewhat risky because, if an interest group's candidate loses, the interest group will likely not have the same access to the winner. The ratings that many public interest and ideological interest groups publish on members of Congress are either a form of endorsement or ammunition for a challenger in the race. Interest groups can help out a campaign by providing mailing lists, by mobilizing volunteers to get out the vote or distribute literature, and, most important, by contributing money largely through political action committees (PACs).

There were just over a hundred PACs in the early 1970s, but that number grew tremendously with changes in the campaign finance laws in 1974. Corporations and labor unions were not permitted to make direct contributions, but they were allowed under the new law to form PACs to raise voluntary contributions for candidates and political parties. Trade associations and similar organizations also created PACs.

Although PACs can be completely unaffiliated, interest groups that want to contribute money to candidates for office must do so through a PAC. In 2007–2008, PACs gave more than $400 million to candidates in the congressional and presidential elections, with the largest amounts coming from trade associations (National Association of Realtors Political Action Committee), unions (International Brotherhood of Electrical Workers Committee on Political Education), corporations (AT&T, Inc., Federal Political Action Committee), and professional organizations (American Dental Political Action Committee).

Data compiled by the Federal Election Commission show that, as a general rule, incumbents get the lion's share of PAC money. This suggests that interest groups want to hedge their bets and prefer to deal with elected officials whom they already know. It's also clear that they reward traditional supporters. Corporate PACs made most of their contributions in 2008 to the Republicans in the Senate, while union money went to Senate Democrats. On the whole, PACs contribute considerably more money to House races than they do to Senate contests. This discrepancy is due at least in part to the fact that Senate campaigns are considerably more expensive. Plus, by focusing on the House, PACs can influence more members of Congress.

Regulating Interest Groups

There is a long-standing concern that interest groups, their lobbyists, and their money have too much influence over politics. In almost every political campaign, one candidate will claim that the other is "a pawn of special interests." Obviously, there is also a concern with outright corruption—bribery of a member of Congress. An early attempt to control undue interest group power was the 1946 Federal Regulation of Lobbying Act. It required lobbyists and/or organizations seeking to influence legislation to register with Congress and submit financial reports. The law was not strictly enforced. The Lobbying Disclosure Act (1995) tightened the old registration and disclosure rules; covered lobbyists working with federal agencies and their staff, as well as members of Congress; and added reporting requirements on clients, issues worked on, and income. Under the legislation, disclosure forms are submitted to both the House and the Senate. Lobbyists who have foreign governments as their clients must register with the Justice Department as agents of those countries. The 2006 scandal involving Jack Abramoff and members of Congress led to new laws placing additional restrictions on the lobbyists' activities. On his first day in office, President Obama issued an executive order with new ethics rules prohibiting members of the administration from accepting gifts from lobbyists or trying to influence their former colleagues for two years after they left the administration.

Another issue that Congress addressed was the so-called **revolving door**, a practice in which former government officials become lobbyists for an industry they may have regulated when on the public payroll. According to the Ethics in Government Act (1978), a former executive-branch employee cannot represent anyone before any agency on a matter that had been within his or her sphere of responsibility for two years after leaving the government, and cannot represent anyone before his or her former agency for one year.

During the debate on campaign financing, there were calls to ban contributions from PACs; indeed, in 1996, Congress considered, but never enacted, such legislation. The Bipartisan Campaign Finance Reform Act leaves the existing limits on PAC donations to candidates or parties unchanged. Eliminating soft money was obviously seen as more effective. But the new law restricts the election activities of interest groups in another way: Corporations, trade associations, and unions can only place ads that refer to a particular candidate for federal office 30 days before a primary and 60 days before a general election. The goal is to limit the influence of potentially large amounts of advertising as the election draws near.

Practice

1. When a political action committee makes a contribution to an elected official, the expectation is that

    A.   The elected official will vote the way the interest group wants.

    B.   The interest group will have access to the elected official.

    C.   The elected official will provide jobs for members of the interest group.

    D.   The elected official will make sure the interest group is not audited by the IRS.

    E.   The elected official will kick back a portion of the contribution to lobbyists.

2. All the following are examples of economic interest groups EXCEPT:

    A.   American Farm Bureau Federation

    B.   Consumer Union of the United States

    C.   Service Employees International Union

    D.   American Bankers Association

    E.   American Federation of Teachers

3. In order to contribute to the campaign of a presidential candidate, an interest group

    A.   can make the donation directly to the candidate

    B.   must earmark money for voter education

    C.   can give the money only to the national party

    D.   must create a political action committee to raise and distribute money

    E.   must approve ads bought with its money

4. The free-rider problem refers to

    A.   candidates for office who face no primary opposition

    B.   candidates with great personal wealth who do not need PAC money

    C.   members of Congress who take gifts from lobbyists

    D.   non-germane amendments added to a bill

    E.   people who benefit from an interest group but do not join the group

5. Lobbyists try to influence public policy by all the following EXCEPT:

    A.   mobilizing grass-roots support

    B.   testifying before congressional committees

    C.   meeting with federal district judges

    D.   speaking with heads of federal agencies

    E.   providing research data to government officials

6. A lobbyist for the National Rifle Association is most likely to get the support of

    A.   a Republican who voted for the Brady Bill

    B.   an incumbent facing a difficult reelection

    C.   a liberal Democrat

    D.   a newly elected senator

    E.   a conservative Republican

7. Which of the following is the Mexican American Legal Defense and Educational Fund LEAST likely to do to achieve its goals?

    A.   lobby Congress on immigration reform

    B.   endorse only Hispanic candidates for office

    C.   file a lawsuit involving immigrant employment discrimination

    D.   challenge local English-only ordinances

    E.   submit a restricting plan to increase Latino voter strength

8. Interest groups participate in electoral politics by

    I.   endorsing candidates

    II.   urging members to vote for a candidate

    III.   running candidates for office

    IV.   lobbying for term limits for Congress

    A.   I only

    B.   I and II only

    C.   I, II, and IV only

    D.   I, II, and III only

    E.   I, II, III, and IV

9. The people attracted to interest groups are most likely

   A. college educated
   B. social conservatives
   C. committed independent voters
   D. liberal activists
   E. racial/ethnic minorities

10. Which one of the following statements about lobbyists is NOT true?

    A. Lobbyists are often former government officials.
    B. Lobbyists must register with the House and the Senate.
    C. Lobbyists cannot represent foreign countries.
    D. Many interest groups have their own lobbyists on staff.
    E. Strong interpersonal skills are important to a lobbyist's success.

11. A former undersecretary in the Department of Energy becomes a consultant for the American Petroleum Institute and testifies before Congress on the regulation of offshore oil drilling. This is an example of

    A. an iron triangle
    B. influence peddling
    C. an issue network
    D. the revolving door
    E. effective lobbying

12. When AARP produces its *Guide to Internet Resources on Aging,* it is supporting which function of an interest group?

    A. member benefits
    B. education
    C. representation
    D. lobbying
    E. electioneering

Contributions by Corporate and Labor PACs to Senate Campaigns, 2008

Candidate	Corporate PAC	Labor PAC
Democratic incumbent	$8,833,380	$2,453,773
Democratic challenger	$660,675	$2,907,048
Open seat	$1,967,283	$1,220,717
Republican incumbent	$18,544,270	$391,150
Republican challenger	$2,101,329	$59,850
Open seat	$1,172,215	$20,500

Source: Federal Election Commission.

13. The above table supports all the following conclusions EXCEPT:

    A. Corporate PACs raise considerably more money than unions.
    B. PACs gave the most money to incumbents.
    C. Corporate PACs supported Republican candidates by a wide margin.
    D. Unions overwhelmingly backed Democrats running for the Senate.
    E. Labor unions are much more willing than corporate PACs to fight for an open seat.

14. Which of the following statements about interest groups is valid?

    A. Interest groups try to influence policymaking only at the federal level.
    B. Interest groups are composed only of individual members.
    C. In almost all cases, the potential membership of an interest group is greater than its actual membership.
    D. Interest groups get all their funding from membership dues.
    E. Interest groups are most effective when they deal with multiple issues.

15. Lobbyists must file reports of their activities, including information about their clients, with the

    A. Federal Election Commission
    B. Justice Department
    C. Securities and Exchange Commission
    D. House of Representatives and Senate
    E. Office of Management and Budget

Answers

1. **B** Studies have shown that campaign contributions do not buy votes or any other direct consideration. Interest groups expect their contribution to get them the opportunity to explain their position on issues of concern to the state legislator or member of Congress, high-level staff in the governor's office, or the executive branch.

2. **B** If you don't realize that the Consumer Union is a public-interest group, you still should be able to get the correct answer by process of elimination. Economic interest groups include trade associations (American Farm Bureau Federation, American Bankers Association), unions (Service Employees International Union), and professional organizations (American Federation of Teachers). Note that you could also consider the AFT as a union.

3. **D** Under current campaign finance laws, an interest group must form a PAC to make political contributions either to an individual candidate or to a national party.

4. **E** This is a straightforward definition question. The other answers are trying to trick you with the idea of a "free ride" or, in the case of **D**, to confuse *free-rider* with a rider that may be attached to a bill as it works its way through the legislative process.

5. **C** Even informal contact between a federal judge and a lobbyist, who presumably would have a case or issue pending before the court, is highly irregular and would be avoided at any cost. Lobbyists do, however, use the judicial system to advance their public policy concerns, either by filing suit or by submitting an amicus brief. Interest groups may be asked to provide input on court nominees and may testify at confirmation hearings.

6. **E** In order to answer this question, you need to know that the Brady Bill was a gun control measure that required a federal three-day waiting period for gun purchases. **B** and **D** are irrelevant to the question; whether the member of Congress is facing reelection or was just elected is meaningless unless you know something about the district or state regarding gun control. Almost all liberal Democrats are in favor of gun control, and a lobbyist for the NRA would not bother meeting with them.

7. **B** The Mexican American Legal Defense and Educational Fund (MALDEF) is the leading Latino civil rights organization. Although it focuses on legal action in areas such as job discrimination, immigrant rights, and education, it also engages in lobbying. MALDEF is certainly interested in increasing the political clout of the Latino community, but it recognizes that supporting only Hispanic candidates is counterproductive. For many offices in many states with a large Latino population, there is no Latino candidate.

8. **B** Although Ralph Nader ran for president in 2000, he did so as the candidate of the Green Party, not of his interest group. Interest groups don't run candidates for office; they aren't political parties. With the exception of public interest groups, most organizations that engage in lobbying depend on developing long-term relationships with members of Congress.

9. **A** Certain interest groups may have a large number of liberal activists (such as Americans for Democratic Action) or social conservatives (such as the Christian Coalition) as members. It's also likely that many people who are involved in an interest group are also committed voters. But the question is broader than that. Studies indicate that well-educated and higher-income individuals tend to join interest groups. Of the choices available, **A** is the best answer.

10. **C** Lobbyists can, in fact, represent foreign governments, but they must register as agents of those countries with the Department of Justice.

11. **D** The two possible confusing answers are **A** and **C**, because the question contains the three elements associated with either an iron triangle or an issue network: a federal agency (Department of Energy), an interest group (American Petroleum Institute [API]), and a congressional committee. But the key point of the statement is that a former Department of Energy official is now working for the API. This is the revolving door, even though the question doesn't tell you whether there was a break between government service and the person's work as a lobbyist.

12. **B** Interest groups are experts in their policy areas, and they see educating their members, elected officials, and the public as a whole as an essential function. *The Guide to Internet Resources on Aging* is information that all these constituencies can use. It isn't a member benefit, because it's accessible to members and nonmembers alike. None of the other answers is relevant.

13. **E** The table shows that union and corporate PACs gave just about the same amount of money to vie for an open seat irrespective of whether it was formerly held by a Democrat or a Republican.

14. **C** Interest groups are active at all levels of government. Although Washington, D.C., gets most of the public attention, interest groups actively lobby in every state capital. An interest group can include institutional/corporate members and/or individual members. Interest groups get funding through grants from foundations, as well as the federal government for certain projects. All the governors of the states and the territories are members of the National Governors' Association, but all women are not members of NOW nor are all consumers members of the Consumer Union of the United States.

15. **D** Disclosure forms and reports must be filed with the clerk of the House of Representatives and the secretary of the Senate under the Lobbying Disclosure Act of 1995.

Civil Liberties

Basic rights that Americans take for granted were not specifically included in the Constitution as ratified. Although trial by jury was guaranteed, and neither the federal government nor the states could revoke habeas corpus, the Constitution didn't mention freedom of religion, speech, or the press. The Antifederalists were quick to point this out, and supporters of the Constitution agreed to remedy the situation through the amendment process as the price for ratification. The terms *civil liberties* and *civil rights* are often used interchangeably, but doing so is incorrect because their definitions are different. Civil liberties are individual protections against actions by the government guaranteed to every citizen by the Bill of Rights and the due process clause of the Fourteenth Amendment. Civil rights, on the other hand, deal with the protection of individuals against discrimination, and are based on the Equal Protection Clause of the Fourteenth Amendment, subsequent amendments, and laws enacted by Congress.

Perspectives on the Bill of Rights

The first ten amendments to the Constitution ratified in 1791 are the Bill of Rights. You should understand, however, that only the first eight pertain to individual rights, such as freedom of religion, protection against unreasonable search and seizure, and the right to counsel. The Ninth Amendment holds out the prospect that there may be other rights not included in the Constitution, and the Supreme Court has found a right to privacy in this language. The Tenth Amendment, on the other hand, doesn't deal with individual liberties at all; instead, it deals with reserved powers of the states. In fact, it became the basis for states' rights arguments and is more relevant to civil rights issues than civil liberties.

The clear purpose of the Bill of Rights was to prevent the abuse of power by the federal government. The First Amendment does not say, "No law shall be made . . . abridging the freedom of speech or of the press. . . ." Instead, it states very specifically that "Congress shall make no law . . . abridging the freedom of speech or of the press. . . ." The Court rejected the notion that the Bill of Rights also applied to the states in *Barron v. Baltimore* (1833) and held to this position throughout most of the 19th century. In its landmark decision in *Gitlow v. New York* (1925), the freedom of speech and press protections of the First Amendment were extended to the states. In a series of cases that followed, the Court held that most, but not all, of the provisions of the Bill of Rights limit municipalities and states, as well as the federal government, through the Fourteenth Amendment. This is known as the **incorporation doctrine**. The parts of the Bill of Rights not incorporated are the Second and Third amendments, as well as indictment by grand jury (Fifth Amendment), trial by jury in civil cases (Seventh Amendment), and excessive bail and fines (Eighth Amendment).

Even through selective incorporation, the Court has expanded considerably the role of the federal government in protecting individual civil liberties.

The First Amendment: Freedom of Religion

The First Amendment spells out what Americans consider their fundamental rights: freedom of religion, speech, and the press (sometimes combined into freedom of expression); the right to assemble; and the right to petition the government. For more than two centuries, the Supreme Court has made it very clear that these rights are not without their restrictions. An individual cannot do anything he or she wants and claim the protection of freedom of religion; a person can't say anything that comes to mind under the guise of free speech. There are limits, and the history of the First Amendment is determining what those limits are.

There are two aspects to freedom of religion:

- The **Establishment Clause**, which pertains to the separation of church and state
- The **Free Exercise Clause**, which prohibits the government from interfering in the way in which religion is practiced

The Establishment Clause

Under the Establishment Clause, the Court has rather consistently ruled that prayer in the public schools is, in effect, state-sponsored prayer and is thereby unconstitutional (*Engel v. Vitale* [1962]). The fact that the prayers were nondenominational or were said at a graduation ceremony is not relevant. At the same time, the Court recognized that interaction between the government and religion is inevitable. In *Lemon v. Kurtzman* (1971), the Court held that a law or state action regarding religion was constitutional if it met three criteria:

■ It had a secular purpose.

■ The primary effect was not to advance or inhibit religion.

■ Government was not excessively entangled with religion.

The criteria are known as the **Lemon test**. In recent years, the Court has moved closer toward accommodation. Use of school facilities can't be denied to religious clubs or groups if those facilities are available to other school or community organizations. Public-school teachers providing remedial services to disadvantaged students in parochial schools is not an "excessive entanglement" with religion (*Agostini v. Felton* [1997]). In *Zelman v. Simmons-Harris* (2002), the Supreme Court upheld an Ohio school voucher program, recognizing that the government may provide financial aid to parents who want to send their children to private schools that may be religious or secular.

The Free Exercise Clause

The government can limit the right of individuals to worship as they wish. For example, judges routinely order autopsies even if a family is opposed on religious grounds when there is a compelling state interest to do so. The need to gather evidence of a crime or to protect the public health are two more instances of compelling state interest. In *Employment Division of Oregon v. Smith* (1990), the Supreme Court upheld an Oregon law that made using illegal drugs in a religious ceremony a crime. The Court pointed out that the Free Exercise Clause protects only against laws intended to disadvantage religion. Many religious groups felt that the ruling weakened the First Amendment protections of religious practices; they worked to reverse the decision in Congress. But the Court found the Religious Freedom Restoration Act unconstitutional as well.

First Amendment: Freedom of Speech and the Press

The basic question is what type of expression is *not* protected under the First Amendment. The Supreme Court has generally found that obscenity, libel, and words that incite are not protected. In *Schenck v. United States* (1919), the **clear and present danger test** was established; a person cannot yell "fire" in a crowded theater. The emphasis has shifted over the years to the direct connection, or proximity, of the words to the danger. "Fighting words" that lead to "an immediate breach of the peace" are an example that the Court noted in *Chaplinsky v. New Hampshire* (1942).

The Court has long considered obscene materials as outside free speech protection. Courts now face the challenge of determining what is obscene. As outlined in *Miller v. California* (1973), a work is obscene if:

■ It appeals to prurient interests based on contemporary community standards.

■ It depicts sexual activity in a patently offensive manner.

■ It does not have "literary, artistic, political, or scientific value" (the so-called **LAPS test**).

Child pornography does not have to meet these tests to be banned.

The government cannot establish rules on what we can or cannot publish (in other words, there is nothing to prevent the publication of obscene materials), because courts consider this to be **prior restraint** or censorship. But the courts can impose punishment after the fact. The same is true for statements that are false or libelous where the intent is to defame the character of an individual.

The most notable case on prior restraint is *The New York Times Co. v. United States* (1971), in which the Court refused to block printing of *The Pentagon Papers,* a collection of classified Department of Defense documents on the history of the Vietnam War. In another case involving *The New York Times,* the Court made it more difficult for public officials to sue for *libel* (defamatory material in print) or *slander* (defamatory speech). The public officials have to show malice—that an editor, for example, knew the information in the story was false but published it anyway, showing a "reckless disregard for the truth" (*The New York Times Co. v. Sullivan* [1964]); this is a higher standard of proof than the courts require of an average person.

Speech is not limited to words, whether spoken or written. Actions are sometimes considered speech that fall under the First Amendment. The right of students to wear black armbands to protest the Vietnam War was upheld as symbolic speech (*Tinker v. Des Moines Independent Community School District* [1969]). Burning an American flag during a demonstration against the policies of the Reagan Administration was also protected by the Court in *Texas v. Johnson* (1989). In the wake of the latter decision, Congress passed the Federal Flag Protection Act, which made desecrating the flag a federal offense; the law was struck down as a violation of free speech, and attempts to get a constitutional amendment on flag burning through Congress have failed. In *R.A.V. v. City of St. Paul* (1992), the Supreme Court struck down a local ordinance that made it a crime to place a symbol such as a burning cross or a Nazi swastika on public or private property.

A number of other issues come up under freedom of expression. Often, a conflict arises between First Amendment rights and other rights. Reporters have claimed that the constitutional guarantees of a free press do not require them to turn over information about confidential sources to a court even though that information may be essential to a fair trial. Courts have consistently ruled against this interpretation, but a number of states have enacted **shield laws** to give journalists a limited degree of protection against the disclosure of sources. Commercial speech is the most regulated form of expression. The First Amendment does not protect false or misleading advertising, but it does permit the ads that ban cigarettes and other tobacco products. Television and radio programming falls under the jurisdiction of the Federal Communications Commission, which controls the time of day when a station can air "indecent speech." During the 1990s, colleges across the country banned offensive speech against racial and ethnic groups, women, and homosexuals on the grounds that it created an intimidating or hostile atmosphere. The courts found many of the codes against **hate speech** unconstitutional.

The Rights of Criminal Defendants

The Fourth, Fifth, Sixth, and Eighth amendments pertain to procedural issues involving suspects in a crime and criminal defendants. They cover search warrants and right to counsel, as well as protection against self-incrimination and cruel and unusual punishment.

The Fourth Amendment protects individuals against "unreasonable search and seizure" and states quite clearly the requirements for obtaining a search warrant. Under the **exclusionary rule**, evidence that is seized illegally is not admissible in court (*Mapp v. Ohio* [1961]). Further, if authorities discover additional evidence by relying on the illegal search, then authorities cannot use that evidence at trial; it is known as the **fruit of the poisonous tree**. In an attempt to balance individual rights with the needs of society, courts have allowed warrantless searches in a variety of instances. The police can search a person who they arrest, and they can take into evidence items that are in plain sight at the time of the arrest. Evidence that authorities obtain through an improper search warrant may be admissible under the **good-faith exception**—if the police believed that the information they used to establish probable cause was valid, but it was not. The Supreme Court has allowed questionable evidence to be used if it "ultimately" would have been found by legal means; this is known as inevitable discovery. There is also an automobile exception: Authorities can search a car and its passenger if there is a valid reason to stop the car in the first place.

A key provision of the Fifth Amendment is the provision against self-incrimination; authorities can't compel a person "to be a witness against himself" in a criminal case. There is a close relationship between this protection and the Sixth Amendment right to counsel. Two landmark cases in the 1960s bear this out. In *Escobedo v. Illinois* (1964), the Court ruled that a confession can't be used against a suspect who asked for, but was refused access to, an attorney. The justices expanded the rights of criminal defendants two years latter in *Miranda v. Arizona* (1966), by requiring the police to inform an individual at the time of arrest of his or her right against self-incrimination and to an attorney. The Court even outlined the essential elements of what became known as the **Miranda warning**:

- The suspect has the right to remain silent.
- Any statements that the suspect gives can be used as evidence against him or her.
- The suspect has the right to have an attorney present during questioning.
- An attorney will be appointed by the court if the suspect cannot afford one.

Miranda not only expanded on *Escobedo* but incorporated the finding in *Gideon v. Wainwright* (1963) that legal counsel is indispensable to a fair trial, and that the state must provide an attorney to poor defendants in criminal cases. Today, this right is required in any case where a prison term is possible.

Cases involving the Eighth Amendment ban on "cruel and unusual punishment" center on the death penalty. The Supreme Court struck down all state death-penalty statutes in *Furman v. Georgia* (1972), because the laws were so unevenly applied. It was much more likely for a poor or African-American defendant convicted of a capital crime to face execution than it was for a white person to do so. New legislation was enacted to address the Court's concerns. In *Gregg v. Georgia* (1976), the Court affirmed the constitutionality of the death penalty per se. In *Atkins v. Virginia* (2002), the Court held that the execution of mentally retarded criminals is cruel and unusual punishment and violates the Eighth Amendment; in 2008, the Court struck down a state law that provided the death penalty for the rape of a child.

Constitutional questions are also raised about the effectiveness of counsel in death penalty cases and whether the common method of execution—lethal injection—is "cruel and unusual punishment." In a number of recent instances, DNA evidence has resulted either in the release of death-row inmates or in new trials.

The Right of Privacy

A right of privacy is not mentioned in the Constitution. The Supreme Court, as it did with judicial review, found that such a right was implied. In *Griswold v. Connecticut* (1965), which struck down a state law that prohibited birth control counseling and made the use of contraceptives by married couples illegal, the Court maintained that privacy was constitutionally protected through the First, Third, Fourth, Fifth, and Ninth amendments. Controversial issues, such as abortion and the right to die, fall under the right of privacy.

A woman's right to an abortion was recognized in *Roe v. Wade* (1973). Although the right is absolute in the first three months of pregnancy, the states can regulate when, where, and how doctors can perform abortions in the second trimester; states can ban abortions in the third trimester except when the health or life of the mother is at stake. The Court has heard numerous abortion cases since *Roe,* imposing additional limits on the procedure. It upheld the ban Congress imposed on the use of Medicare funds for abortion. States can now prohibit abortions in public hospitals or other medical facilities, again with the health-of-the-mother exception (*Webster v. Reproductive Health Services* [1989]). States can impose other types of restrictions that do not impose an "undue burden" on women seeking an abortion; these include a mandatory 24-hour waiting period and parental consent from a minor seeking an abortion (*Planned Parenthood of Southeastern Pennsylvania v. Casey* [1992]). Attempts to get around *Roe* through a constitutional amendment have gotten nowhere in Congress, but pro-choice groups are concerned that a change in the composition of the Court could lead to a reversal of the decision.

In 2000, the Supreme Court found a state ban on so-called partial-birth abortion (a type of late-term abortion) unconstitutional because no exception was provided for the health of the mother. Congress passed the Partial-Birth Abortion Ban Act in 2003, which the Court upheld four years later in *Gonzales v. Carhart* (2007).

Advances in medical technology—for example, fetal viability tests in the second trimester—have impacted the abortion debate and have raised the constitutional question of the right to die. The fact is that technology can keep a person "alive" on various life support systems indefinitely. To avoid such an end or the agony that can accompany a terminal illness, many people have living wills or sign Do Not Resuscitate (DNR) orders, stating that no extraordinary measures should be taken to prolong their lives. The key case on the right to die is *Cruzan v. Director, Missouri Department of Health* (1990). Although the Court refused to allow the parents of a comatose patient to remove a feeding tube, the Court did indicate that competent individuals could refuse medical treatment though a living will or a similar document such as a DNR order. On the other hand, laws that prohibit physician-assisted suicide are constitutional because there is a difference between refusing treatment and intervening to bring about a person's death (*Vacco v. Quill* [1997]). The Supreme Court supported Oregon's Death with Dignity Act, which allowed physician-assisted suicide, in *Gonzales v. Oregon* (2006).

Civil Liberties after September 11

Serious civil liberties concerns were raised by the federal government's response to the events of September 11, 2001. President George W. Bush initiated a widespread warrantless wiretap program to identify potential terrorist threats, bypassing the procedures established for reliance of the Foreign Intelligence Surveillance Act (FISA) Court. The USA Patriot Act (2001) significantly expanded the government's ability to gather information. E-mail could be monitored by showing it was relevant to an ongoing criminal case, and the use of sneak-and-peek warrants, which allowed searches without a person's knowledge, was expanded. Some of the civil liberties issues were corrected when the legislation was reauthorized in 2006.

The Bush Administration's policy toward terror suspects held at the U.S. naval base in Guantánamo, Cuba, came under scrutiny by the Supreme Court. The president was forced to go back to Congress to get approval for military tribunals to try suspected terrorists (2006), and the Court ruled that the Guantánamo prisoners had the right to challenge their detention in the federal courts (2008).

Practice

1. Which of the following Supreme Court decisions dealt with the issue of prior restraint?

   A. *The New York Times Co. v. Sullivan*
   B. *United States v. Nixon*
   C. *The New York Times Co. v. United States*
   D. *Miller v. California*
   E. *Near v. Minnesota*

2. The recent trend of the courts with respect to the rights of criminal defendants can best be described by which of the following?

   A. Police and prosecutors have greater flexibility in collecting evidence.
   B. Courts are reluctant to grant warrants because of police corruption.
   C. The police are permitted to ignore the Fourth Amendment.
   D. The use of confidential informants by the police is unconstitutional.
   E. Individuals placed under arrest no longer have to be given the Miranda warning.

3. The Religious Freedom Restoration Act was intended to

   A. restore prayer to the public schools
   B. weaken the application of the Lemon test
   C. approve Sunday closing laws in several states
   D. make sure courts use the compelling state interest test
   E. allow public schools to be used by religious groups

4. Which of the following basic liberties was NOT protected by the Constitution before the adoption of the Bill of Rights?

   A. There can be no religious test for holding elected office.
   B. Trial by jury was guaranteed in criminal cases.
   C. The right to vote was recognized for all citizens.
   D. Neither Congress nor the states could enact ex post facto laws.
   E. The writ of habeas corpus was protected.

5. In *Griswold v. Connecticut,* the Court found a constitutionally protected right of privacy in all of the following EXCEPT:

   A. Third Amendment
   B. Fourth Amendment
   C. Fifth Amendment
   D. Ninth Amendment
   E. Tenth Amendment

6. Under the exclusionary rule,

   A. Evidence seized illegally cannot be used in court.
   B. The police must have a search warrant before collecting evidence.
   C. A search is legal only if there is probable cause.
   D. Evidence collected by federal authorities cannot be used in state courts.
   E. The only evidence that cannot be used is from a forced confession.

7. The Supreme Court opposed a state law requiring displaying the Ten Commandments in school classrooms because

   A. It might offend atheists.
   B. It represented an unnecessary state involvement with public education.
   C. The law had no secular purpose.
   D. It violated the Free Exercise Clause.
   E. The cost was a burden on school districts.

8. Which of the following statements about a pornographic magazine is valid?

   A. The state can prevent its publication.
   B. The publishers can be prosecuted for violating state law after publication.
   C. The content of the magazine must contain violent photographs.
   D. Even obscene materials are protected under the First Amendment.
   E. Obscenity is judged by national standards alone.

9. The main concern of the Supreme Court with the death penalty is that

A. The death penalty must be applied equitably without regard to race or income.

B. Methods of execution other than lethal injection are "cruel and unusual punishment."

C. The death penalty itself is a violation of the Eighth Amendment.

D. A defense attorney in a death penalty case must have previous experience in a capital case.

E. States cannot drop the death penalty without the approval of Congress.

10. Recent Supreme Court decisions on abortion have

A. expanded the rights granted women under *Roe v. Wade*

B. allowed the states to impose restrictions on abortion

C. outlawed abortions for minors or the mentally ill

D. required federal funding for abortions for women on Medicare

E. allowed abortion only in cases of rape or incest

11. Which one of the following forms of expression is NOT protected under the First Amendment?

A. a newspaper ad that makes inaccurate statements about a product

B. a statement by a member of Congress against the president

C. defacing an American flag during a political demonstration

D. pornographic photographs published in an adult magazine

E. a speech by a religious leader urging opposition to war

12. All the following statements about the Bill of Rights are accurate EXCEPT:

A. The Bill of Rights was added to the Constitution after ratification.

B. The protections provided by the Bill of Rights are not absolute.

C. The Bill of Rights recognizes that there might be additional rights beyond those mentioned.

D. The first eight amendments are applicable to the states through the Fourteenth Amendment.

E. Most of the Bill of Rights relate to the rights of suspects and criminal defendants.

13. The Miranda warning that police are required to give a person placed under arrest is based on

A. the probable cause requirement for a search warrant

B. freedom-of-speech protection in the First Amendment

C. protection against self-incrimination in the Fifth Amendment

D. the right to be represented by an attorney at trial

E. the right to know the charges brought against you

14. Celebrities and other public figures who bring libel actions against publications

A. have a higher burden of proof than the average citizen

B. usually win the lawsuit without great difficulty

C. have to show only that what was written was false

D. almost never win because judges decide the cases

E. look to settle quickly because they're afraid of the publicity

15. The scope and extent of the civil liberties that Americans enjoy under the Constitution are determined by

A. laws enacted by Congress

B. the president under the authority to see that laws are faithfully executed

C. the Supreme Court through its decisions

D. the Bill of Rights

E. the Department of Justice

Answers

1. **C** *The New York Times Co. v. United States* (1971) is *The Pentagon Papers* case in which the Supreme Court refused to prevent the publication of classified documents relating to the Vietnam War despite the government's claims that public disclosure would damage national security.

2. **A** Several court decisions that more loosely interpret the Fourth Amendment or make exceptions to the exclusionary rule have certainly given government officials greater freedom to collect evidence. These include the good-faith exception, the automobile exception, and, particularly, the concept of "inevitable discovery." All the other answers are incorrect. Indeed, the Supreme Court upheld the Miranda warning in a 2000 decision.

3. **D** The Religious Freedom Restoration Act, which numerous religious groups supported, was Congress's response to the decision in *Employment Division of Oregon v. Smith* (1990), in which the Court allowed a lower standard than "compelling state interest" to limit the right of an individual to the free exercise of his or her religion. A person's religious beliefs can't be used as an excuse for engaging in conduct that the state has the right to prohibit.

4. **C** There is no guarantee of the right to vote in the Constitution as ratified. The Constitution makes voting a state matter, with the states responsible for determining the qualifications for voters. Voting was initially limited to white male property owners. The first time the Constitution discusses a "right to vote" is in the Fourteenth Amendment (1868), which implies universal male suffrage for all citizens 21 years of age or older. African Americans were given the right to vote in the Fifteenth Amendment (1870).

5. **E** In *Griswold v. Connecticut,* the justices found a constitutionally protected right of privacy in the shadows, or "penumbras," of the First, Third, Fourth, Fifth, and Ninth amendments. The Tenth Amendment deals principally with the rights of states (reserved powers), not the rights of individuals.

6. **A** Although recognized in 1914 with respect to the federal government, *Mapp v. Ohio* (1961) extends the exclusionary rule to the states. In recent years, the more conservative Supreme Courts under chief justices Warren Burger and William Rehnquist have weakened the exclusionary rule with numerous exceptions. Warrantless searches are allowed; authorities can search a person under arrest without a warrant and can seize items in "plain sight" at the time of the arrest.

7. **C** The law failed to meet the standards set down in *Lemon v. Kurtzman,* particularly that the Court could find in it no secular purpose. This is clearly an Establishment Clause question dealing with the separation of church and state; it doesn't fall under the Free Exercise Clause. None of the other answers is a constitutional question that the Court would address.

8. **B** If the content of the magazine was determined to be obscene, the publishers would face prosecution after the fact. The magazine's publication can't be prevented under prior restraint. The Court has clearly defined *obscenity* only in terms of sexual content, not violence per se, and has recognized that community standards (as opposed to national standards) apply. In *Roth v. United States* (1957), the Court affirmed that the First Amendment doesn't protect obscene materials.

9. **A** This was the Court's reasoning in striking down Georgia's death penalty statute in *Furman v. Georgia* (1972); it halted executions in 39 states until their laws were rewritten to conform to the decision. The death penalty is a matter of criminal procedure that is solely within the power of the states to determine; there is a federal death penalty statute. The Court also upheld the death penalty per se in *Gregg v. Georgia* (1976).

10. **B** Recent Supreme Court decisions have imposed restrictions on the right to an abortion. Upholding limits on both federal and state funding for abortions, fetal survivability tests, parental permission of minors, a 24-hour waiting period, and the ban on late-term abortions (so-called partial-birth abortions) are all examples of the ways in which the Court has made it more difficult for a woman to get an abortion.

11. **A** Newspaper advertising is an example of commercial speech, and the First Amendment doesn't protect false or misleading ads. The First Amendment, does, however protect all the other examples. *Remember:* Pornographic photographs are not necessarily obscene, and the First Amendment protects them as long

as they are not obscene. Defacing the flag in the context given is clearly symbolic speech in the sense of *Texas v. Johnson* (1989).

12. **D** Not all the first eight amendments have been "incorporated" by the Supreme Court. The right to bear arms (Second Amendment), the ban on the quartering of troops in times of peace (Third Amendment), indictment by a grand jury, trial by jury in civil cases, and excessive bail and fine do not apply to the states.

13. **C** The Miranda warning includes the right to say nothing to the police after the arrest; it is clearly a protection against self-incrimination found in the Fifth Amendment. It also includes the right to have an attorney present during questioning; because it isn't clear that a suspect will even go to trial at the time of arrest, the purpose of having the attorney present is to make sure that the person under arrest doesn't say or do anything that may be used against him or her.

14. **A** People in the public eye have a higher burden to prove. It isn't enough for them to demonstrate that the information in the story is false; they must prove that the reporter and/or editors knew it was false and published it anyway, with malice and complete disregard for the truth. Libel cases are usually heard by a jury, and, because of the higher burden, these suits are not easy to win.

15. **C** It should be clear from the number of Supreme Court decisions cited in this chapter that the Court determines what the civil liberties granted through the Bill of Rights actually mean. In areas as different as search and seizure and the right to an abortion, the position of the Court changes with the judicial philosophy and the perspective of the justices.

Civil Rights

Civil rights are policies that protect individuals against discrimination in such areas as voting, accessibility to housing, employment and job opportunities, to name a few. Throughout most of our history, civil rights have focused on the status of African Americans. Women began to demand equal treatment in the mid-19th century, and that goal remains elusive to a degree. More recently, victims of discrimination based on their age, physical or mental disability, and sexual preference have begun to speak up.

From Slavery to Jim Crow

Although the Confederation Congress prohibited slavery in the Northwest Territory (Northwest Ordinance [1787]), the framers somewhat reluctantly recognized the institution in the Constitution. Slaves were counted as three-fifths a person for taxation and representation purposes. The international slave trade was permitted at least until 1808, and slaves who ran away to a free state had to be returned. Although slavery gradually ended in the North (New York became the last northern state to formally emancipate all its slaves in 1827), free blacks were routinely denied the right to vote in the North and several states barred them from settling. Meanwhile, in the southern states, slavery became entrenched as the cotton kingdom grew. In the decades before the Civil War, the expansion of slavery into the lands in the West divided the country.

Abolitionists demanded the immediate emancipation of the slaves. The publication of *Uncle Tom's Cabin* (1852), a best-selling attack on the injustices of slavery, and the Supreme Court's decision in *Dred Scott v. Sanford* (1857), which denied citizenship to African Americans, heightened tensions on both sides of the issue. The election of Abraham Lincoln in 1860 tipped the scales, and the Civil War began in the spring of 1861.

The first steps toward recognizing the civil rights of African Americans came during the immediate aftermath of the Civil War. Lincoln's Emancipation Proclamation (January 1, 1863) granted freedom to slaves still under the Confederacy, but it did not apply to the border states that remained in the Union. Slavery in the United States did not end completely until the adoption of the Thirteenth Amendment in 1865. The Fourteenth Amendment (1868) granted African Americans citizenship; it strongly suggested that black men 21 years of age or older had the right to vote, and it prohibited the states from denying individuals "equal protection under the law." Under the Fifteenth Amendment (1870), Americans could not be denied the right to vote.

Congress also took action. The Civil Rights Act of 1875 sought to protect blacks against discrimination in public accommodations such as hotels and public transportation. Under the law, for example, an African American could not be denied service in a restaurant solely on the basis of his or her race, color, or previous condition of servitude. But the legislation was struck down by the Supreme Court in *The Civil Rights Cases* (1883), which found that the Equal Protection Clause applied only to actions by the state and was not meant to regulate private conduct. If state laws denied blacks access, it might be another matter.

Following the end of Reconstruction, the southern states enacted laws that were intended to severely limit the newly won rights of African Americans. The Jim Crow laws not only established a rigidly segregated society but took away the vote of most blacks through such devices as the poll tax, the literacy test, and the grandfather clause. The literacy test required proof of an ability to read and/or write before a person would be allowed to vote. The grandfather clause was meant to exclude African Americans but still allow poor, illiterate whites to vote, because they all presumably had relatives who were eligible to vote in the past.

Segregation was challenged first. A test case was brought over the constitutionality of a Louisiana statute that required railroads to have separate cars for blacks and whites. In *Plessy v. Ferguson* (1896), the Court argued that the fact that the races were separated did not mean one race was inferior to the other. It established the "separate but equal" doctrine, which effectively approved **de jure segregation** (segregation based on law).

In the first half of the 20th century, civil rights for African Americans slowly advanced through the actions of the Supreme Court and the executive branch. The grandfather clause was struck down in *Guinn v. United States* (1915). The so-called **white primary**, which barred black voters from participating in a primary election, was declared unconstitutional in *Smith v. Allwright* (1944). The Democratic Party was so strong in the South in the late 19th and early 20th centuries that whoever won the Democratic nomination through the primary was guaranteed of winning the general election; denying African Americans to vote in the primary was seen as critical. In *Sweatt v. Painter* (1950), the Court indicated that the "separate but equal" doctrine was not valid in law schools and other professional schools. Congress took no action on discrimination during this time, but President Franklin Roosevelt prohibited employment discrimination based on race by defense contractors during World War II, and President Truman ordered the desegregation of the armed forces by executive order in 1948.

The Struggle for Equality

After 1950, the courts and Congress took the lead in advancing equality against the backdrop of the civil rights movement. The Supreme Court struck down the concept of "separate but equal" public schools in 1954 in *Brown v. Board of Education of Topeka, Kansas.* In the following year, the Court directed local school districts to develop desegregation plans, which federal district courts needed to review *(Griffin v. County School Board of Prince Edward County,* known as *Brown II).* Although the process was expected to move ahead "with all deliberate speed," integration proceeded slowly until the early 1970s. The Court recognized in *Swann v. Charlotte-Mecklenburg County Board of Education* (1971) that, in school districts where there was a history of segregation, busing students within the respective school district was a legitimate tool to achieve a degree of racial balance. The case also raised the issue of **de facto segregation** (segregation based on living patterns). It was certainly true in many states in the North that blacks and whites attended separate schools, not because the law required it, but because of where they lived. Court-ordered busing in many northern cities in the 1970s was extremely controversial.

Just as the Court was moving to dismantle segregation in public schools, African Americans directly challenged discrimination in other areas. The Montgomery, Alabama, bus boycott and the sit-in demonstrations at lunch counters across the South showed the power of nonviolent protest as well as the economic clout of the black community. The civil rights demonstrations in Birmingham, Alabama, and the police violence they provoked— as well as the August 1963 March on Washington for jobs and freedom—brought blacks' struggle for equality to the nation's attention. The civil rights movement did not involve just African Americans, however; whites from around the country participated as well. It was in the context of these developments that Congress took action.

President Kennedy submitted a comprehensive civil rights bill to Congress in 1963, but he made little headway with it. Three factors ultimately led to the passage of the Civil Rights Act of 1964: growing public support for equal treatment for African Americans, Kennedy's assassination, and the political skill of his successor, Lyndon Johnson. The wide-ranging new law

- Prohibited discrimination in hotels, restaurants, and similar places of public accommodation, based on the power to regulate interstate commerce
- Prohibited discrimination in employment based on race, color, religion, natural origins, and sex
- Authorized the Department of Justice to take legal action to desegregate public schools
- Withheld federal funds from state and local programs that discriminated on the basis of race

While far reaching in its scope, the law was just a first step. Congress passed the landmark Voting Rights Act the following year, which effectively ended the use of literacy tests and similar means to deny African Americans access to the polls. It also required the federal government to approve any changes in voter qualifications and/or procedures, and promoted voter registration in areas with historically low turnout. The Civil Rights Act of 1968 prohibited discrimination in housing based on race, religion, ethnicity, or sex.

The Twenty-fourth Amendment (1964) outlawed the poll tax in state and federal elections. The combined result was a significant increase in African-American participation in politics in the South by the 1970s and in the number of black elected officials. Other racial/ethnic minorities—Mexican Americans, Native Americans, Asian Americans—also benefited from the gains the civil rights movement made in both Congress and the courts. These groups pushed their own political agendas through such organizations as the Mexican American Legal Defense and Education Fund (MALDEF); the Organization of Chinese Americans (OCA), which now embraces all Asian-Pacific Americans; and the American Indian Movement (AIM).

The 1975 amendments to the Voting Rights Act required that election materials be made available in minority languages (such as Spanish and Chinese), where the number of minority voters justified such an accommodation. The Civil Liberties Act of 1988 provided restitution to Japanese Americans and those of Japanese ancestry interned in the United States during World War II.

Women's Rights

The women's movement began in July 1848 when a group of reform-minded men and women drafted the Seneca Falls Declaration of Rights and Sentiments. Modeled after the Declaration of Independence, it was, in many ways, a very contemporary document. Besides demanding women's right to vote, the declaration called for equal access to employment and education, and a greater role for women in organized religion. The first demand was realized comparatively early.

Fourteen states granted women full suffrage and 12 others allowed them to vote for presidential electors before the Nineteenth Amendment was ratified in 1920. The role women played during World War I, serving in the military for the first time and taking nontraditional roles in factories, convinced many people that they deserved the vote. President Wilson supported the Nineteenth Amendment. Although an Equal Rights Amendment (ERA) was introduced in 1923, no considerable progress was made on gender equality issues until the 1960s. The National Organization for Women (NOW) was founded in 1966, and Congress formally proposed a new ERA in 1972. The amendment faced well-organized opposition and was not approved by three-quarters of the state legislatures, even though the deadline for ratification was extended. There have been no serious attempts in recent years to revive the ERA; court decisions and legislation have filled the gap to a degree.

The battle for women's rights was fought out in the courts, at first with little success. Judges either maintained that the Equal Protection Clause of the Fourteenth Amendment applied only to African Americans or found discrimination against women—for example, not allowing women to practice law—"reasonable." This is known as the minimum rationality test, which means that discrimination against women was constitutional if there was some "rational" basis for it. That rational basis was often found in stereotypes about women's roles, such as "her place was in the home." Things began to change in the 1970s. In *Reed v. Reed* (1971), the Supreme Court struck down a state law that gave preference to men over women as administrators of an estate, arguing that the distinction was arbitrary. A key change came in 1976, when the Court abandoned the rationality test in favor of **heightened scrutiny** (*Craig v. Boren* [1976]), where classifying individuals based on gender must be related to an important government objective. Under the new standard, the Court found that both men and women were entitled to alimony but that women may be excluded from the draft.

The 1964 Civil Rights Act prohibited gender-based discrimination in employment. The courts have also recognized that sexual harassment in the workplace is a form of discrimination. Under Title IX of the Education Amendments of 1972, educational programs receiving federal funds cannot discriminate on account of gender. The Title IX legislation is responsible for bringing a degree of equality to men's and women's sports at the high school and collegiate levels. Businesses cannot refuse to hire or promote pregnant women, and a company's sick leave and health benefits package must cover pregnancy and childbirth (Pregnancy Discrimination Act of 1978). The Civil Rights and Women's Equity in Employment Act (1991), which effectively overturned several Supreme Court decisions in the area of employment discrimination, allows significant damage awards in instances of intentional discrimination and shifts the burden of proof from the employee to the employer in certain types of cases.

In 1963, Congress passed the Equal Pay Act, which required employers to pay men and women the same compensation for the same work. Women's groups recognized, however, that the wages for traditional women's jobs (secretary, for example) remained significantly lower than jobs held by men that required comparable skill. This discrepancy led to the concept of **comparable worth** or pay equity—in other words, compensation based on the worth of the job not the job title or classification. Determining comparable worth is a complicated process; although it has been adopted by several states and municipalities, it has found little support in Congress or the federal courts. In 2009, the Lily Ledbetter Fair Play Restoration Act gave victims of pay discrimination greater opportunity to file a claim.

Age, Disability, and Sexual Orientation

Racial and ethnic minorities and women are not the only groups that have successfully demanded recognition of their rights. Congress and the courts have addressed discrimination based on age, physical or mental disability, and sexual orientation.

The "graying of America" refers to the fact that the population of the United States is getting older. The post–World War II baby boom generation is reaching retirement age. Because older Americans vote in large numbers and have effective lobbying organizations, it isn't surprising that issues such as Social Security, Medicare, and age discrimination are important. The Age Discrimination in Employment Act (1967) protects all workers over the age of 40 and prohibits a company from denying benefits to older employees. Discrimination on account of age in any program receiving federal funds was prohibited in 1975. A mandatory retirement age, unless justified by the nature of the work, no longer exists for most jobs. In a recent decision, the Supreme Court held that employers must show that factors other than age are involved when a large number of older workers are laid off.

At first, the most pressing issue for disabled Americans was access to public places, addressed through the Rehabilitation Act of 1973. Congress passed more extensive legislation in 1990. The Americans with Disabilities Act (ADA) bans discrimination in employment and promotion, as long as a disabled person can perform a particular job with "reasonable accommodations." Public transportation and public accommodations must be made or designed so that they're accessible, and devices for the hearing and/or speech impaired must be made available. The Supreme Court, however, has narrowed the scope of the ADA through a series of recent rulings. In *Toyota Motor Manufacturing, Kentucky, Inc. v. Williams* (2002), the Court held that the law only covers impairments that affect a person's daily life, not whether a worker can perform a particular job. Congress specifically rejected this ruling and other Court decisions that narrow the number of people who can make effective claims under the ADA, through the ADA Amendments Act of 2008; the new legislation makes it clear that Congress's intent was to define *disability* in such a way as to give broad coverage to the disabled.

Civil rights for gays and lesbians have advanced over the last quarter-century. States and municipalities have passed laws prohibiting discrimination based on sexual orientation. The Supreme Court held in *Bowers v. Hardwick* (1986) that a constitutionally protected right of privacy did not extend to consensual homosexual activity, but it reversed that decision in *Lawrence v. Texas* (2003), striking down state sodomy laws. Although under review by the Obama Administration, the "Don't Ask, Don't Tell" policy continues to prevent gays from serving openly in the military.

A highly controversial issue is the right of same-sex couples to marry. In 2000, Vermont recognized civil unions, which give gay and lesbian couples nearly the same rights and benefits as heterosexual couples; several other states followed suit. Domestic partnerships, which may be available to both same-sex and opposite-sex couples, usually offer fewer rights than civil unions, and their scope is set by state law or municipal ordinance. A number of states, beginning with Massachusetts in 2004, have recently recognized same-sex marriages either by legislative or court action. Other states have enacted laws or amendments to the state constitution defining marriage as a union between one man and one woman.

Under the **Full Faith and Credit Clause** of the Constitution (Article IV, Section 1), marriages recognized in one state are valid in all states. In response to the issue of gay marriage, Congress passed the Defense of Marriage Act in 1996. The legislation allows states to ignore same-sex marriages legal in other states, and defines marriage in federal law as a legal union between one man and one woman.

Affirmative Action

One of the most controversial civil rights issues is **affirmative action**. This policy, which the Johnson Administration introduced in the mid-1960s, refers to the broad range of programs intended to correct the past effects of discrimination. Over the years, those programs have included preferential recruitment and treatment, numerical quotas, numerical goals, and set-asides in such areas as employment, contracting, and university and professional school admissions. There is no doubt that affirmative action brought sweeping changes to the workplace and public institutions, but it also generated numerous lawsuits.

The Supreme Court's landmark decision on affirmative action was *Regents of the University of California v. Bakke* (1978), which involved **reverse discrimination**. A white applicant who was twice denied admission to the medical school at the University of California, Davis, claimed that his rights were violated because 16 slots in the entering class were reserved for minority students. The Court agreed and ordered Bakke admitted. It also found the rigid quota unconstitutional, but it recognized that race could be taken into account as a factor in admissions, because a diverse student body is a legitimate educational goal. The ruling in *Bakke* did not settle the matter at all; indeed, the Court has heard numerous affirmative action cases since the 1978 decision. In *Grutter v. Bollinger* (2003), the Court upheld the use of race in admissions decisions at the University of Michigan Law School, but it required changes in the undergraduate admissions program at the school that awarded points to minority applicants in a related case, *Gratz v. Bollinger* (2003).

Practice

1. Under *Regents of the University of California v. Bakke,* colleges can consider race a factor in admissions because

    A.   Reverse discrimination is constitutional.
    B.   Such consideration is a remedy for contemporary discrimination.
    C.   A diverse student body is a legitimate educational goal.
    D.   Racial minorities are economically disadvantaged.
    E.   Numerical quotas are acceptable in certain circumstances.

2. The abolition of the poll tax in federal elections was accomplished through the

    A.   Voting Rights Act of 1965
    B.   1964 executive order issued by President Johnson
    C.   Supreme Court decision in *Smith v. Allwright*
    D.   Civil Rights Act of 1964
    E.   Twenty-fourth Amendment

3. Until the 1970s, claims of gender discrimination were routinely rejected by the Supreme Court because

    A.   Women were not citizens within the meaning of the Constitution.
    B.   The Court had no female members.
    C.   Limitations on women's rights were usually considered "reasonable."
    D.   The women's movement was not well organized.
    E.   The justices did not believe that the Fourteenth Amendment applied to women.

4. The status of gays and lesbians is best described by which of the following statements?

    A.   Same-sex marriages are widely recognized throughout the United States.
    B.   The Supreme Court has struck down laws criminalizing homosexual behavior.
    C.   Homosexuals are screened out of the military during the enlistment process.
    D.   Gays and lesbians have not yet organized to push their civil rights claims.
    E.   Neither Congress nor the courts is willing to extend civil rights protections on the basis of sexual orientation.

5. In the first half of the 20th century, which institution was most responsible for advancing the civil rights of African Americans?

    A.   Congress
    B.   state legislatures
    C.   the presidency
    D.   the Supreme Court
    E.   state courts

6. All the following statements about the civil rights movement in the South between 1955 and 1965 are true EXCEPT:

    A.   Boycotts and sit-ins were effective techniques for achieving the movement's goals.
    B.   The federal government took a hands-off policy throughout the period.
    C.   Blacks and whites marched and demonstrated together.
    D.   Desegregation and voter registration were key issues.
    E.   Violence against civil rights demonstrators increased public support for the movement.

7. The ability of the federal government to prohibit discrimination in private businesses such as motels and restaurants derives from

    A.   the Equal Protection Clause of the Fifth Amendment
    B.   its implied powers under the Elastic Clause
    C.   the Privileges and Immunities Clause
    D.   the Supremacy Clause
    E.   its power to regulate interstate commerce

8. A controversial civil rights issue during the 1970s was

    A.   the integration of public universities in the South
    B.   the right of homosexuals to serve in the military
    C.   granting resident aliens the right to vote
    D.   de facto segregation in the North
    E.   the constitutionality of single-sex colleges

9. Under the heightened scrutiny test, distinctions based on gender

   A. are treated the same as those based on race
   B. are always resolved to the benefit of women
   C. come up only in cases involving employment discrimination
   D. are acceptable if they serve an important government objective
   E. are not permitted under federal law

10. The most important consequence of the Voting Rights Act of 1965 was

   A. extending the right to vote to Native Americans
   B. a shift in African-American voting patterns to the Democratic Party
   C. an increase in African-American voter registration in the South
   D. an increasing liberal bent in Southern politics
   E. the use of race in legislative redistricting

11. In *Dred Scott v. Sanford* (1857), the Supreme Court held that African Americans were not citizens of the United States. The decision was effectively overturned by the

   A. Thirteenth Amendment
   B. Fourteenth Amendment
   C. Fifteenth Amendment
   D. Sixteenth Amendment
   E. Seventeenth Amendment

12. Which one of the following statements about women's suffrage is valid?

   A. Women were not allowed to vote in the United States until 1920.
   B. The key factor in the ratification of the Nineteenth Amendment was the service of women during World War I.
   C. Granting women the right to vote dramatically changed U.S. politics in the 1920s.
   D. The Equal Rights Amendment was not proposed until the 1970s.
   E. Women were united in seeking other rights once they won the right to vote.

13. Which of the following civil rights policies were enacted through executive order?

   I. desegregation of the military
   II. creation of the Equal Employment Opportunity Commission
   III. affirmative action
   IV. eliminating the grandfather clause

   A. I and III only
   B. I and II only
   C. II, III, and IV only
   D. I only
   E. I, II, III, and IV

14. The white primary was an effective way of disenfranchising African Americans because

   A. Only those who voted in the primary could vote in the general election.
   B. Voters in the primary did not pay the poll tax.
   C. In the Democratic South, whoever won the primary was guaranteed to win the general election.
   D. Federal officials did not supervise primaries.
   E. Voter turnout was usually low in a primary.

15. Which of the following was NOT a provision of the Civil Rights Act of 1964?

   A. Discrimination in the sale and rental of housing was prohibited.
   B. Gender discrimination in employment was banned.
   C. Discrimination in public accommodations was prohibited.
   D. Federal funds were to be cut off for programs that discriminate.
   E. The Department of Justice was given more authority to end school desegregation.

Answers

1. **C** In *Regents of the University of California v. Bakke,* the Court rejected the rigid quota in place at the University of California, Davis, Medical School that reserved 16 places in the incoming class for minority applicants. However, the Court did recognize the validity of taking race into account in admissions to foster a diverse student population. Several cases on affirmative action programs that are based on this diversity argument are coming to the Court.

2. **E** The Twenty-fourth Amendment (1964) outlawed the poll tax or any tax as a requirement for voting in a primary or general election for the president or a member of Congress. The Court declared poll taxes in state elections unconstitutional in *Harper v. Virginia Board of Elections* (1966).

3. **C** Although there was some thought by the Supreme Court in the late 19th century that the Fourteenth Amendment only applied to African Americans, this was certainly not the case throughout the entire period. The Court was consistent, however, in applying a "reasonableness" test in cases involving women's rights. The decision in *Reed v. Reed* (1971) was based on this standard—it was not "reasonable" to give preference to men over women as the executors of an estate.

4. **B** In *Lawrence v. Texas* (2003), the Supreme Court ruled that state laws against sodomy were unconstitutional. Some states allow same-sex marriage, but it is certainly not "widely recognized" and a number of states specifically define marriage as a union between one man and one woman. Both Congress and the courts, as well as state and local governments, treat sexual orientation as a civil rights issue.

5. **D** With Congress unsympathetic and the executive branch limited to occasional executive orders, the strategy of the NAACP's Legal Defense and Education Fund was to challenge the Jim Crow laws through the federal courts. A string of Supreme Court decisions—from *Guinn v. United States* (1915) to *Brown v. Board of Education* (1954)—validated this approach.

6. **B** The federal government played a significant role in the civil rights struggles of the period. President Eisenhower federalized the Arkansas National Guard and sent U.S. Army troops to Little Rock in 1957 to guarantee that his desegregation order was carried out. President Kennedy sent federal troops to ensure that James Meredith could enroll at the University of Mississippi in 1962; he also sent officials of the Department of Justice to Birmingham, Alabama, to work out a compromise between city officials and black civil rights leaders in the following year. With the passage of the Civil Rights Act of 1964 and the Voting Rights Act of 1965, the federal government assumed a major role in advancing civil rights.

7. **E** The Commerce Clause was the key element ending discrimination in public accommodations, which the Supreme Court recognized. In *Heart of Atlanta Motel v. United States* (1964), the Court found that the motel was subject to congressional regulation because it served interstate travelers. In the case of a local restaurant (*Katzenbach v. McClung* [1964]), the Court held that it obtained its supplies through interstate commerce.

8. **D** The integration of public schools in the North was a key political issue of the 1970s. The issue was segregation based on housing patterns, rather than laws mandating separate schools. Although busing students out of neighborhood schools was extremely controversial, other solutions to racial imbalance—such as free choice, in which school students could attend magnet schools—were gradually accepted.

9. **D** Distinctions based on gender are less suspect than those based on race. "Heightened scrutiny" is a middle ground or intermediate test between "strict scrutiny" (used for classifications based on race) and "reasonableness"; it is used by the courts today on issues relating to discrimination based on age and disability.

10. **C** The Voting Rights Act of 1965 targeted practices such as the literacy test, which prevented African Americans from exercising their right to vote and recognized that there was a significant disparity between white and black voter registration in the South. Increased African-American voter registration was a critical factor because it translated into greater black political strength and the election of black officials. Native Americans were granted the right to vote by Congress in 1924, and African Americans had already thrown their lot to the Democratic Party. In one sense, Southern politics became more conservative; at least the Republican Party gained support from the 1960s on.

11. **B** The Fourteenth Amendment granted citizenship to African Americans by defining a citizen as anyone born in the United States. You should know that the Thirteenth, Fourteenth, and Fifteenth amendments are the so-called "Civil War Amendments" and that they deal with the rights of African Americans. The Thirteenth Amendment ended slavery and said nothing about citizenship, and the Fifteenth Amendment granted blacks the right to vote.

12. **B** Although there was growing political pressure on the federal government from women's groups, the role of women during World War I—serving in the military for the first time and taking jobs in factories in record numbers—convinced President Wilson to support women's suffrage. You should know that many states had already granted women the right to vote before the Nineteenth Amendment, and that the vote did not, in fact, alter U.S. politics immediately. The initial Equal Rights Amendment was introduced in 1923.

13. **A** President Truman issued an executive order in 1948 to desegregate the armed forces, and President Johnson initiated federal affirmative action programs in 1965 with an executive order that directed federal contractors to give minority applicants a slight edge over non-minority applicants bidding for jobs.

14. **C** The South, particularly in state and local elections, was solidly Democratic from the Reconstruction into the 1960s. Prohibiting African Americans from participating in the Democratic primary effectively gave them no voice in selecting the governor, members of the state legislature, and a host of municipal officials. Although the Supreme Court acted against the white primary on several occasions, it was not until 1944 in *Smith v. Allwright* that the Court declared the practice a violation of the Fifteenth Amendment.

15. **A** The Civil Rights Act of 1964 did not ban discrimination in housing; however, the Civil Rights Act of 1968 did, in the hope that this would lead to the creation of integrated neighborhoods. Integration did not happen in the short run, because most African Americans couldn't afford to move into predominantly white neighborhoods at the time the law went into effect.

Public Policy

Public policy refers to the actions taken by governments, principally the legislative and executive branches, from federal to local governments, to deal with a broad range of issues. The discussion here focuses on public policy from a federal perspective. Areas of public policy include regulating business and managing the economy, protecting the American people at home and abroad, and providing assistance—whether to states and local communities for highway construction or to individuals who can't help themselves. Public policy doesn't just happen; it's the end result of a process that begins with identifying the issues that the government has to tackle and ends with an evaluation of the policy and its possible termination.

The Process of Making Public Policy

Identifying the problems the government has to deal with is known as **agenda setting**. There are various ways in which an issue gets the attention of the public and politicians alike. The bombing of the World Trade Center in 1993 and the 1995 attack on the Oklahoma City Federal Building heightened awareness of terrorism in the United States, but no one seriously thought of the need for "homeland security" until the events of September 11, 2001. On a much less dramatic level, the media plays a role in establishing the political agenda. Rachel Carson's 1962 bestseller *Silent Spring* about the dangers of the pesticide DDT led to the environmental movement. In the same way, Ralph Nader's *Unsafe at Any Speed* (1965) raised consumer product safety concerns that Congress had to address. Earlier, Jacob Riis's *How the Other Half Lives* (1890) pushed the need for housing reform by pointing out the overcrowded living conditions of the poor, immigrant neighborhoods of New York. *The Other America* (1962) by Michael Harrington pointed out that 20 percent of Americans lived in poverty, despite the general affluence of the country; the book influenced President Lyndon Johnson's Great Society's War on Poverty. Healthcare was a major public policy issue for the Clinton Administration and was one of the first major domestic issues tackled by President Barack Obama.

Once a problem is identified, the next step is to come up with an approach to solve it. This step is known as **policy formulation**. Congress, the president, interest groups, and their lobbyists may all have ideas on the best way to address the issue. Their ideas may be contradictory, or they may demand cooperation to develop an effective policy.

In the 1980s, Mothers Against Drunk Driving (MADD) recognized that the disparity in drinking ages from state to state contributed to highway fatalities. Instead of trying to get individual states to raise their drinking age, MADD turned to Congress for a national solution. The response was a bill that provided for a cutoff of a portion of federal highway funds to states that did not set the minimum drinking age at 21 years old. Policy formulation has a direct consequence—a bill is introduced as in this case, a federal agency begins to draft new regulations, and the president issues an executive order. After the bill passes and the president signs it, the *Federal Register* publishes the new regulations, and the executive order goes into effect—the policy is adopted.

Administrative agencies typically implement public policies. Congress may pass amendments to the Clean Air Act, but the Environmental Protection Agency (EPA) develops the specific standards that conform to the legislation and assumes responsibility for the inspection/monitoring of the new standards. The 2008 amendments to the Americans with Disabilities Act required the Equal Employment Opportunity Commission to revise its rules. Litigation may delay the implementation phase of policymaking. The requirement that states raise their minimum drinking age to 21 did not go into effect until the Supreme Court, in *South Carolina v. Dole* (1987), ruled that the statute did not violate states' rights. You should keep in mind here that the Court has no power to enforce its decisions. Although stating the desegregation should move ahead "with all deliberate speed" in *Griffin v. County School Board of Prince Edward County* (1955), also known as *Brown II,* the fact is that the integration proceeded slowly. Actual implementation of the ruling required the cooperation of the states, local school boards, and parents, all of whom were reluctant to comply with the order.

Policy evaluation examines how well a policy is working. Through **cost-benefit analysis**, officials hope to determine if the amount spent on a program brings positive returns. For example, is the expense imposed on electric utilities for anti-pollution devices worth the improvement in air quality that results? Often, it's difficult to evaluate policies because of ideological or political factors. Looking at the same data, proponents and opponents of the death penalty may well come to completely different conclusions on the effectiveness of capital punishment. A program that is politically popular may survive even if no one can demonstrate that it's working as expected.

Policies are terminated because original policy goals were achieved, they are obsolete, clearly are not effective, or lose the support of the politicians, interest groups, and bureaucrats that put them on the agenda in the first place. Mandatory busing was an important tool for challenging de facto segregation in the public schools outside the South in the 1970s. Opposition to this approach was significant, and white flight from the public schools became an issue in many communities. In time, the policy was abandoned in favor of voluntary programs such as magnet schools and open districts that allowed students to attend almost any school. The need to regulate railroad rates did not have the constituency in the 1980s, when *deregulation* was the policy watchword of the Reagan Administration, as it had been when the Interstate Commerce Commission (ICC) was established. By the 1990s, the ICC had few powers left and those were easily transferred to other agencies. The ICC was formally terminated at the end of 1995.

The Politics of Policymaking

The very structure of our political system—checks and balances and federalism—guarantees that formulating a coherent policy is difficult at best and often contentious. So many individuals and groups are usually involved in the policymaking process that it isn't surprising that politics plays a key role. For example, when the AIDS crisis hit in the early 1980s, the federal government was slow to respond, in part because the Reagan Administration was sensitive to its conservative supporters' views on homosexuality. There are numerous other examples. From a national perspective, programs that promote clean air and water or provide greater access for the disabled seem like sound public policy. States and municipalities that have the financial responsibility for implementing them, however, can be less than supportive given their budget limits. The Unfunded Mandates Reform Act (1995) required Congress to take this issue into account. The act's purpose was to slow down or halt altogether the creation of new unfunded mandates by having the Congressional Budget Office review the economic impact of legislation on state and local governments; federal agencies were required to do the same with new regulations. The effectiveness of the law is a matter of debate.

There is also the question of internal politics, as noted in "The Bureaucracy," earlier in this book. An array of federal agencies frequently has responsibility for implementing and evaluating policy, but each may be jealous of its own turf and unwilling to fully cooperate with others. The task of the Department of Homeland Security in developing a coherent policy to protect the United States against a terrorist attack is particularly daunting because the activities of numerous federal, state, and local agencies have to be coordinated.

In the wake of September 11, 2001, for example, there was broad bipartisan support for President George W. Bush's foreign policy, particularly in respect to the War on Terror. The fact that the president enjoyed record-high approval ratings at that time was certainly a factor. While that support carried over to domestic policy after September 11, working out differences between the White House and Congress on a broad range of issues is more difficult in a government that is divided in several ways—Democrats in control of the Senate and Republicans in control of the House with a Republican president. Another example is how the Bush Administration was criticized for both the way it developed its energy policy and the substance of that policy. It appears that energy companies were consulted for their input, but environmental groups were largely left out of the process. While there is general agreement that the United States must become less dependent on foreign sources of oil, particularly in light of the situation in the Middle East, the administration's proposals to drill for oil in wilderness areas of Alaska brought a strong attack from Democrats and the environmental lobby.

Congress is made up of representatives and senators, each of whom has his or her own agenda. The fact that there may be agreement in times of large budget deficits to cut spending (the question is where to make the cuts) does not prevent them from proposing legislation or amendments to bills that benefit their own districts or states.

Members of Congress also want to push for their pet projects in periods of budget surpluses when questions surface about whether, where, and how much to spend. In both cases, very narrow concerns may undermine a broader policy initiative.

Elected officials are not the only ones involved in the politics of policymaking. The common denominator in both **iron triangles** and **issue networks** are interest groups and their lobbyists, who together can mount a very effective campaign for or against a particular policy direction. Organized labor's opposition to the North American Free Trade Agreement (NAFTA), although ultimately unsuccessful, is an illustration. The agreement created a free trade zone between the United States, Canada, and Mexico. Today, there are a myriad of groups and think tanks that produce volumes of data concerning existing public policies or new ideas for the policy agenda.

The Development of Regulatory Policy

Regulatory policy refers to the supervision of the actions of individuals, businesses, and government institutions. Although state and local governments have their own regulatory responsibility, this section of this chapter focuses on the federal regulatory effort. Historically, regulatory policy came as a response to abuses. The Interstate Commerce Commission was created in 1887 (and is now defunct) because of the discriminatory rates and other unfair practices of the railroads, and—over time—the scope of its activities extended to all common carriers. The national system of meat inspection was prompted by an exposé of the unsanitary conditions in the meatpacking industry by the writer Upton Sinclair (*The Jungle* [1906]). Other factors have played a role in making policy regulations as well. Because radio stations can't broadcast on the same frequency (the signals will cancel each other out), the Federal Radio Commission (predecessor to the Federal Communications Commission) was established in 1927 to award licenses and frequencies to radio stations. The high point of regulation came in the 1960s and early 1970s as new issues such as civil rights, consumer rights, and the environment became important items on the political agenda. With respect to the environment, this period saw Congress pass the National Environmental Policy Act (1969) and the Endangered Species Act (1973), as well as create the Environmental Protection Agency (1970). Under the National Environmental Policy Act (NEPA), environmental impact statements must be filed with the EPA before federal funds can be expended on a project and federal agencies must examine the effect their activities have on the environment.

Regulatory agencies often have more than one function and carry out regulatory policy in a variety of ways. One of the goals of regulation is to set the cost for service or a commodity. The Federal Energy Regulatory Commission (FERC), for example, oversees wholesale prices of electricity and the sale of natural gas; it also is responsible for the licensing of the nation's hydroelectric plants. Another regulatory objective is establishing standards. The Occupational Safety and Health Administration (OSHA) develops limits for workplace exposure to such toxins as asbestos and lead. Over 15,000 household products come under the jurisdiction of the Consumer Product Safety Commission (CPSC), which has standards for age-appropriate toys and the flammability of children's clothing. The EPA imposes limits on pollutants allowed in the air but leaves monitoring and enforcement to the individual states.

In the mid to late 1970s, the attitude toward regulation began to change. For economic as well as political reasons, the value of regulation in some areas came into question. In a period of high inflation, for example, rules that business had to adhere to often added to costs; moreover, there were questions as to whether regulation represented an unwanted and unwarranted government intrusion, and if the benefits that regulation often promised were worth that intrusion. For example, up until 1978, the Civil Aeronautics Board regulated airfares and airline routes. That changed with enactment of the Airline Deregulation Act, which was expected to lower fares and increase competition by bringing new airlines into the system. Studies done in the 1990s indicated that fares dropped overall with some regional variations. Many airlines, however, were forced out of business, small communities lost air service altogether, and there is less competition today than in 1978. The deregulation of other industries has not gone smoothly either. In California, deregulation of the investor-owned electrical utility industry led to skyrocketing prices for consumers, rolling blackouts, and the near financial collapse of the state's two major providers of electrical service. Many blame the deep recession the country entered in late 2007, as well as the bursting of the housing bubble and the worldwide financial crisis in 2008, on lax regulation.

Social Policy

Social policy addresses the needs of many Americans, including the poor, elderly, disabled, and children in poverty. While the Constitution recognizes a federal role "to promote the general welfare," throughout most of the country's history this responsibility fell to private groups, local government, and the states. Child labor and mandatory education laws adopted during the Progressive Era (1900–1920) were the products of state legislatures. Most states adopted some type of old-age pension by the onset of the Depression, as well as programs to provide some help to widows and orphans. Federal involvement in developing social welfare policy and providing services came with Franklin Roosevelt's New Deal.

The Social Security Act of 1935 probably remains the single most important piece of social legislation. What is typically called "Social Security" is actually Old Age, Survivors, and Disability Insurance, which provides money to Americans who stop working at their full retirement age, paid for by a payroll tax paid by employees and employers. The 1983 Social Security Amendments set the eligible age for those born before 1937 at 65; the eligibility age gradually increased for those born between 1938 and 1959, and those born after 1959 can collect Social Security at 67. These benefits are extended to the retirees' dependents, to surviving dependents in the event of death, and to the permanently disabled irrespective of age. Even with cost-of-living adjustments that subsequent legislation added to the program, Social Security payments were never intended to cover all the expenses a retired person may have. Originally, Social Security was not available to all workers—domestics, farm workers, and government employees, for example, were excluded. A payroll tax by employers finances unemployment insurance and provides payments to workers who lose their jobs through no fault of their own. In contrast to Social Security, the states completely administer this program. Coverage runs for a maximum of 26 weeks, but Congress extends benefits under special circumstances.

During the 2000 campaign and more forcefully in his second term, President George W. Bush pushed for a partial privatization of Social Security. The plan would have allowed workers to invest a small percentage of their payroll taxes in stocks, bonds, and government securities through private retirement accounts. There was little support for the program in Congress or the country generally.

The Social Security legislation also provided for two assistance programs: Supplemental Security Income (SSI) and Aid to Families with Dependent Children (AFDC). Although everyone is eligible for Social Security and unemployment insurance, there is a **means test**; for example, income must be below a certain level, which the government determines, in order to qualify for benefits under SSI and AFDC. SSI originally provided help to the poor, the elderly, and the blind, but the government expanded it to include the permanently disabled.

AFDC was initially a small program, but the number of people whom it had to serve grew. With the increase in the divorce rate and the climbing number of unwed mothers came the charge that the AFDC was creating a permanent class of welfare recipients, and demands for reform. In 1988, Congress passed the Family and Child Support Act, which focuses on moving people from welfare into the workforce through job training and educational programs. There was also an emphasis on **workfare**, making at least part-time work for one member of the family a requirement for receiving benefits.

President Clinton came into office with the pledge to "end welfare as we know it." When the Republicans took control of Congress in 1994, a major overhaul of welfare was high on their legislative agenda, which they called the Contract with America. With support for welfare reform in the White House and Congress, the Personal Responsibility and Work Opportunity Reconciliation Act was passed in 1996. Essentially, the new law eliminated AFDC and made federal money available to the states in a block grant to provide poor families with funding for a five-year period with clear work requirements; this program is known as Temporary Assistance for Needy Families (TANF). In addition to getting families off welfare, there were social goals—such as the prevention of teen pregnancy (unmarried teen parents had to stay in school) and the encouragement of two-parent families. Under the program, recipients of benefits had to work a maximum of two years after they started receiving benefits, albeit with exemptions for families with very young children or families who could not find child care. By all accounts, welfare reform has been a success. The number of people receiving assistance under the program declined dramatically between 1997 and 2007. TANF was reauthorized through fiscal year 2010 by the Deficit

Reduction Act of 2005. In light of the severe impact of the recession on states, President Obama's American Recovery and Investment Act (2009) provided $5 billion in emergency funds for the states for TANF.

Another program to help move poor Americans off welfare is the earned income tax credit (EITC), in which the amount of the tax benefit is tied to the amount of money that an individual earns annually. The EITC can be more than $3,500. Eligibility for food stamps is also based on a means test. It makes it possible for the working poor to buy food to ensure a balanced diet with the use of food coupons or electronic debit cards issued by the Department of Agriculture. The monthly benefit for a family of four can run over $650 (as of 2009–2010) in what is now called the Supplemental Nutrition Assistance Program (SNAP). There has been a noticeable decline in the number of recipients since the introduction of welfare reform.

Healthcare Policy

Legislators considered including healthcare benefits for the elderly and poor in the Social Security Act, but they dropped the matter as too controversial. President Truman's call for national health insurance was strongly opposed by the American Medical Association, which branded the proposal "socialized medicine." But Lyndon Johnson's landslide victory in 1964 gave his administration the political clout to push the idea through Congress in 1965. Two types of coverage were provided: Medicare (for Americans who get Social Security benefits) and Medicaid (for those covered by SSI and AFDC); both programs are administered by the states, even though more than half of the costs are paid for by the federal government. Unlike Medicare, there is a means test to qualify for Medicaid. Basic Medicare payments cover hospitalization, but most beneficiaries take the optional program that provides for regular doctor visits, X-rays, and other diagnostic tests. Medicare has become extremely expensive as the number of eligible Americans increases and healthcare costs continue to rise.

Congress enacted legislation in 2003 that added a prescription drug benefit to Medicare. Medicare Part D is insurance that covers both name-brand and generic drugs. Those Medicare recipients who participate in Part D pay a monthly premium and an annual deductible.

A number of ongoing policy questions relate to healthcare, most important, the availability of health insurance and rising healthcare costs; approximately 46 million Americans do not have health insurance. The Clinton Administration unsuccessfully tried to address these issues in 1994 through the Health Security Act, the product of a task force headed by then First Lady Hillary Clinton. The plan, which required all Americans to have health insurance, was opposed as another complex and costly federal program. President Obama is also committed to healthcare reform that expands coverage and lowers cost. Instead of developing the program within the White House, he has given Congress the responsibility for developing healthcare legislation that meets his goals. As of this book's publication, the results are still unknown.

Practice

1. The Supreme Court's decision in *Griffin v. County School Board of Prince Edward County* (1955), also known as *Brown II,* illustrates

    A. the difficulty in implementing policy
    B. the power of the federal courts to enforce their decision
    C. the role that the Supreme Court plays in educational programming
    D. the reliance of the Supreme Court on precedent
    E. the importance of a unanimous decision in advancing public policy

2. Which one of the following statements about Social Security is accurate?

    A. Social Security covered all American wage earners from its inception.
    B. Social Security is financed by a payroll tax paid by both the workers and their employers.
    C. The amount of money an individual contributes to Social Security is put into his or her designated account.
    D. Social Security benefits alone provide adequate retirement income for most Americans.
    E. There will always be enough money available in Social Security to pay benefits.

3. To determine eligibility for benefits, a means test is used for

    A. Medicaid
    B. Medicare
    C. state unemployment insurance
    D. Social Security
    E. veterans' health coverage

4. Which of the following books is identified with the WRONG public policy area?

    A. *Unsafe At Any Speed,* consumer protection
    B. *The Other America,* urban crime
    C. *Silent Spring,* the environment
    D. *The Jungle,* food safety
    E. *How the Other Half Lives,* urban poverty

Poverty Rates By Age: 1959 to 2000

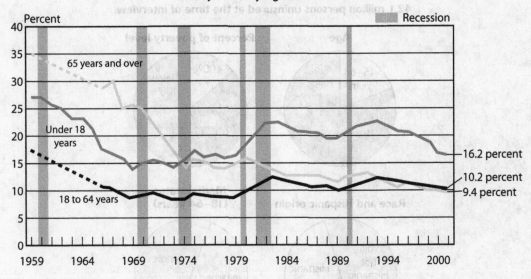

Source: U.S. Census Bureau.

5. What conclusions are supported by the above chart's data?

   I.   Poverty levels for all age groups declined dramatically during the 1960s.

   II.   Children are most affected by poverty.

   III.   There has been a relatively steady decline in poverty among the elderly since the late 1970s.

   IV.   The poverty rate is not affected by economic conditions.

  A.   I only

  B.   I and II only

  C.   I, II, and III only

  D.   III and IV only

  E.   II and III only

6. The fact that today all states have a minimum drinking age of 21 shows the influence of which institution in agenda setting?

  A.   Congress

  B.   interest groups

  C.   the Supreme Court

  D.   state legislatures

  E.   the Department of Transportation

7. The principal goal of welfare reform was to

  A.   increase benefits to single-parent families

  B.   provide college tuition tax credits to low-income families

  C.   increase Department of Health and Human Services oversight of state programs

  D.   move individuals from reliance on public assistance to reliance on a paycheck

  E.   make food stamps easier to use by the introduction of debit cards

8. The development of public policy includes all the following EXCEPT:

  A.   identification of a problem

  B.   developing a solution to the problem

  C.   determining the effectiveness of the solution

  D.   providing the funds to carry out the solution

  E.   testing the legality of the solution through the courts

Uninsured population under 65 years, 2005
42.1 million persons uninsured at the time of interview

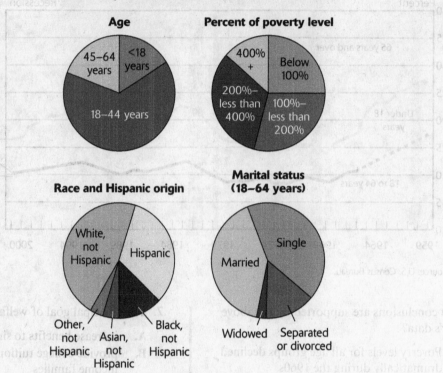

Source: *Health, United States, 2007, with Chartbook on Trends in the Health of Americans.* **Hyattsville, MD: National Center for Health Statistics, 2007.**

9. Based on the above pie charts, which of the following statements is accurate?

   A. Most of the uninsured live below the poverty line.

   B. Hispanics are the largest minority group without health insurance.

   C. Older Americans and children make up the highest percentage of uninsured.

   D. Most unmarried people are insured.

   E. Women are more likely to have health insurance than men.

10. In developing his administration's energy policy, President George W. Bush was strongly criticized for

   A. refusing to consider additional oil drilling in Alaska

   B. giving particular weight to the input from major energy companies

   C. downplaying the need to diversify energy supplies in light of problems in the Middle East

   D. meeting with Ralph Nader to get the perspective of the environmental movement

   E. increasing the regulatory authority of the Environmental Protection Agency

11. All the following statements about Social Security are true EXCEPT:

   A. Workers who retire before the age of 65 can't receive benefits.

   B. Both employers and employees contribute to Social Security.

   C. There is a limit on how much a person can earn in income and still receive full benefits.

   D. Monthly payments for Social Security are paid for through the Social Security Trust Fund.

   E. There is no means test for Social Security.

12. As a result of the National Environmental Policy Act,

   A. A moratorium was imposed on the construction of new nuclear plants.

   B. Municipalities were required to chlorinate their water supplies.

   C. Federal agencies had to consider the environmental impact of their actions.

   D. The Department of the Interior was directed to develop a list of animals and plants threatened with extinction.

   E. States were required to budget money for environmental protection.

13. Larger payouts for Social Security and increasing Medicare costs are expected because

   A. Americans are living longer because of advances in medicine.

   B. The cost of medical treatment is declining, but administering the programs is expensive.

   C. More Americans continue to work after age 65 than ever before.

   D. Lobbying groups are very successful in getting Congress to increase benefits.

   E. Projected budget surpluses have allowed coverage of more Americans.

14. Which of the following is NOT an argument usually made in support of deregulation?

   A. It increases competition.

   B. It increases services to consumers.

   C. It reduces costs.

   D. It reduces the size of government.

   E. It corrects abuses that hurt consumers.

15. An important element of any workfare program aimed at single mothers is

   A. an increase in the minimum wage

   B. the availability of child care

   C. policies that promote affirmative action

   D. training for nontraditional jobs

   E. college credit for parenting classes

Answers

1. **A** Although the Supreme Court clearly played a major role in civil rights policy, its decision in *Brown II* shows the difficulty in implementing that policy. By making local school boards responsible for developing desegregation plans, it had to rely on the willingness of the members of the boards to move forward "with all deliberate speed," which they clearly did not.

2. **B** Social Security is, in fact, financed by a payroll tax that both employees and employers contribute to. This answer may be obvious from looking at the choices or through the process of elimination. Farm workers, domestic workers, and the self-employed are not covered under the Social Security Act of 1935. The contributions made go into a general Social Security Trust Fund; the monies collected today are paid out in benefits to current recipients and are not held for the contributor until he or she retires. Social Security was always considered supplemental income, and whether there will always be enough money in the Social Security Trust Fund depends on too many variables to give a definitive answer.

3. **A** Medicaid, which provides health coverage to individuals who receive federal welfare benefits, is the only program on the list that relies on a means test. A person qualifies for the other programs either by age (Medicare or Social Security) or by status (unemployed or armed-services veteran).

4. **B** *The Other America* by Michael Harrington exposed poverty that existed in the United States with a focus on Appalachia. It had an influence on the social welfare policies of Kennedy's New Frontier and Johnson's Great Society.

5. **C** The graph clearly indicates a significant drop in the poverty rate for all groups during the 1960s, as well as the high poverty rate for children. Poverty rates are susceptible to changes in the economy, although the impact is not always dramatic. The decline in the rates for all three age groups during the high-employment period from the mid-1990s is proof.

6. **B** It was Mothers Against Drunk Driving that recognized the need for a uniform national drinking age and worked hard to get Congress to enact the necessary legislation. The Department of Transportation was responsible for implementing and enforcing the policy, particularly with respect to the release of federal highway funds to the states.

7. **D** The nation's welfare program has long been criticized for supporting welfare cheats—people who are getting benefits but are able to work. The phrase *workfare rather than welfare* was key. If anything, the overhaul of the welfare system in 1996 with its reliance on block grants was intended to shift responsibility from the federal government to the states.

8. **E** Public policy at all levels of government is susceptible to court challenge, and litigation is the most important factor that delays the implementation of policy, but it isn't an inevitable part of the process. All the other possible choices are, however. Providing funds to carry out the solution (for example, budgeting) falls either to Congress or to the state legislature.

9. **B** Hispanics account for about a third of the uninsured population. It is clear from the pie chart on percent of poverty level that most of the uninsured earn more—as much as 400 percent more—than the poverty level. The largest age group of those without health insurance are young adults, ages 18 to 44; children comprise less than 20 percent of the uninsured. Sixty percent of the unmarried people—single, divorced, separated, or widowed—are uninsured. A married couple has two possible sources of insurance. The charts do not break down the uninsured by gender.

10. **B** Vice President Dick Cheney headed the Bush Administration's Energy Policy Task Force and met personally with a number of energy-industry executives. The administration initially refused to release information about these meetings. Bush consistently stressed the need for energy diversity, including nuclear power, and was a strong advocate in favor of drilling in the Arctic National Wildlife Refuge.

11. **A** An individual can retire at age 62 and receive reduced benefits. For people between the ages of 65 and 69, the amount of money they can earn and still receive full benefits is higher than for people who retire early. There is no limit on the amount of unearned income a Social Security recipient can receive; unearned income comes from dividends and interest payments.

12. **C** The legislation, better known by its acronym NEPA, required federal agencies to submit an environmental impact statement (EIS) on the likely consequences for the environment of a project financed with federal funds. The states quickly adopted similar statutes, but they aren't required under federal law to budget money specifically for environmental protection. Unfunded environmental mandates are another matter.

13. **A** Because Americans are living longer, more money has to be paid out for more years; the older a person is, the more likely he or she is to need medical care that Medicare will fund, at least in part. The healthcare costs across the board are increasing.

14. **E** Many regulatory policies were adopted in order to correct abuses; for example, the rate discrimination practiced by the railroads led to the creation of the Interstate Commerce Commission (ICC). Advocates of deregulation used the other possible answers. Deregulation resulted in some minor shrinking of the size of the federal government, the elimination of the Civil Aeronautics Board by the Airline Deregulation Act, and the phasing out of the ICC as well. Conservatives, who support deregulation, argue that any reduction in the role of government in business is beneficial.

15. **B** The key term in the question is *single mothers.* Those dealing with welfare reform, both at the state and federal levels, realized that the lack of affordable day care would limit the likelihood that welfare recipients would actively seek employment.

Economic Policy

Economic policy consists of **fiscal policy** and **monetary policy**. Fiscal policy deals with taxation and government spending at the local, state, and federal levels. Monetary policy is set by the federal government through the Federal Reserve Board and concerns the control of the money supply. The United States is an important player in the global economy and deals with a number of international economic organizations such as the International Monetary Fund (IMF), the World Bank, and the World Trade Organization. The goals of economic policy are stable prices, low unemployment, and economic growth.

The Goals of Economic Policy

Stable prices mean that inflation is under control. This has been an important objective of the federal government's economic policy since the 1970s, a period in which the rate of inflation moved into double digits and high prices were sometimes accompanied by high unemployment; this unusual combination was called **stagflation**. There is general agreement that the Federal Reserve Board, which is discussed in the next section, did an effective job of keeping prices at the same level through its control over interest rates. But there are circumstances that neither the Federal Reserve nor the other agencies that deal with economic policy can influence—events in the Middle East may lead to a spike in oil prices; a drought in the Midwest or a freeze in California can impact the cost of groceries at the supermarket.

Low unemployment is the sign of a sound economy. Between 1990 and 1999, for example, the national **unemployment rate** (the percentage of the civilian labor force out of work) dropped from more than 5.5 percent to just over 4 percent. The rate was either somewhat higher or lower depending on the sector of the economy, the type of occupation, and the region of the country. Generally, however, the problem that faced the nation was that there were not enough people to take the jobs that were available. This is a potentially dangerous situation because it forces employers to raise wages to attract workers and contributes to inflationary pressures in the process. Conversely, an early sign that the economy may be headed for a recession is an increase in the number of unemployed people. As the recession that began in late 2007 deepened, the unemployment rate rose from just under 5 percent to just over 10 percent in October 2009.

The basic measure of economic growth is the **gross domestic product** (GDP), which is the market value of all final goods and services that the United States produces in a year. When the GDP grows around 3 percent a year, the economy is considered strong; if the percentage drops below 2 percent, it's a sign that the economy is weakening. A standard definition of a **recession** is a decline in the real GDP for two consecutive quarters.

For a good part of the 20th century, the federal budget ran a deficit—in other words, government expenditures exceeded revenues. The deficit grew dramatically during the 1980s for a variety of reasons: First, a recession cut into revenues that a large tax cut further reduced. At the same time, the Reagan Administration increased defense spending significantly, and the funding for **entitlements** expanded rapidly. Entitlements are benefit programs like Social Security and Medicaid that individuals qualify for by age, income, or a similar criteria; their costs are set by law and are not subject to congressional action. Attempts to shrink the deficit through legislation were not very successful. A combination of a robust economy and political compromise between the Clinton Administration and the Republican Congress on the budget finally generated a surplus in 1998. The surplus grew over the next two years and then disappeared as the country entered a brief recession. Deficits returned after 2001 due to a combination of Bush Administration tax cuts and the increased spending associated with homeland security and the Iraq War.

Economic Policy in Theory

Various theories and models attempt to explain how the economy works and how to make it work better. The first, and for a long time the only, widely accepted economic theory was outlined by Adam Smith in his *Wealth of Nations* (1776). A product of its time, Smith's ideas emphasized low taxes, free trade, and, quite importantly, a minimal role for the government. **Laissez-faire economics** held that the government should not interfere in the economy; there are inevitable booms and busts in the business cycle, and the market will self-correct if it's left alone. A pure laissez-faire approach never really existed in the United States. The federal government encouraged business with high protective tariffs and subsidized the railroads with land grants; when railroads and monopolies proved incapable of acting in the public interest, the federal government stepped in again with regulations and legislation designed to curb the worst abuses.

Writing in the midst of the Depression, the British economist John Maynard Keynes argued for a much more active government role. He saw the key fact of the worldwide economic collapse during the 1930s as largely a problem of demand. Government action such as public works projects and cutting taxes can stimulate demand. Public works projects open up new jobs, and tax cuts put money in people's pockets. As spending power increases, factories hire more workers to meet the demand for more goods. Under **Keynesian economics**, deficit spending is acceptable. Keynes also recognized that the economy may get overheated—demand is too great, threatening inflation. The solution is to reduce federal spending and increase taxes. Using taxes and spending to impact the economy is also known as fiscal policy.

Monetarism ties a healthy economy to the ability to control the supply of money; the institution largely responsible for implementing monetary policy is the Federal Reserve System. Twelve regional banks under the jurisdiction of a board of governors compose the Federal Reserve System. The president appoints and the Senate confirms the seven members of the Federal Reserve Board for a 14-year term, which effectively insulates the board from any single administration. The Federal Reserve Board's chair is one of the most influential economists in the country. A key way in which the Federal Reserve controls the money supply is through the **discount rate**, which is the interest rate that the Federal Reserve banks charge to their member banks for loans. When the discount rate is low, banks across the country are more likely to borrow money and to have more money to lend to businesses. In other words, the Federal Reserve can stimulate the economy by lowering the discount rate. It can also operate in the other direction: Raising the discount rate has the effect of restricting the amount of money available and cools down the economy as a check on inflation.

A model popular in the 1980s was **supply-side economics**. The argument was that a combination of tax cuts—particularly for corporations and wealthier Americans—and deregulation would lead to economic growth. Tax cuts would give companies incentive to expand and put more money in the hands of individuals likely to invest and/or spend. Businesses would hire more workers and develop new products. Deregulation was a means of decreasing the cost of doing business and stimulating competition, which, in turn, would improve efficiency. The Reagan Administration adopted this approach in some respects. While tax cuts and deregulation went forward, so did federal spending on a massive defense build-up. Supply-side economics did not assume deficit spending on that scale.

The Budget Process

Under the Budget and Accounting Act of 1921, the president was given the authority to prepare the budget. The legislation created the Bureau of the Budget to provide assistance to the president; it became the Office of Management and Budget (OMB) in 1970. The budget year runs from October 1 to September 30. Work on the budget begins at least nine months before the OMB actually submits the budget to Congress. The OMB reviews and modifies funding requests submitted by executive departments and federal agencies. The OMB modifies the requests, if necessary, to conform to the administration's spending priorities. The final product, the Budget of the United States Government, is sent to the Congress early in the new year. It's important to emphasize that the budget is only a request at this point.

The budget committees of the House and Senate hold hearings on the president's proposal and listen to a wide range of testimony from inside and outside the government. The Congressional Budget Office (CBO) provides both committees with reports on the economic outlook for the country and an analysis of the budget itself. Based on this information, budget resolutions are prepared for action by the full House and Senate. A budget resolution includes total spending broken down by function (for example, defense, natural resources and the environment, and Social Security), total revenues, and information on the anticipated deficit or surplus. Members can make amendments during the floor debates. A conference committee must reconcile the House and Senate budget resolutions that ultimately pass.

With a concurrent budget resolution adopted (usually, but not always, by April 15), the House and Senate appropriations committees and their subcommittees develop the actual spending bills for the areas of government for which they are responsible. They act within the limits set for **discretionary spending** in the resolution. (Discretionary spending is not required by law.) A conference works out the differences between the appropriation bills that each house passes, and the president ultimately receives the final legislation for action. But additional legislative action may be necessary to make sure that the budget targets are met. The budget resolution often includes reconciliation instructions, which are directives to the congressional committees that have jurisdiction over mandatory spending (for example, entitlements such as Social Security or veterans' benefits) and taxes to make changes in existing laws. Reconciliation legislation may cut benefits under Medicare or raise taxes. There is still no guarantee that the targets of the budget resolutions will be met. The rise in unemployment and the significant increase in spending in the wake of September 11, 2001, are a case in point.

Taxation and Tax Policy

Until the beginning of the 20th century, the federal government relied on revenues from two sources: *tariffs* (taxes on goods imported into the country) and the sale of public lands. In 1895, the Supreme Court struck down an early federal income tax enacted by Congress, and it took the Sixteenth Amendment (1913) to restore it. Most Americans paid little or no federal income tax until World War II when rates rose significantly. Even today, we pay less in taxes than most other industrialized nations. Personal income tax is, however, the single most important source of receipts for the federal government; it accounted for over 50 percent of revenues in 2000.

The income tax is an example of a **progressive tax**, which means that the amount of tax owed varies with income—the more money you make, the higher your tax rate. A **regressive tax** falls more heavily on the poor. A sales tax is an example of a regressive tax; the rich and poor pay the same local sales tax on a new television, but the cost is a greater burden on a poor individual. Federal excise taxes that fall on airline tickets and commodities such as gasoline are also regressive. Such taxes on alcohol and tobacco are sometimes called "sin taxes" because the purpose is not just to raise revenue, but to increase the price to the point where people think twice about using them.

Tax policy is the litmus test of U.S. politics. Republicans often attack Democrats as the "tax and spend" party, while Democrats criticize Republicans for giving tax breaks to corporations and the rich. President George H. W. Bush broke his pledge not to raise taxes during his administration, and he suffered serious political consequences.

Taxes always figure prominently in presidential elections. Steve Forbes made the **flat tax** the focus of his 1996 campaign for the Republican nomination. A flat tax sets a single low rate for all Americans, irrespective of income, coupled with the elimination of all exemptions. Proponents claimed that this radical change in the tax system would allow individuals to file their taxes on a postcard and eliminate the need for the Internal Revenue Service (IRS). When budget deficits were high, there was a proposal for a **value-added tax** (VAT), which taxes an item at each stage of its production, distribution, and sale. This is essentially a national sales tax, and is extremely regressive. Conservatives have called for significantly reducing the **capital-gains tax**, which is a tax on the income derived from the sale of real estate or stock, and for the elimination of the estate tax, the so-called "death tax."

Over the last 20 years, there have been dramatic changes in tax policy. Early in the Reagan Administration, Congress approved the largest tax cut in U.S. history. This was followed by the 1986 Tax Reform Act, which consolidated and lowered individual tax brackets and lowered the top rate for corporations. While key deductions such as home mortgage interest were kept in the legislation, many other deductions were eliminated. In 1997, President Clinton agreed to a number of tried-and-true Republican tax issues in the Taxpayer Relief Act, including a cut in capital gains tax and the child tax credit. The Bush Administration's Economic Growth and Tax Relief Reconciliation Act (2001) provided Americans with a tax rebate; reduced tax rates significantly; provided numerous tax breaks for families, education, and those with retirement plans; and provided for the phased elimination of the estate tax by 2010. Critics claim that the 2001 tax cuts primarily benefited the wealthy and contributed to the return of deficits.

Housing Collapse, Financial Crisis, and Recession

Home ownership and home values increased dramatically during the George W. Bush Administration. To bring more people into the market, banks relaxed their lending requirements and developed new types of loans, such as subprime mortgages, which have high interest rates because the borrowers don't have the income or the creditworthiness to qualify for traditional loans. By 2007, many people with sub-prime mortgages were unable to meet their obligations; the housing bubble burst as foreclosures rose and home prices began to fall.

The housing crisis became a financial crisis in 2008. Many financial institutions in the United States and abroad invested heavily in questionable home mortgages, which led to the failure or government bailout of investment banks, mortgage companies, and insurance firms. The federal government was forced to take over mortgage giants Fannie Mae (Federal National Mortgage Association) and Freddie Mac (Federal Home Loan Corporation) in September of that year. As a result of these developments, credit dried up, stock prices fell, and unemployment increased.

Faced with the most serious economic crisis since the Great Depression, the federal government responded in several ways: Tax rebates to individuals and tax breaks to businesses in the spring of 2008 were intended to stimulate the economy. A much larger stimulus package was provided for in the American Recovery and Reinvestment Act (2009), which earmarked over $700 billion for spending on highways, bridges, and other infrastructure projects, as well as money for the states and tax cuts. The Federal Reserve cut its interest rates to half a percent or less to encourage banks to extend credit. Most significantly, the crisis led to an unprecedented level of involvement of the federal government in the economy. Through the Troubled Asset Relief Program (TARP), hundreds of billions of dollars were provided to banks and other companies who were considered "too big to fail," with the government often getting an ownership share in return for the funding. The best example: The federal government owns 60 percent of General Motors.

International Economic Policy

Globalization is the key economic fact of the early 21st century; there is no getting around the fact that the United States is part of a global economy, and the economic crisis certainly bore this out. The roots of the financial collapse may have been in the United States, but it impacted most countries around the world. By the same token, events in Japan, South Asia, Europe, and South America impact U.S. businesses, financial institutions, and the stock market. The United States is an important member of international organizations such as the International Monetary Fund (IMF) and the World Bank. The IMF promotes monetary cooperation around the world, encourages international trade, and provides assistance to countries that need help paying their international obligations. The World Bank provides loans and technical assistance for economic development programs in member states. The United States is a member of the **Group of Eight** (G8), which also includes Canada, France, Germany, Italy, Japan, the United Kingdom, and Russia; the heads of these leading industrial countries meet periodically to discuss economic policy questions. The Group of Twenty (G20) is made up of the finance ministers and central bank governors of 19 countries; the European Union is the twentieth member. It was founded in 1999 to bring important industrialized and developing countries together to discuss the global economy.

The principal international economic issue facing the United States is trade. After World War II, the General Agreement on Tariffs and Trade (GATT) was established to promote free trade through international agreements.

The World Trade Organization (WTO), which replaced GATT in 1995, is committed to breaking down protectionism (high tariffs and similar barriers), which limits the flow of goods, services, and intellectual property. The United States is generally supportive of the WTO and actively promotes free trade under both Democratic and Republican presidents. Despite strong opposition from organized labor and environmental groups, the Clinton Administration pushed through the North American Free Trade Agreement (1993), which created a free trade zone between the United States, Canada, and Mexico. President George W. Bush sought **fast-track authority** from Congress to help achieve his goal of the Free Trade Area of the Americas, essentially the expansion of NAFTA throughout the Western Hemisphere. Fast track authorizes the president to negotiate trade agreements that Congress can only vote up or down, not amend.

Despite a strong commitment to free trade, the United States will act to protect important sectors of the economy if necessary. This is exactly what President George W. Bush did in the spring of 2002 when a flood of foreign steel imports threatened to further weaken the domestic steel industry. The safeguards put in place were strongly criticized by the European Union and there was some talk of retaliation; a trade war did not materialize. In the United States, opponents of the president's action claimed he was really more interested in the votes in steel-producing states like Ohio, Pennsylvania, and West Virginia in the midterm elections than in the future of American steel. The fact that politics shapes policy is no surprise.

The Office of the U.S. Trade Representative (USTR) is responsible for shaping our international trade policy. It works with individual countries, the United Nations Conference on Trade and Development, and the WTO; the deputy U.S. trade representative in Geneva is our ambassador to that organization. The fact that the trade representative has cabinet rank is a statement about the importance attached to this area of economic policy. An agency that works closely with the USTR is the Commerce Department's International Trade Administration (ITA), which actively promotes U.S. non-farm exports; it has offices around the world that provide assistance to U.S. companies and monitors compliance with trade agreements to which we are a party. Complaints about a country dumping goods in the United States at less than fair market value are fully investigated. Another pertinent organization is the National Economic Council, which includes among its responsibilities coordinating policymaking on international economic issues. Staff that deal with international questions report as well to the National Security Advisor within the Executive Office of the President.

Practice

1. A key difference between laissez-faire and Keynesian economics is

   A. the importance of easy credit for business
   B. the response to "boom and bust" business cycles
   C. the way budget surpluses are spent
   D. how each deals with inflationary pressures
   E. the value of printing more money

2. The largest share of expenditures in the federal budget is earmarked for

   A. defense
   B. farm subsidies
   C. Social Security
   D. veterans' services
   E. education

3. A budget deficit occurs when

   A. exports exceed imports
   B. taxes and spending are reduced
   C. unemployment increases
   D. the amount of money in circulation increases
   E. federal outlays are greater than receipts

4. The federal agency that has the most independence in shaping economic policy is the

   A. National Economic Council
   B. Internal Revenue Service
   C. Federal Reserve Board
   D. Office of the U.S. Trade Representative
   E. Department of the Treasury

5. All the following statements about the budget process are valid EXCEPT:

   A. The Budget of the United States Government is a proposal developed by the executive branch.
   B. The Congressional Budget Office provides analysis to the budget committees of Congress.
   C. The president can reject a budget resolution that increases spending.
   D. Government programs are actually funded by appropriations bills.
   E. A budget reconciliation may involve raising taxes or reducing entitlement benefits.

6. The combination of factors that plagued the economy in the 1970s was

   A. high inflation and high unemployment
   B. tight money supply and trade deficit
   C. high taxes and low unemployment
   D. high stock prices and high credit card debt
   E. high savings rates and low bond sales

7. To ensure a healthy economy, supply-side economists support

   A. maintaining a trade balance
   B. cutting individual and corporate taxes
   C. deficit spending to ensure high employment
   D. increasing taxes on the wealthiest Americans
   E. increasing government regulation of business

8. A recession is characterized by

   I. rising interest rates
   II. increase in the unemployment rate
   III. a trade deficit greater than $10 billion
   IV. a negative GDP

   A. I only
   B. II only
   C. II and III only
   D. II and IV only
   E. II, III, and IV only

9. The principal way in which the Federal Reserve Board has impacted the economy in recent years is through

   A. controlling speculation in the stock market
   B. raising and lowering interest rates
   C. encouraging Americans to save more by increasing insurance on deposits
   D. increasing the number of banks that are part of the Federal Reserve System
   E. allowing banks to sell mutual funds and other investments

U.S. International Trade in Goods and Services

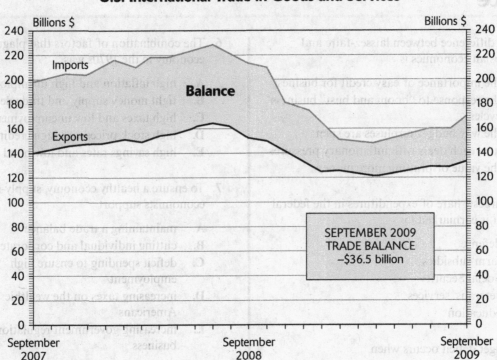

SEPTEMBER 2009
TRADE BALANCE
−$36.5 billion

Source: U.S. Census Bureau.

10. All the following statements are supported by the above chart EXCEPT:

   A. The U.S. trade imbalance continued throughout the recent recession.

   B. Trade continued to increase gradually even after the recession officially began.

   C. U.S. imports declined more rapidly than exports due to the recession.

   D. The volume of trade declined because of the recession.

   E. The principal trading partner of the United States through the recession was China.

11. Taxes make up the lion's share of the money used to fund the federal government. Most of the tax revenue comes from

   A. corporations
   B. retail sales
   C. taxes on commodities
   D. payroll taxes
   E. individuals

12. The Department of Commerce helps implement U.S. economic policy by

   A. regulating the rates charged by investor-owned electric utilities

   B. setting high protective tariffs for vital industries such as computers

    C. promoting the export of U.S. products around the world

   D. overseeing the activities of the National Weather Service

   E. representing U.S. interests in the World Trade Organization

13. The key idea behind a progressive tax is that

   A. The money raised is used only for social programs.

   B. The rich pay proportionately more than the poor.

   C. Deductions allow all Americans to pay.

   D. A single rate applies to everyone.

   E. The tax burden should be as low as possible.

14. Responsibility for ensuring that the administration's budget priorities are adhered to by individual federal agencies falls to the
    A. Council of Economic Advisers
    B. Office of Management and Budget
    C. Congressional Budget Office
    D. House and Senate budget committees
    E. Joint Economic Committee

15. Monetarists are most concerned with
    A. deficits
    B. high taxes
    C. trade imbalances
    D. regulation
    E. inflation

Answers

1. **B** Proponents of laissez-faire believe that the ups and downs of the business cycle are inevitable and that the market is self-correcting; Keynesians have no such confidence, and support government intervention to create demand, particularly during periods of severe recession or depression.

2. **C** Mandatory spending takes up two-thirds of the federal budget outlays, and the largest single component is Social Security. Social Security costs grew significantly during the 1990s, while defense spending declined. Before the end of the Cold War, defense accounted for a greater share of expenditures than Social Security did.

3. **E** Don't let the terms *outlays* and *receipts* fool you. They mean expenditures and revenues and are the only factors involved in determining the size of a budget deficit.

4. **C** The Internal Revenue Service has little or no policymaking functions; it collects taxes and enforces the tax laws enacted by Congress. The president appoints the National Economic Council and the U.S. trade representative, and both are expected to carry out the president's policies. The Department of the Treasury is somewhat more independent for no other reason than that it is a large bureaucracy with its own agenda; the president expects the secretary of the treasury to manage the department in line with administration goals. The very structure of the Federal Reserve Board is intended to promote independence. Although appointed by the president, the 14-year staggered term allows the board as a whole not to feel beholden to any one president.

5. **C** The budget resolution is a concurrent resolution of the Congress; it is not a law, and the president does not have to sign it, nor can the president veto it. Office of Management and Budget staff and cabinet secretaries testify before the budget committees, and there is a considerable amount of direct negotiation between the White House and Congress on the budget, but the president can't take any formal action against the budget resolution.

6. **A** The question is asking you to recognize that, in the 1970s, the economy experienced *stagflation* (a weak economy characterized by high unemployment and high inflation).

7. **B** Supply-side economics is based on the premise that tax cuts encourage work, savings, and investment. If individuals and corporations have more money to spend, they'll invest in companies or expansion, which, in turn, will produce more jobs and additional revenue for the government. Government interference, either in the form of such programs as public works or federal regulation, represents the worst way to approach the economy.

8. **D** Many economists define a recession as two consecutive quarters with a negative GDP; unemployment will rise during a recession as well. An interest rate boost is the opposite of what the Federal Reserve Board would do in a recession; interest rates are lowered to encourage expansion. There is no trade deficit target that signals the onset of a recession.

9. **B** The Federal Reserve Board uses monetary policy to regulate the economy. In periods of recession, it lowers the discount rate, which ultimately makes it cheaper for businesses to borrow money that they can use to increase production and hire new workers. Raising the discount rate has the opposite effect and is intended to cool down the economy and prevent inflation from getting out of control. Although several of the other answers deal with banking generally, the Federal Reserve Board does not have any responsibilities in these areas.

10. **E** The graph shows the value of all imports and exports from September 2007 to September 2009; it does not provide information on imports to and exports from specific countries. In fact, the top trading partner of the United States during the period was Canada. All the other statements are correct. Answer **B** does require you to know that the recession began in the fourth quarter of 2007.

11. **E** Individual income taxes account for most of the revenue of the federal government. The balance is largely made up of payroll taxes for Social Security and similar programs, corporate income taxes, and *excise taxes* (taxes on commodities). Retail sales are not a factor because states, not the federal government, collect sales taxes.

12. **C** A vital responsibility of the Department of Commerce is to promote the sale of U.S. products on the world market; it does this through the International Trade Administration. Although the U.S. Census Bureau is part of the Department of Commerce and provides important statistical data on the economy, that fact is hardly as important as international trade. Congress sets tariff policy through legislation, and the Office of the U.S. Trade Representative provides our personnel to the World Trade Organization.

13. **B** The essence of progressive taxation is that the tax rate goes up with income. **D** is a simple definition of the flat tax, and **A** tries to trick you by suggesting that the term *progressive* should be thought of in political terms (as in the Progressive Movement).

14. **B** In preparing the president's budget, federal agencies are in regular contact with the OMB, which is responsible for keeping these spending requests within the parameters set by the president. Agencies may try to appeal to the president's top aides regarding an OMB decision that calls for a cut in spending in some area. The Congressional Budget Office really is a check on the OMB and works closely with the House and Senate budget committees; in a divided government, the members of these committees may well be antagonistic to the administration. Neither the Joint Economic Committee in Congress nor the Council of Economic Advisers has a key role in the budget process.

15. **E** The focus of monetarists is obvious—to control the money supply. Prior to the onset of the major recession in late 2007, the Federal Reserve Board was most concerned with using interest rates to keep inflation in check.

Foreign Policy

The foreign policy of the United States involves promoting our national interests in negotiations and relationships with other countries, protecting the security of Americans at home and abroad, and participating in international organizations. There is a very close connection between our foreign policy and our defense posture, as well as the economic health of the nation. Diplomatic efforts, military force, and economic assistance may advance the interests of the United States in the world, either singly or in combination. Today, foreign policy faces new challenges from international terrorism, globalization, and the environment.

Overview of U.S. Foreign Policy

The United States had a foreign policy before it was a nation. Benjamin Franklin represented American interests in France during the revolution, and the two countries entered into an alliance in 1778. The Department of State was the first of the three executive departments formally established after the ratification of the Constitution. Nonetheless, the importance of the president in setting the direction of U.S. foreign policy was clear from practically the beginning of the country. In his Farewell Address (1796), President George Washington clearly warned the nation about the dangers of permanent alliances: "The great rule of conduct for us in regard to foreign nations is in extending our commercial relations, to have with them as little political connection as possible."

For most of the 19th century, U.S. energy focused on westward expansion. Thomas Jefferson bought the Louisiana Territory from France (1803), and war and diplomacy added the Southwest, California, and the Pacific Northwest. U.S. foreign policy did, however, look beyond what became the continental United States. Diplomatic relations and trade were established with China and Japan, and Alaska was purchased from the Russians. But it was the Spanish-American War that put the United States on the world stage. As a result of the war, Guam, the Philippines, and Puerto Rico, former Spanish possessions, came under U.S. control, as did the Hawaiian Islands. In 1903, the United States acquired the rights to build a canal across the Isthmus of Panama. The construction of the canal extended U.S. influence in the Caribbean, Central America, and South America.

U.S. troops played a decisive role in bringing World War I to an end. Although the Senate rejected the Treaty of Versailles and with it, membership in the League of Nations, which was the brainchild of President Woodrow Wilson, the United States did not retreat into isolationism after the conflict. Instead, the United States took the lead in pressing for naval disarmament; tried to resolve the conflict over war reparations and war debts between Germany, France, Great Britain, and itself; and initiated a new policy in the Western Hemisphere. Improved relations with the nations in the Caribbean, Central America, and South America began with President Hoover, and President Roosevelt pledged an end to U.S. intervention in the region through the Good Neighbor Policy. As the threat of war in both Europe and Asia gathered during the 1930s, Congress passed a series of Neutrality Acts between 1935 and 1937 in the hope of keeping the United States out. But once war was declared in Europe, in September 1939, U.S. foreign policy shifted. Through the **cash-and-carry** provisions of the Neutrality Act of 1939, the country's first peacetime draft (1940), and the Lend-Lease Act (1941), the United States sided with allies against Germany.

With the Japanese attack on Pearl Harbor on December 7, 1941, the United States formally entered the war and the alliance that included Great Britain, Free France, China, and the Soviet Union. The wartime conferences between the allied leaders—Casablanca (January 1943), Tehran (November 1943), Yalta (February 1945), and Potsdam (July–August 1945)—set the military strategy for the defeat of Germany and Japan and helped shape the postwar world. When the conflict ended in 1945, the United Nations stood as the hope for an enduring peace, but the United States had a monopoly on the atomic bomb, and Russian troops were in control of Eastern Europe. Within just a few years, the hot war was replaced by the Cold War.

The reaction of the United States to the threat from the Soviet Union was the **containment policy**—in other words, any aggressive moves by the U.S.S.R. would be met by a U.S. counterforce. The Truman Doctrine (1947), under which the United States provided assistance to Greece and Turkey, and the Berlin Airlift (1948–1949)—in which the Russian effort to force the United States, Great Britain, and France out of West Berlin was thwarted—are early examples of containment in practice. Under the Marshall Plan (1947), the United States funneled billions of dollars into Western Europe for reconstruction. The United States recognized the value of economic assistance in undercutting the appeal of communism around the world, and such foreign aid became an integral part of U.S. foreign policy. Containment was also expressed through multilateral agreements. A network of military and political alliances was created, the most important of which was the North Atlantic Treaty Organization (NATO) founded in 1949.

The early years of the Cold War in Asia saw China come under communist control (1949) and a military stalemate between East and West in the Korean War (1950–1953), which the United States fought under United Nations auspices. Here, the **domino theory** held that if one country in a region "fell to communism," the others would soon follow. This thinking led to U.S. involvement in Southeast Asia after 1954 and the Vietnam War, the longest and most divisive conflict in U.S. history. The Cold War also undercut the Good Neighbor Policy in the Western Hemisphere. In 1954, the United States supported the overthrow of a left-wing government in Guatemala, and the Central Intelligence Agency was involved in the planning of the abortive Bay of Pigs Invasion of Castro's Cuba in 1961. The Soviet Union placed medium-range nuclear weapons on the island in the wake of the invasion, precipitating the Cuban Missile Crisis (1962) that brought the U.S. and the U.S.S.R. to the brink of war. Positive results did come of this, however. The Limited Nuclear Test Ban Treaty (1963), which prohibited testing in the atmosphere, under water, or in outer space, was signed by the United States, Great Britain, and the Soviet Union.

As the United States became more involved in Vietnam during the 1960s, the arms race between the superpowers was in full swing; tensions eased somewhat through summit diplomacy—face-to-face meetings between U.S. and Soviet leaders. The election of Richard Nixon in 1968 brought a new direction to U.S. foreign policy. **Détente**, which replaced confrontation with cooperation and negotiation, led to the Strategic Arms Limitation Treaty (SALT I), which froze the number of long-range nuclear missiles for five years, and a presidential visit to the People's Republic of China (1972). President Jimmy Carter incorporated a concern for human rights into the global policy of the United States; he had two major successes—the Panama Canal Treaties (1977), which returned control over both the canal and the Panama Canal Zone to Panama, and the Camp David Accords (1978), which brought peace between Egypt and Israel after 30 years. But the invasion of Afghanistan by the Soviet Union in 1979 put a halt to any further improvement in relations, and Carter was not able to win the release of Americans seized during the takeover of the U.S. embassy in Iran.

The election of Ronald Reagan seemed a throwback to the most frigid days of the Cold War. Reagan returned to an interventionist policy in the Caribbean and Central America with the invasion of Grenada (1983) and support for the right-wing government in El Salvador. Congress supported his call for a major increase in defense spending that included money for an anti-missile defense system known officially as the Strategic Defense Initiative but more popularly known as Star Wars. Despite tough talk, Reagan was willing to return to summit diplomacy. His meetings with Soviet leader Mikhail Gorbachev during his second term led to the Intermediate Nuclear Force Treaty in 1987, which banned intermediate-range missiles from Europe. In just a few years, the fall of the communist governments in Eastern Europe and the collapse of the Soviet Union itself brought an end to the Cold War and a different set of international problems.

While the threat of nuclear war was significantly reduced during the 1990s, the world saw no end to conflict. The Iraqi invasion of Kuwait (1990) prompted President George H. W. Bush to build a coalition of European and Arab states that successfully drove Saddam Hussein's forces out during the Persian Gulf War (1991). The world community was much slower to respond to the bitter ethnic fighting that broke out in Yugoslavia during that decade. The United States belatedly arranged a settlement in the region known as the Dayton Accords (1995), which led to U.S. troops serving as peacekeepers under the United Nations. The agreement did not prevent a war from breaking out over the province of Kosovo between Serbia and NATO, the first time NATO forces went into combat on European soil. It's important to note here that the United States supported the expansion of NATO, which Poland, the Czech Republic, and Hungary joined in 1998.

The United States responded to the attacks of September 11, 2001, with the destruction of an Al-Qaeda terrorist base in Afghanistan and the overthrow of the Taliban government in that country. In his 2002 State of the Union address, President George W. Bush identified Iraq, Iran, and North Korea as an "axis of evil" supporting terrorism and seeking weapons of mass destruction (WMDs)—biological, chemical, or nuclear. According to the Bush Doctrine (2002), the United States had the right to use force preemptively against countries that posed a threat to us and were attempting to acquire WMDs.

In the fall of 2002, growing concern about Iraq's WMD program led Congress to grant the president authority to use force against Iraq. U.S. forces, along with a contingent of troops from other countries, most notably Great Britain, invaded Iraq in March 2003. Although no WMDs were found, Iraqi dictator Saddam Hussein was overthrown. But the fighting continued against Al-Qaeda in Iraq, and sectarian violence between Shiites and Sunnis raged even as a new democratically elected government was instated. The level of violence declined significantly by the end of Bush's second term; President Obama is committed to removing all U.S. troops from Iraq by 2011 but has increased U.S. forces to Afghanistan to defeat a resurgent Taliban.

Although Iraq and Afghanistan remain an important focus, they aren't the only foreign policy issues facing the country. The United States continues to oppose Iran's ongoing nuclear program, which United Nations sanctions have failed to slow down. Tensions with North Korea over its nuclear and missile program remain high despite the six-party talks, which involved the United States, China, Russia, Japan, South Korea, and North Korea. North Korea tested nuclear devices in 2006 and 2009.

The Bush Administration was often criticized for its go-it-alone approach in foreign affairs (known as *unilateralism*). Bush's rejection in 2001 of the Kyoto treaty on global warming, which committed the industrialized nations to legally binding reductions in greenhouse gases, is a case in point.

Making Foreign Policy

Both the president and the Congress have responsibility for foreign policy under the Constitution. The president negotiates treaties, appoints and receives ambassadors from around the world, and is the commander-in-chief of the armed forces. From Thomas Jefferson and the North African Barbary pirates, presidents have involved the United States in conflicts without the benefit of a formal declaration of war by Congress by using their control over the military. For its part, Congress has one clear foreign policy responsibility: Treaties do not go into effect unless ratified by a two-thirds vote of the Senate. The Senate exercised this authority most notably in 1920 when it rejected the Treaty of Versailles, which ended World War I. In addition, the Senate has to approve the appointment of the key members of the president's foreign policy team, and Congress as a whole controls appropriations. Only Congress, of course, can formally declare war. The president and Congress have assumed additional foreign policy authority either by precedent or by statute.

There is no doubt that the president is the nation's chief diplomat. He or she meets regularly with world leaders and the heads of other nations on issues of mutual concern, decides through the budget process spending priorities in terms of defense and foreign aid, and uses the presidency as a bully pulpit (relying on the power of persuasion) to press for support for actions from the American people and the international community. The president makes broad policy statements that give direction to U.S. diplomacy.

The United States responded quickly to the Soviet Union's invasion of Afghanistan in December 1979. Referring specifically to the invasion in his State of the Union address in January 1980, President Carter committed the United States to the defense of the Persian Gulf against an outside threat; this policy position became known as the Carter Doctrine. The president has access to a tremendous amount of information and advice on which to base decisions from an extensive foreign policy/national security/military bureaucracy. Although it rarely handles cases that deal with foreign policy questions, the Supreme Court has shown considerable deference to the president's authority. In *United States v. Curtiss-Wright Export Corp.* (1936), the Court recognized the broad discretion of the president because he or she is the only person who can speak for the country. An executive agreement negotiated between the president and another head of state does not require Senate approval on these grounds. The president can also bypass Congress by relying on special envoys to represent or negotiate for the United States rather than members of the formal foreign policy establishment, and use discretionary funds outside of the appropriations process to finance special programs. Of course, such "creative financing" can lead to problems. During the Reagan Administration, money from the sale of arms to Iran, which was intended to buy help in freeing U.S. hostages held in other parts of the Middle East, actually supported the Contras who were fighting the left-wing government in Nicaragua.

In August 1964, Congress gave President Johnson sweeping authority to involve the United States in Vietnam in response to an alleged attack by North Vietnam on U.S. ships in the Gulf of Tonkin. The **Gulf of Tonkin Resolution** allowed the United States to commit 500,000 troops to a protracted war in Southeast Asia; as that war came to an end, Congress thought better of that action. In 1973, Congress passed, over the veto of President Nixon, the **War Powers Act**, which provided the following:

- The president must inform Congress within 48 hours of introducing U.S. troops into combat or into an area where combat is imminent.
- Congress must approve of the continued use of U.S. troops in combat within 60 days.
- If Congress does not provide such authorization, the troops must be withdrawn.
- The president must comply with a concurrent resolution requiring the removal of U.S. troops.

The Supreme Court struck down the provision in the original statute that allowed Congress to use the legislative veto to prevent the sale of arms overseas in *Immigration and Naturalization Service v. Chadha* (1983). Despite the rhetoric at the time that it became law, the War Powers Act has not hampered the president's ability to conduct foreign policy. Either the reporting terms have been complied with or the president has asked Congress for a specific grant of authority. President George W. Bush had little trouble getting Congress to authorize the use of force in Iraq in the fall of 2002.

Congress has additional authority over foreign policy through its appropriation and oversight functions. It can reduce the amount of foreign aid that the president asks for or cut the budget for, or eliminate altogether funding for, a defense project. Congress holds hearings regularly to hear from the secretaries of state and defense as well as the director of the Central Intelligence Agency (CIA) and the National Security Advisor. In addition to getting special briefings, the House and Senate committees with jurisdiction over foreign relations and intelligence can turn their investigative eyes onto foreign policy questions. This is exactly what was done in the 1970s and 1980s about the Iran-Contra affair and actions taken by the CIA.

Except in time of war or heightened tensions, Americans focus more on bread-and-butter issues than foreign policy. Nonetheless, public opinion can shape decision making. News coverage of the Vietnam War, particularly on television, brought about a shift in attitudes in favor of withdrawal. On the other hand, images of starvation in Somalia and stories about "ethnic cleansing" in Bosnia and Kosovo, built up pressure for U.S. intervention. In the wake of the terrorist attacks of September 11, 2001, President George W. Bush initially received broad public support for the War on Terror. That support waned when no WMDs were found in Iraq, the conflict dragged on, and U.S. casualties mounted. Opposition to the war was one of the factors that cost Republicans control of Congress in the 2006 midterm elections.

The Institutions of Foreign Policy

The executive branch develops and implements U.S. foreign policy, primarily through the Department of State, the Department of Defense, the National Security Council (NSC), the CIA, the Director of National Intelligence, and the National Economic Council. Institutionally, the War on Terror has blurred to some degree the distinction between foreign and domestic terrorism. The FBI has agents in Pakistan investigating terrorist links, and the Department of Health and Human Services is preparing to respond to bioterrorism.

The Department of State is the lead agency responsible for foreign policy. Through its embassies in foreign countries and missions to international organizations such as the United Nations, it is responsible for communicating the position of the United States on issues to the world community. It negotiates treaties covering *biodiversity* (maintaining the diversity of plant and animal life on the planet), international trade, nuclear weapons proliferation, and a myriad of other subjects. The Department of State is also a service agency in a sense, protecting and providing assistance to Americans overseas, supporting commerce, and informing the public at home and abroad about our foreign policy. The secretary of state is a close advisor to the president, the chief spokesperson for U.S.

foreign policy rather than an independent voice, and the manager of an executive department. Relations between the secretary and the other members of the foreign policy team are not always smooth. Early on, President Nixon relied more heavily on his National Security Advisor, Henry Kissinger, than on Secretary of State William Rogers; President Carter and Secretary of State Cyrus Vance broke over the best way to handle the Iran hostage crisis. There is evidence that, in the Bush Administration, the Department of State and Department of Defense held differing views on the Middle East and Iraq.

The Department of Defense was created in 1947 through the consolidation of the Department of the Army and the Department of the Navy, both of which were cabinet-level departments, as well as the U.S. Air Force. Each service retained its own secretary who reported to the secretary of defense. This arrangement was intended to reduce or eliminate interservice rivalries. The secretary of defense is obviously an important policymaker and advisor to the president, as well as the manager of a huge agency (almost 2.5 million civilian and military employees) that is responsible for spending a significant percentage of the federal budget. The president also receives military advice from the Joint Chiefs of Staff (JCS), which is composed of the heads of the four services (Army, Navy, Marines, and Air Force), and a chair and vice-chair appointed by the president and confirmed by the Senate. The chair of the JCS is officially designated as the president's principal military advisor. George W. Bush's secretary of state, Colin Powell, held this position during the George H. W. Bush Administration and developed the overall planning for the Persian Gulf War. George W. Bush's vice president, Dick Cheney, was secretary of defense under the George H. W. Bush Administration.

The NSC is made up of the president and vice president; the secretaries of defense, state, and treasury; the chair of the Joint Chiefs of Staff; the Director of National Intelligence, and the director of the CIA. Its relatively small staff is headed by the president's National Security Advisor. The president's closest White House advisors— including the chief of staff—usually attend meetings, and the director of the Office of Management and Budget and the attorney general are invited if the subject falls within their areas of responsibility. The purpose of the NSC is to provide the president with a forum to consider strategic and foreign policy options; it also helps to coordinate the implementation of policy. As noted earlier, the council can become a rival to the Department of State.

The CIA principally serves two functions: the collection and analysis of intelligence relating to the national security of the United States, and counterintelligence. Over the last 30 years, the CIA has come under both public and congressional scrutiny on a number of occasions. In the 1970s oversight committees in Congress looked into the agency's covert operations, particularly its role in destabilizing legitimate governments; in the 1990s, there were revelations about a major spy scandal.

The CIA came under strong criticism after September 11 for its failure to fully appreciate the terrorist threat to the United States. The 9/11 Commission emphasized the need to restructure intelligence activities to bring about greater coordination among the various agencies involved. This was accomplished by the creation of the position of director of national intelligence in 2004. The director is the principal advisor to the president, the NSC, and the Department of Homeland Security on intelligence matters. He or she is also the head of the Intelligence Community, which includes the intelligence branches of the armed services, the FBI, the CIA, the National Security Agency, the Defense Intelligence Agency, and key executive departments in addition to homeland security— energy, state, and treasury.

As noted in the preceding chapter, the National Economic Council is involved in international economic policy. Created by President Clinton in 1993, it is part of the Executive Office of the President along with the NSC. The key cabinet heads that deal broadly with economic issues—the secretaries of commerce, labor, and the treasury— along with the director of the OMB, the U.S. trade representative, and the chair of the Council of Economic Advisers are members.

Practice

1. The president's civilian advisor on military force strength is the

   A. secretary of defense
   B. chair of the Joint Chiefs of Staff
   C. secretary of the Army
   D. chief of staff of the Army
   E. director of the CIA

2. All the following statements about the War Powers Act are true EXCEPT:

   A. The War Powers Act was a response to the limited control Congress had over the Vietnam War.
   B. Under the legislation, the president must inform Congress that troops are being sent overseas.
   C. It allows Congress to effectively limit the president's powers as commander-in-chief.
   D. The commitment of U.S. troops can be extended if Congress acts within 60 days.
   E. A president can't ignore a joint resolution call for the removal of U.S. troops.

3. The Korean War can be considered a victory for the containment policy because

   A. The fighting was authorized by the United Nations.
   B. It did not lead to a wider war with the Soviet Union.
   C. China was forced to withdraw its support for North Korea.
   D. Nuclear weapons did not have to be used.
   E. North Korea did not conquer South Korea.

4. Which of the following geographic areas has U.S. foreign policy generally neglected?

   A. Western Europe
   B. Eastern Europe and Russia
   C. Africa
   D. Asia
   E. Central America and the Caribbean

5. Concerned about the expansion of the Soviet Union into South Asia, the Senate exercised its constitutional power to offer "advice and consent" and rejected which of the following treaties?

   A. Intermediate Nuclear Force Treaty
   B. SALT I Treaty
   C. Chemical Weapons Convention
   D. Nuclear Non-Proliferation Treaty
   E. SALT II Treaty

6. According to critics, granting the president fast-track trade authority weakens which constitutional authority of the Congress?

   A. the right to regulate foreign and interstate trade
   B. the right of the Senate to ratify treaties entered into by the United States
   C. the right of the Senate to confirm cabinet-rank officials like the U.S. trade representative
   D. its oversight role over foreign policy
   E. the power of Congress to authorize expenditures

7. With the end of the Cold War, which of the following was NOT a concern of U.S. foreign policy?

   A. nuclear proliferation
   B. ethnic conflicts
   C. human rights in China
   D. the global environment
   E. the future of Berlin

8. The term *peace dividend* refers to

   A. the reductions in defense spending anticipated with the end of the Cold War
   B. the trade opportunities that will develop with the end of the crisis in the Middle East
   C. the prosperity that the United States experienced after World War II
   D. the benefits that veterans expected to receive after World War I
   E. the healing of divisions within the United States once the Vietnam War ended

9. *Unilateralism* refers to a nation relying on its own resources to achieve a foreign policy objective. Which of the following fits this definition?

   A.   Persian Gulf War
   B.   Korean War
   C.   NATO
   D.   Vietnam War
   E.   War in Kosovo

10. The U.S. commitment to defend the Persian Gulf against a threat from outside the region was the

   A.   Truman Doctrine
   B.   Carter Doctrine
   C.   Eisenhower Doctrine
   D.   Nixon Doctrine
   E.   Reagan Doctrine

11. Rejecting the interventionist policies of the past, the Carter Administration demonstrated a new approach to the Western Hemisphere through the

   A.   Good Neighbor Policy
   B.   Panama Canal Treaties
   C.   Alliance for Progress
   D.   Camp David Accords
   E.   North American Free Trade Agreement

12. An important reason behind the organizational changes in the U.S. military since the end of World War II is to

   A.   respond to the shift from a conscription to an all-volunteer army
   B.   better integrate minority groups and women into units
   C.   improve cooperation between the four branches of the service
   D.   make it easier to downsize with the end of the Vietnam War
   E.   utilize U.S. forces more effectively within NATO

13. When it comes to the exercise of presidential authority in foreign affairs, the Supreme Court

   A.   has no role to play
   B.   supports all attempts by Congress to limit the president's power
   C.   encourages U.S. participation in international organizations
   D.   recognizes that the president needs flexibility to implement policy
   E.   supports an end to civilian control over the armed forces

14. Congress has all the following responsibilities related to foreign/military policy EXCEPT:

   A.   to declare war on other countries
   B.   to appoint ambassadors to foreign countries and international organizations
   C.   to authorize expenditures by the military
   D.   to confirm the president's choice for secretary of state
   E.   to revive the draft through legislation

15. Which action by the Reagan Administration best expresses concern with the nuclear threat from the Soviet Union?

   A.   assistance to right-wing groups in Central America
   B.   the invasion of Grenada
   C.   support for the Strategic Defense Initiative
   D.   negotiation of the Intermediate-Range Nuclear Forces Treaty
   E.   commitment of troops to Lebanon

Answers

1. **A** This is a trick question. The key word is *civilian* rather than *military force strength.* If you miss the word *civilian,* you might well answer the chair of the Joint Chiefs of Staff, who was designated the official military advisor to the president under 1986 Department of Defense reorganization legislation.

2. **C** There is general consensus that the War Powers Act has not restricted the president's power to commit U.S. troops abroad to any meaningful degree. With the obvious exception of the wars in Iraq and Afghanistan, the military engagements that the United States has been involved in since the passage of the law have been brief; the Persian Gulf War is a case in point.

3. **E** The purpose of the containment policy was to limit the expansion of communism or the Soviet Union. The fact that the war ended in a stalemate with the armistice line essentially at the border that existed between North Korea and South Korea in 1950 meant that communist expansion had been contained.

4. **C** In comparison to the other regions listed, the United States has no long involvement with Africa, particularly sub-Saharan Africa. After World War II, the principal issue was the end of colonialism that involved the former European colonial powers, not the United States. President George W. Bush's efforts to curb AIDS and other diseases in Africa were well received; the administration had no success in limiting the violence in the Darfur region of Sudan.

5. **E** The SALT II Treaty is the only one of the choices that Congress did not ratify. The treaty, which the Carter Administration negotiated, went to the Senate after the Soviet Union invaded Afghanistan. Distrust of the U.S.S.R. was high at that time.

6. **B** Although Congress's oversight functions are not specifically provided for in the Constitution, all the possible answers are powers that Congress has. Confirmation of the U.S. trade representative is not relevant to the question. Fast-track authority requires Congress to simply vote a trade agreement up or down without amendment, which is seen as a serious limitation on the right of the Senate to ratify treaties.

7. **E** The status of Berlin was one of the most serious issues of the Cold War. When the Russians instituted a land blockade of Berlin in 1948, the United States responded with the Berlin Airlift. U.S. presidents, including Ronald Reagan, made the Berlin Wall, which was constructed in 1961, a symbol of the rift that separated East and West. When the Berlin Wall fell in 1989, the reunification of Germany quickly followed. The fate of the city was determined and was no longer an issue.

8. **A** Keep in mind that defense spending increased significantly during the first term of the Reagan Administration, and the inability of the Soviet Union to compete with that buildup was considered a factor in the end of the Cold War. Although the budget windfall that some expected never materialized, defense spending was cut during the 1990s.

9. **D** Although there were troops from other countries in Vietnam, most notably from Australia, the Vietnam War, both militarily and diplomatically, was a U.S. operation. NATO is obviously a multinational organization, and the other conflicts listed were either sanctioned by the United Nations and included a coalition of forces (the Korean War and the Persian Gulf War) or by NATO, again with a military coalition (Kosovo).

10. **B** This was President Carter's response to the invasion of Afghanistan by the Soviet Union in 1979, which he believed posed a genuine threat to other countries in the region—namely, India and Pakistan. The other choices are all policy statements associated either directly or indirectly with a particular administration:

    - Truman Doctrine (1947): U.S. commitment to aid countries threatened by "armed minorities" within their own country or outside pressure

    - Eisenhower Doctrine (1957): United States to aid any country in the Middle East threatened with communist aggression

    - Nixon Doctrine (1969): Policy of disengagement; nations threatened by aggression must provide for their own defense

    - Reagan Doctrine (1980–1988): Never formally adopted by the administration, but supported by conservatives; destabilization of governments that were communist or pro–Soviet Union

11. **B** The Panama Canal Treaties provided for turning over the operation of the Panama Canal and sovereignty over the canal to the Panamanians on December 31, 1999. With the exception of the Camp David Accords, all the other choices refer to noninterventionist policies affecting the Western Hemisphere. The Alliance for Progress (1961) was developed during the Kennedy Administration and provided for substantial economic assistance to countries through Central America and South America.

12. **C** Promoting greater interservice cooperation was a factor in consolidating the services into the Department of Defense in 1947. The 1986 reorganization of the department created seven regional commanders (commanders-in-chief) responsible for the military in their respective sectors, regardless of the branch of service involved.

13. **D** The handful of cases that have come to the Supreme Court that deal at all with foreign policy issues have a constitutional basis in the doctrine of the separation of powers. Here, the Court has been willing to recognize that the president has broader authority than the Constitution may specifically grant to him or her.

14. **B** Congress has no power to appoint ambassadors; the Senate has the power only to confirm ambassadors whom the president nominates.

15. **C** During his first term, President Reagan's foreign policy generally was affected by his views on the threat from the Soviet Union. The most serious threat that remained, as in the worst days of the Cold War, was a nuclear attack, and the response to that possibility was the Strategic Defense Initiative.

PART II

AP U.S. GOVERNMENT AND POLITICS PRACTICE TESTS

Practice Test 1

Answer Sheet

Remove this sheet and use it to mark your answers for the multiple-choice section of Practice Test 1.

1 Ⓐ Ⓑ Ⓒ Ⓓ Ⓔ	21 Ⓐ Ⓑ Ⓒ Ⓓ Ⓔ	41 Ⓐ Ⓑ Ⓒ Ⓓ Ⓔ
2 Ⓐ Ⓑ Ⓒ Ⓓ Ⓔ	22 Ⓐ Ⓑ Ⓒ Ⓓ Ⓔ	42 Ⓐ Ⓑ Ⓒ Ⓓ Ⓔ
3 Ⓐ Ⓑ Ⓒ Ⓓ Ⓔ	23 Ⓐ Ⓑ Ⓒ Ⓓ Ⓔ	43 Ⓐ Ⓑ Ⓒ Ⓓ Ⓔ
4 Ⓐ Ⓑ Ⓒ Ⓓ Ⓔ	24 Ⓐ Ⓑ Ⓒ Ⓓ Ⓔ	44 Ⓐ Ⓑ Ⓒ Ⓓ Ⓔ
5 Ⓐ Ⓑ Ⓒ Ⓓ Ⓔ	25 Ⓐ Ⓑ Ⓒ Ⓓ Ⓔ	45 Ⓐ Ⓑ Ⓒ Ⓓ Ⓔ
6 Ⓐ Ⓑ Ⓒ Ⓓ Ⓔ	26 Ⓐ Ⓑ Ⓒ Ⓓ Ⓔ	46 Ⓐ Ⓑ Ⓒ Ⓓ Ⓔ
7 Ⓐ Ⓑ Ⓒ Ⓓ Ⓔ	27 Ⓐ Ⓑ Ⓒ Ⓓ Ⓔ	47 Ⓐ Ⓑ Ⓒ Ⓓ Ⓔ
8 Ⓐ Ⓑ Ⓒ Ⓓ Ⓔ	28 Ⓐ Ⓑ Ⓒ Ⓓ Ⓔ	48 Ⓐ Ⓑ Ⓒ Ⓓ Ⓔ
9 Ⓐ Ⓑ Ⓒ Ⓓ Ⓔ	29 Ⓐ Ⓑ Ⓒ Ⓓ Ⓔ	49 Ⓐ Ⓑ Ⓒ Ⓓ Ⓔ
10 Ⓐ Ⓑ Ⓒ Ⓓ Ⓔ	30 Ⓐ Ⓑ Ⓒ Ⓓ Ⓔ	50 Ⓐ Ⓑ Ⓒ Ⓓ Ⓔ
11 Ⓐ Ⓑ Ⓒ Ⓓ Ⓔ	31 Ⓐ Ⓑ Ⓒ Ⓓ Ⓔ	51 Ⓐ Ⓑ Ⓒ Ⓓ Ⓔ
12 Ⓐ Ⓑ Ⓒ Ⓓ Ⓔ	32 Ⓐ Ⓑ Ⓒ Ⓓ Ⓔ	52 Ⓐ Ⓑ Ⓒ Ⓓ Ⓔ
13 Ⓐ Ⓑ Ⓒ Ⓓ Ⓔ	33 Ⓐ Ⓑ Ⓒ Ⓓ Ⓔ	53 Ⓐ Ⓑ Ⓒ Ⓓ Ⓔ
14 Ⓐ Ⓑ Ⓒ Ⓓ Ⓔ	34 Ⓐ Ⓑ Ⓒ Ⓓ Ⓔ	54 Ⓐ Ⓑ Ⓒ Ⓓ Ⓔ
15 Ⓐ Ⓑ Ⓒ Ⓓ Ⓔ	35 Ⓐ Ⓑ Ⓒ Ⓓ Ⓔ	55 Ⓐ Ⓑ Ⓒ Ⓓ Ⓔ
16 Ⓐ Ⓑ Ⓒ Ⓓ Ⓔ	36 Ⓐ Ⓑ Ⓒ Ⓓ Ⓔ	56 Ⓐ Ⓑ Ⓒ Ⓓ Ⓔ
17 Ⓐ Ⓑ Ⓒ Ⓓ Ⓔ	37 Ⓐ Ⓑ Ⓒ Ⓓ Ⓔ	57 Ⓐ Ⓑ Ⓒ Ⓓ Ⓔ
18 Ⓐ Ⓑ Ⓒ Ⓓ Ⓔ	38 Ⓐ Ⓑ Ⓒ Ⓓ Ⓔ	58 Ⓐ Ⓑ Ⓒ Ⓓ Ⓔ
19 Ⓐ Ⓑ Ⓒ Ⓓ Ⓔ	39 Ⓐ Ⓑ Ⓒ Ⓓ Ⓔ	59 Ⓐ Ⓑ Ⓒ Ⓓ Ⓔ
20 Ⓐ Ⓑ Ⓒ Ⓓ Ⓔ	40 Ⓐ Ⓑ Ⓒ Ⓓ Ⓔ	60 Ⓐ Ⓑ Ⓒ Ⓓ Ⓔ

Section 1: Multiple-Choice Questions

Time: 45 minutes
60 questions

Directions: Each of the questions or incomplete statements below is followed by five suggested answers or completions. Select the one that is best in each case, and then fill in the corresponding oval on the answer sheet.

1. Which of the following is a matter area that states are NOT responsible for?

   A. education
   B. police
   C. health
   D. interstate commerce
   E. taxation

2. Politicians are concerned about the "graying of America" because

   A. Older Americans do not contribute as much as they can to political campaigns.
   B. Older Americans are politically engaged and vote in high numbers.
   C. Older Americans are single-issue voters and care only about foreign policy.
   D. Older Americans are apathetic and don't bother to vote.
   E. Older Americans are not well organized politically compared to other groups.

3. The functions of the Senate include

   I. ratifying treaties
   II. approving presidential appointments
   III. oversight over federal agencies
   IV. introducing revenue bills

   A. I only
   B. II only
   C. I and II only
   D. I, II, and III only
   E. I, II, and IV only

4. All the following were methods used to deny African Americans the right to vote in the South EXCEPT

   A. poll tax
   B. grandfather clause
   C. requirement to register
   D. good-character test
   E. literacy test

5. A closed rule means that

   A. No amendments to a bill are allowed on the House floor.
   B. No amendments to a bill are allowed on the Senate floor.
   C. The bill can't be filibustered in the Senate.
   D. Unlimited debate on the bill is allowed.
   E. The House Committee on Rules took no action.

6. What is the concern that is often raised about an open primary?

   A. An open primary costs more to run than a closed primary.
   B. Cross-party voting allows one party to influence the nominee of the other party.
   C. The most ideologically committed party members vote in an open primary.
   D. An open primary requires a winner-take-all system.
   E. An open primary benefits third-party candidates.

7. Which of the following officials of the Congress is provided for in the Constitution?

   A. clerk of the House
   B. Senate majority leader
   C. House minority leader
   D. president pro tempore
   E. majority whip

8. The idea behind revenue sharing was to

   A. give the states greater control over the use of federal money.
   B. resolve the long-standing problem of unfunded mandates.
   C. allow the federal government to determine the specific needs of the states.
   D. decrease the amount of federal money available to the states.
   E. heighten support for the administration in upcoming elections.

Section I: Multiple-Choice Questions

Time: 45 minutes
60 questions

Directions: Each of the questions or incomplete statements below is followed by five suggested answers or completions. Select the one that is best in each case, and then fill in the corresponding oval on the answer sheet.

1. Which of the following is a policy area that states are NOT responsible for?

   A. education
   B. police
   C. health
   D. interstate commerce
   E. taxation

2. Politicians are concerned about the "graying of America" because

   A. Older Americans do not contribute as much as they can to political campaigns.
   B. Older Americans are politically engaged and vote in high numbers.
   C. Older Americans are single-issue voters and care only about foreign policy.
   D. Older Americans are apathetic and don't bother to vote.
   E. Older Americans are not well organized politically compared to other groups.

3. The functions of the Senate include

   I. ratifying treaties
   II. approving presidential appointments
   III. oversight over federal agencies
   IV. introducing revenue bills

   A. I only
   B. II only
   C. I and II only
   D. I, II, and III only
   E. I, II, and IV only

4. All the following were methods used to deny African Americans the right to vote in the South EXCEPT:

   A. poll tax
   B. grandfather clause
   C. requirement to register
   D. good-character test
   E. literacy test

5. A closed rule means that

   A. No amendments to a bill are allowed on the House floor.
   B. No amendments to a bill are allowed on the Senate floor.
   C. The bill can't be filibustered in the Senate.
   D. Unlimited debate on the bill is allowed.
   E. The House Committee on Rules took no action.

6. What is the concern that is often raised about an open primary?

   A. An open primary costs more to run than a closed primary.
   B. Cross-party voting allows one party to influence the nominee of the other party.
   C. The most ideologically committed party members vote in an open primary.
   D. An open primary requires a winner-take-all system.
   E. An open primary benefits third-party candidates.

7. Which of the following officials of the Congress is provided for in the Constitution?

   A. clerk of the house
   B. Senate majority leader
   C. House minority leader
   D. president pro tempore
   E. majority whip

8. The idea behind revenue sharing was to

   A. give the states greater control over the use of federal money
   B. resolve the long-standing problem of unfunded mandates
   C. allow the federal government to determine the specific needs of the states
   D. decrease the amount of federal money available to the states
   E. strengthen support for the administration in upcoming elections

9. Under the War Powers Act (1973), the president must

   A. get a joint resolution from Congress before sending U.S. troops into combat
   B. pay for the deployment of U.S. troops with funds already budgeted for the Department of Defense
   C. notify Congress if U.S. troops are under United Nations or NATO command
   D. receive approval from Congress to keep troops deployed for more than 60 days
   E. direct the Joint Chiefs of Staff to testify before Congress on the purpose of military operations

10. All the following are powers that Congress has over the federal courts EXCEPT:

    A. The Senate confirms nominees to the federal courts.
    B. Congress can change the jurisdiction of the federal courts through legislation.
    C. Congress can reduce the salaries paid to federal judges.
    D. A federal judge can be impeached by the House of Representatives.
    E. Congress can change the number of federal courts.

11. Which policy identifies President George W. Bush as a "compassionate conservative"?

    A. additional oil drilling in Alaska
    B. support for the Kyoto Protocol
    C. federal role in education
    D. increase in defense spending
    E. work requirements for welfare recipients

12. Under the Articles of Confederation, Congress had the power to

    A. impose taxes on the businesses involved in interstate trade
    B. amend the articles by a two-thirds vote
    C. select the executive authority
    D. settle disputes between two or more states
    E. impeach and remove from office a governor of a state

13. The responsibilities of the vice president in an administration are determined by

    A. the provisions of the Constitution
    B. the relationship with the president
    C. polls indicating the popularity of the vice president
    D. the size of the election victory
    E. which party is in control of Congress

14. Which of the following is LEAST likely to have an impact on political attitudes?

    A. race
    B. marital status
    C. gender
    D. education
    E. socioeconomic class

15. Civilian control over the military is based on

    A. legislation that created the Department of Defense
    B. an executive order issued by George Washington
    C. the fact that the president is commander-in-chief of the armed forces
    D. a Supreme Court decision written by Chief Justice John Marshall
    E. custom that dates back to British policy

2008 Presidential Primaries and Caucuses by Month

Month	Number of Primaries and Caucuses
January	8
February	37
March	7
April	2
May	7
June	4

Source: Federal Election Commission.

16. What conclusions can be drawn from the above data?

    A. Presidential campaigns have become longer.
    B. The cost of running for president has increased.
    C. The South has a disproportionate impact on determining presidential candidates.
    D. The nominees for both parties are likely determined before the primary season ends.
    E. The number of primaries is a disadvantage to third-party candidates.

17. The growth of the federal bureaucracy can be attributed to all the following EXCEPT:

    A. the need to regulate business
    B. responsibility of the government for the welfare of the people
    C. administrators who push for larger budgets and staff
    D. creation of new agencies to give policy a high profile
    E. Supreme Court decisions on federal-state relations

18. The Supreme Court's decision in *McCulloch v. Maryland* concerned which of the following issues?

    I. the right of the federal government to control interstate commerce
    II. the authority of a state to tax an agency of the federal government
    III. the right of the states to declare a federal law null and void
    IV. the right of the federal government to create the Bank of the United States under the Necessary and Proper Clause

    A. I and II only
    B. II only
    C. II and IV only
    D. I and III only
    E. IV only

19. The idea that parties are dangerous to political freedom is associated with

    A. Andrew Jackson
    B. James Madison
    C. Franklin Roosevelt
    D. Thomas Jefferson
    E. Abraham Lincoln

20. An example of unconventional political participation is

    A. writing a letter to an elected official
    B. blocking the entrance to an abortion clinic
    C. making "get out the vote" calls for a candidate
    D. contributing to a political campaign
    E. registering to vote for the Libertarian Party

21. The only organization outside the government that has played a direct role in the selection of federal judges is the

    A. AFL-CIO
    B. American Civil Liberties Union
    C. American Bar Association
    D. National Governors Association
    E. Association of Trial Lawyers of America

22. *The Literary Digest*'s prediction of the winner of the 1936 presidential election was wrong because

    A. Not enough people were included in its survey.
    B. Exit-poll data was used to determine the results.
    C. Most people surveyed actually did not vote.
    D. The survey questions were not clear.
    E. The survey sample was biased.

23. An example of a non-means-tested benefit program is

    A. COLAs
    B. Supplemental Security Income
    C. Medicaid
    D. food stamps
    E. Aid to Families with Dependent Children

24. President Bush stated during the 2000 campaign that he did not have a "litmus test" for the appointment of justices to the Supreme Court. This means:

    A. He would consider appointing a Democrat.
    B. He was interested in making the Court as diverse as possible.
    C. A nominee's previous judicial experience was important.
    D. He was looking for a loose constructionist.
    E. He would consider a nominee that may not share his views on controversial issues.

25. The Fourteenth Amendment effectively overturned which 19th-century Supreme Court decision?

    A. *Dred Scott v. Sanford*
    B. *Fletcher v. Peck*
    C. *Plessy v. Ferguson*
    D. *Barron v. Mayor of Baltimore*
    E. *The Civil Rights Cases*

26. The election of Ronald Reagan is not an example of party realignment because

    A. The Republicans were not able to hold onto the presidency in 1992.
    B. The Democratic Party remained strong in the South.
    C. The Republicans did not get control of both houses of Congress.
    D. Reagan's policies were not supported by the majority of Americans.
    E. The election victory in 1984 was smaller than it was in 1980.

27. The most important responsibility of a cabinet member is to

    A. provide advice to the president
    B. manage the department that he or she heads
    C. appoint staff to positions within the department
    D. work with the president's staff to develop policy
    E. testify before Congress on the department's budget

28. Which of the following is NOT an example of successful use of the media by a political figure?

    A. Nixon's 1952 Checkers speech
    B. Roosevelt's fireside chats
    C. Nixon's performance in the 1960 presidential debates
    D. Kennedy's news conferences
    E. Kennedy's performance in the 1960 presidential debates

29. Which of the following statements about the use of executive agreements in the conduct of foreign policy are valid?

    I. Executive agreements do not require the approval of the Senate.
    II. The president must disclose the terms of an executive agreement to Congress.
    III. Executive agreements are relied on much less frequently than formal treaties.
    IV. An executive agreement is only binding on the administration that negotiates it.

    A. I only
    B. I and II only
    C. I, II, and III only
    D. I, II, and IV only
    E. I, II, III, and IV

30. What is the main difference between political parties and interest groups?

    A. Interest groups are not concerned with the electoral process.
    B. Interest groups have more members than political parties.
    C. Interest groups are concerned with a limited range of issues.
    D. Only dues-paying members of an interest group benefit from its activities.
    E. Political parties don't rely on their members for financial support.

31. The individuals whom the president appoints to key positions in the executive branch

    A. are always members of the president's party
    B. have held jobs in both government and the private sector
    C. must be approved by party leaders
    D. have little experience in government
    E. must have held elective office at the state or federal level

32. Even a scientifically conducted telephone poll can include a sample bias because

    A. Many people refuse to participate in political surveys.
    B. A higher percentage of minority groups do not have telephones.
    C. People confuse pollsters with telephone solicitations.
    D. People prefer face-to-face interviews.
    E. Telephone interviewers don't go through rigorous training.

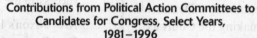

Contributions from Political Action Committees to Candidates for Congress, Select Years, 1981–1996

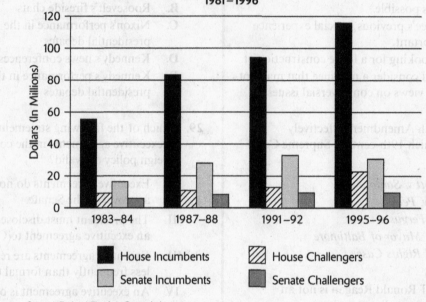

Source: Federal Election Commission.

33. Which of the conclusions is NOT supported by the graph above?

    A. Contributions from political action committees to congressional candidates have increased over the years.
    B. Candidates for House seats receive considerably more money than those running for the Senate.
    C. Contributions for the Senate are lower in non-presidential-election years.
    D. In both houses, incumbents receive more money than challengers.
    E. Since 1987–1988, the amount of money received by incumbent senators has remained relatively stable.

34. The Supreme Court is most likely to hear a case when

    A. two courts of appeals have ruled in different ways on the same issue
    B. directed to do so by the solicitor general of the United States
    C. the Congress indicates that the issue is important
    D. the president expresses an opinion on a matter on appeal
    E. the Court's calendar has an open date for oral argument

35. In recent years, delegates to the Democratic National Convention

   A. were more conservative than Democratic voters generally
   B. were more liberal than the electorate as a whole
   C. were strongly in favor of restrictions on immigration
   D. were less diverse as a group than delegates to the Republican National Convention
   E. were opposed to any reduction in defense spending

36. Federal agencies can't spend money unless

   A. the expenditure is approved by the Office of Management and Budget
   B. the president directly approves the funding
   C. the funds are authorized and appropriated by Congress
   D. the agency head explains to Congress how the money will be spent
   E. the agency has enacted a rule detailing the spending

37. Which of the following is the most regulated type of speech?

   A. political speech
   B. commercial speech
   C. hate speech
   D. symbolic speech
   E. religious speech

38. A reporter's refusal to turn over confidential information to the police

   A. is protected by freedom of the press
   B. was upheld by the Supreme Court
   C. is a violation of unreasonable search and seizure
   D. is protected in a limited way by state shield laws
   E. is sanctioned by legislation enacted by Congress

39. The Consumer Price Index is an important measure of

   A. employment
   B. interest rates
   C. inflation
   D. spending
   E. savings

40. Which of the following is an accurate characterization of an issue network?

   A. An issue network usually dissolves after the goal is achieved.
   B. An issue network includes fewer participants than an iron triangle.
   C. Issue networks only engage in outside lobbying.
   D. In an issue network, all the participants have political clout.
   E. Issue networks focus their activity on a single congressional committee.

41. All the following statements about the influence of constituents on the voting patterns of members of Congress are valid EXCEPT:

   A. Members who ignore their constituents' views on major issues are not reelected.
   B. Most of the votes that members of Congress make are irrelevant to constituents.
   C. A legislator who considers himself or herself a delegate is not concerned with the opinion of the voters.
   D. Members can try to gauge the views of their constituents through polls and questionnaires.
   E. A politico tries to balance constituent views with his or her own.

42. What do constitutional courts, with the exception of the Supreme Court, and legislative courts have in common?

   A. Both are mentioned in the Constitution.
   B. Both are created by legislation enacted by Congress.
   C. Judges in both serve for life.
   D. The jurisdiction of both types of courts is the same.
   E. Both deal only with cases under civil law.

43. Which of the following did NOT lead to a weakening of political machines?

   A. welfare state
   B. primary elections
   C. civil service reform
   D. public opinion polls
   E. secret ballot

44. The idea that the media acts as a scorekeeper in covering political campaigns is associated with what type of journalism?

    A. muckraking
    B. horse-race journalism
    C. investigative reporting
    D. yellow journalism
    E. tabloid journalism

45. If the case of a poor criminal defendant is granted a writ of certiorari, the Supreme Court

    A. asks an interest group like the ACLU to represent the individual
    B. allows the defendant to give the oral argument
    C. appoints an attorney to handle the case
    D. still requires all fees and costs to be paid
    E. asks the Department of Justice to provide counsel

46. Which of the following statements is an accurate characterization of the federal bureaucracy?

    A. The president appoints a majority of the staff of the federal agencies.
    B. The number of federal employees has grown steadily since World War II.
    C. It is easy to fire a federal bureaucrat under the civil service rules.
    D. Half of all federal jobs are based on a competitive merit process.
    E. Individuals appointed by the president are completely independent from the White House.

47. Attempts to ensure minority representation by relying on race as the key factor in drawing congressional district lines are

    A. legal under the Voting Rights Act of 1965
    B. permissible under affirmative action guidelines set by the Federal Election Commission
    C. allowed only to remedy obvious instances of past discrimination
    D. the responsibility of the states and cannot be challenged in the federal courts
    E. unconstitutional under a ruling of the Supreme Court

48. What happens to representation in Congress as the population increases?

    A. The total number of representatives in Congress goes up.
    B. The number of people each member of Congress represents increases.
    C. States with a large population will continue to gain seats in Congress.
    D. States will be forced to abandon single-member districts.
    E. A constitutional amendment providing for term limits will be enacted.

49. The "Don't Ask, Don't Tell" policy initiated by President Clinton refers to

    A. the sex scandals that plagued his two terms
    B. the administration's response to the impeachment proceedings
    C. the campaign contributions received from foreign nationals
    D. the treatment of homosexuals in the armed forces
    E. the Office of Management and Budget's response to the budget impasse in 1993

50. The programs of the Great Society, which included the War on Poverty and Medicare, were adopted in the 1960s primarily because

    A. The Democratic Party gained control of Congress in 1964.
    B. Active lobbying by the urban poor and senior citizens was successful.
    C. Strong presidential leadership was provided by Lyndon Johnson.
    D. Supreme Court decisions supported an expanded federal role on social issues.
    E. The administration needed to divert public attention from the Vietnam War.

CPS Turnout Rates by Race/Ethnicity

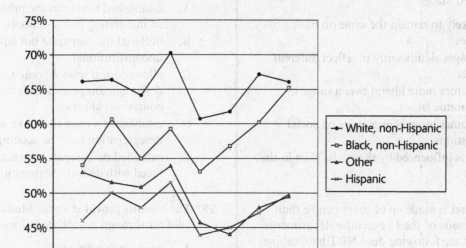

Source: United States Election Project: 2008 Current Population Survey Voting and Registration Supplement.
http://elections.gmu.edu/CPS_2008.html.

51. Based on the above graph, which of the following is NOT valid?

   A. White voter turnout declined in 2008.
   B. All racial/ethnic groups showed an increase in turnout in 2008 as compared to 2004.
   C. The most dramatic increase in turnout in 2008 was among African-American voters.
   D. Hispanic and Asian-American turnout was about the same in 2008.
   E. Whites historically have the highest voter turnout rates.

52. Although it is well established that obscene materials are not protected under the First Amendment, the problem the Supreme Court has faced is

   A. establishing community standards
   B. preventing the publication of such materials
   C. defining what obscenity is
   D. closing establishments that distribute such materials near schools
   E. expanding rulings on obscenity to include violence

53. A whistleblower is

   A. a member of Congress who does not vote with his or her party
   B. a presidential aide who leaks a story to the press
   C. the head of a federal agency who asks for additional funding
   D. a bureaucrat who informs the public about waste in the government
   E. a union leader who accepts a management settlement offer

54. All the following statements about presidential popularity are true EXCEPT:

   A. A president's popularity is highest right after the inauguration.
   B. A president's popularity generally declines over his or her term.
   C. World events have little impact on a president's standing with the public.
   D. A strong economy leads to an increase in the president's approval rating.
   E. A president's popularity does not necessarily translate into success for his or her party.

55. Looking over the long term, public opinion in the United States

   A. is likely to remain the same on basic policy issues
   B. changes significantly to reflect different times
   C. becomes more liberal over a range of economic issues
   D. becomes more conservative on social questions
   E. is less influenced by the media than in the past

56. The cabinet is made up of more people than just the heads of the 15 executive departments. Which of the following does NOT have cabinet rank?

   A. director of the Central Intelligence Agency
   B. U.S. trade representative
   C. director of the Office of Management and Budget
   D. administrator of the Environmental Protection Agency
   E. vice president

57. In order to be considered a member of a political party, a person must

   A. make a contribution to the party as a form of membership dues
   B. register to vote with the party
   C. serve on the party's county committee
   D. volunteer for a local party campaign
   E. vote for candidates of the party

58. In *Brown II* (1955), the Supreme Court

   A. established busing as the principal means of integrating public schools
   B. declared the "separate but equal" doctrine unconstitutional
   C. allowed local school boards to develop desegregation plans that federal district courts would review
   D. established a rigid timetable within which desegregation must be accomplished
   E. extended desegregation to school districts faced with de facto segregation

59. The benefits provided under Medicare that are paid for through payroll taxes include

   A. prescription drugs
   B. regular physician visits
   C. hospitalization
   D. diagnostic tests
   E. dental care

60. An example of the activity of an intergovernmental lobby is

   A. seeking an increase in foreign aid to a particular country
   B. pressing Congress for limits on unfunded mandates
   C. contacting the House Budget Committee about additional funding for a federal agency
   D. speaking to the White House staff about an upcoming appointment to the Supreme Court
   E. testifying before the Senate Appropriations Committee on a new Navy ship

IF YOU FINISH BEFORE TIME IS CALLED, CHECK YOUR WORK ON THIS SECTION ONLY. DO NOT WORK ON ANY OTHER SECTION IN THE TEST.

Section II: Free-Response Questions

Time: 100 minutes

4 questions

Directions: You have 100 minutes to answer all four of the following questions. Unless the directions indicate otherwise, respond to all parts of all four questions. It is suggested that you take a few minutes to plan and outline each answer. Spend approximately one-fourth of your time (25 minutes) on each question. Illustrate your essay with substantive examples where appropriate. Be sure to number each answer in the same way the question is numbered below.

1. From the Constitutional Convention through the 2000 election, Americans have debated the proper relationship between the states and the federal government.

   a. Describe two models or theories of federalism.
   b. Discuss two advantages and two disadvantages of federalism.

2. The graphs below show the amount of money raised by the Democratic and Republican parties from the 1992 election cycle through the 2000 election cycle.

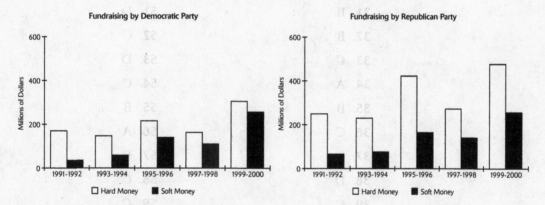

Using this information and your knowledge of recent U.S. politics, do the following:

   a. Identify two trends that the graphs show.
   b. Define hard money and soft money, and how each is used.
   c. Discuss how recent changes in campaign finance law are likely to impact party fundraising.

3. The legislative process takes place inside and outside of Congress. Explain the role of each of the following in enacting legislation:

   a. committee system
   b. interest groups
   c. the president

4. Although relations between the media and the government are often called adversarial, the two institutions actually have a symbiotic relationship. Describe how their relationship is symbiotic, and provide two examples for the media and two examples for the government that demonstrate their relationship.

IF YOU FINISH BEFORE TIME IS CALLED, CHECK YOUR WORK ON THIS SECTION ONLY. DO NOT WORK ON ANY OTHER SECTION IN THE TEST.

Answer Key

Section I: Multiple-Choice Questions

1. D	21. C	41. C
2. B	22. E	42. B
3. D	23. A	43. D
4. C	24. E	44. B
5. A	25. A	45. C
6. B	26. C	46. D
7. D	27. B	47. E
8. A	28. C	48. B
9. D	29. D	49. D
10. C	30. C	50. C
11. C	31. B	51. D
12. D	32. B	52. C
13. B	33. C	53. D
14. B	34. A	54. C
15. C	35. B	55. B
16. D	36. C	56. A
17. E	37. B	57. B
18. C	38. D	58. C
19. B	39. C	59. C
20. B	40. A	60. B

Section II: Free-Response Questions

Student essays and analyses begin on page 198.

Answer Explanations

Section I: Multiple-Choice Questions

1. **D** This is a question about federalism. Health and taxation are concurrent powers of both the federal government and the states; education and police are largely the responsibility of the states and local government. Interstate commerce is specifically a federal responsibility under the Constitution.

2. **B** Voter turnout is consistently high for older Americans, and they have a very effective lobby—the AARP, which claims to represent all Americans over 50. If they're single-issue voters, that issue is certainly not foreign policy. As a group, they're concerned with the solvency of Social Security and Medicare and the related problem of prescription drugs.

3. **D** Choices I and II are powers specific to the Senate; both the House and the Senate, through standing and select committees, play an oversight role. Revenue bills, on the other hand, must be introduced in the House under the Constitution.

4. **C** The requirement to register to be eligible to vote was not a method of restricting the voting rights of African Americans; all the other choices were. The good-character test required that African Americans get two or more registered voters to vouch for them.

5. **A** The student should know that only the House of Representatives has a Committee on Rules; the term *closed rule* can apply only to actions in the House. This eliminates answers **B** and **C**. Only the Senate has unlimited debate, and it is clear that the House Committee on Rules did take action by issuing a closed rule.

6. **B** The concern is that activists from the other party will try "to do mischief"—in other words, vote for the weakest candidate in the primary field so that their candidate will have a better choice. However, it's extremely difficult, if not impossible to organize such an effort.

7. **D** The only officers of Congress mentioned in the Constitution are the Speaker of the House, the president of the Senate, and the president pro tempore. The majority and minority leaders, along with the whip, reflect the organization of Congress along party lines that were not envisioned by the framers of the Constitution. The position of clerk of the House was created under the House rules.

8. **A** The basic premise behind revenue sharing was that the states knew best how to most effectively use federal dollars; it also reflected a belief that the federal government had become too powerful, and it was time for power to flow from Washington to the states and not the other way around.

9. **D** The War Powers Act has two main provisions: (1) The president must consult with Congress before committing U.S. troops to likely combat situations overseas and must formally notify Congress of such a mission within 48 hours, and (2) troops must be brought home within 60 days unless the United States declares war or Congress approves and extends the mission deadline.

10. **C** Article III of the Constitution specifically provides that the salaries of federal judges cannot be reduced. The purpose behind this provision is to protect the independence of the courts from political influence. Naturally, Congress can increase the salary of the judges (and it has done so on several occasions).

11. **C** All the other policies are fully consistent with a conservative agenda. Liberals, for example, oppose additional drilling in Alaska because, for them, environmental concerns outweigh the possible energy benefits. Conservatives, on the other hand, focus the argument on greater independence for overseas sources of energy. Federal support for education was long a Democratic position; conservative Republicans like Ronald Reagan, for example, even considered abolishing the Department of Education. President George W. Bush, on the other hand, increased the federal role considerably with the No Child Left Behind Act (2002).

12. **D** Among the enumerated powers granted to Congress under the articles was the authority to resolve disputes among the states as a sort of "court of last resort." All the other choices are clearly powers Congress did not have—there was no executive authority, Congress did not have the power to tax, amending the articles required a unanimous vote of the states, and the governors were sometimes responsible to the state legislatures but not the Congress.

13. **B** The actual responsibilities of the vice president are determined by the president. Keep in mind that the vice president's constitutional functions are limited—president of the Senate who only votes in the event of a tie, next in line to the president, and a role in determining the president's ability to serve under the Twenty-fifth Amendment. In recent years, vice presidents have been given important jobs within the administration and have been close advisors to the president. This is certainly the case with Bill Clinton and Al Gore and George Bush and Dick Cheney.

14. **B** All the other choices are important elements in the process of political socialization. A person's overall political attitude is unlikely to change, for example, simply because he gets a divorce. Certain issues—such as taxation, child support, and child care—may be viewed differently.

15. **C** The provision is clearly stated in the first draft of the Constitution and in the Constitution as enacted. None of the other choices is even remotely possible.

16. **D** The chart clearly shows the results of frontloading—states moving primary elections and/or caucuses to early in the election year so that they can have a say in the selection process. It's clear from the number of primaries and caucuses in February that most of the delegates were chosen by the early spring.

17. **E** It is difficult to see how decisions of the Supreme Court could affect the size of the bureaucracy. All the other choices, particularly the role of the "ambitious administrator," are factors. For example, the abuses of the railroads in the late 19th century led to the creation of the Interstate Commerce Commission (1887), while the government's responsibility to protect the health and welfare of the public saw the formation of the Food and Drug Administration.

18. **C** The Supreme Court made it clear that the establishment of the Bank of the United States was a legitimate function of the government under the Elastic Clause and that the states could not tax federal institutions—"The power to tax is the power to destroy." The issue of interstate commerce is addressed in *Gibbons v. Ogden.*

19. **B** James Madison presented a clear argument in *Federalist No. 10* that what he called "factions" were dangerous to freedom and stable government.

20. **B** Unconventional participation in politics is an action that is outside or a challenge to established institutions; civil disobedience qualifies as unconventional participation. The only choice that fits this definition is **B**. All the other choices are examples of conventional political participation.

21. **C** The American Bar Association's Standing Committee on the Federal Judiciary has been responsible for ranking candidates for the federal courts. Candidates are rated as Well Qualified, Qualified, or Not Qualified.

22. **E** *The Literary Digest* poll had a very large sample; the problem was that the names were drawn from automobile registrations and telephone directories. In the midst of the Depression, those sources skewed the poll in favor of wealthy Americans who were more likely to vote for the Republican candidate. In addition, the survey was done relatively early in the fall campaign.

23. **A** A COLA is a cost of living adjustment that is attached to federal benefit programs to take into account the impact of inflation. While the program that has a COLA may be means tested, the COLA itself is not. All beneficiaries receive it.

24. **E** Voters may apply a litmus test to candidates, or a litmus test may be applied to judicial appointments. In either case, it means the same. A person will vote for a candidate or a president will appoint a judge if that person takes the correct position on an issue like abortion. Bush indicated that he would not necessarily use abortion as a litmus test, but he would support judges who took a strict constructionist view of the Constitution.

25. **A** *Dred Scott v. Sanford* (1857) is the famous Dred Scott case. The key ruling by Chief Justice Taney was that Scott, as an African American, was not a citizen of the United States and, therefore, did not have standing to bring suit in the federal courts. Under the definition in the Fourteenth Amendment, Scott was, indeed, a citizen since he was born in the United States.

26. **C** While Reagan's victory in 1980 was significant, a strong case can be made that it was more a vote against Carter than for the conservative Republican Party that he represented. Comparing 1980 to 1932, it is

significant that Reagan's coattails were not long enough for the Republicans to gain control of both houses of Congress; the party did win the Senate, however.

27. **B** Although the president will turn to members of the cabinet for advice in their area of policy expertise, the basic responsibility of the cabinet secretaries is to manage what are, in fact, very large bureaucracies.

28. **C** There was a general consensus among people who watched the first televised presidential debate in 1960 that Kennedy won the debate in part because he looked better on the screen. Nixon's Checkers speech was a masterful use of the media not because of how he looked (there was no one to compare him with), but because of what he said; the speech allowed him to stay on the ticket as Eisenhower's vice president. Kennedy had a very good relationship with the press, which is seen very clearly in his press conferences, and Franklin Roosevelt's fireside chats on radio during the Depression were critical to explaining his policies to the American people.

29. **D** The fact is that executive agreements are much more common than treaties. During the Clinton Administration, executive agreements outnumbered treaties by a ratio of ten to one. In 1995, for example, Clinton used an executive agreement for a $20 billion loan to Mexico.

30. **C** Interest groups, even those that are broadly based or are committed to public interest questions, still focus on a rather narrow range of issues—the elderly (AARP), women's rights (NOW), or the status of minorities (NAACP). As a glance at either the Democratic or Republican platform will show, parties take positions on a variety of issues. Interest groups, through their political action committees, certainly participate in the electoral process; you don't have to pay dues to an interest group to benefit from its activities. This is the free-rider problem.

31. **B** The typical presidential appointee has served in government before and has had a career in the private sector. This includes, but does not exclude, close associates who worked on the campaign. Important campaign staff usually stay with the president and take jobs in the West Wing of the White House. Presidents often appoint members of the opposite party to posts within their administration in a show of bipartisanship. President George W. Bush appointed Democrat Norman Mineta as secretary of transportation and President Obama named Republican Congressman Ray LaHood to the same post.

32. **B** This should be an obvious answer. The fact that people will refuse to participate in a survey does not create a sample bias. Techniques such as random-digit dialing will ensure that an adequate number of people are in the survey, which is the only way a hang-up can have an impact.

33. **C** The table, in fact, charts presidential election-year cycles; there is no data presented on off-year elections.

34. **A** The Supreme Court, unlike the U.S. Courts of Appeals, has discretion on those cases it hears on appeal. You should be able to rule out **B**, **C**, and **D** because these all challenge the concept of the separation of powers and suggest a degree of influence by the other branches of government that does not exist. Choice **E** seems like a silly reason to hear a case. The other substantive answer is **A**.

35. **B** Delegates to a party's national convention typically are the most active and ideologically committed. Democratic delegates would be very liberal and Republican delegates would be very conservative. The two policy positions listed are, in fact, better identified with the Republican Party, and since the reforms in the wake of the 1968 convention, the Democratic Party has stressed bringing to the convention younger party activists, minorities, and women.

36. **C** Authorization (done through standing committees) and appropriation (done through the House and Senate appropriations committees) are two fundamental responsibilities of Congress. Agency heads routinely testify before Congress as part of the process. Once the funds are authorized and appropriated, no further action by the president or the Office of Management and Budget (OMB) is necessary. Any approvals by the OMB are given as part of the process of developing the administration's budget proposal.

37. **B** It is generally recognized that commercial speech receives less protection under the First Amendment than other types of speech, including those listed as the other possible choices. Commercial speech is largely regulated by the Federal Trade Commission, which is responsible for seeing that commercial advertising is not false and misleading. In recent years, the Supreme Court has moved toward greater protection of commercial speech. The basic rule emerging is that truthful advertising about a lawful product, service, or activity is protected.

38. **D** A reporter does not have an absolute right not to disclose information collected for a story. A state shield law does not prevent a judge from issuing a subpoena for information in every instance, nor is that subpoena always squashed because of the shield law. The Supreme Court has ruled that a defendant's right to a fair trial outweighs a reporter's right to keep sources confidential.

39. **C** The Consumer Price Index (CPI) is a measure of the average change in the prices of a "market basket" of goods and services over time. It is published by the Bureau of Labor Statistics and covers such items as food, clothing, shelter, fuel, transportation fares, dental and medical expenses, and prescriptions.

40. **A** Issue networks are much more broadly based than the traditional iron triangle and may include individuals far removed from the political process—academics, for example. While an iron triangle maintains its relationship over the long term, an issue network is often informally created just to get a particular piece of legislation passed or a new rule adopted, and it dissolves once the goal is achieved.

41. **C** This question addresses how a member of Congress views her relationship with constituents. A delegate takes the views of constituents to heart and tries to reflect those views through voting; a trustee, on the other hand, is more independent and relies on his or her judgment about what is good for the district and the nation.

42. **B** The only similarity is that both legislative courts and constitutional courts are created by acts of Congress—legislative courts under the authority granted by Article I and constitutional courts under Article III. Federal courts below the Supreme Court were established by the Judiciary Act of 1789. The crucial difference is that judges who sit on legislative courts serve for a fixed term. Their jurisdictions vary considerably, and both courts deal with civil and criminal matters.

43. **D** The secret ballot and the primary elections took some of the political power from the machine; primaries allowed reformers within a party to challenge the candidates hand-picked by the machine. The rise of the welfare state and the civil service undermined both the social services and the patronage system that the political machine often relied on to keep itself in power.

44. **B** Horse-race journalism focuses on which candidate is ahead rather than the issues the candidates are trying to address. Muckraking and investigative reporting and yellow journalism and tabloid journalism are clearly related to each other, but they don't have anything to do with the scorekeeper concept.

45. **C** When petitions to hear a case are submitted to the Supreme Court *in forma pauperis,* the Court will appoint an attorney. In the landmark *Gideon v. Wainwright* (1963), which dealt with the right of an indigent defendant to counsel, the Court appointed well-known Washington attorney Abe Fortas, who was subsequently appointed to the Court himself.

46. **D** In fact, civil service rules make it a very difficult and time-consuming process to fire a member of the federal civil service. The president appoints a very small fraction of the personnel in the executive branch, and the size of the federal government has remained relatively stable since the end of World War II. Those whom the president does appoint are expected, in most instances, to follow and support administration policy.

47. **E** The key case is *Shaw v. Reno* (1993), where the Supreme Court dealt with the creation of a strangely shaped congressional district in North Carolina that was created to elect an African American to the seat. This was a clear case of racial gerrymandering; the Court noted that race was the sole criteria used, and more traditional guidelines in redistricting such as compactness were ignored.

48. **B** Following the 2000 census, each member of Congress represents 650,000 to 700,000 people. This number will go up as the population grows. The total number of members of Congress is fixed at 435 through the Reapportionment Act of 1929. The only way that number can go up is if Congress increases the ceiling, which is a possibility in the long term. New York is a state with a large population that has lost seats in Congress recently because the number of people living in the state declined from one census to another.

49. **D** In 1992, Clinton made a campaign promise for a more open policy with regard to homosexuals in the military. At the time, homosexuality was grounds for immediate dismissal from the armed services. Opposition from all branches of the service to any significant change was strong, causing a major political problem for the administration early in its first term. The compromise that was ultimately worked out was "Don't Ask, Don't Tell." This meant that the military could not inquire into a person's sexual preference

and military personnel were not allowed to say anything about their sexual orientation. The policy has not prevented the dismissal of gay men and women from the military.

50. **C** The Great Society was Lyndon Johnson's program, and it harked back to the New Deal of the Roosevelt Administration where Johnson had begun his career. The president believed that he could fight the Vietnam War and provided the spending required by the Great Society; many of the programs were begun before opposition to the war became strong.

51. **D** While the "Other" category likely includes Asian Americans, it might include other minorities as well (Native Americans, for example). The conclusion that Asian Americans and Hispanic Americans had the same voter turnout can't be supported by the graph.

52. **C** Justice Stewart Potter raised the problem of defining what is and what is not obscene in his famous concurring opinion in *Jacobellis v. Ohio* (1964), in which he said, "I know it when I see it."

53. **D** A whistleblower is someone in government who reports waste, fraud, or other improper or illegal activity. In the past, such individuals often lost their jobs when they came forward about a serious problem. The Whistleblower Protection Act protects federal employees against retaliation. They can seek protection from the Office of Special Counsel and the Merit Systems Protection Board, which can order reinstatement, reversal of suspensions, disciplinary action against supervisors, and reimbursement for legal fees, medical costs, and other damages. Protections for public officials were somewhat limited by the Supreme Court's decision in *Garcetti v. Ceballos* (2006); here, the Court held that speech by a public official is not protected when made in the context of official duties. Congress is considering legislation to strengthen protections through the Whistleblower Protection Enhancement Act.

54. **C** As both President George H. W. Bush (Persian Gulf War) and President George W. Bush (September 11, 2001) came to know very well, a president's popularity and approval ratings soar during an international crisis. With President George H. W. Bush, those high marks proved fleeting in the face of a worsening economy.

55. **B** This is really a common sense question. Clearly, public opinion changes over time and in dramatic ways. Attitudes toward African Americans and civil rights issues generally are much different today from what they were 50 years ago. During the Vietnam War, opinion shifted gradually from strong support for U.S. policy to demands that the United States withdraw as quickly as possible.

56. **A** Although the director of the Central Intelligence Agency is certainly invited to cabinet meetings and is a full member of the National Security Council, the position does not have cabinet rank. Giving a non-executive-department head cabinet rank is a sign of how important the administration views that particular policy area.

57. **B** Although a case can be made that just voting for a party makes you a member of that party, it probably is not a strong enough commitment. Do you have to vote for all the candidates of that party in every election? Registering to vote with a particular party is obviously a clear statement of support. Saying you're a registered Democrat is more of a sign of membership than saying you usually vote Democratic.

58. **C** The issue in the 1954 *Brown* decision was that it struck down the "separate but equal" doctrine but did not provide any guidance on the implementation of that ruling. *Brown II* addressed implementation. The Court specifically did not issue a definite timetable, but it urged instead that desegregation be accomplished "with all deliberate speed."

59. **C** Although additional coverage for tests and doctor visits is available for an additional fee, and most of those eligible for Medicare take advantage of that option, basic coverage is limited in light of the choices given here to hospitalization.

60. **B** An intergovernmental lobby represents states and local governments (cities and counties), as well as various employee groups that fall within those levels of government (for example, chiefs of police). Given what an intergovernmental lobby represents, the only issue that they would really be interested in is unfunded mandates—in other words, where a law or regulation requires states and municipalities to take some action, but no federal money is provided to pay for that action.

Section II: Free-Response Questions

Question 1

Scoring Guidelines

Part (a): 4 points (2 points for each model discussed)

Part (b): 4 points (2 points for each advantage and 2 points for each disadvantage)

Total: 8 points

Models/theories of federalism

- Dual federalism
- Cooperative federalism
- Fiscal federalism
- Creative federalism
- New Federalism

Advantages of federalism

- Encourages greater political participation
- Allows for greater access to government
- Promotes policy innovation
- Encourages policy diversity

Disadvantages of federalism

- Fragments U.S. politics (works against greater participation)
- Promotes inequity
- Challenges the national majority

Sample Answer

Over the last 200-plus years, both politicians and political scientists have come up with models that claim to explain the relationship between the states and the federal government. Two such models are dual federalism, which was popular throughout the 19th century and up to the beginning of the New Deal, and creative federalism, which is associated with the policies of President Lyndon Johnson.

Under dual federalism, the states and the federal government are each supreme in its own sphere. Because of this rigid separation, dual federalism is often compared to a layer cake. The relationship between the two spheres in this model is characterized by tension—the states try to protect areas of policy that they consider their own from federal intrusion. Dual federalism, which emphasizes the importance of the Tenth Amendment and downplays the Elastic Clause, fit well with states' rights arguments on issues such as nullification and slavery in the decades before the Civil War and the desegregation of public schools in the mid-20th century.

Creative federalism significantly increased the power of the federal government at the expense of the states. Not only did it give priority to programs that Washington thought important, but it was based on the belief that the states had long demonstrated an unwillingness or inability to tackle these problems—assistance to the poor, urban renewal, and minorities. President Johnson's Great Society provided federal money directly to the cities (Model Cities) or to local nongovernmental agencies, intentionally bypassing state legislatures and/or municipalities completely. States were sometimes made responsible for implementing federal programs such as Medicaid, but they had little or no say in whether this type of spending best met their needs. An important consequence of creative federalism was that the states became more and more dependent on federal funding for social programs. The Washington-knows-best premise of the Johnson era led to a reaction under Richard Nixon—the so-called New Federalism, which gave states much greater freedom in determining how best to use available federal dollars.

Federalism is not a perfect political system; there are both advantages and disadvantages. On the plus side, the fact there are multiple levels of government allows policies to be pursued at the local, state, or national level, whichever offers the best opportunity for success. Mothers Against Drunk Driving, for example, would have had to mount lobbying efforts in numerous states to get the national drinking age raised to 21; it was more effective for them to turn to Congress. Federalism also allows greater participation in politics. Not only do Americans have the opportunity to vote for national and state leaders, but they can vote for representatives to the city council, the school board, and even the county party committee. The system also makes it easier for people to become more involved by volunteering for a local campaign or running for office. At the same time, there is a downside. The sheer number of government units—there are almost 90,000 nationwide at the local level—makes government very confusing. Instead of encouraging political participation, federalism may well have the opposite effect. The fact is, for example, that voter turnout is often much lower in local elections than it is in state and federal elections.

Reader Commentary

The student starts out strong but ends weak. The descriptions of dual federalism and creative federalism are sound, although the examples that the student gives for each could have been fleshed out a little better. It is note-worthy that the student did not just compare dual and cooperative federalism, which is the approach taken in most textbooks; the student also commented on the reaction that sets in with the Nixon Administration. The answer to part (b) gives the impression that time was a factor. The student didn't mention a second disadvantage at all, and the examples for the multiple levels of government could have been clearer. What is the impact of frag-mented government? If the student had used the civil rights movement in the example—for example, civil rights was pressed in the federal courts and Congress as opposed to state legislatures in the South—it may have been easier to discuss a disadvantage of federalism where the states can block or delay national policy priorities. Again, civil rights is a good example here. Score = 5.

Question 2

Scoring Guidelines

Part (a): 2 points (1 point for each trend identified)

Part (b): 2 points (1 point for each definition)

Part (c): 4 points

Total: 8 points

Trends on graph

- Republicans raise more money than Democrats.
- The amount of soft money raised has increased.
- Soft money as a percentage of total raised has increased.
- The total amount of money raised by both parties has increased.

Definitions

- **Hard money** is regulated under campaign-finance law; it is used in a candidate's campaign for advertising.
- **Soft money** is not subject to campaign-finance laws; it is used for "party building" and issue ads.

Changes in campaign finance law

- Must focus on Bipartisan Campaign Finance Reform Act.

Sample Answer

The graph on fundraising by the Republican and Democratic parties shows several clear trends. First, the Republicans are able to raise considerably more money than the Democrats over the years. This is due less to the fact that supporters of the Republicans have more money than to the party's highly computerized system of tracking donors both large and small. The second obvious trend is the growing importance of soft money for both parties. Indeed, it was the growth of soft money that led to demands for campaign finance reform.

Hard money is the money raised under the limitations of existing campaign finance law and is regulated by the Federal Election Commission (FEC). Before the enactment of the Bipartisan Campaign Finance Reform Act (discussed below), individuals could contribute a maximum of $1,000 per election to candidates for federal office (Congress or the presidency) and political action committees, representing corporations, unions, or other interest groups, could contribute a maximum of $5,000 to a candidate.

Both individuals and PACs can make regulated contributions to the national party. In addition to donation limits, there are disclosure requirements that must be followed. Hard money is used directly by the candidate for advertising, as well as campaign expenses including staff salaries, travel, and polling. Changes in the Federal Election Campaign Act in 1979 allowed political parties to raise money for what were called "party-building activities" such as voter registration and "get out the vote" drives; the money raised for this purpose was called soft money because there were no limits on the amounts that could be raised and the fundraising was effectively unregulated. While soft money was not supposed to be used to directly influence federal election campaigns, it was used to run issue ads that clearly supported one candidate over another.

The tremendous growth in the amount of soft money raised between the 1996 and 2000 elections and allegations of fundraising abuses in 1996, led to demands for a major overhaul of campaign financing. The focus of the debate was on soft money, and in the spring of 2002, Congress passed and the president signed legislation to address this and related issues. The new law, which did not go into effect until after the 2002 midterm elections, was the Bipartisan Campaign Finance Reform Act.

Under the act, soft money is banned completely. Not surprisingly, both parties significantly increased the use of soft money in the 2002 midterm elections when the control of Congress was up for grabs. The soft money ban did not apply to those campaigns. While the limitations on the amount of money that PACs could contribute remained unchanged, limits on individual contributions were increased for both donations to candidates and to national parties; the maximum amount an individual candidate can receive is $2,000 per election (primary and general election). The increase in individual contributions was meant to offset the loss of soft money.

The most controversial part of the law was the limit on advertising for a specific candidate by corporations, trade associations, and labor unions toward the end of a primary or general election campaign. This provision was challenged in the courts on First Amendment grounds. The Supreme Court ruled in *Federal Election Commission v. Wisconsin Right to Life, Inc.* (2006) that the issue ads in question were protected as political speech. In light of the data from the graph, it seems likely that the Republicans may benefit from these changes more than the Democrats will. The Republican Party has shown an ability to raise considerably more money within the current limits on individual contributions; it is certain that they will encourage their supporters to support the party right up to the higher limits established by the 2002 law.

Reader Commentary

This is a very good essay. The focus on Republican fundraising success and soft money in the brief discussion of the data is brought up again in the body of the essay. The definitions of hard and soft money are succinct, and there is a good transition to the third part of the question. The Bipartisan Campaign Finance Reform Act is summarized quite well; the student could have gone into the limitations on campaign advertising in more depth, but this is a complicated part of the legislation and time must be considered. The two points made on the influence of the legislation are well taken—the bill did not have an effect on soft money in the 2002 election because of the stakes involved, and Republican fundraising success makes the party better able to increase hard money to make up for the loss of soft money. Bringing in the Supreme Court decision in *Federal Election Commission v. Wisconsin Right to Life, Inc.,* was helpful as well. Score = 8.

Question 3

Scoring Guidelines

Total: 6 points (2 points for each explanation—at least two roles must be discussed for each)

Committee system

- Legislative gatekeeper
- Amend bills
- Report bills
- House Committee on Rules
- Conference committee

Interest groups

- Draft legislation
- Provide information
- Develop strategy
- Iron triangles/issue networks

President

- Propose legislation
- Congressional liaison/personal contact
- Veto

Sample Answer

Enacting a law is a complex process that involves numerous actors. Although the party leadership in both the House and the Senate is clearly important, the committees that consider legislation, interest groups that try to influence the legislative agenda, and clearly the president all have a major role.

There are political scientists who suggest the party leadership and special party task forces are undermining the legislative role of committees. While the power of committees may be somewhat diminished, they are still essential to the legislative process. Thousands of bills are introduced in every session of Congress; legislative work would quickly come to a standstill if there were not a mechanism that determined which bills should get a thorough examination and which should not. The vast majority of bills that are introduced "die" in committee; they never get to the point where hearings are held or they are not reported out favorably by committee. The committee is recognized as the expert in the policy area of the legislation it considers; its views are given great weight by other members of Congress and even the courts. Bills rarely leave the committee in the same form in which they came to it. Bills are amended in committee to reflect political compromises with other members and the White House, information that came out of the hearings, and work done by committee staff. The committee plays a key role in determining the final shape of legislation as well; its members participate in the conference committee that reconciles versions of the bill that come out of the House and the Senate.

Interest groups are involved in the work of Congress in several ways, all of which fall under the general heading of lobbying. Although only a member of Congress can formally introduce a bill, it is very common for an interest group to actually write the legislation. A lobbyist may work alone or together with members of Congress and their staff or the administration and executive-branch agency. Once a bill is before a committee, interest groups will testify, presenting their perspective on the legislation as well as factual information that the committee might want to consider. Interest groups representing different constituencies might come together to form an issue network to push a bill that is beneficial to them all.

The president has been called the "legislator in chief." It is also said that "The president proposes; the Congress disposes." Both of these statements emphasize how involved the president is in the legislative process. Under the Constitution, the president clearly has authority to propose legislation and a vehicle for doing so—the State of the Union address. The fact is that the president will usually outline his legislative agenda at the beginning of each session of Congress. Very much like an interest group, congressional liaison staff within the White House translate the president's ideas into draft legislation, finalize the bills with the leaders of the president's party in Congress, and closely monitor the progress of the bills. The president will use the bully pulpit to build public support for legislative programs that are particularly important to the administration. While the president may engage in personal lobbying—calling up a member of Congress to discuss a vote—this type of pressure is usually left to high-level staff. The president does not act alone; in addition to consulting with key figures in Congress, interest groups are brought in to give advice. In a very controversial move, the Bush Administration involved energy corporations in the planning of energy policy that would need to be translated into legislation.

Reader Commentary

The committee system and the president are handled well. It is interesting that the student chooses not to include the veto power but discusses the president as a legislator in broad political terms. Additional factual information might have been helpful, however—for example, extension of presidential power through budget authority and line-item veto, and the fact that the Supreme Court declared the line-item veto unconstitutional.

The student doesn't discuss interest groups as fully. The student could have expanded on the suggestion that presidential and interest group lobbying are similar. The reader doesn't get a clear idea of what lobbying entails or how close the relationship between lobbyists and Congress can be. Because the student mentions the looser issue networks, he should mention iron triangles as well. Score = 4.

Question 4

Scoring Guidelines

Total: 5 points (1 point for each relationship description; 1 point for each example)

Media examples

- Press releases
- News conferences/briefings
- Interviews

Government examples

- Media events
- Trial balloons
- Leaks

Sample Answer

The relationship between the media and the government, particularly the administration, is symbiotic simply because both need and use the other. Political reporters rely on the government for a considerable amount of the information they use for their stories despite the distrust that Watergate, Iran-Contra, and the recent revelations about the information that the administration had before September 11, 2001, created.

The government, on the other hand, needs the media to explain its policies to the American people, to influence public opinion on a critical issue, and to put the president in the best possible light.

Reporters gather information about the government from a variety of sources, with news conferences/briefings and interviews with government officials the most important. Members of the White House press corps are briefed every day by the president's press secretary and provided with news releases or press kits that contain background information. There are also regular briefings at the departments of State and Defense, at other federal agencies, and by members of Congress and the congressional leadership. While reporters are free to ask questions, it is doubtful that much more information than the government wants to get out will be forthcoming. One source of information that has become less frequent in recent years is the presidential news conference. Interviews with government officials allow the reporter to dig a bit deeper into the story. But there are guidelines for such interviews. Not everything that an official says may be quoted directly or directly attributed. A "highly placed White House source" may be the president's chief of staff or a special assistant to the president. Government officials will often give greater access to reporters who file favorable stories about the administration than those who are constantly critical.

The government uses the media to convey the best possible image to the public. One of the ways to accomplish this is through a media event, a staged political activity that is meant to be covered by the press. TV cameras and reporters are called in to see President George W. Bush reading to a group of first graders — the president is actually pushing his education program about "leaving no child behind." Media events don't always work. During the 1988 campaign, Democratic candidate Michael Dukakis was filmed driving a tank; the purpose was to demonstrate his concern with defense, but he looked uncomfortable and ridiculous. An administration might also leak information to a reporter. This is not the type of leak the government wants to prevent; it doesn't involve sensitive information or something that the administration would rather keep under wraps. Such a planned leak is known as a trial balloon; its purpose is often to float a policy idea through the media, and gauge both the public and political reaction. If there seems to be support for the idea, the administration may go ahead with it.

Reader Commentary

This question is about how the news is presented. The student certainly presents the basic facts, and gives two good examples for media events, but it could have moved a bit beyond the basics. What does the fact that reporters get much of their information from "official sources" mean? It is one of the factors, for example, that mitigates against the so-called liberal bias in the media. What is the media's response when the government wants to limit the flow of information, as it did during the Persian Gulf War? Are the media and government really adversaries despite their symbiotic relationship? The student could have raised these questions. Score = 4.

Practice Test 2

Answer Sheet

Remove this sheet and use it to mark your answers for the multiple-choice section of Practice Test 2.

1 Ⓐ Ⓑ Ⓒ Ⓓ Ⓔ	21 Ⓐ Ⓑ Ⓒ Ⓓ Ⓔ	41 Ⓐ Ⓑ Ⓒ Ⓓ Ⓔ
2 Ⓐ Ⓑ Ⓒ Ⓓ Ⓔ	22 Ⓐ Ⓑ Ⓒ Ⓓ Ⓔ	42 Ⓐ Ⓑ Ⓒ Ⓓ Ⓔ
3 Ⓐ Ⓑ Ⓒ Ⓓ Ⓔ	23 Ⓐ Ⓑ Ⓒ Ⓓ Ⓔ	43 Ⓐ Ⓑ Ⓒ Ⓓ Ⓔ
4 Ⓐ Ⓑ Ⓒ Ⓓ Ⓔ	24 Ⓐ Ⓑ Ⓒ Ⓓ Ⓔ	44 Ⓐ Ⓑ Ⓒ Ⓓ Ⓔ
5 Ⓐ Ⓑ Ⓒ Ⓓ Ⓔ	25 Ⓐ Ⓑ Ⓒ Ⓓ Ⓔ	45 Ⓐ Ⓑ Ⓒ Ⓓ Ⓔ
6 Ⓐ Ⓑ Ⓒ Ⓓ Ⓔ	26 Ⓐ Ⓑ Ⓒ Ⓓ Ⓔ	46 Ⓐ Ⓑ Ⓒ Ⓓ Ⓔ
7 Ⓐ Ⓑ Ⓒ Ⓓ Ⓔ	27 Ⓐ Ⓑ Ⓒ Ⓓ Ⓔ	47 Ⓐ Ⓑ Ⓒ Ⓓ Ⓔ
8 Ⓐ Ⓑ Ⓒ Ⓓ Ⓔ	28 Ⓐ Ⓑ Ⓒ Ⓓ Ⓔ	48 Ⓐ Ⓑ Ⓒ Ⓓ Ⓔ
9 Ⓐ Ⓑ Ⓒ Ⓓ Ⓔ	29 Ⓐ Ⓑ Ⓒ Ⓓ Ⓔ	49 Ⓐ Ⓑ Ⓒ Ⓓ Ⓔ
10 Ⓐ Ⓑ Ⓒ Ⓓ Ⓔ	30 Ⓐ Ⓑ Ⓒ Ⓓ Ⓔ	50 Ⓐ Ⓑ Ⓒ Ⓓ Ⓔ
11 Ⓐ Ⓑ Ⓒ Ⓓ Ⓔ	31 Ⓐ Ⓑ Ⓒ Ⓓ Ⓔ	51 Ⓐ Ⓑ Ⓒ Ⓓ Ⓔ
12 Ⓐ Ⓑ Ⓒ Ⓓ Ⓔ	32 Ⓐ Ⓑ Ⓒ Ⓓ Ⓔ	52 Ⓐ Ⓑ Ⓒ Ⓓ Ⓔ
13 Ⓐ Ⓑ Ⓒ Ⓓ Ⓔ	33 Ⓐ Ⓑ Ⓒ Ⓓ Ⓔ	53 Ⓐ Ⓑ Ⓒ Ⓓ Ⓔ
14 Ⓐ Ⓑ Ⓒ Ⓓ Ⓔ	34 Ⓐ Ⓑ Ⓒ Ⓓ Ⓔ	54 Ⓐ Ⓑ Ⓒ Ⓓ Ⓔ
15 Ⓐ Ⓑ Ⓒ Ⓓ Ⓔ	35 Ⓐ Ⓑ Ⓒ Ⓓ Ⓔ	55 Ⓐ Ⓑ Ⓒ Ⓓ Ⓔ
16 Ⓐ Ⓑ Ⓒ Ⓓ Ⓔ	36 Ⓐ Ⓑ Ⓒ Ⓓ Ⓔ	56 Ⓐ Ⓑ Ⓒ Ⓓ Ⓔ
17 Ⓐ Ⓑ Ⓒ Ⓓ Ⓔ	37 Ⓐ Ⓑ Ⓒ Ⓓ Ⓔ	57 Ⓐ Ⓑ Ⓒ Ⓓ Ⓔ
18 Ⓐ Ⓑ Ⓒ Ⓓ Ⓔ	38 Ⓐ Ⓑ Ⓒ Ⓓ Ⓔ	58 Ⓐ Ⓑ Ⓒ Ⓓ Ⓔ
19 Ⓐ Ⓑ Ⓒ Ⓓ Ⓔ	39 Ⓐ Ⓑ Ⓒ Ⓓ Ⓔ	59 Ⓐ Ⓑ Ⓒ Ⓓ Ⓔ
20 Ⓐ Ⓑ Ⓒ Ⓓ Ⓔ	40 Ⓐ Ⓑ Ⓒ Ⓓ Ⓔ	60 Ⓐ Ⓑ Ⓒ Ⓓ Ⓔ

Section I: Multiple-Choice Questions

Time: 45 minutes
60 questions

Directions: Each of the questions or incomplete statements below is followed by five suggested answers or completions. Select the one that is best in each case, and then fill in the corresponding oval on the answer sheet.

1. According to the language of the First Amendment, which institution of government cannot limit freedom of religion?

   A.   state legislatures
   B.   the executive branch
   C.   the Supreme Court
   D.   state courts
   E.   Congress

2. The Great Compromise, also known as the Connecticut Compromise, concerned

   A.   the power of the president
   B.   representation in Congress
   C.   continuation of the slave trade
   D.   the organization of the federal courts
   E.   the right to vote

3. The federal debt is best described as

   A.   the amount of money paid out to foreign countries
   B.   the difference between the money coming into the treasury and the money going out
   C.   the shortfall in the payment of federal income taxes
   D.   the total of all the money borrowed by the United States that remains unpaid
   E.   the money owed the states by the federal government

4. Which of the following statements about the cabinet is NOT valid?

   A.   The cabinet is too large to be an effective policymaking body.
   B.   The president can give officials other than the heads of the executive departments cabinet rank.
   C.   The cabinet is made up of close associates of the president who worked on the election campaign.
   D.   Recent presidents have made cabinet appointments with an eye toward diversity.
   E.   Cabinet members are primarily responsible for managing their departments.

5. Incumbent members of the House of Representatives are likely to get reelected when

   A.   Casework for the constituency is done well.
   B.   The country faces a foreign policy crisis.
   C.   The president from their party is not popular.
   D.   The economy is in recession.
   E.   They're faced with wealthy challengers.

6. Which provision of the Constitution is the Defense of Marriage Act based on?

   A.   Necessary and Proper Clause
   B.   Privileges and Immunities Clause
   C.   Tenth Amendment
   D.   Full Faith and Credit Clause
   E.   Supremacy Clause

7. The social welfare programs of the Great Society included

    I.   Head Start

    II.   Peace Corps

    III.   Earned Income Tax Credit

    IV.   Model Cities

    A.   I only

    B.   I and IV only

    C.   I and III only

    D.   II and IV only

    E.   I, II, and IV only

8. Redistricting, the redrawing of congressional district lines to reflect changes in population, is

    A.   done every four years following the presidential election

    B.   the responsibility of the special commissions appointed by the governors of each state

    C.   a highly political process, with each party trying to protect its interests

    D.   subject to review by the Supreme Court before going into effect

    E.   the way a state's representation in the House increases or decreases

9. As primaries grew in importance in determining the party's presidential nominee,

    A.   Fewer politicians decided to run for the office.

    B.   The media paid less attention to the primaries.

    C.   Raising money became increasingly important.

    D.   The party organization played a greater role in the campaigns.

    E.   Candidates took more moderate positions to appeal to more voters.

10. Term limits can't be imposed on members of Congress through legislation because

    A.   Such action violates the separation of powers.

    B.   The expertise in Congress on policy matters is reduced.

    C.   It's prohibited under the Supremacy Clause.

    D.   It's tantamount to adding a qualification for serving in Congress.

    E.   Congress will never vote for such a law.

11. Under the Constitution, the federal government and the states

    A.   cannot grant titles of nobility

    B.   can enter into any treaty or alliance

    C.   can extradite a person to a foreign country

    D.   can coin money

    E.   cannot impose tariffs on imports

12. All the following are legislative courts EXCEPT:

    A.   U.S. Court of Federal Claims

    B.   U.S. Court of International Trade

    C.   U.S. Court of Appeals for Veterans Claims

    D.   U.S. Tax Court

    E.   U.S. territorial courts

13. The first expansion of the right to vote was the result of

    A.   constitutional amendments ratified after the Civil War

    B.   state legislatures granting suffrage to women

    C.   Supreme Court decisions striking down Jim Crow laws

    D.   legislation passed by Congress after the Civil War

    E.   state legislatures eliminating property qualifications

14. The incumbency effect is more pronounced for members of the House than for members of the Senate because

    A.   The franking privilege is not available in the Senate.

    B.   Senate challengers always outspend a senator running for reelection.

    C.   Senators consider themselves trustees rather than delegates.

    D.   Senators have less contact with their constituents than representatives do.

    E.   Senators spend less time campaigning for reelection than representatives do.

15. The concept of strict scrutiny is applied by

    A. the OMB reviewing budget requests from federal agencies

    B. the federal courts in discrimination cases where race is used as a classification

    C. the Equal Employment Opportunity Commission when looking into disability-based discrimination

    D. the Department of Defense in examining proposals for defense contracts

    E. the House and Senate budget committees when considering the president's budget proposal

16. In *Clinton v. Jones,* the issue that the Supreme Court decided was

    A. whether a president could be sued while in office

    B. if there were adequate grounds for impeachment

    C. the constitutionality of the line-item veto

    D. the validity of the sexual harassment claims against the president

    E. whether sending troops to Bosnia was covered by the War Powers Act

17. Which political institution gets the most attention from the national media?

    A. Congress

    B. municipal governments

    C. state governments

    D. the president

    E. the Supreme Court

18. Which of the following positions is/are most likely to be included in a Democratic Party platform?

    I. the need to address the underlying causes of crime

    II. support for right to life

    III. stricter environmental protection

    IV. increased spending on missile defense

    A. I and II only

    B. II and III only

    C. III only

    D. I and III only

    E. I and IV only

19. The General Accountability Office is

    A. responsible for reviewing the accounting practices of federal agencies

    B. an investigative arm of Congress that evaluates federal programs

    C. part of the Executive Office of the President, headed by the chief accountant

    D. an independent regulatory agency that establishes rules for the financial industry

    E. the coordinator of economic policy between Congress and the White House

20. Newly elected members of Congress indicate the committees they prefer to serve on. Which is a logical choice for a new senator from Texas?

    A. Veterans' Affairs

    B. Governmental Affairs

    C. Energy and Natural Resources

    D. Labor and Human Resources

    E. Appropriations

21. All the following statements about school desegregation between 1950 and 1975 are true EXCEPT:

    A. Despite Supreme Court decisions, the pace of integration was very slow in the South.

    B. In *Griffin v. County School Board of Prince Edward County* (known as *Brown II*), the Supreme Court relied on local school boards to develop desegregation plans.

    C. The only method of desegregation that the Supreme Court recognized was busing.

    D. School desegregation was an issue in the North even in the absence of laws requiring separate schools.

    E. "White flight" from public schools was often a response to desegregation orders.

22. To win a libel judgment, a private person must show that

    A. The newspaper article contained false statements.

    B. The newspaper knew that the statements were false and published them anyway.

    C. The newspaper refused to print a retraction.

    D. The words were spoken with malice.

    E. The broadcast included misleading information.

Cases before the Supreme Court, 1980–1998									
Action	1980	1990	1995	1999	2000	2001	2002	2003	2004
Appellate cases granted review	167	114	92	78	85	82	83	74	69
Pauper cases granted review	17	27	13	14	14	6	8	13	11
Original cases granted review*	24	14	11	8	9	8	7	6	4

*Cases of original jurisdiction

Source: Statistical Abstract of the United States. Washington, D.C.: Government Printing Office, 2006.

23. All the following statements are supported by the above table EXCEPT:

   A. The caseload of the Supreme Court has declined since the 1980s.
   B. The number of *in forma pauperis* petitions that the Supreme Court receives has decreased.
   C. The majority of the cases that the Supreme Court hears fall under its appellate jurisdiction.
   D. The Supreme Court had its lightest caseload in almost 20 years in 2004.
   E. Original jurisdiction cases are comparatively rare.

24. In order to get federal matching funds in presidential primaries, a candidate must

   A. file an application with the Federal Election Commission
   B. pledge to accept donations only from individuals not political action committees
   C. raise $5,000 in each of 20 states in contributions of $250 or less
   D. agree not to use money to run negative campaign ads
   E. commit to use part of the federal money for voter registration drives

25. President Reagan's ability to influence votes in Congress declined dramatically in 1988 because

   A. The country was turning away from his policies.
   B. Congress was in Democratic hands.
   C. The Republican leadership in Congress was weak.
   D. The influence of lobbyists for liberal groups was too strong.
   E. He was a lame-duck president.

26. The greatest asset that the representatives who met in Philadelphia had as they drafted the Constitution was

   A. business success
   B. intellectual abilities
   C. political experience
   D. religious convictions
   E. military exploits

27. The fact that the Senate is less centralized than the House is shown by

   A. the length of the member's terms
   B. the absence of a Committee on Rules
   C. its role in foreign policy
   D. the authority to give "advice and consent"
   E. the salary of its members

28. A claim of executive privilege, where the president refuses to divulge communications with advisors, is

   A. specifically granted in the Constitution
   B. authorized under federal law
   C. unconstitutional under a Supreme Court ruling
   D. recognized when necessary to protect military/diplomatic information
   E. used more by Democratic than Republican presidents

29. The New Hampshire presidential primary is important because

   A. It's an early test of candidate support.
   B. The candidates get to meet many people face to face.
   C. The focus is on issues rather than the candidates' personalities.
   D. The media coverage is less intense than it is in other primaries.
   E. The state represents a good cross section of the country.

30. Which of the following activities is the Speaker of the House NOT responsible for?

   A. presiding over the House of Representatives
   B. participating in determining presidential disability
   C. appointing members to committees
   D. assigning bills to committees
   E. determining who will serve in party leadership posts

31. While interest groups testify before Congress and meet with the staff of a federal agency, how do they influence the courts?

   A. They speak directly with judges about their concerns.
   B. They try to determine how Supreme Court justices are leaning from their law clerks.
   C. They organize letter-writing campaigns against unfavorable Supreme Court decisions.
   D. They file briefs with the Supreme Court to get their views before the justices.
   E. They call for the impeachment of a federal judge who consistently rules against their position.

32. Under the Constitution as ratified, members of the Senate were

   A. chosen by the state legislatures
   B. appointed by the governor
   C. elected by the people
   D. selected by the House of Representatives
   E. chosen through the Electoral College

33. Which of the following statements about organized labor is true?

   A. Unions can't establish political action committees.
   B. Union membership has declined in recent years.
   C. Unions support right-to-work laws.
   D. There is little the president can do to prevent a major strike.
   E. Unions support free trade agreements to boost U.S. exports.

34. An important distinction between a categorical grant and a block grant is that

   A. States must provide matching funds for a block grant.
   B. States have more freedom in determining how to use block grants.
   C. Block grants are more numerous than categorical grants.
   D. Categorical grants have comparatively few restrictions.
   E. Block grants are targeted to very specific program goals.

35. A conference committee is responsible for

   A. investigating an issue such as illegal campaign contributions
   B. providing oversight of the operations of a federal agency
   C. working out the differences between the House and Senate version of a bill
   D. providing information to members on broad policy areas
   E. examining the administration's budget proposal

36. The most publicized issue under Title IX of the Education Act of 1972 is

   A. busing to achieve public school integration
   B. affirmative-action programs in university faculty hiring
   C. gender discrimination in collegiate athletic programs
   D. access to public schools for the disabled
   E. equal pay for women teachers in public schools

37. The Contract with America refers to

   A.   the 2000 Democratic Party platform
   B.   Ralph Nader's campaign slogan for the
        Green Party
   C.   the Republican legislative agenda in 1994,
        the year the party gained control of
        Congress
   D.   the strong economic ties between the
        United States and the European Union
   E.   the foreign aid package that the Bush
        Administration proposed for Africa

38. The cooperative federalism model was a
   response to

   A.   the need to pass civil rights legislation
   B.   the increasing number of immigrants
        coming into the country
   C.   conditions in the South after the Civil War
   D.   the end of the Cold War
   E.   the economic conditions that the United
        States faced during the Depression

39. Polls show that most reporters, in both print
   and electronic journalism, consider themselves

   A.   liberals
   B.   moderates
   C.   conservatives
   D.   libertarians
   E.   apolitical

40. Which of the following is NOT a controversial
   issue in the development of the nation's energy
   policy?

   A.   the cost of renewable energy sources
   B.   the need to diversify energy resources
   C.   the safety of nuclear power
   D.   the impact of energy development on the
        environment
   E.   regulation of the energy industry

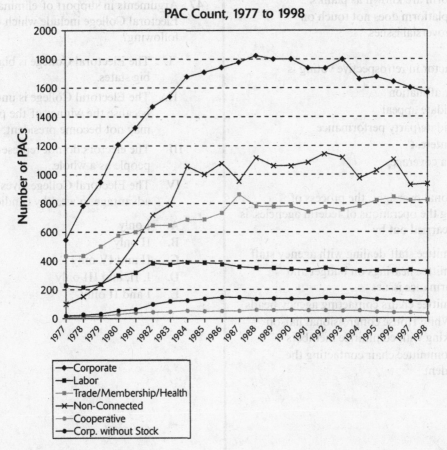

PAC Count, 1977 to 1998

Source: Federal Election Commission.

41. The graph on the preceding page indicates that

    A. Overall, the number of PACs has declined in this time period.
    B. Groups that don't represent economic interests have the smallest number of PACs.
    C. Labor PACs contributed the most money to congressional campaigns.
    D. All U.S. public corporations have a PAC.
    E. The most dramatic growth was in cooperative PACs.

42. All the following statements about the party platform are valid EXCEPT:

    A. The candidate is bound by the platform if elected.
    B. The platform provides a guide to voters on the issues.
    C. The platform is adopted at the national party convention when the presidential candidate is formally nominated.
    D. The individual issues covered in the platform are known as planks.
    E. The platform does not touch on controversial issues.

43. The key factor in retrospective voting is

    A. party affiliation
    B. candidate appeal
    C. candidate/party performance
    D. self-interest
    E. media coverage

44. Congressional oversight, the process of monitoring the operations of federal agencies, is primarily carried out by

    A. committee staff dealing with agency staff
    B. committee hearings on budget and performance issues
    C. committee chairs contacting agency heads
    D. the White House congressional liaison speaking with committee members
    E. the committee chair contacting the president

45. The theoretical justification for the break with Great Britain presented in the Declaration of Independence drew heavily on the ideas of

    A. James Madison
    B. Thomas Hobbes
    C. John Locke
    D. John Marshall
    E. Adam Smith

46. A drastic and never implemented solution to the fact that Congress seemed unable to control spending was

    A. legislation that required caps on spending
    B. a change in how the federal budget was prepared
    C. a constitutional amendment requiring a balanced budget
    D. an executive order that made federal agencies cut their budgets by 10 percent
    E. the elimination of federal agencies that did not meet budget targets

47. Arguments in support of eliminating the Electoral College include which of the following?

    I. The Electoral College is biased in favor of big states.
    II. The Electoral College is undemocratic because the winner of the popular vote may not become president.
    III. The electors do not represent the American people as a whole.
    IV. The Electoral College gives an unfair advantage to wealthy candidates.

    A. I only
    B. II only
    C. II and IV only
    D. I, II, and III only
    E. I and II only

48. What do *Griswold v. Connecticut* and *Cruzan v. Director, Missouri Department of Health* have in common?

    A. Both were early decisions on abortion.
    B. Both struck down state laws prohibiting physician-assisted suicide.
    C. Congress tried to get around both decisions through legislation.
    D. Both dealt with the right of privacy.
    E. The Supreme Court rejected precedent in both cases.

49. During the Cold War, the expansion of the Soviet Union into Europe was checked by

    A. United Nations peacekeepers
    B. SEATO
    C. the European Union
    D. CENTO
    E. NATO

50. All the following statements about nominating federal officials are valid EXCEPT:

    A. The Senate rarely fails to confirm a president's nominee for the cabinet.
    B. Delays in the confirmation process of presidential nominees are not uncommon.
    C. The president can try to bypass the Senate by making an appointment when Congress is not in session.
    D. Cabinet nominees get more scrutiny by the Senate than nominees for the Supreme Court do.
    E. The president has the option of withdrawing a nomination that generates strong opposition.

51. Which of the following social programs is paid for by taxes on employers only?

    A. Supplemental Security Income
    B. unemployment insurance
    C. Supplemental Nutrition Assistance Program
    D. Medicare Part B
    E. Old Age, Survivors, and Disability Insurance

52. The military-industrial complex, which President Eisenhower warned against when he left office, refers to

    A. the close relationship between the Department of Defense and defense contractors
    B. the planned economy of the Soviet Union that gave priority to military spending
    C. the large civilian and military bureaucracy of the Pentagon
    D. the fact that many corporate executives served in the military
    E. the idea that spending on defense does not result in a decline in spending on consumer goods

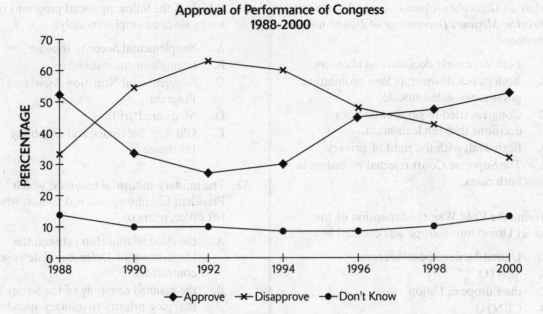

Source: The American National Election Studies (www.electionstudies.org). The ANES Guide to Public Opinion and Electoral Behavior. Ann Arbor, MI: University of Michigan, Center for Political Studies [producer and distributor].

53. Which of the following statements is supported by the graph?

- A. The approval rating of Congress declined during a period of divided government.
- B. Congress's standing declined during the impeachment of President Clinton.
- C. There was a significant improvement in public support for Congress when the Republicans gained control of the House and the Senate.
- D. Americans thought Congress performed very well during the Persian Gulf War.
- E. As the 2000 election approached, the public became uncertain of where it stood with Congress.

54. The 1993 Federal Employees Political Activities Act liberalized the provisions of the

- A. Pendleton Act
- B. Hatch Act
- C. National Labor Relations Act
- D. Whistleblower Protection Act
- E. Fair Labor Standards Act

55. The purpose of a filibuster is to

- A. add non-germane amendments to a bill
- B. prevent a bill from coming to a vote
- C. force a committee to report a bill out
- D. end debate on a bill in the Senate
- E. have a roll-call vote in the House

56. No poll is 100 percent accurate. This is reflected in the concept of a

- A. sampling error
- B. question bias
- C. random sample
- D. margin of error
- E. ideological bias

57. In what way did the Supreme Court decision in *Buckley v. Valeo* help the presidential aspirations of Ross Perot in 1992?

- A. The amount of money a corporation could contribute to a candidate increased.
- B. It became easier for a candidate to get on the ballot in all 50 states.
- C. Limits on the money individuals could contribute to their own campaigns were eliminated.
- D. Federal matching funds were approved for presidential primaries.
- E. Soft money could not be used for issue ads.

58. As the head of a political party, the responsibilities of the president include

    I. appointing the majority or minority members in Congress

    II. raising money for the party and individual candidates

    III. selecting the chair of the party's national committee

    IV. campaigning for the party's candidates

    A. I and II only
    B. II and III only
    C. III and IV only
    D. I, II, and III only
    E. II, III, and IV only

59. The 1974 reform of the budget process did all the following EXCEPT:

    A. It limited the president's ability not to spend money appropriated by Congress.
    B. It gave the Office of Management and Budget responsibility for developing the administration's budget.
    C. It established budget committees in both the House and the Senate.
    D. It set the calendar for the completion of the federal budget.
    E. It created the Congressional Budget Office to advise Congress during budget deliberations.

60. The form of government outlined in the Virginia Plan gave the power to veto state laws to the

    A. national legislature
    B. national executive
    C. national judiciary
    D. Council of Revision
    E. state governors

IF YOU FINISH BEFORE TIME IS CALLED, CHECK YOUR WORK ON THIS SECTION ONLY. DO NOT WORK ON ANY OTHER SECTION IN THE TEST.

Section II: Free-Response Questions

Time: 100 minutes

4 questions

Directions: You have 100 minutes to answer all four of the following questions. Unless the directions indicate otherwise, respond to all parts of all four questions. It is suggested that you take a few minutes to plan and outline each answer. Spend approximately one-fourth of your time (25 minutes) on each question. Illustrate your essay with substantive examples where appropriate. Be sure to number each answer in the same way the question is numbered below.

1. Political attitudes, including the way an individual votes, are shaped by a variety of factors, some early in life, some later.

    a. Discuss the impact of two of the following on political attitudes.
        ▪ Family
        ▪ Education
        ▪ Media

    b. Discuss the impact of two of the following on voting patterns.
        ▪ Race/ethnicity
        ▪ Age
        ▪ Gender

2. Independent regulatory agencies play an important role in controlling a sector of the economy in the public interest.

    a. Identify two independent regulatory agencies and describe the functions of each.
    b. Describe two ways in which an independent regulatory agency is similar to an independent executive agency or a cabinet department and two ways in which it is different from an independent executive agency or cabinet department.

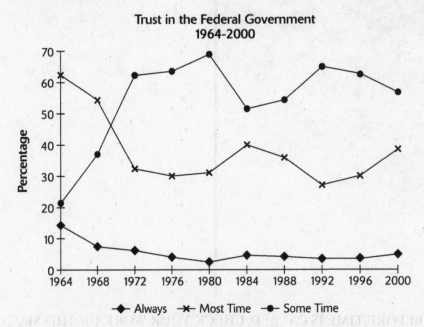

Trust in the Federal Government
1964-2000

◆ Always ✕ Most Time ● Some Time

Source: The American National Election Studies (www.electionstudies.org). The ANES Guide to Public Opinion and Electoral Behavior. Ann Arbor, MI: University of Michigan, Center for Political Studies [producer and distributor].

3. Based on the chart on the preceding page and your knowledge of U.S. politics during the period 1964 to 2000, perform the following tasks:

a. Identify three trends that are supported by the data.

b. For two of the trends you've identified, discuss two factors that explain each trend.

4. African Americans and women successfully relied on the Supreme Court and Congress to expand their rights. Discuss how the federal government has responded to discrimination in two of the following areas:

- Age
- Disability
- Sexual orientation

IF YOU FINISH BEFORE TIME IS CALLED, CHECK YOUR WORK ON THIS SECTION ONLY. DO NOT WORK ON ANY OTHER SECTION IN THE TEST.

Answer Key

Section I: Multiple-Choice Questions

1. E	21. C	41. A
2. B	22. A	42. A
3. D	23. B	43. C
4. C	24. C	44. B
5. A	25. E	45. C
6. D	26. C	46. C
7. B	27. B	47. E
8. C	28. D	48. D
9. C	29. A	49. E
10. D	30. B	50. D
11. A	31. D	51. B
12. B	32. A	52. A
13. E	33. B	53. C
14. D	34. B	54. B
15. B	35. C	55. B
16. A	36. C	56. D
17. D	37. C	57. C
18. D	38. E	58. E
19. B	39. A	59. B
20. C	40. B	60. A

Section II: Free-Response Questions

Student essays and analyses begin on page 224.

Answer Explanations

Section I: Multiple-Choice Questions

1. **E** The First Amendment clearly states, "Congress shall make no law respecting an establishment of religion, or prohibiting the free exercise thereof. . . ." In the 19th century, it was assumed that other civil liberties listed in the First Amendment were similarly protected against action by the federal government. The key word in the question is *language;* absent that word, all the possible choices are right.

2. **B** The Great Compromise reconciled the major difference between the Virginia Plan and the New Jersey Plan submitted at the Constitutional Convention: the structure of the legislative branch. It provided for a bicameral legislature with the representation in the House of Representatives based on population and equal representation among the states in the Senate.

3. **D** This is a straightforward definition question. The only really tricky choice you're presented with is **B**, which explains the federal deficit. The federal debt is essentially the accumulated federal deficit.

4. **C** Although cabinet appointments are sometimes made for political reasons, it is rare, particularly over the last 30 years or so, for a cabinet secretary to be a close campaign associate. People whom the president trusts and who played a major role in the election are much more likely to take positions on the White House staff. All the other choices are accurate statements about the cabinet.

5. **A** National affairs, whether domestic issues or foreign policy questions, play a much less significant role for members of Congress than they do for the president. The key advantage an incumbent has over a challenger is access to money; facing a wealthy challenger obviously means that the chances for reelection go down somewhat. If the incumbent is from the same party as the president, a president's popularity may work against reelection. In a bad economy, voters may place blame on those in Congress for getting the country into the mess or not doing enough to get the country out of it. Doing casework well—in other words, providing constituents with services—is the logical answer.

6. **D** The Full Faith and Credit Clause (Article IV) provides that the public records, laws, and judicial proceedings of one state shall be recognized in every other state. In response to indications that Hawaii was going to recognize gay and lesbian marriages, Congress passed the Defense of Marriage Act in 1996. The statute states that states are not required to give effect to laws or judicial proceedings in other states that permit same-sex marriages. The Full Faith and Credit Clause does give Congress a role to play on such state-to-state issues.

7. **B** Even if you don't know that Head Start and Model Cities are Great Society programs, chronology may help you out. The Peace Corps was established during the Kennedy Administration; it deals with sending Americans in a variety of fields to work in other countries and is not a social welfare program. Although the Earned Income Tax Credit is a social welfare program, it was established in 1975 to help the working poor.

8. **C** Redistricting is done by the state legislatures following reapportionment. The party that controls the state legislature tries to maximize the chances for party members to get elected to Congress by the way the congressional district lines are drawn. The Supreme Court has ruled on a number of landmark cases dealing with congressional districts and redistricting, most notably *Westberry v. Sanders* (1964) and *Shaw v. Reno* (1993), but a review by the Court is not automatic as **D** suggests.

9. **C** Although the field becomes smaller very quickly, it is not uncommon in recent elections to have as many as nine or ten candidates announce that they're running for the presidency. Having more primaries basically means that the race for the White House is more expensive; a candidate must run in more states, have a larger staff, and buy more television time. The contemporary presidential campaign, which is candidate centered, is less, not more, controlled by the party. Candidates typically appeal more to the committed elements in their party because they're the likely primary voters.

10. **D** The Supreme Court struck down term limits on Congress that state legislation imposed in *U.S. Term Limits, Inc. v. Thornton* (1995). Congress itself recognized that legislation could not impose term limits. The issue was part of the Republican Contract with America in 1994, but the House of Representatives rejected four proposals for a constitutional amendment that would have limited the number of terms a member could serve.

11. **A** Only the federal government can do choices **B** through **E**. The only answer that is true for both the federal government and the states is **A**; neither can grant titles of nobility.

12. **B** This is the type of question for which you either know the answer or you don't. The U.S. Court of International Trade is a constitutional court that deals with cases arising out of tariffs or other trade statutes; decisions of the Court of International Trade are appealed to the Court of Appeals for the Federal Circuit.

13. **E** Don't make the mistake of thinking that the first expansion of the right to vote was when African Americans were granted suffrage through the Fifteenth Amendment (1870). The franchise expanded significantly in the 1820s as state legislatures eliminated all property and/or tax qualifications for voting and established the principle of universal white male suffrage.

14. **D** Because of the size difference between the two constituencies, a senator cannot maintain the same contact with the voters that a member of the House can. House members come before the voters every two years, while the Senate term is six years. All members of Congress enjoy the *franking privilege* (the right of members of Congress to free use of the mail for official business). The money gap between an incumbent senator and a challenger may not be that great, but incumbents still enjoy a financial advantage.

15. **B** Strict scrutiny is the highest standard the courts apply to cases where a distinction based on race or fundamental civil liberties are involved (for example, freedom of religion, speech, and the press). In order to be upheld, the distinction must be necessary to accomplish a compelling state interest. The heightened scrutiny test is applied to distinctions based on gender, while the reasonableness test is used for classifications based on age, disability, and sexual preference.

16. **A** Paula Jones sued President Clinton for civil damages over allegations of sexual harassment when he was governor of Arkansas. The issue before the Supreme Court was whether a sitting president could be sued; the Court had no jurisdiction to decide the merits of the sexual harassment claims. Watch out for the trick in **C**, which is a reference to the 1998 *Clinton v. City of New York* decision.

17. **D** News coverage focuses on leaders, and the president is the leader of the nation. This holds true for other branches of the federal government, as well as state and local governments. Coverage of Congress emphasizes the views of the majority and minority leaders in the House and the Senate. State news looks more closely at the governor than the state legislature.

18. **D** The choices lay out basic conservative and liberal positions on issues that reflect the thinking of the major parties. On crime, Republicans support stiffer sentencing, while Democrats argue that getting at the social roots of crime is critical. Democrats favor, for example, rehabilitation over incarceration for drug use. Democrats also favor strict environmental laws, while Republicans emphasize the need to balance environmental protection with economic growth.

19. **B** The key to this question is knowing that the General Accountability Office (GAO) is under the Congress. The GAO examines the use of public funds, evaluates federal programs, and provides analysis to Congress in connection with its oversight and appropriations functions. It conducts financial audits, reviews programs, and issues legal opinions. The comptroller general heads the GAO.

20. **C** A new senator is interested in a committee assignment in a policy area of interest that will give him or her high visibility and that will provide an opportunity to help his or her constituents. Texas is a state where the oil and natural gas industries, as well as energy service companies, are central to the economy.

21. **C** All the other statements provide accurate information about the state of desegregation between 1950 and 1975. Even in *Brown II,* the Court implied that local conditions varied so much that there was not just one remedy to end segregation. In *Swann v. Charlotte-Mecklenburg Board of Education* (1971), for example, reassignment of students and teachers and changing school district boundaries were mentioned in addition to busing.

22. **A** The fact that it is a private person, not a political figure or celebrity, who is bringing the action makes all the difference. A private person has to demonstrate only that the printed statement was false. The higher standard that the Supreme Court established for public officials in *The New York Times Co. v. Sullivan* (1964) is presented in **B**. Choice **D** refers to slander (spoken words) not libel (written words).

23. **B** The chart deals with cases that the Supreme Court decided to hear; it says nothing about how many petitions for review came to the Court. In fact, the number of *in forma pauperis* cases coming to the Supreme Court increased from roughly 2,400 in 1980 to over 6,500 in 1998.

24. **C** The matching funds apply only to the primaries, and qualified candidates receive federal money only for individual contributions of $250 or less. The major-party candidates receive a fixed amount of federal money to cover expenses during the general election campaign. This question should not present any difficulty if you know the terms of the 1974 Federal Election Campaign Act. Candidates who receive matching funds must agree to certain limits on spending during the primaries.

25. **E** The date is critical. You need to know that 1988 was Reagan's last full year in office. You should also be aware that he faced a Congress where the Democrats controlled the House throughout his two terms, but Republicans had a majority in the Senate for part of the time. There is evidence that support was low for Reagan's policies during his years in office, although he was extremely popular.

26. **C** Most of the delegates to the Constitutional Convention had either served in the Continental Congress and the Confederation Congress or had experience in their state legislatures. They were experienced politicians who knew the value of compromise, which was crucial in the drafting of the Constitution. Keep in mind that the question does not address the idea that the delegates represented the merchant/planter elite as historian Charles Beard argues in *An Economic Interpretation of the Constitution* (1913).

27. **B** This is another way of saying that there is no limit on debate in the Senate, in contrast to the House. Although not addressed in the choices, you should be aware that the constitutional leadership in the Senate—for example, the president of the Senate and the president pro tempore—have little real authority in comparison to what the House rules give the Speaker of the House.

28. **D** During the Watergate scandal, President Nixon tried to use a claim of executive privilege to refuse to turn over to a special prosecutor tapes of conversations between the president and his advisors. The Supreme Court in *United States v. Nixon* (1974) ruled that, while presidents did not enjoy a blanket form of executive privilege, particularly in instances where a crime may have been committed, the concept was valid regarding national security concerns.

29. **A** As the "first-in-the-nation primary," New Hampshire gives candidates their first opportunity to go before voters. This is what's important about New Hampshire, and the media coverage of the campaign and the results are extensive. It's true that, given its small population, candidates do get to meet many voters one on one. The principal criticism of the fact that New Hampshire has such a tremendous impact on the nomination process is that the state is not very representative of the country as a whole. It has no major urban area, and its minority population is small. In fact, how a candidate does in New Hampshire is not a very good barometer of how he or she may do in other parts of the nation.

30. **B** Under the Twenty-fifth Amendment, the Speaker does not play a direct role in determining presidential disability. That responsibility falls to either the president or the vice president and the cabinet. The Speaker is notified in the event of a declaration of disability. Disputes over presidential disability are ultimately resolved by the Congress as a whole.

31. **D** Choices **A** and **B** are highly irregular and simply would not take place. Organizing public opinion against the Court has been tried—there was considerable opposition to the rulings of the Court under Chief Justice Earl Warren, and there were frequent calls for his impeachment. The most often used technique is for interest groups to submit *amicus curiae* (friend of the court) briefs in cases in which they have an interest; in one sexual harassment case, over 50 organizations submitted such briefs. Another obvious option is for the interest groups to become a party to the litigation; groups like the American Civil Liberties Union and Common Cause, a public interest group, have done this on numerous occasions.

32. **A** The Constitution originally set up an indirect system of electing senators—specifically, through the state legislatures. This indirect system reflected a similar concern with the people of the United States as the election of the president through the Electoral College. The Seventeenth Amendment (1913) provided for the direct election of senators. The Virginia Plan provided for the election of members of the upper house of the bicameral legislature by the lower house (**D**).

33. **B** Although union membership is up for public sector workers, overall union membership has declined over the last 25 years. Unions have opposed right-to-work laws, which prohibit companies from requiring that workers join unions, and have raised concerns about trade agreements that may result in the loss of U.S. jobs to other countries. The latter was a factor in union opposition to the North American Free Trade Agreement. The president has authority under the Taft-Hartley Act to order a 90-day cooling-off period in the event of a major strike. A significant number of the top 50 political action committees (in terms of contributions to candidates) represents labor unions.

34. **B** The key feature of block grants is that there are few federal strings attached. Block grants are made in broad public policy areas such as policing and healthcare, and the states are presumed to know how to use the money most effectively.

35. **C** The answer choices present simple definitions of the various types of committees in Congress—select committee is **A**, standing committee is **B**, conference committee is **C**, joint committee is **D**, and budget committee is **E**.

36. **C** Title IX of the Education Act of 1972 prohibits gender discrimination in education programs that receive federal funds. Without question, the most publicized issue surrounding the legislation is the matter of equality of the athletic programs offered to men and women. In recent years, colleges and universities operating within budget constraints have had to eliminate men's intercollegiate sports programs so that women's programs could be expanded to meet the requirements of Title IX.

37. **C** The Contract with America is associated with then House Minority Leader Newt Gingrich. It was a legislative program unveiled before the 1994 midterm elections by which the Republicans gained control of the House and the Senate, and included such elements as the line-item veto, tax cuts, a balanced budget, and welfare reform.

38. **E** Meeting the challenges of the Great Depression led to a considerable expansion of the power of the federal government, which challenged the concept of separate spheres embodied in dual federalism. In cooperative federalism, no clear-cut lines exist between the states and the federal responsibility, and it's assumed that the latter will be involved in areas that previously may have been reserved for the states.

39. **A** Polls over the years clearly show that journalists take liberal positions on a wide range of issues intended to gauge an individual's ideological bent. To those who claim there is a liberal bias in the media, these studies are proof of that bias. Others argue that other factors, such as a reporter's objectivity, keep any bias in check.

40. **B** There is general agreement on the need to diversify energy sources if only to make the United States more energy self-sufficient. All the other issues are controversial. Conservatives argue that renewable sources such as solar and wind are not cost-effective. They may support the further development of nuclear plants, which liberals reject on safety and environmental grounds: What do you do with spent nuclear fuel? Conservatives favor less regulation of the energy industry to promote exploration and development, while liberals favor maintaining regulation in the public interest.

41. **A** Although most noticeable with corporate PACs, it's clear that the total number of PACs declined slightly in this time period. There is no way of knowing how much union PACs contributed based on the data, nor is it possible to say that all U.S. public corporations have PACs.

42. **A** The influence of the platform on voters is hard to gauge, but it's clear that the voters don't read the platform statement. The platform does tackle controversial questions such as abortion, crime prevention, and gun control, but it doesn't offer detailed solutions to these problems. The most important thing that delegates to the convention do is vote for the presidential and vice presidential nominees of their party. Studies have shown that there is a strong correlation between the platform and a successful president's legislative agenda. This is due largely to the fact that the presumptive nominee's supporters control the Platform Committee at the convention.

43. **C** Retrospective voting means that the voter looks back at the record of the candidate and/or party to see if he or she fulfilled his or her promises. An incumbent who lives up to commitments is going to get the nod from a retrospective voter.

44. **B** While congressional staff certainly play a role in the oversight process, it's during the hearing process of standing committees that the routine monitoring of federal agencies and programs take place. An obvious opportunity to question agency heads comes when they outline their appropriations needs before Congress, but oversight also takes place during routine testimony on how the executive department or agency is functioning, as well as when critical issues arise.

45. **C** Thomas Jefferson, the principal draftsman of the Declaration of Independence, drew heavily on the ideas in Locke's *Second Treatise on Civil Government* (1689), particularly the concepts of natural rights, consent of the governed, and limited government.

46. **C** Between 1974 and 1988, no less than 32 states called for a constitutional convention to draft a balanced budget amendment. Congress tried but failed to pass such an amendment in 1995.

47. **E** Whoever wins the popular vote in a state gets all the electoral votes. Winning big states, therefore, is more important than building up large pluralities in small states. In conception, the Electoral College demonstrates the distrust of the founders for the people and democracy—a distrust that has no place in today's world. The fact that the electors do not represent the American people is not relevant. Respective parties choose the electors, usually as a reward for party service.

48. **D** In *Griswold,* the Supreme Court established a constitutionally protected right to privacy; *Cruzan* applied this concept to a case involving the right to die. The Court recognized that a competent person could choose to reject medical measures intended to extend his or her life.

49. **E** The North Atlantic Treaty Organization (NATO) was established in 1949 to protect Western Europe from possible aggression from the Soviet Union. With the exception of recent conflicts in the former Yugoslavia, the United Nations has not played a peacekeeping role in Europe. While similar in concept to NATO, the Central Treaty Organization (CENTO) pertains to the Middle East and the Southeast Asia Treaty Organization (SEATO) pertains to South Asia and Southeast Asia, not to Europe. The European Union is the organization through which the economic integration of most of Europe has been accomplished.

50. **D** Everyone involved in the process recognizes that the most important nominations that a president makes are justices to the Supreme Court. Supreme Court nominees get much more careful scrutiny by the press, the Senate Judiciary Committee (which oversees the confirmation process), and the full Senate. Supreme Court justices serve for life and can affect the direction of the Court for decades.

51. **B** Supplemental Security Income (SSI) and the Supplemental Nutrition Assistance Program (SNAP) are paid for out of general revenues. Old Age, Survivors, and Disability Insurance, which is Social Security, is paid for by a payroll tax by both employees and employers. Beneficiaries themselves pay for Medicare Part B benefits, which is a supplement to the hospitalization paid for under Medicare.

52. **A** The danger of the military-industrial complex is that spending on hardware for the armed services will have no bearing on the actual threats that the United States faces around the world.

53. **C** The period of divided government began in 1994 when the Republicans took control of Congress, and the approval rating of Congress rose during this period. It continued to go up through the impeachment crisis, even though polls showed that Americans supported the president. Congress's standing declined during the year of the Persian Gulf War (1990–1991), and the public became increasingly uncertain about its attitude toward Congress in the last years of Clinton's presidency.

54. **B** The Hatch Act prohibited federal employees from becoming involved in political campaigns; they could not make financial contributions, work for a party, or campaign for a particular candidate. These limitations have been largely removed by the new legislation, which allows federal employees to run in nonpartisan elections. They can't, however, engage in any political activity on the job or collect political contributions from the general public.

55. **B** Because debate is unrestricted in the Senate, non-germane amendments (riders) can and often are added on the floor. A House committee can force a bill out of committee through a discharge petition signed by a majority of the members of the House. Answer **D** refers to cloture.

56. **D** The margin of error is a measure of the accuracy of a poll and is expressed as a +/− percentage. A margin of error of +/−3 percent is considered highly reliable. If the poll results are close—for example, if Candidate A is supported by 49 percent of likely voters and Candidate B is backed by 52 percent—the election is too close to call with a +/−3 percent margin of error.

57. **C** The Supreme Court rejected any limits on how much an individual could contribute to his or her campaign as a violation of the First Amendment's free speech protections. This allowed Ross Perot to spend his considerable personal wealth to buy large blocks of television time needed to get his message across to the American people and to pay for the other expenses involved in running a national campaign without the support of a political party.

58. **E** Although sometimes candidates don't want the president to campaign for them, this remains one of the functions of the president as party leader. Unlike the chair of the party national convention, the president has no direct role in determining party leadership in Congress. If the party in control in the House or Senate changes, then the leadership changes as well. When the Republicans lost control of the Senate in 2001 with the defection of Senator Jim Jeffords, Democrat Tom Daschle replaced Republican Trent Lott as Senate majority leader.

59. **B** The Office of Management and Budget has been developing the administration's budget since 1921, when its predecessor, the Bureau of the Budget, was created. The purpose of the 1974 reforms was to increase Congress's role in the budget process and to place limits on the ability of the president to *impound* (refuse to spend) money that was appropriated.

60. **A** The terms used here are those in the Virginia Plan as presented in the records of the Constitutional Convention. The Virginia Plan outlined a structure of government that was expected to strengthen the federal government at the expense of the states. This was reflected in the power of the National Legislature to "negative" laws passed by the states. The Council of Revision, made up of the National Executive and members of the National Judiciary, were given authority to veto federal laws.

Section II: Free-Response Questions

Question 1

Scoring Guidelines

Part (a): 4 points (2 points for each factor discussed)

Part (b): 4 points (2 points for each factor discussed)

Total: 8 points

Political attitudes

- Family
  - Informal education
  - Party identification
  - Generation gap
- Education
  - Formal education
  - Political participation
- Media
  - Source of political information
  - Differences in media
  - Role in setting political agenda
  - Bias in media

Voting patterns

- Race/ethnicity
  - Voter registration and voting
  - Party identification by group
  - Diversity within groups
- Age
  - Voter registration and voting by age group
  - Graying of America
- Gender
  - Gender gap
  - Women and political parties

Sample Answer

Political socialization is the process by which an individual learns about politics and his or her political views take form. Two critical early factors are the influence of the family and the role of education.

Political socialization begins at home. A child sitting at the dinner table hears things about politics, candidates running for office, the government, and elections. These facts and opinions are absorbed. Studies show that there is a high correlation between the political views of the parents and the political views of their children, particularly with respect to party identification. If both parents, for example, are committed Democrats, the likelihood is that the children will also consider themselves Democrats. Children from a "mixed marriage"—one parent a Democrat and the other a Republican—tend to be more politically independent. Political socialization is a lifelong process, and other factors such as age and income can change a person's political orientation.

Education about politics becomes more formal in school. From elementary school through high school, students learn the facts about U.S. history and how the government works. High school community service project requirements often encourage political participation. Students at a very young age get hands-on experience in the political process by participating in class or school elections. These activities introduce them to such basic concepts as campaigning for office and voting. Studies show that the more education a person has (i.e., through college), the more likely that person is to vote and become involved in politics.

Despite voter education efforts, racial/ethnic minorities are less likely to vote than whites are. When factors other than race are added, however, the picture becomes less clear. Voter turnout among highly educated and well-to-do members of minority groups is much higher, suggesting that education and income are more important variables than race. African Americans are the most liberal of all racial/ethnic minorities, and support the Democratic Party in overwhelming numbers. African-American voter turnout in 2008 jumped significantly over 2004 because an African American was the Democratic candidate. Hispanic Americans usually vote Democratic as well, but within the group there is a distinctly Republican faction. Cuban Americans, largely concentrated in South Florida, are strongly Republican because of the party's long-standing anti-Communist and anti-Castro position. Cuban Americans also tend to be economically better off than Mexican Americans and recent immigrants from Central America.

Women are the majority of the population, and their voter registration and voter turnout have been consistently higher than men's over the last two decades. Politicians often refer to the gender gap with respect to women voters. The term has two meanings: (1) Men and women take different positions on key political issues, (2) Women support the Democratic Party over the Republicans by a margin of 5 percent to 7 percent. Women tend to support "compassion" issues—in terms of federal spending priorities, they want less spent on defense and more on social programs, and they support stricter gun control laws but don't favor the death penalty to the same extent as men. These positions more closely reflect what the Democratic Party stands for and explains the support that Democratic presidential candidates have received from women. The gender gap was a factor in the magnitude of Bill Clinton's electoral victory in 1996; significantly, President Bush did not appreciably close the gap in the 2000 election.

Reader Commentary

Although the student touches on the major points, the essay is not as strong as it could be. The relationship between the family and party identification needs more development, particularly on the issue of whether children rebel against their parents' politics. Certainly more could have been done with education and political attitudes. With more education, does a person become more conservative or more liberal? Is there a correlation between education and income level? The treatment of race/ethnicity should have included a statement about Asian Americans, who tend to be more politically conservative than either African Americans or Hispanics. There are African-American Republicans (for example, Alan Keyes, who ran for the Republican nomination for president in 1996 and 2000, and former Representative J. C. Watts of Oklahoma). Score = 6.

Question 2

Scoring Guidelines

Part (a): 4 points (1 point for each independent executive agency and 1 point for each description)

Part (b): 4 points (1 point for each similarity and 1 point for each difference)

Total: 8 points

Independent regulatory agencies

- Federal Reserve Board
- Federal Communications Commission
- Federal Trade Commission
- Federal Energy Regulatory Commission
- Nuclear Regulatory Commission
- Securities and Exchange Commission

Similarities

- Created by Congress
- Administrative heads appointed by the president
- Senate confirmation
- Not part of executive department like independent executive agencies

Differences

- Administered by board or commission
- Term of board or commission members fixed by law
- Board or commission members can't be removed except for cause
- Regulatory vs. service function

Sample Answer

Since the creation of the Interstate Commerce Commission in 1887, federal agencies have been responsible for protecting the public interest by regulating the activities of businesses in key sectors of the economy. Two prominent independent regulatory agencies are the Federal Reserve Board and the Federal Communications Commission.

The Federal Reserve Board oversees the activities of the Federal Reserve System, the 12 regional banks created in 1913. It is primarily responsible for managing monetary policy through affecting how much money is in circulation and interest rates. The board accomplishes this through its control of reserve requirements and the discount rate. Reserve requirements refers to the amount of money member banks of the Federal

Reserve System must keep on hand to back their outstanding loans. If the reserve requirements are increased, the member banks have less money available to make loans. The impact of that is to slow down the economy. Lowering the reserve requirements has the opposite effect. The discount rate is the interest rate charged by Federal Reserve banks to member banks for loans. Raising or lower the discount rate has the same effect as raising or lowering the reserve requirements. If the Federal Reserve Board wants to stimulate the economy (for example, the country is in the midst of a recession with high unemployment), it lowers the discount rate to encourage business to borrow money for new equipment or facilities that will ultimately result in hiring more workers. During the major recession that began late in President George W. Bush's second term and continued into President Obama's presidency, the Federal Reserve lowered its interest rates to less than 1 percent and was given greater authority to deal with the nation's economic problems. Raising the discount rate is intended to check inflation by making it more expensive for businesses to expand their operations.

The Federal Communications Commission was established during the New Deal as the successor to the Federal Radio Commission. It is responsible for regulating radio, television, telephone, telegraph, and satellite and cable communications; the FCC has no jurisdiction over the Internet. The commission issues operating licenses to radio and broadcast television stations and the renewal of these licenses, and ensures that the rates charged for telephone and cable services, for example, are reasonable. Throughout most of its history, the commission was concerned with the concentration of control of communications, particularly the electronic media. Limits were imposed by the commission on the number of radio and/or television stations that a single company could own. Most of those regulations ended with the Telecommunications Act of 1996, which emphasized a major deregulation of the industry. Restrictions on how many stations can be owned in a single market remain in effect, however. The commission has some influence over the content of the broadcast media, particularly television, with rules regarding public service and children's programming. In the political arena, the FCC also requires radio and television stations to make airtime available to candidates for political office on an equal basis and to give individuals a right to respond to comments made about them on the air.

Like independent executive agencies and cabinet departments, independent regulatory agencies are the product of legislation. The Federal Reserve Board and the FCC were established through the Federal Reserve Act (1913) and the Federal Communications Act (1934), respectively. While the president can certainly outline the need for a new federal agency, it is up to Congress to work out the details. Congress can change the scope of the responsibilities of any entity that it creates through new legislation. The other obvious similarity is that those who run agencies within the executive branch—whether it is the secretary of defense, the administrator of NASA (an independent executive agency), or a member of the Federal Energy Regulatory Commission—are appointed by the president and confirmed by the Senate. But while the appointment process is the same, the term and relationship with the president is much different.

The chief difference between an independent regulatory agency and other institutions within the executive branch is that they're run by multi-person boards or commissions whose members serve for fixed terms that range from 4 to 14 years. The terms overlap, and there may be requirements that a certain number of members can't be from the same party. This is the case with the Federal Communications Commission. Both the length of the terms and the fact that they are staggered emphasize the fact that the president has less control over these appointments than he or she does to other agencies. Although both the Federal Trade Commission and NASA are independent in the sense that they are not under an executive department, an FTC commissioner can be removed only for cause, while the NASA administrator, like any cabinet member, serves at the pleasure of the president. This degree of independence is intended to free the independent regulatory agencies as much as possible from political interference.

Reader Commentary

The student does a good job with this question. The treatment of the Federal Reserve Board and the FCC are sound, although a little elaboration would have made the answer better. Under the Federal Reserve Board, the role of the Open Market Committee and the impact of buying and selling government securities might have been mentioned. It was important to bring the 1996 Telecommunications Act in, but some discussion of its impact on the deregulation of telephone service would have been helpful. An argument could certainly be made that the "chief difference" between an independent regulatory agency and an independent executive agency is their functions and how they carry them out, but the student gets points for the approach taken, which is certainly correct. Score = 7.

Question 3

Scoring Guidelines

Part (a): 1 point for each trend identified (total of 3 points)

Part (b): 1 point for each factor identified (total of 4 points)

Total: 7 points

Trends

- Sharp decline in trust, 1964–1972
- Less dramatic decline, 1972–1980
- Increase in trust, 1980–1984
- Decline in trust, 1984–1992
- Increase in trust, 1992–2000

Factors explaining decline

- Vietnam War
- Watergate scandal
- Energy crisis and stagflation
- Iran hostage crisis
- High deficits
- Iran-Contra scandal
- Tax increases

Factors explaining increase

- Reagan popularity
- Tax cuts
- Improvements in economy
- Full employment
- Budget surplus

Sample Answer

The data clearly show a dramatic decline in the trust the American people had in the federal government following the 1964 presidential election. That trend is most evident between 1964 and 1972, but it continued until 1980. While the level of trust rebounded with the election of Ronald Reagan in 1980, it declined again with his second term. There was a steady improvement in trust during the Clinton Administration (1993–2001).

The sharp decline in trust between 1964 and 1972 can largely be attributed to the growing opposition to the Vietnam War. The credibility of the Johnson Administration, which emphasized that we were winning the war, was undermined by the success of the 1968 North Vietnamese/Viet Cong Tet Offensive. Despite the fact that U.S. troops were withdrawn rather rapidly under Nixon, the publication of *The Pentagon Papers,* a secret history of U.S. involvement in Vietnam, and particularly the expansion of the war into Cambodia, intensified feelings that the administration was not completely candid with the American people. What the graph shows is a continuing decline in trust after 1972; it is surprising that it did not drop further. The Watergate scandal, which uncovered illegal activities reaching into the White House and resulting in the resignation of a president, seems to have affected public attitudes toward government less than the handling of the war. The other issues that probably contributed to the modest decline was the difficulty that the government had in dealing with a variety of economic programs, including the energy crisis of the early 1970s and the combination of high unemployment and high inflation.

The election of Ronald Reagan clearly made the American people feel better about the government. But this did not last very long. The downward trend resumed during Reagan's second term and reached a low point in the early 1990s. Major foreign policy successes apparently did not have a positive effect on the attitude toward the federal government. The collapse of the Soviet Union and the end of the Cold War, as well as the victory in the Persian Gulf War, were not enough to overcome the obvious failure to bolster trust on domestic issues. Tax cuts and a large boost in defense spending coupled with an economic slowdown led to large and growing federal deficits in the late 1980s and early 1990s that neither the Congress nor the administration seemed able to control. More important perhaps, George H. W. Bush flip-flopped on the issue of taxes. During the 1988 presidential campaign, he made a clear pledge to the American people not to raise taxes. He went back on that pledge in 1990 and agreed to a moderate tax increase on wealthy Americans in light of the fact that the federal deficit continued to increase. That decision not only contributed to his defeat in 1992 but was obviously a factor in the continuing decline in trust in the government.

Americans traditionally are more concerned with domestic issues than foreign policy. This certainly was the case between 1984 and 1992. Important, even historic, foreign policy achievements evidently did not instill a sense of confidence in the government on the part of the American people. Trying to explain the data on the graph for this period, it seems appropriate to say, "It's the economy, stupid."

Reader Commentary

Interpreting the graph is not particularly challenging, but the question does require familiarity with important political developments over the past 40 years. The student provides a sound summary of the factors that contributed to the fluctuations in the level of trust in the government. Two good points are made: (1) The Watergate scandal did not impact trust as dramatically as one may have expected, and (2) Trust in government declined during Reagan's second term and during the George H. W. Bush Administration because of the handling of domestic concerns, despite a number of diplomatic and military successes. It is not clear that the student has addressed two factors for the 1984–1992 period. The student does not mention the Iran-Contra scandal, perhaps because it does not fit into the argument that domestic matters are more important than foreign policy. But the student could have presented the Iran-Contra scandal as another White House cover-up/lying-to-Congress scandal certainly reminiscent of Watergate. Score = 5.

Question 4

Scoring Guidelines

Total: 8 points (4 points for each of the two areas selected)

Age

- Role of Congress
  - Age Discrimination in Employment Act (1967)
  - Age Discrimination Act (1975)
  - Age limits and mandatory retirement

Disability

- Role of Congress
  - Rehabilitation Act of 1973
  - Americans with Disabilities Act (1990)
- Supreme Court decisions on scope of Americans with Disabilities Act

Sexual orientation

- Supreme Court decisions
  - *Bowers v. Hardwick*
  - *Romer v. Evans*
  - *Lawrence v. Texas*
- "Don't Ask, Don't Tell" policy
- Local anti-discrimination ordinances
- Domestic partnerships and same-sex marriages

Sample Answer

The rights of disabled Americans are protected through legislation—most notably the Rehabilitation Act of 1973 and the Americans with Disabilities Act (1990). In recent years, however, the Supreme Court has narrowed the definition of *disabled,* and thereby limited the scope of the legislation; Congress responded to that change. Recognition of the civil rights of gays and lesbians, on the other hand, made headway primarily at the state and local levels. Gains made are limited to the inclusion of sexual orientation or sexual preference in anti-discrimination ordinances and state action on issues such a domestic partnerships and same-sex marriages.

Under the Rehabilitation Act of 1973, discrimination against people with disabilities was prohibited by federal agencies, institutions receiving federal funds (for example, colleges and universities), and private companies doing business with the federal government. Not only was employment discrimination prohibited, but all programs and institutions covered by the legislation were expected to take "affirmative action" with regard to the disabled. Other provisions of the law required that steps be taken to ensure the accessibility of buildings and other facilities for the disabled. The Americans with Disabilities Act requires businesses to make reasonable accommodations for the disabled, which may include restructuring jobs and modifying equipment that employees use.

Public transportation systems must be accessible to the disabled, and accommodations for the disabled must be available in hotels, restaurants, and retail stores. Telecommunication devices for the deaf must be made available by telephone companies.

The key Supreme Court rulings on the ADA relate to defining who is disabled. In recent rulings, the Court has indicated that determining whether an individual qualifies as disabled under the law depends on the extent to which the disability is affected by things like glasses or medication. A person who doesn't face a serious limitation in any "major life activity" when using such things would not be considered disabled. In 2008, however, amendments to the Americans with Disabilities Act looked toward a broader definition of disability and the Equal Employment Opportunity Commission revised its rules to take the new legislation into account.

It has taken the Supreme Court 20 years to decriminalize homosexual behavior. In *Bowers v. Hardwick* (1986), the Court held that consensual homosexual acts between two adults were not protected under the right of privacy and could be considered illegal by the states. That decision was reversed in *Lawrence v. Texas* (2003), which struck down stated sodomy laws as unconstitutional.

Gay rights have made no real progress in Congress. Indeed, faced with the prospect that Hawaii might approve same-sex marriages, Congress enacted the Defense of Marriage Act (1996), which effectively freed the states from recognizing such marriages under the Full Faith and Credit Clause of the Constitution. Half the states have passed similar legislation of their own. Over the last decade, however, states have adopted domestic partnership laws that give individuals in a homosexual relationship some of the rights enjoyed by married couples. More significantly, a small number of states have legalized same-sex marriage, either as the result of court rulings or legislative action. It should also be noted that other states have amended their constitutions to define marriage as a union between one man and one woman.

When President Clinton attempted to change the policy toward gays in the military early in his first term, it resulted in a firestorm of controversy; Congress, the armed services, and the administration came up with the "Don't Ask, Don't Tell" policy, under which homosexuals can still be discharged from the service for their sexual orientation. During the 2008 campaign, Barack Obama pledged to end the policy but was slow to take action after he came into office.

In a sense, the efforts of gays and lesbians to gain recognition for their civil rights have taken the opposite track of African Americans, for example. Blacks knew that they could make no headway in breaking down Jim Crow laws at the local or state level, so they focused their attention on the federal courts and Congress. Recognition of sexual orientation or sexual preference as a group entitled to civil rights protection has made no headway with the federal government, but it has succeeded in municipalities and states.

Reader Commentary

The essay is good. It offers considerable factual information and demonstrates a sound mastery of the subject. The comparison made between African Americans and gays and lesbians is well taken; it's an example of one of the advantages of federalism and could have been made with disabled Americans as well. The introductory paragraph sets up the balance of the essay. The student, though, raises a point here that is not followed up in the body—state domestic partner legislation. The student should have fleshed this out a bit, even though the question focuses on federal action. Score = 7.

Practice Test 3

Answer Sheet

Remove this sheet and use it to mark your answers for the multiple-choice section of Practice Test 3.

1 Ⓐ Ⓑ Ⓒ Ⓓ Ⓔ	21 Ⓐ Ⓑ Ⓒ Ⓓ Ⓔ	41 Ⓐ Ⓑ Ⓒ Ⓓ Ⓔ
2 Ⓐ Ⓑ Ⓒ Ⓓ Ⓔ	22 Ⓐ Ⓑ Ⓒ Ⓓ Ⓔ	42 Ⓐ Ⓑ Ⓒ Ⓓ Ⓔ
3 Ⓐ Ⓑ Ⓒ Ⓓ Ⓔ	23 Ⓐ Ⓑ Ⓒ Ⓓ Ⓔ	43 Ⓐ Ⓑ Ⓒ Ⓓ Ⓔ
4 Ⓐ Ⓑ Ⓒ Ⓓ Ⓔ	24 Ⓐ Ⓑ Ⓒ Ⓓ Ⓔ	44 Ⓐ Ⓑ Ⓒ Ⓓ Ⓔ
5 Ⓐ Ⓑ Ⓒ Ⓓ Ⓔ	25 Ⓐ Ⓑ Ⓒ Ⓓ Ⓔ	45 Ⓐ Ⓑ Ⓒ Ⓓ Ⓔ
6 Ⓐ Ⓑ Ⓒ Ⓓ Ⓔ	26 Ⓐ Ⓑ Ⓒ Ⓓ Ⓔ	46 Ⓐ Ⓑ Ⓒ Ⓓ Ⓔ
7 Ⓐ Ⓑ Ⓒ Ⓓ Ⓔ	27 Ⓐ Ⓑ Ⓒ Ⓓ Ⓔ	47 Ⓐ Ⓑ Ⓒ Ⓓ Ⓔ
8 Ⓐ Ⓑ Ⓒ Ⓓ Ⓔ	28 Ⓐ Ⓑ Ⓒ Ⓓ Ⓔ	48 Ⓐ Ⓑ Ⓒ Ⓓ Ⓔ
9 Ⓐ Ⓑ Ⓒ Ⓓ Ⓔ	29 Ⓐ Ⓑ Ⓒ Ⓓ Ⓔ	49 Ⓐ Ⓑ Ⓒ Ⓓ Ⓔ
10 Ⓐ Ⓑ Ⓒ Ⓓ Ⓔ	30 Ⓐ Ⓑ Ⓒ Ⓓ Ⓔ	50 Ⓐ Ⓑ Ⓒ Ⓓ Ⓔ
11 Ⓐ Ⓑ Ⓒ Ⓓ Ⓔ	31 Ⓐ Ⓑ Ⓒ Ⓓ Ⓔ	51 Ⓐ Ⓑ Ⓒ Ⓓ Ⓔ
12 Ⓐ Ⓑ Ⓒ Ⓓ Ⓔ	32 Ⓐ Ⓑ Ⓒ Ⓓ Ⓔ	52 Ⓐ Ⓑ Ⓒ Ⓓ Ⓔ
13 Ⓐ Ⓑ Ⓒ Ⓓ Ⓔ	33 Ⓐ Ⓑ Ⓒ Ⓓ Ⓔ	53 Ⓐ Ⓑ Ⓒ Ⓓ Ⓔ
14 Ⓐ Ⓑ Ⓒ Ⓓ Ⓔ	34 Ⓐ Ⓑ Ⓒ Ⓓ Ⓔ	54 Ⓐ Ⓑ Ⓒ Ⓓ Ⓔ
15 Ⓐ Ⓑ Ⓒ Ⓓ Ⓔ	35 Ⓐ Ⓑ Ⓒ Ⓓ Ⓔ	55 Ⓐ Ⓑ Ⓒ Ⓓ Ⓔ
16 Ⓐ Ⓑ Ⓒ Ⓓ Ⓔ	36 Ⓐ Ⓑ Ⓒ Ⓓ Ⓔ	56 Ⓐ Ⓑ Ⓒ Ⓓ Ⓔ
17 Ⓐ Ⓑ Ⓒ Ⓓ Ⓔ	37 Ⓐ Ⓑ Ⓒ Ⓓ Ⓔ	57 Ⓐ Ⓑ Ⓒ Ⓓ Ⓔ
18 Ⓐ Ⓑ Ⓒ Ⓓ Ⓔ	38 Ⓐ Ⓑ Ⓒ Ⓓ Ⓔ	58 Ⓐ Ⓑ Ⓒ Ⓓ Ⓔ
19 Ⓐ Ⓑ Ⓒ Ⓓ Ⓔ	39 Ⓐ Ⓑ Ⓒ Ⓓ Ⓔ	59 Ⓐ Ⓑ Ⓒ Ⓓ Ⓔ
20 Ⓐ Ⓑ Ⓒ Ⓓ Ⓔ	40 Ⓐ Ⓑ Ⓒ Ⓓ Ⓔ	60 Ⓐ Ⓑ Ⓒ Ⓓ Ⓔ

Section I: Multiple-Choice Questions

Time: 45 minutes

50 questions

Directions: Each of the questions or incomplete statements below is followed by five suggested answers or completions. Select the one that is best in each case, and then fill in the corresponding oval on the answer sheet.

1. The best way to gauge the mood of voters during a political campaign is through a

    A. tracking poll
    B. straw poll
    C. focus group
    D. exit poll
    E. online poll

2. Pundits say that 60 votes are needed to pass a bill in the Senate

    A. under the rules of the Senate
    B. in order to demonstrate bipartisan support
    C. to end a filibuster through cloture
    D. to prevent a presidential veto
    E. to persuade the House to accept the Senate version

3. The president's approval rating will likely go up when

    A. He or she has been in office a year
    B. There is an increase in the unemployment rate
    C. He or she is in the midst of a reelection campaign
    D. The administration is faced with a scandal
    E. The country is dealing with an international crisis

4. Which of the following best describes the Blue Dog Coalition?

    A. House Democrats from the South
    B. Healthcare-reform advocates among the Senate Republicans
    C. Members of Congress who support global warming legislation
    D. Fiscally conservative Democrats in the House
    E. Senate Democrats who favor increased defense spending

5. In our federal system, taxation can example of a(n)

    A. concurrent power
    B. implied power
    C. inherent power
    D. reserved power
    E. enumerated power

6. The Equal Rights Amendment did not become part of the Constitution because

    A. It was vetoed by the president.
    B. It was withdrawn from Congress.
    C. It was not ratified by three-fourths of the state legislatures.
    D. It failed to pass the Senate by a two-thirds vote.
    E. It was rejected by the state constitutional conventions.

7. President George W. Bush was criticized for limiting the scope of legislation passed by Congress through

    A. pocket vetoes
    B. executive orders
    C. signing statements
    D. line-item vetoes
    E. executive agreements

8. Efforts to increase voter turnout have focused on

    A. giving people time off to vote
    B. making it easier for people to register to vote
    C. passing laws that make voting mandatory
    D. lowering the voting age to 16
    E. providing people with more information about elections

Section I: Multiple-Choice Questions

Time: 45 minutes

60 questions

Directions: Each of the questions or incomplete statements below is followed by five suggested answers or completions. Select the one that is best in each case, and then fill in the corresponding oval on the answer sheet.

1. The best way to gauge the mood of voters during a political campaign is through a
   A. tracking poll
   B. straw poll
   C. focus group
   D. exit poll
   E. online poll

2. Pundits say that 60 votes are needed to pass a bill in the Senate
   A. under the rules of the Senate
   B. in order to demonstrate bipartisan support
   C. to end a filibuster through cloture
   D. to prevent a presidential veto
   E. to persuade the House to accept the Senate version

3. The president's approval rating will likely go up when
   A. He or she has been in office a year.
   B. There is a an increase in the unemployment rate.
   C. He or she is in the midst of a reelection campaign.
   D. The administration is faced with a scandal.
   E. The country is dealing with an international crisis.

4. Which of the following best describes the Blue Dog Coalition?
   A. House Democrats from the South
   B. Healthcare-reform advocates among the Senate Republicans
   C. Members of Congress who support global-warming legislation
   D. Fiscally conservative Democrats in the House
   E. Senate Democrats who favor increased defense spending

5. In our federal system, taxation is an example of a(n)
   A. concurrent power
   B. implied power
   C. inherent power
   D. reserved power
   E. enumerated power

6. The Equal Rights Amendment did not become part of the Constitution because
   A. It was vetoed by the president.
   B. It was withdrawn from Congress.
   C. It was not ratified by three-fourths of the state legislatures.
   D. It failed to pass the Senate by a two-thirds vote.
   E. It was rejected by the state constitutional conventions.

7. President George W. Bush was criticized for limiting the scope of legislation passed by Congress through
   A. pocket vetoes
   B. executive orders
   C. signing statements
   D. line-item vetoes
   E. executive agreements

8. Efforts to increase voter turnout have focused on
   A. giving people time off to vote
   B. making it easier for people to register to vote
   C. passing laws that make voting mandatory
   D. lowering the voting age to 16
   E. providing people with more information about elections

9. Block grants are sometimes criticized because

    A.   They focus on very specific policy concerns.

    B.   It is difficult to determine if the funded programs are successful.

    C.   There are too many strings attached.

    D.   They account for the majority of federal aid to the states.

    E.   They give local officials limited authority.

10. The Supreme Court's decisions on affirmative action confirm that

    A.   Race can be a factor in college admissions.

    B.   Numeric quotas based on race or gender are acceptable.

    C.   Public schools can use race classifications in assigning students.

    D.   Busing students is the only remedy for de facto segregation.

    E.   Numerical set-asides for minority businesses are constitutional.

11. Superdelegates at Democratic Party nominating conventions are

    A.   required to vote for the candidate they first endorsed

    B.   delegates from states with a large number of electoral votes

    C.   elected public officials and party leaders

    D.   chosen to represent specific interest groups

    E.   a very small percentage of the convention delegates

Gains and Losses of the President's Party in Midterm Elections			
President	**Year**	**House**	**Senate**
Lyndon Johnson	1966	−47	−4
Richard Nixon	1970	−12	+2
Gerald Ford	1974	−48	−5
Jimmy Carter	1978	−15	−3
Ronald Reagan	1982	−26	+1
Ronald Reagan	1986	−5	−8
George H. W. Bush	1990	−8	−1
Bill Clinton	1994	−52	−8
Bill Clinton	1998	+5	−8
George W. Bush	2002	+8	+2
George W. Bush	2006	−30	−6

12. Which of the following conclusions is supported by the table?

    A.   The president's party gains seats when he is a lame duck.

    B.   The results of midterm elections always lead to divided government.

    C.   Republican presidents lose more seats in the House than Democratic presidents do.

    D.   Foreign policy issues are the main reasons that the president's party loses seats.

    E.   The president's party doesn't always lose seats in both houses.

13. Which political cause usually associated with liberals have some religious conservatives recently come to support?

    A.   school vouchers

    B.   the environment

    C.   stem-cell research

    D.   increases in domestic spending

    E.   same-sex marriage

14. The Intelligence Community is a federation of executive branch agencies headed by

    A. the director of the Central Intelligence Agency
    B. the president
    C. the National Security Advisor
    D. the Director of National Intelligence
    E. the chair of the Joint Chiefs of Staff

15. When an independent regulatory commission engages in rule making, it is exercising its

    A. executive power
    B. constitutional power
    C. legislative power
    D. judicial power
    E. fiduciary power

16. Fear that concentration of the electronic media in a few hands will limit the range of political opinion available is challenged by

    A. the prevalence of political blogs
    B. the number of newspapers in the country
    C. the 24-hour news cycle of cable stations
    D. effective federal regulation
    E. the popularity of network news programming

17. If the president elect dies in January, before the inauguration but after the electoral votes have been submitted to Congress, what happens?

    A. The leadership of the successful party selects a new president.
    B. Congress calls a new election.
    C. The vice president elect becomes president.
    D. The decision is left to Congress under the Twenty-fourth Amendment.
    E. The candidate who received the second most electoral votes becomes president.

18. At a party's national convention, issues relating to the status delegates are decided by the

    A. credentials committee
    B. party's nominee
    C. chair of the party's national committee
    D. rules committee
    E. majority of the delegates

19. Through a discharge petition, members of the House can

    A. end a filibuster
    B. impose a time limit on amendments from the floor
    C. call for new elections of the Speaker
    D. force a bill out of committee
    E. require an immediate role-call vote

20. Given the current demographic trends, the concerns of which group will become increasingly important to politicians?

    A. African Americans
    B. younger Americans
    C. Hispanic Americans
    D. Asian Americans
    E. white non-Hispanic Americans

21. Which of the following would not be considered a single-issue interest group?

    A. NARAL Pro-Choice America
    B. National Rifle Association
    C. Mothers Against Drunk Driving
    D. People for the Ethical Treatment of Animals
    E. National Association of Manufacturers

22. In a presidential election, which of the following is numerically the largest?

    A. registered voters
    B. voting-age population
    C. voter turnout
    D. eligible voters
    E. votes cast

23. For a person convicted in a state court of a crime, what are valid grounds for an appeal to the Supreme Court?

    I. The conviction was based on a state law that violated the Constitution.

    II. There is new evidence that the individual did not commit the crime.

    III. The individual did not receive a fair trial because of the way the jury was selected.

    IV. The state Supreme Court refused to review the conviction.

    A. I only
    B. I and III only
    C. II and III only
    D. I, III, and IV only
    E. I, II, and III only

24. Through the 1950s, the NAACP was most effective in advocating for civil rights through

    A. holding nonviolent protests
    B. lobbying Congress to pass civil rights laws
    C. mounting legal challenges to discrimination
    D. conducting voter registration drives in the South
    E. supporting candidates running for office

25. A COLA was added to Social Security in 1973 to

    A. expand those eligible for the program
    B. increase the money in the Social Security Trust Fund
    C. reduce benefits to keep the program solvent
    D. take into account the impact of inflation on benefits
    E. allow workers to open up private retirement accounts

26. The ongoing shift of population to the South and West has meant

    A. Democratic majorities in Congress
    B. more federal money to those regions
    C. greater attention paid to education issues
    D. increases in defense spending
    E. stricter enforcement of immigration laws

27. The responsibility of the FISA Court is to

    A. approve wiretap warrants requested in national-security investigations
    B. try U.S. citizens accused of terrorist acts
    C. serve as an appeals court for military tribunals
    D. decide whether a foreign terror suspect is subject to extradition
    E. rule on whether national-security information can be presented at trial

28. The order of presidential succession is provided for in

    A. the Constitution
    B. the Twenty-fifth Amendment
    C. an executive order
    D. a joint congressional resolution
    E. a federal law

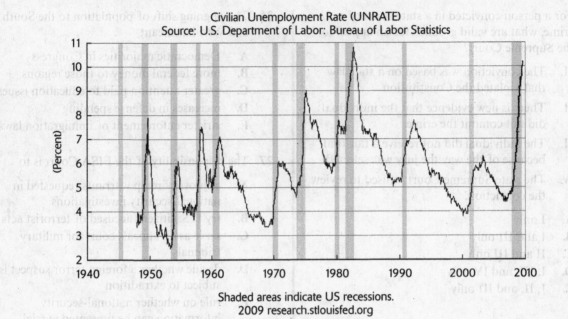

Civilian Unemployment Rate (UNRATE)
Source: U.S. Department of Labor: Bureau of Labor Statistics

Shaded areas indicate US recessions.
2009 research.stlouisfed.org

Source: Federal Reserve Bank of St. Louis. http://research.stlouisfed.org/fred2/series/UNRATE.

29. What conclusion can you draw about the unemployment rate and recessions from the above graph?

   A. The unemployment rate often peaks after a recession.
   B. The length of recessions are becoming longer.
   C. Teenagers have the highest unemployment rate.
   D. The range of the unemployment rate is between 3 percent and 10 percent.
   E. There is no relation between recession and the unemployment rate.

30. If Congress objects to a decision of the Supreme Court,

   A. It can refuse to enforce the decision.
   B. It can impeach and remove the chief justice.
   C. There is no legislative remedy.
   D. It can pass a law to get around the decision.
   E. It can only propose a constitutional amendment.

31. In shaping an individual's political outlook, the LEAST important factor is

   A. family
   B. level of education
   C. race and religion
   D. place of residence
   E. the media

32. All the following statements about focus groups are valid EXCEPT:

   A. They allow the campaign to take the pulse of likely voters.
   B. Participants are usually paid for their time.
   C. They're used to evaluate campaign ads or candidate positions.
   D. They're made up of individuals who have similar backgrounds.
   E. They can influence the direction a campaign takes.

33. The term *straight ticket* refers to

    A. a party's candidates for president and the Senate sharing the same views
    B. voting for all the candidates from one party running for office
    C. a member of Congress voting for a bill supported by the majority party
    D. voting for candidates based on their stands on the issues rather than their party affiliations
    E. a delegate to the national convention supporting one candidate on all ballots

34. Which of the following Supreme Court decisions limited the power of the federal government with respect to municipalities?

    A. *Gibbons v. Ogden*
    B. *South Dakota v. Dole*
    C. *United States v. Lopez*
    D. *McCulloch v. Maryland*
    E. *Heart of Atlanta Motel v. United States*

35. In an iron triangle, what does an interest group provide to both the federal agency and the congressional committee?

    A. campaign contributions
    B. information
    C. proposals on rule making
    D. help with constituents
    E. draft legislation

36. A member of the House of Representatives who considers himself or herself a delegate is most likely to

    A. follow the party leadership on all votes
    B. vote his or her conscience most of the time
    C. give weight to the views of the administration
    D. gauge the views of constituents before casting an important vote
    E. listen carefully to the arguments of lobbyists

37. Which group of Franklin Roosevelt's New Deal coalition have Democrats lost support of in recent years?

    A. organized labor
    B. immigrants
    C. southerners
    D. African Americans
    E. liberals

38. The healthcare debate during the Obama Administration focused on what issues?

    I. healthcare costs
    II. training of physicians
    III. expanding health insurance coverage
    IV. the role of the federal government

    A. I and III only
    B. I, II, and III only
    C. I, II, III, and IV
    D. I, III, and IV only
    E. II, III, and IV only

39. Which of the following appointments made by the president does NOT require Senate approval?

    A. director of the Office of Management and Budget
    B. White House chief of staff
    C. chair of the Federal Communications Commission
    D. deputy secretary of defense
    E. director of the Central Intelligence Agency

40. In a unitary government, education policy is

    A. set at the local level
    B. a shared responsibility of central and regional authorities
    C. established and implemented by the central government
    D. in the hands of a private corporation
    E. decided by the political leader

41. When nominating a judge to the federal courts, presidents take into account all the following EXCEPT:

    A. judicial philosophy
    B. marital status
    C. party affiliation
    D. experience
    E. gender

42. Under the Bush Doctrine, the United States can use force

    A. when attacked by another country
    B. only in consultation with our allies
    C. with the consent of Congress
    D. in the fact of a threat to U.S. security
    E. with the formal approval of an international organization

43. A bankruptcy case involving U.S. citizens on the island of Guam would be heard in a(n)

    A. U.S. district court
    B. territorial court
    C. appellate court
    D. international tribunal
    E. state bankruptcy court

44. Which of the following statements does NOT reflect the Supreme Court's position on the death penalty?

    A. Electrocution is cruel and unusual punishment.
    B. Minors who commit a capital offense are not subject to the death penalty.
    C. The death penalty must be applied evenly.
    D. Mentally retarded people cannot be executed.
    E. The rape of a child does not warrant the death penalty.

45. In a period of high inflation, the federal government would likely

    A. raise interest rates
    B. reduce taxes
    C. increase spending
    D. expand exports
    E. lower interest rates

46. The results of a public opinion poll can be invalid for all the following reasons EXCEPT:

    A. The number of those polled is too small.
    B. The sample polled is biased in some way.
    C. Random-digit dialing only contacts home phones.
    D. The poll questions are poorly worded.
    E. The margin of error is plus or minus 3 percent.

47. The Supreme Court's ruling in *Lawrence v. Texas* dealt with

    A. free speech
    B. the right to counsel
    C. the right to privacy
    D. extradition
    E. affirmative action

48. After the Persian Gulf War (1990–1991), the George H. W. Bush Administration was criticized for

    A. its unilateral approach to the conflict
    B. not invading Iraq to topple the regime
    C. inadequate military forces
    D. failing to get United Nations approval
    E. the heavy U.S. casualties

49. The purpose of a presidential primary is to

    A. determine the party's candidate for vice president
    B. discuss issues relevant in the general election
    C. raise money for the eventual nominee
    D. select delegates to the party's national convention
    E. determine the party platform

50. President George W. Bush expanded the role of the federal government in which policy areas?

    I.   national security
    II. public works
    III. healthcare
    IV. education

    A. I and II only
    B. I, II, and III only
    C. II, III, and IV only
    D. I, III, and IV only
    E. III and IV only

51. Looking at presidential elections between 1976 and 2000, voters chose candidates who

    A. had executive experience
    B. were foreign policy experts
    C. had a moderate political outlook
    D. believed that government was the solution to the country's problems
    E. ran as political outsiders

Party Identification 3-Point Scale, 1952–2004

Source: The American National Election Studies (www.electionstudies.org). The ANES Guide to Public Opinion and Electoral Behavior. Ann Arbor, MI: University of Michigan, Center for Political Studies [producer and distributor].

52. What conclusions can you draw about party identification among Democrats from the above graph?

   I.   Party identification rises and falls with presidential elections.

   II.   Party identification among Democrats has decreased.

   III.   Most Americans consider themselves independents.

   IV.   Party identification is affected by midterm elections.

   A.   II only

   B.   I and II only

   C.   I, II, and III only

   D.   I, II, and IV only

   E.   I, II, III, and IV

53. A judge who believes in *stare decisis*

   A.   is considered a judicial activist

   B.   also follows the plain meaning rule

   C.   is cautious in overturning precedents

   D.   is a strict constructionist

   E.   would not be qualified to serve on the Supreme Court

54. Members of the Senior Executive Service

   A.   are the highest ranking employees in the federal civil service

   B.   are easily fired from their positions

   C.   are paid comparable to other government employees

   D.   are appointed by the president

   E.   are the spokespersons for their agencies

55. All the following are restrictions the Supreme Court has allowed on abortions EXCEPT:

   A.   use of federal funds for abortions

   B.   parental notification for minors seeking abortions

   C.   protesters limiting access to abortion clinics

   D.   a ban on late-term abortions (sometimes referred to as "partial-birth abortions")

   E.   a waiting period before a woman can have an abortion

56. The concept of separation of powers in the Constitution refers to relations between

   A.   the states and the federal government

   B.   the executive, legislative, and judicial branches

   C.   the executive departments

   D.   the executive branch and Congress only

   E.   the states and the executive branch

57. The power of the vice president was expanded under the Twenty-fifth Amendment to include

   A. presiding over the Senate
   B. serving as the chief foreign policy envoy of the president
   C. voting to break a tie in the Senate
   D. leading his or her party in the Senate
   E. helping to determine whether the president can continue to serve

58. What term best characterizes U.S. foreign policy after World War II?

   A. unilateralism
   B. containment
   C. isolationism
   D. collective security
   E. human rights

59. The Reform Party, which sought to attract voters from the Democrats and Republicans, was identified with which candidate?

   A. George Wallace
   B. Ralph Nader
   C. Ross Perot
   D. John Anderson
   E. Eugene V. Debs

60. A seat in the House of Representatives is said to be open when

   A. The incumbent is not running for reelection.
   B. The incumbent and a challenger are even in the polls.
   C. The incumbent has no challenger.
   D. There is no party primary for the seat.
   E. The seat covers a new district because of reapportionment.

IF YOU FINISH BEFORE TIME IS CALLED, CHECK YOUR WORK ON THIS SECTION ONLY. DO NOT WORK ON ANY OTHER SECTION IN THE TEST.

Section II: Free-Response Questions

Time: 100 minutes
4 questions

Directions: You have 100 minutes to answer all four of the following questions. Unless the directions indicate otherwise, respond to all parts of all four questions. It is suggested that you take a few minutes to plan and outline each answer. Spend approximately one-fourth of your time (25 minutes) on each question. Illustrate your essay with substantive examples where appropriate. Be sure to number each answer in the same way the question is numbered below.

---

1. The Fifteenth Amendment (1870) expanded the right to vote to African Americans, but it took a century for that right to be fully realized.

   a. Describe two ways in which African Americans were denied the right to vote in the decades after the ratification of the amendment.
   b. Explain two ways by which the federal government protected voting rights for African Americans.
   c. Explain two ways the civil rights movement advocated for voting rights for African Americans.

2. The recent recession was the worst economic crisis the United States faced since the Great Depression. The federal government used the tools of fiscal and monetary policy to try to put the economy back on track.

   a. Identify three indications of an economic slowdown.
   b. Explain two fiscal policy actions that might help in a recession.
   c. Explain two monetary policy actions that might help in a recession.

3. Interest groups play an important role in U.S. politics. They contribute to political campaigns, help shape legislation before Congress, and have input on federal regulations. Some people say interest groups have too much influence on the political process.

   a. Identify two types of interest groups and provide one example for each.
   b. Explain two reasons why individuals join an interest group.
   c. Describe two ways in which the federal government has tried to limit the influence of interest groups.

4. The Constitution creates three coequal branches of government, but the judiciary is treated differently from either Congress or the president.

   a. Identify two ways in which federal judges differ from both members of Congress and the president.
   b. Discuss two ways in which Congress can affect the federal courts.
   c. Discuss two ways in which the president can affect the federal courts.

IF YOU FINISH BEFORE TIME IS CALLED, CHECK YOUR WORK ON THIS SECTION ONLY. DO NOT WORK ON ANY OTHER SECTION IN THE TEST.

Answer Key

Section I: Multiple-Choice Questions

1. A	21. E	41. B
2. C	22. B	42. D
3. E	23. B	43. B
4. D	24. C	44. A
5. A	25. D	45. A
6. C	26. B	46. E
7. C	27. A	47. C
8. B	28. E	48. B
9. B	29. A	49. B
10. A	30. D	50. D
11. C	31. D	51. A
12. E	32. A	52. D
13. B	33. D	53. C
14. D	34. C	54. A
15. C	35. B	55. C
16. A	36. D	56. B
17. C	37. C	57. E
18. A	38. B	58. B
19. D	39. B	59. B
20. C	40. C	60. A

Section II: Free-Response Questions

Student essays and analyses begin on page 249.

Answer Explanations

Section I: Multiple-Choice Questions

1. **A** A tracking poll is conducted on a regular basis, often daily as an election approaches, and can detect changes in support for a candidate or an issue like a proposition on the ballot. Telephone polls are a polling method, and tracking polls are conducted by telephone.

2. **C** Although legislation can pass with a simple majority, the notion that 60 votes are needed is because of the possibility of a filibuster in the Senate. A filibuster is unlimited debate and can be ended through a cloture vote that requires 60 votes. Once cloture is voted, the bill can be enacted by a simple majority.

3. **E** Public opinion rallies behind a president in times of international tension; President George H. W. Bush's approval rose dramatically after the Persian Gulf War as did his son's approval in the wake of September 11. If the crisis costs lives and drags on as the Iraq War did, presidential approval falls just as dramatically.

4. **D** Although some of its members are from the South, the coalition includes representatives from the Midwest, Northeast, and West. Formed in 1995, it has over 50 members committed to financial stability and national security.

5. **A** A concurrent power is one shared by all levels of governments—federal, state, and local. There is a federal income tax and most states have a state income tax, as do cities like New York. Just like the federal government, the states rely on taxation to fund programs they're responsible for—education, police, health, and social welfare, for example.

6. **C** The Equal Rights Amendment was approved by Congress and sent to the states for ratification in 1972. The required three-fourths of the state legislatures did not ratify the amendment within the seven-year time limit. Congress extended the time limit to June 30, 1982, and the amendment still did not have support in the required number of states.

7. **C** Signing statements are written comments made by the president when a bill is signed into law. President Bush's statements often indicated that he would not implement parts of the law that he believed undermined executive authority or national security. The Supreme Court declared the presidential line-item veto unconstitutional in 1998.

8. **B** The National Voter Registration Act (1993) and state laws that allow same-day registration and voting are examples of ways to make it easier for people to vote.

9. **B** Block grants cover broad policy areas such as public health, education, or crime prevention rather than specific programs. They give local officials much broader discretion on the use of funding, and the very lack of comprehensive federal oversight is considered a potential problem in determining how well the money is used.

10. **A** The decision in *Gratz v. Bollinger* (2003) upheld this key point that was originally included in *Regents of the University of California v. Bakke* (1978). The Supreme Court ruled the opposite of the statements in choices **B** through **E**. In *Parents Involved in Community Schools v. Seattle School District No. 1* (2007), the Court specifically held that race could not be used in assigning pupils to schools.

11. **C** Superdelegates are present or former elected officials—members of Congress or governors—or individuals selected by the state party organizations. In 2008, many superdelegates originally came out for Hillary Clinton but switched to Barack Obama later in the primary campaign. They represented about 20 percent of the delegates at the Democratic National Convention.

12. **E** Republicans gained seats in both houses in 2002, while Democrats lost eight Senate seats in 1998 but picked up five in the House. Republicans lost heavily in the House in 1982 but gained one seat in the Senate. Domestic issues explain the Republican loses under Gerald Ford in 1974 and Democratic losses under Clinton in 1994.

13. **B** The answer should be easy to identify even if you aren't aware that a growing number of conservative religious leaders maintain that caring for the earth is an obligation. School vouchers is not a liberal cause,

and conservatives oppose embryonic stem-cell research and same-sex marriage. Small government is a basic conservative belief.

14. **D** The Director of National Intelligence is the highest intelligence official in the United States. The position was created by Congress in 2004, and the director is responsible for providing objective intelligence to the president, the executive departments, the Joint Chiefs of Staff, and the Congress.

15. **C** In rule making, independent regulatory commissions hear from those affected by the proposed rule in hearings that are similar to a legislative process. Commissions carry out executive functions when they see that their rules are properly executed.

16. **A** Hundreds of political blogs are on the Internet, and they range in terms of content and slant across the political spectrum.

17. **C** The Twentieth Amendment states: "If, at the time fixed for the beginning of the term of the president, the president elect shall have died, the vice president shall become president."

18. **A** In 2008, Florida and Michigan moved their presidential primaries up to January against Democratic Party rules and were stripped of their delegates to the convention. The status of the delegates from the two states became an issue during the primary campaign. Although both the chair of the Democratic National Committee and Barack Obama played a role here, it was ultimately the credentials committee that decided to seat the delegations at the convention.

19. **D** It takes a majority of the members of the House to successfully get a discharge petition to bring a bill to the floor for a vote. The filibuster is allowed only in the Senate. Election of the Speaker is up to the members of the majority party.

20. **C** Hispanics are the largest single racial/ethnic minority in the United States, and their numbers are expected to increase significantly over the next 40 years. White non-Hispanics are declining as a percentage of the population. Younger Americans historically do not turn out to vote.

21. **E** The National Association of Manufacturers is the oldest industrial trade association (1895). Its members are concerned with a much broader range of issues (including the environment, tax policy, and international trade) than the more focused agendas of the other interest groups listed.

22. **B** The voting-age population is all people living in the United States 18 years of age or older; it includes individuals who cannot vote—noncitizens and felons. The number of votes cast is also smaller than any of the other measures except voter turnout, which is the same but usually expressed as a percentage.

23. **B** The Supreme Court hears cases from the state court only if a "federal question" is involved (a claim that a state law violated the Constitution or the trial violated the defendant's rights). The refusal of the state supreme court to act is, by itself, not grounds for the case going before the Supreme Court.

24. **C** The NAACP won a number of major cases that eliminated the white primary, segregation on interstate transportation, segregation in graduate schools, and the separate-but-equal doctrine in public education in *Brown v. Board of Education* (1954).

25. **D** This question requires that you know that COLA stands for cost of living adjustment. COLAs are tied to the annual increase in the Consumer Price Index.

26. **B** Population is an important element in federal funding formulas. Since the regions have more members in the House, they can direct more federal projects to their districts. In 2004, California, the most populous state with the largest congressional delegation, received the most federal money.

27. **A** If you know that FISA stands for Foreign Intelligence Surveillance Act, the answer is obvious. The court's only function is to authorize surveillance and it has almost always agreed to the government's request for a warrant. It is not a trial court.

28. **E** The Presidential Succession Act of 1947 established the order of success when there are vacancies in the offices of president and vice president. The order is Speaker of the House, president pro tempore of the Senate, followed by the members of the Cabinet in the order in which their executive department was created, beginning with the Secretary of State. The 1947 law has been amended to account for the creation

of new executive departments such as the Department of Homeland Security. Article III, Section 1 of the Constitution states only that the powers and duties of the office of president shall devolve on the vice president. The Twenty-fifth Amendment clarifies that in the event of the death or resignation of the president, the vice president becomes president.

29. **A** It is clear from the graph that unemployment continues to rise after a recession is officially over. The unemployment rate has dropped below 3 percent and risen above 10 percent. While teenagers do have the highest unemployment rate, the graph doesn't break down categories of unemployed.

30. **D** Congress does pass legislation in response to Supreme Court decisions. The Lilly Ledbetter Fair Pay Act (2009) specifically referred to the ruling in *Ledbetter v. Goodyear Tire & Rubber Co.* (2007), which Congress felt restricted the protections against pay discrimination.

31. **D** Americans are a very mobile people. If a person moves from one part of the country to another, it's unlikely that his or her political views will change very much because of the change in locale.

32. **A** A focus group is not a scientific poll or survey. It's a small group, usually no more than a dozen people. A focus group is considered a qualitative rather than a quantitative measure—predictions about the views of a larger group cannot be made from a focus group.

33. **B** When an individual votes a straight ticket, he or she votes for all the Democratic or Republican candidates on the ballot. This is the opposite of ticket splitting, in which a person votes for a candidate from one party for president and a candidate from another party for another office.

34. **C** In *United States v. Lopez,* the Court held that Congress exceeded its authority when it banned guns near school based on the Commerce Clause. All the other landmark cases expanded federal authority. *Heart of Atlanta Motel v. United States* upheld the use of the Commerce Clause in the 1963 Civil Rights Act to ban discrimination in places of public accommodation.

35. **B** While proposed rules and draft legislation might be shared with agency and committee staff, respectively, information is a commodity that an interest group will always share with the other members of an iron triangle.

36. **D** Delegates see themselves as the voice of the people who elected them and try to reflect their views in voting. A trustee would vote his or her conscience even if that meant going against the will of his or her constituents.

37. **C** The Democrats lost the "Solid South" because of inroads make by George Wallace in the 1960s and the concerted effort of Republicans to win over more conservative Southern voters. All the other groups.are still firmly in the Democratic camp.

38. **D** Although concern was expressed whether there are enough primary-care doctors, physician training was not a significant issue. Controlling the rising cost of healthcare and providing coverage to the 47 million Americans without health insurance was the focus of the debate. Republicans and conservatives expressed serious concern about the federal government becoming the health provider of choice.

39. **B** All members of the White House staff do not require Senate confirmation. Appointments to various offices with the Executive Office of the President, the heads of regulatory agencies, and many sub-cabinet positions in the executive departments do.

40. **C** In a unitary system, power is held almost exclusively by the central government. In our federal system, education largely falls to state departments of education and local school boards, but with the Congress and the executive branch having influence, particularly in funding. Answer **E** suggests that all unitary governments are dictatorships.

41. **B** The only irrelevant factor is marital status. A president would take into consideration all the other choices. For example, Ronald Reagan pledged to appoint a woman to the Supreme Court during the 1980 campaign.

42. **D** Preemption justified the Iraq War based on the perceived threat from the WMD program Saddam Hussein was expected to have. Preemption does not require an attack on the United States or its allies or action by an international body; it is unilateral action.

43. **B** There are three U.S. territories that have territorial courts: Guam, the Virgin Islands, and the Northern Mariana Islands. While similar to U.S. district courts, judges on the territorial courts do not have life tenure. Answer **D** suggests that Guam is a sovereign country, which it is not.

44. **A** The Nebraska State Supreme Court struck down electrocution as the method of execution because of the pain it inflicted; it has not been found unconstitutional by the U.S. Supreme Court. All the other answers are positions that the Court has taken.

45. **A** Raising interest rates discourages spending and is a means of slowing down the economy. Increasing spending and lowering interest rates are policies adopted to end a recession. The federal government can impact imports through tariff policy, but it has less influence over exports, and trade balance is usually not an anti-inflation measure. Lower taxes might add to inflation.

46. **E** The margin of error given is standard for polls with a sample size of 1,000. It's difficult to make predictions based on a poll with a sample less than 1,000. Younger voters rely heavily on cellphones and may not be captured in a telephone poll using random-digit dialing.

47. **C** In *Lawrence v. Texas,* the Court struck down Texas's sodomy law, which effectively criminalized homosexual behavior between consenting adults in private.

48. **B** Some people in and out of government believed that the successful conclusion of the war was an opportunity to topple Saddam Hussein. The war was fought by a coalition with significant contributions from Arab states. Over 500,000 troops were involved, U.S. casualties were limited, and the U.N. supported the action.

49. **D** The purpose of a presidential primary is to select delegates to the party's national convention who will vote for the presidential candidate they represented in the primary. The party platform is hammered out by the Platform Committee and is voted on at the convention. The party's vice-presidential candidate is chosen by the presidential candidate and is approved by the delegates at the convention.

50. **D** The key programs were the creation of the Department of Homeland Security, the No Child Left Behind Act (having to do with education), and the prescription drug benefit in Medicare.

51. **A** Jimmy Carter, Ronald Reagan, Bill Clinton, and George W. Bush all served as governors. Only President George H. W. Bush had a strong foreign policy background. Carter and Clinton were hardly conservatives, but neither were they traditional liberal Democrats.

52. **D** No conclusions can be drawn about independent voters, since the data only concerns Democrats. Party identification is clearly impacted by whether Democrats win or lose elections, and the trend on the graph is toward less party identification for Democrats.

53. **C** This is a definition question. *Stare decisis* means "let the decision stand"; it indicates the attitude toward precedent or previous decisions of a court.

54. **A** Members of the Senior Executive Service serve in positions just below presidential appointees. Civil service rules make it difficult to fire any federal bureaucrat, and members of the Senior Executive Service are among the highest paid civil servants.

55. **C** The Court has supported limited restrictions on the actions of protesters—*Madsen v. Women's Health Center, Inc.* (1994) and *Hill v. Colorado* (2000). Congress passed the Freedom of Access to Clinic Entrances Act in 1994.

56. **B** Separation of powers refers to the three coequal branches of government. Although most separation-of-powers issues involve the president and Congress, it's certainly possible for the courts to encroach on the powers given to the president or Congress.

57. **E** This question is more about the Twenty-fifth Amendment than about the vice president. If you know that the amendment deals with presidential disability, the answer is obvious. Answers **A** and **C** are provided for in Article I, Section 3 of the Constitution; the majority and minority leaders are selected by their respective party caucus.

58. **B** Although U.S. membership in NATO is an example of collective security, NATO itself was a key element of the containment policy that sought to prevent the expansion of the Soviet Union.

59. **C** Ross Perot ran for president as an independent in 1992 with no party affiliation; he formed the Reform Party for his second run for the presidency in 1996.

60. **A** When a vacancy occurs due to the death of a member of Congress, the governor of his or her state calls a special election. That election is for a vacant seat. But an open seat is also created when an incumbent decides not to run for reelection.

Section II: Free-Response Questions

Question 1

Scoring Guidelines

Part (a): 2 points (1 point for each method discussed)

Part (b): 2 points (1 point for each action taken by the Supreme Court or Congress)

Part (c): 2 points (1 point for each action taken by the civil rights movement)

Total: 6 points

Methods

- Grandfather clause
- White primary
- Poll tax
- Literacy test
- Complex registration procedures

Supreme Court decisions

- *Guinn v. United States* (1915)
- *Smith v. Allwright* (1944)
- *Harper v. Virginia Board of Elections* (1966)

Congressional actions

- Twenty-third Amendment (1961)
- Twenty-fourth Amendment (1964)
- Voting Rights Act (1965)
- Voting Rights Act Amendments (1970)

Civil rights movement

- Legal challenges to Jim Crow laws
- Protest demonstrations over voting rights
- Voter registration drives

Sample Answer

  After Reconstruction, the states of the former Confederacy enacted laws intended to prevent or severely restrict African Americans from voting. The legislation was part of a larger pattern of discrimination known as the Jim Crow laws, which maintained the segregated society in the South into the 1960s.

  The grandfather clause and the literacy test were two ways in which Southern legislatures used to keep African Americans from exercising their right to vote. Under the grandfather clause, a person who was entitled to vote or whose ancestor was entitled to vote before the Civil War did not have to take the literacy test or pay the poll tax. Since no African Americans in the South had the vote prior to Reconstruction, they would have to meet these other qualifications for voting. Many Africans Americans had very little if any education in the decades after the Civil War and were very poor. In some Southern states, people had to pass a literacy test in order to register to vote. The test often involved reading and understanding part of the state constitution. The test was administered by local election officials in such a way as to guarantee that African Americans would not pass.

Both the Supreme Court and Congress took action to guarantee African Americans the right to vote. An important early decision of the Supreme Court came in *Guinn v. United States* (1915), which struck down Oklahoma's voter registration law because the grandfather clause discriminated against African Americans in violation of the Fifteenth Amendment. Congress passed the landmark Voting Rights Act of 1965. The legislation effectively outlawed the literacy test as a means of qualifying voters. It also required that any changes in voting laws and procedures in certain parts of the country had to be cleared by either the Department of Justice or the U.S. District Court for the District of Columbia to ensure that they did not discriminate.

The civil rights movement used a variety of means to ensure that African Americans could vote throughout the country. They challenged discriminatory laws in the courts; for example, the NAACP played a key role in bringing *Guinn v. United States* to the Supreme Court. The civil rights movement also organized voter registration drives in the South during the 1960s; Freedom Summer in Mississippi in 1964 is a good example. The voter registration drive involved a number of civil rights groups, including the NAACP, CORE, and SNCC.

Reader Commentary

This answer certainly meets the requirements of the question. There are no factual errors, but the response could have been fleshed out just a bit more. The provisions of the Voting Rights Act could have been expanded on, and the student should have at least mentioned that the act was amended and extended several times after its original passage. It certainly would have been useful if the student had mentioned the recent Supreme Court challenge to the law, *Northwest Austin Municipal Utility District No. 1 v. Holder* (2009), and that African-American voter registration increased significantly after the passage of the law. The reference to Freedom Summer could have been expanded on as well. Why the focus on Mississippi? Score = 5.

Question 2

Scoring Guidelines

Part (a): 3 points (1 point for each indicator)

Part (b): 2 points (1 for each fiscal policy action)

Part (c): 2 points (1 for each monetary policy action)

Total: 7 points

Indicators of economic slowdown

- Gross domestic product
- Unemployment
- Industrial production
- Retail sales
- Stock market
- Home construction

Fiscal policy

- Responsibility of the executive branch and Congress
- Increase federal spending
- Lower taxes

Monetary policy

- Responsibility of the Federal Reserve System
- Money supply
- Interest rates

Sample Answer

A slowdown in the economy is going to be signaled by a variety of factors. The most important is the gross domestic product (GDP), which is the market value of all goods and services produced within a country during a year. Economists define a recession as two consecutive quarters of negative GDP. In addition to the GDP, policymakers will also look at unemployment data, particularly new claims for unemployment benefits. If this number is increasing month to month, it is obvious that businesses are laying off workers because there is limited demand for their products or services. The construction industry is another significant indicator. A decline in building permits indicates that new homes are not being built again because demand is not there. A couple who was planning to buy a new house decides not to because one spouse is out of work or the economic future looks uncertain.

Fiscal policy involves federal spending and taxation. Faced with an economy slipping into recession, the president and Congress most likely would decide to increase federal spending and cut taxes. In the spring of 2008, President George W. Bush's plan to stimulate the economy included a tax rebate—a maximum of $600 to individuals and $1,200 to couples. The idea behind the rebate was that people would spend the money and that buying would stimulate the economy. Concern over the future made many Americans save the rebate or use it to pay off credit card debt. When President Obama took office, the country was in the worst recession since the 1930s. His American Recovery and Reinvestment Act was an $800 billion program that included tax rebates, tax cuts, expansion of unemployment benefits, and billions of dollars earmarked for states and localities for construction and other projects. Again, the hope is that the additional money put in people's hands by rebates and tax credits will boost spending and the direct federal project money will create jobs and begin to reduce the high unemployment numbers.

Monetary policy refers to controlling the amount of money in circulation and this is the responsibility of the Federal Reserve System (the Fed). To get the economy back on track during a recession, the Fed will follow a loose monetary policy. It will encourage banks to lend by lowering the two interest rates it controls—the discount rate and the federal funds rate. During the recent recession, both of these rates were less than 1 percent. The idea here is that businesses will find credit cheap and decide that now is the time to borrow to expand their plants or buy new equipment. The factory producing the new equipment will hire back workers it may have let go when business was slow.

Reader Commentary

The student's answer is clearly weaker on monetary policy than it is on fiscal policy. The essay shows a good knowledge of the response of the president and Congress to economic crisis as well as the Fed's interest rate policy. But if the discount rate and federal funds rate are mentioned, they should be defined. Simply, the discount rate is the interest rate the Fed charges to member banks, and the federal funds rate is the interest rate commercial banks charge each other. The student does not mention the Fed's control over reserve requirements—the amount of cash a bank must have available—and how that might fit into a recession analysis. These are not fatal flaws in the essay, however. Score = 6.

Question 3

Scoring Guidelines

Part (a): 2 points (1 point for each example of a type of interest group)

Part (b): 2 points (1 point for each reason provided)

Part (c): 2 points (1 point for each way interest groups are controlled)

Total: 6 points

Types of interest groups

Acceptable examples are not limited to the following; business, labor, and agricultural interest groups may be included under the broader category of economic interest groups.

- Business
  - U.S. Chamber of Commerce
  - National Association of Manufacturers
- Labor
  - AFL-CIO
  - Teamsters
- Agriculture
  - American Farm Bureau Federation
  - American Dairy Association
- Public interest
  - Common Cause
  - League of Women Voters
- Environment
  - Sierra Club
  - Environmental Defense Fund
- Ethnic, racial, gender
  - NAACP
  - National Organization for Women
- Single issue
  - National Rifle Association
  - NARAL-Pro Choice America
- Governmental
  - National Association of Counties
  - National Governors Association

Reasons for joining

Students should note in their answer that reasons for an individual joining an interest group may differ from a business's reasons.

- Sense of belonging
- Material benefits
- Joint action

Regulation of interest groups

Students must point out that regulation occurs when interest groups try to influence public policy either through lobbying Congress or federal agencies or by participating in the electoral process.

- Registration of lobbyists
- Reports on lobbying activities
- Limitations on gifts to members of Congress
- Restrictions on members of Congress or other government officials lobbying
- Campaign contributions by political action committees

Sample Answer

   The number of interest groups in the U.S. has grown dramatically over recent decades and can be broken down into a variety of types; two of these are economic interest groups and single-issue interest groups. Economic interest groups can represent various types of businesses or entire industries (such as the American Petroleum Institute), workers through their labor unions, or farmers. One of the oldest and largest interest groups in this category in the National Association of Manufacturers. It represents its company members on a broad range of issues such as tax policy, environmental regulation, international trade, and energy. While the National Rifle Association provides its members with information and training on the safe use of firearms, it's best known for its effects at the local, state, and federal levels on gun control legislation.

   Individuals join interest groups for many reasons. One important incentive is the direct benefits of membership. These can include discounts on travel, group health insurance plans, and reduced costs for publications. The state chapters of the National Education Association, which represents teachers in the public schools, offer professional liability insurance. Trade associations offer somewhat different benefits to their company or corporate members. For example, the National Association of Manufacturers offers its members discounts on office supplies and shipping rates, as well as drug discount plans for employees and retirees through agreements with various vendors.

   Another reason for joining an interest group is to accomplish the goals or objectives that the group stands for. Individuals who feel strongly about an issue—abortion, global warming, tax policy—join interest groups so that they can help change policy. They understand that their dues and their voices joined with others who share their views can have an impact. No interest group is going to have every individual who supports its cause join the interest group; for many corporations joining a trade association or another business interest group may be essential and it's an expense that is well worth it. This is certainly the case for companies that can't afford to mount their own lobbying effort.

   An interest group's message is not subject to regulation, but its actions are. When an interest group tries to influence legislation or the decisions of a federal agency (lobbying) or when it puts money into electoral politics through its political action committee, it's subject to regulation. Congress enacted numerous laws in this area, and the most recent legislation (2007) tightened up rules in place since 1995. Lobbyists must register with Congress and have to submit reports on their activities more frequently than in the past. They also have to report their campaign contributions over $200 to a candidate, political action committee, or party. Members of Congress and their staff are prohibited from accepting gifts from lobbyists, including private travel.

Reader Commentary

The student should have defined, even briefly, an interest group. The essay makes a good point on the differences between an individual and a company joining an interest group, but these certainly could have been made clear. How important are the material incentives an interest group might offer to a company? If the student had been able to bring in the 2007 lobbying legislation, mention of the strict ethics and lobbying rules adopted early in the Obama Administration would have been welcome. Score = 5.

Question 4

Scoring Guidelines

Part (a): 2 points (1 point for each difference for both members of Congress and the president)

Part (b): 2 points (1 point for each way in which Congress can affect the federal courts)

Part (c): 2 points (1 point for each way the executive branch can affect the federal courts)

Total: 6 points

Differences

Difference	Courts *	Congress	President
Qualifications	None	Age, citizenship, residency	Age, natural-born citizen, residency
Term	In good behavior (for life)	Two years for the House, six years for the Senate	Four years
Salary	Can't be reduced during service	Can't be changed during term	Can't be increased or decreased during term

* Students must note that the above applies only to constitutional courts established under Article III, Section 1 of the Constitution; Congress has more control over the term and salary of judges who serve on legislative courts created under Article I, Section 8.

Congress and the federal courts

- Establishes federal courts below the Supreme Court
- Establishes the jurisdiction of the federal courts
- Congress sets the budget and appropriates money for the federal courts
- Senate confirms nominees for the federal courts
- Congress can sometimes reverse a federal court decision

The president and the federal courts

- Nomination of federal judges
- Enforcement of the decision of the federal courts

Sample Answer

The most obvious differences between federal judges who serve on constitutional courts—the U.S. Supreme Court, U.S. courts of appeals, and U.S. district courts—and members of Congress and the president relate to qualifications and term. Article III of the Constitution provides no specific qualifications for federal judges. In theory at least, a person appointed to the federal bench doesn't even have to be a lawyer and certainly doesn't need to have prior judicial experience. Earl Warren, who became chief justice of the Supreme Court, was the attorney general and governor of California but never heard a case. In contrast, Article I and Article II of the Constitution list specific age, citizenship, and residency requirements for those who serve in Congress and for the president; the qualifications are slightly different for members of the House and Senate, and only the president must be a natural-born citizen of the United States. Federal judges serve for life; although life tenure is not mentioned in Article III, this was stated as the meaning of "in good behavior" by Alexander Hamilton in *The Federalist Papers*. Judges can certainly retire early, as Justice David Souter recently did. The Constitution includes specific year terms for Congress and the president.

Congress has broad authority over the federal courts. It can, under Article III, increase the number of U.S. district courts or courts of appeals, and create new courts under the power granted in Article I, Section 8. The latter are known as legislative courts and include U.S. territorial courts and the FIS Court. In recent years, federal judges have complained about their heavy workload and have asked Congress to create additional courts; Congress has been reluctant to do this due to budget considerations. The Senate has the authority to confirm federal judicial appointments made by the president. The Senate Judiciary Committee holds major hearings on appointments to the Supreme Court; it is rare for the Senate to reject a presidential nominee, but the hearings give the public the opportunity to get to know the next Supreme Court justice and for senators to question the direction the Court might take. The Senate may delay confirmation of lower federal court judges for political reasons, forcing the president to make a recess appointment.

The president nominates all federal judges. It is generally recognized that the appointments to the Supreme Court are the most important for any administration. The selection is done very carefully with a variety of factors figuring into the mix—including qualifications, judicial philosophy, ethnicity, and gender. President Reagan made a campaign pledge to appoint the first woman to the Supreme Court and President Obama was interested in appointing the first Hispanic. Presidents almost always choose nominees from within their own parties.

Reader Commentary

The first two parts of the question are handled well. The student could have mentioned that judges in legislative courts typically serve for a fixed term, but that's a rather minor matter. The answer to the third section only addresses one way in which the executive branch affects the federal courts, and the most obvious one. The federal courts have no enforcement power of their own; instead, they rely on the president to enforce the law. President Andrew Jackson's opposition to John Marshall's decision in *Worcester v. Georgia* (1832) and President Eisenhower's use of federal troops to implement a lower federal court ruling on desegregation in Little Rock, Arkansas, in 1957 should remind us of that fact. Score = 5.

PART III

APPENDIXES

Glossary of Key Terms

administrative discretion The flexibility a federal agency can exercise in implementing legislation through its rules and regulations.

affirmative action A program intended to give a boost or preference to minority applicants over white applicants in contracting, employment, housing, and college or professional school admissions.

agenda setting Identification of the problems and/or issues that require the attention of the government to resolve.

amicus curiae brief A brief submitted to the court by an interested third party that outlines issues it thinks are important in the case. *Amicus curiae* literally means "friend of the court."

Antifederalists Those opposed to the ratification of the Constitution because it gave too much power to the central government at the expense of the states and because of the lack of a bill of rights. Notable Antifederalists were Patrick Henry and Thomas Jefferson.

appellate jurisdiction The power that a court has to review the decision of a lower court. The Supreme Court exercises appellate jurisdiction in the overwhelming majority of the cases it hears.

Articles of Confederation The first written constitution of the United States, which went into effect in 1781. It created a unicameral legislature (Confederation Congress), in which each state had one vote but no executive or judicial authority. The power of the central government was extremely limited; for example, Congress did not have the authority to tax or control foreign or interstate commerce.

bicameral legislature A two-house legislature. Congress and all the state legislatures with the exception of Nebraska are bicameral.

bill A proposed law.

bill of attainder A law that makes a person guilty of a crime without a trial. Neither Congress nor the states can enact such a law under the Constitution.

Bill of Rights The first ten amendments to the Constitution, ratified in 1791, which protect basic civil liberties.

blanket primary A primary election in which candidates from all parties are on the ballot, and a registered voter can vote for the Democratic candidate for one office and the Republican candidate for another.

block grants Federal funds given to the states for programs in broad policy areas such as law enforcement, with few, if any, restrictions on how the money is used.

brief A written document submitted to a court that presents the facts and legal reasoning of a party to the lawsuit.

capital gains tax A tax on the sale of stock or real property.

casework Services performed by an elected official for constituents. Examples of casework are a member of Congress getting tickets to tour the White House for a family from his or her district, or contacting the Department of Veterans Affairs for a person in his or her district.

cash-and-carry Provided for in the Neutrality Act of 1939, it stipulated that the United States could provide goods to countries at war if those countries paid cash and transported the goods in their own ships.

categorical grants Federal funds given to state and local governments for specific programs that usually require the recipient to match the money provided and have other strings attached.

caucus A group of members of Congress who may or may not be from the same party but who share common policy concerns; the Congressional Black Caucus is an example. The term also refers to a meeting of all the members of a party in Congress.

centralized federalism *See* creative federalism.

checks and balances A system in which each branch of the government has the power to limit the other branches of government so that one is not dominant; for example, the president can veto a bill passed by Congress, but Congress can override the veto. Related to the separation of powers.

clear and present danger test Established in *Schenck v. United States* (1919), it limits speech that is a "clear and present danger." The famous example of that type of speech cited in the decision is that a person cannot yell "Fire!" in a crowded theater.

closed convention A party national convention at which the nominee has already been determined through the primaries (one candidate won a majority of the delegates before the convention).

closed primary A primary election that is limited to registered voters of a particular political party.

closed rule A rule issued by the House Committee on Rules, in which there is a strict time limit for debate and no amendments can be offered.

cloture A method for cutting off a filibuster in the Senate. The Senate needs 16 votes to call for cloture and 60 votes to end a filibuster.

coattail effect The ability of a strong or popular candidate to get other candidates on the ticket elected. It is a term most often used in connection with a presidential candidate helping other members of the party to win an election.

confederal system A political system in which the states are sovereign and determine what authority the central government has.

committee report A report issued by the standing committee that examined a bill. It includes the text of the bill as reported by the committee, a summary of its provisions, and reasons for committee approval.

comparable worth A method for determining what compensation an employee should receive based on a calculation of the worth of that job. It is intended to eliminate the discrepancies in salaries paid to women and men. Also known as pay equity.

concurrent powers Powers that are shared by both the federal government and the states; taxation and the creation of courts are examples.

concurring opinion An opinion written by one or more judges in an appellate case that agrees with the decision but presents a different legal argument.

conference committee A committee made up of members of the House and the Senate that is responsible for reconciling the differences when two versions of the same bill pass both houses of Congress.

congressional review Congress's authority to review a new federal regulation and overrule it through a joint resolution.

congressional-executive agreement A trade agreement that requires approval of only a majority of both houses of Congress and not a two-thirds vote of the Senate.

Connecticut Compromise *See* Great Compromise.

constitutional courts Courts created by Congress under Article III, in which the judges serve for life; the U.S. courts of appeals are an example.

containment policy The policy adopted by the United States toward the Soviet Union after World War II, in which any attempt by the Soviet Union or communism to expand would be met by U.S. counterforce.

cooperative federalism A model of the relationship between the federal government and the states that developed during the 1930s. The power of the federal government expands into areas that the states are usually responsible for. Sometimes referred to as marble-cake federalism.

cost-benefit analysis A method of evaluating a public policy by determining whether the benefits of the policy outweigh its costs.

creative federalism A type of federalism identified with President Lyndon Johnson's Great Society. Under creative federalism, the federal government determines the needs of the states. Also known as centralized federalism.

cross-ownership In the mass media, when a corporation owns a broadcast outlet (for example, a television or radio station) and a print outlet in the same market.

de facto segregation Segregation that results from living patterns rather than law.

de jure segregation Segregation that results from law. For example, the Jim Crow laws in the South required racial segregation in public schools, public accommodations, public transportation, and many other areas.

delegate An elected official who considers it an obligation to vote the way the majority of his or her constituents wants.

delegated powers *See* enumerated powers.

deregulation The process of reducing or completely eliminating federal government oversight of an industry so as to allow it to operate more freely. Deregulation is supposed to encourage competition and reduce costs to consumers.

détente The U.S. policy of easing tensions with the Soviet Union during the Nixon Administration. The policy led to increased trade, cultural exchanges, and arms control agreements.

discount rate The interest rate that the Federal Reserve charges to member banks for loans. The discount rate is set by the Federal Reserve Board.

discretionary spending Federal spending that is authorized through the appropriations process. The amount included in the defense budget for personnel is an example.

dissenting opinion An opinion by a judge who voted in the minority, explaining the reasons for opposing the majority opinion.

divided government A situation that occurs when the president is from one party and Congress is controlled by the other party. This also occurs if the House is controlled by one party and the Senate by the other party.

domino theory A Cold War argument that if one country in a region fell to communism, the other countries in the region would quickly follow.

double jeopardy A rule that says that a person can't be tried by the same court under the same charges twice. Provided for in the Fifth Amendment.

dual federalism A model of the relationship between the federal government and the states in which each is supreme in its own sphere and tension exists between them. States' rights are emphasized, and the federal government is limited to the enumerated powers. Also known as layer-cake federalism.

due process Protection against the arbitrary loss of life, liberty, and property provided for under the Fifth and Fourteenth amendments.

Elastic Clause *See* Necessary and Proper Clause.

Electoral College A group of people, known as electors, who officially elect the president and vice president of the United States. The number of electors each state has is equal to the total number of representatives in Congress—two senators plus the number of representatives in the House. To be elected president, the candidate needs a majority vote of the Electoral College.

eminent domain The power of government at all levels to take private property for public use, as long as just compensation is paid.

entitlements Government benefits provided to Americans who qualify because of their age, income, and/or status (for example, children living below the poverty line, the disabled, and veterans).

enumerated powers Powers that the Constitution specifically grants to the federal government (Congress). Also known as delegated powers.

equal access rule A rule that says that the broadcast media must give all candidates for political office the same opportunity to be heard under Federal Communications Commission rules.

Equal Rights Amendment A proposed amendment to the Constitution that provided that equal rights "shall not be denied or abridged" on account of sex. It passed the Congress in 1972 but failed to be ratified by three-fifths of the state legislatures despite an extension of time to do so.

Establishment Clause First Amendment freedom-of-religion protection that focuses on the separation of church and state.

ex post facto law A law that makes an action a crime even though it was legal when it was committed or increases the penalty for a crime after it has been committed. Under the Constitution, neither the states nor Congress can pass such a law.

exclusionary rule A rule that says that evidence that is obtained illegally is not admissible in court.

executive agreement An agreement between the United States and another country that does not require approval of the Senate. An executive agreement is different from a treaty.

executive branch In the federal government; the executive branch consists of the president; the vice president; the Executive Office of the President; the executive departments; numerous independent federal agencies and government corporations; and various boards, commissions, and committees.

executive order Action by the president that does not require the approval of Congress.

executive privilege A claim by the president or a member of the executive branch that information or documents requested by Congress or the courts do not have to be turned over because of the separation of powers. The Supreme Court has limited the claim to national security matters.

exit poll A poll conducted on election day to determine how people voted.

fairness doctrine A doctrine that required the broadcast media to present opposing sides of controversial issues. It was abolished by the Federal Communications Commission in 1985.

fast-track authority Authority granted to the president to negotiate trade agreements that Congress must vote up or down without any amendments.

federal budget deficit The difference in any year between government spending and government revenue. The national debt is the cumulative unpaid total of the annual deficit.

federal system A political system in which power is divided between the national government and other governmental units.

Federalists Those who favored a stronger central government and supported the ratification of the Constitution. George Washington, James Madison, and Alexander Hamilton were Federalists.

filibuster Talking a bill to death on the Senate floor so that no other business can be conducted. Only a cloture vote can end a filibuster.

fiscal federalism A type of federalism that deals with the flow of funds through grants and other means from the federal government to the states and municipalities.

fiscal policy How the government uses taxes and spending to impact the economy. Associated with Keynesian economics.

flat tax A single low tax rate on all taxpayers coupled with the elimination of all or most exemptions.

formula grants Noncompetitive federal grants in which funding is determined by certain applied criteria: age group, per-capita income, percentage of population below the poverty line.

franking privilege The right of members of Congress to free use of the mail for official business.

Free Exercise Clause First Amendment freedom-of-religion protection against interference with the practice of religion.

free rider An individual who benefits from the activities of an interest group but does not support the group either financially or through active participation.

front loading The practice of bunching presidential primaries early in the year so that a majority of the delegates are selected by March.

fruit of the poisonous tree Additional evidence that is discovered from evidence obtained through an illegal search, which is also not admissible in court.

Full Faith and Credit Clause Article IV, Section 1 of the Constitution states that laws, records, and court decisions of one state are recognized and valid in every other state.

gender gap A situation in which men and women hold different positions on a wide range of political issues. In the United States, women tend to vote for the Democratic Party more than men do.

gerrymandering The redrawing of legislative district lines in such a way as to favor one political party over the other. Racial gerrymandering refers to creating districts that guarantee the election of a minority candidate.

good-faith exception A rule of evidence that says that if the authorities act "in good faith," evidence that otherwise might have been excluded may be admissible.

government corporation A corporation that may receive part of its funding from Congress and is managed by a board appointed by the president. The function that it performs could be carried out by private enterprise. The U.S. Postal Service is an example.

grass-roots lobbying Organizing a letter-writing campaign or taking out advertisements to influence public opinion and persuade elected officials to support a particular policy.

Great Compromise A solution to the problem of representation at the Constitutional Convention, in which the number of members that each state would have in the House of Representatives is determined by population, while each state would have equal representation in the Senate (two senators from each state).

gross domestic product The total output of goods and services produced in the United States, which is a measure of the health of the economy.

Group of Eight The world's major industrial nations—Canada, France, Germany, Great Britain, Italy, Japan, and the United States—plus Russia. The Group of Eight meets regularly to discuss global economic issues. Often referred to as the G8.

Gulf of Tonkin Resolution A joint resolution of Congress passed on August 4, 1964, in response to alleged attacks on U.S. naval vessels by North Vietnam. It authorized the president to use U.S. military force to respond to aggression in Southeast Asia. The resolution provided the justification for the increased involvement of the U.S. in the Vietnam War.

hard money Money used directly by a candidate running for office. It is subject to campaign finance laws and Federal Election Commission regulations.

Hatch Act (1939) A law that limits partisan political activity by federal employees.

hate speech Offensive speech against racial or ethnic minorities, women, and homosexuals that creates a hostile environment.

heightened scrutiny A standard adopted in *Craig v. Boren* (1976), in which classification of individuals based on gender must be related to an important government objective. It replaced the minimum rationality standard.

implied powers Powers of the federal government not specifically mentioned in the Constitution but derived from the Necessary and Proper Clause.

incorporation doctrine A doctrine that says that the Bill of Rights, with certain exceptions, applies to states and localities as well as the federal government through the Fourteenth Amendment.

independent executive agency An agency that is part of the executive branch but not included in any executive department. The head of the agency is appointed by the president and serves at the pleasure of the president. NASA and the CIA are examples.

independent regulatory agency An agency that is part of the executive branch and responsible for regulating and oversight of a segment of the economy. It is managed by a board or commission appointed by the president for a fixed term. The Federal Communications Commission (FCC) is an example.

inherent powers Powers, usually claimed by the president, that are implied but not specifically stated in the Constitution or are derived from the office.

interest group An organization whose members share the same concerns and try to influence public policy that impact those concerns.

interstate compact An agreement between two or more states approved by the Congress. The Colorado River Compact (1922), which divided water from the Colorado River between Arizona, California, Colorado, Nevada, New Mexico, Utah, and Wyoming, is a good example.

iron triangle The relationship that develops between interest groups, federal agencies, and the committee or sub-committees of Congress that have oversight over those agencies.

issue network The numerous people who are involved in the formulation of policy, including the president, members of Congress, the cabinet, lobbyists, interest groups, government agencies, and scholars and academics. A looser relationship than the iron triangle.

Jim Crow laws Laws passed by state legislatures in the South in the late 19th and early 20th centuries to create a racially segregated society and deprive African Americans of the right to vote.

joint committee A committee of Congress made up of members of both houses that focuses on issues of general concern but does not propose legislation. The Joint Economic Committee is an example.

judicial activism A judicial philosophy that holds that courts have a more expansive role to play in shaping public policy.

judicial branch Responsible for interpreting and applying the laws; in the federal government, it consists of the U.S. district courts, the U.S. appellate courts, various specialized courts, and the U.S. Supreme Court.

judicial restraint A judicial philosophy that holds that policymaking is the responsibility of the legislature not the courts.

judicial review The power of the Supreme Court to declare a law passed by Congress or the state legislatures or an executive action unconstitutional. Established in *Marbury v. Madison* (1903).

Keynesian economics An economic philosophy associated with the ideas of British economist John Maynard Keynes, in which economic slumps are seen as the result of too little demand, and government can stimulate demand by increasing spending and cutting taxes, even if this results in growing deficits.

laissez-faire economics An economic philosophy that says that the government should keep its hand off the economy and not interfere with business. This was a popular concept in the 19th century, when the federal government actually helped business through land grants to the railroads and high protective tariffs.

LAPS test Part of the criteria for determining obscenity, established in *Miller v. California* (1973). Work is considered obscene if it lacks "literary, artistic, political," or "scientific" value.

layer-cake federalism *See* dual federalism.

leak An unauthorized release of information to the press from someone in the government.

legislative branch Under Article I of the Constitution, the legislative branch consists of the House of Representatives and the Senate, which taken together form the U.S. Congress. The prime responsibility of the legislative branch is to enact laws.

legislative courts Courts created by Congress under Article I that deal with specialized cases. Judges serve in legislative courts for a fixed term.

legislative veto When Congress rejects an action of the president by a majority vote of both houses. Legislative veto was declared unconstitutional by the Supreme Court in *Immigration and Naturalization Service v. Chadha* (1983).

Lemon test Criteria established in *Lemon v. Kurtzman* (1971) concerning a law or government action dealing with religion. According to the Lemon test, such laws or actions are constitutional if they serve a secular purpose, do not inhibit or advance religion, and do not entangle the government with religion.

line-item veto When the president selectively vetoes parts of a bill without vetoing the entire bill. The line-item veto was declared unconstitutional by the Supreme Court in *Clinton v. City of New York* (1998).

lobbying The way an interest group tries to influence public policy.

logrolling An agreement between two or more members of Congress to vote for each other's bills.

mandate A law, regulation, or court decision that compels a state or local government to do something under the threat of legal action or the cutoff of federal funds.

mandatory spending Federal spending that is required by law (for example, for entitlement programs such as Social Security and veterans' benefits).

marble-cake federalism *See* cooperative federalism.

margin of error The percentage that a scientific poll is likely to be off. A margin of error of +/–3 percent is common.

means test A test used when income must be at a certain level to qualify for benefits from federal or state programs. There are means tests for such programs as the Supplemental Nutrition Assistance Program and Medicaid.

media event A staged public event that gives the press the opportunity to see an elected official in action and that presents the politician in a good light.

midterm elections Congressional elections held between presidential elections. The president's party usually loses seats in Congress in a midterm election.

minimum rationality standard In the 19th and through most of the 20th century, the standard used by the courts to determine if discrimination based on gender was valid. Also known as the reasonableness test. *See also* heightened scrutiny.

Miranda warning The warning that an individual must be read at the time of arrest and questioning, letting him know his Fifth and Sixth Amendment rights — his right to remain silent, the fact that anything he says may be used against him in court, his right to have an attorney present during questioning, and his right to have an attorney appointed if he can't afford one.

monetary policy Control of the growth of the monetary supply by the Federal Reserve System.

muckrakers During the Progressive Era (1900–1920), journalists committed to bringing political corruption and unsavory business practices to the public's attention. Today they are known as investigative reporters.

Necessary and Proper Clause A clause in Article I, Section 8 of the Constitution that enables the Congress to enact laws "necessary and proper" to carry out the enumerated powers. Also known as the Elastic Clause because it expands the power of the federal government.

New Deal Coalition A political coalition created by Franklin Roosevelt in the 1930s that included the South, organized labor, urban voters, and racial and ethnic minorities, including Catholics, Jews, and African Americans.

New Federalism A concept identified with Richard Nixon, in which power and money was supposed to flow from Washington, D.C., back to the states and municipalities.

nonpartisan election An election in which candidates run as independents without party affiliation.

North American Free Trade Agreement A treaty that established a free trade zone between the United States, Canada, and Mexico.

off the record Information provided in an interview that a reporter cannot directly use.

Office of Personnel Management An independent agency responsible for the federal civil service system; established in 1979, the OPM is the successor of the U.S. Civil Service Commission.

on background Information provided in an interview that a reporter can quote but can't attribute specifically to the interviewee.

on deep background Information provided in an interview that a reporter can use but can't make even an indirect reference to the source.

on the record Information provided in an interview that a reporter can quote and attribute to the source, referring to the source by name.

open convention A party national convention at which no candidate has won a majority of the delegates in the primaries. The candidate is chosen by the convention.

open primary A primary election in which an individual does not have to be a registered voter in a particular party to vote for candidates of that party. A registered Democrat can vote in the Republican primary, and vice versa.

open rule In the House of Representatives, a rule that allows any amendments to a bill, regardless of whether they're relevant to the legislation.

original jurisdiction The first court to hear a case. The Supreme Court has original jurisdiction in cases involving two or more states, the United States and a state, a state and the citizens of another state, and foreign diplomats.

party dealignment Weakening of ties between the voters and the two major parties. A situation in which voters increasingly identify themselves as independents.

party machine A political organization, typically at the local level, that wielded considerable power through its ability to get out the vote. The party machine relied heavily on patronage and providing services to constituents and was often corrupt.

party realignment A shift in voter loyalty in response to critical events. This occurred in 1932 with the election of Democrat Franklin Roosevelt.

pay equity *See* comparable worth.

plain meaning When the language of legislation under review by a court is clear and means what it says.

platform A statement of a political party on the issues facing the country, adopted at the national convention. Each issue position is known as a plank.

plurality opinion An opinion that presents the judgment of an appellate court that is not supported by a majority of the justices; in the Supreme Court, there have been plurality opinions issued by three or four justices.

pocket veto When the president takes no action on a bill within ten days of Congress adjourning, the bill does not become law. The pocket veto is provided for in Article I, Section 7 of the Constitution.

policy formulation The development of an approach to solving a problem that is on the political agenda. Congress, the president, federal agencies, and interest groups may each be involved in the process.

political action committee An organization established by a corporation, labor union, or other interest group to raise and contribute money to the campaigns of candidates for office or to a national party.

political agenda The issues that the American people believe are important for the government to handle.

political ideology A coherent set of beliefs about politics and the role of government.

political socialization The process by which people learn about the political system and develop their political views.

pork-barrel legislation Legislation that brings a federal program or project to the district or state of a member of Congress. Examples include the expansion of a military base, a new dam or other public works project, or a new highway.

prior restraint Action by the government to prevent the publication of material; censorship. The Supreme Court rejected the attempt by the Nixon Administration to prevent the publication of *The Pentagon Papers* on the Vietnam War in *The New York Times Co. v. United States* (1971).

progressive tax A tax that is higher for those who make more money. The federal income tax is an example of a progressive tax.

project grants Federal funding given for specific projects and awarded through a competitive process to states, local government, and individuals.

proportional representation When the delegates in a presidential primary are divided among the candidates based on the percentage of the votes received, as long as a minimum threshold (usually 15 percent) is achieved.

proposition A proposed law submitted to the voters for approval.

random sampling A statistical technique that gives everyone in the target group (for example, all eligible voters) the same opportunity to participate in a poll.

random-digit dialing The method often used to select households for a telephone poll.

reapportionment The states' loss or gain of seats in the House of Representatives based on the population changes between the decennial census.

reasonableness test *See* minimum rationality standard.

recall The process by which voters can decide to remove from office an elected official at the local or state level.

recess appointment A presidential appointment made when Congress is not in session. It does not require immediate confirmation.

recession A downturn in the economy; two consecutive quarters of a negative gross domestic product.

redistricting The process of redrawing congressional and state legislative district boundaries to reflect population changes in the decennial census; responsibility for redistricting usually falls to the individual state legislatures. *See also* reapportionment.

referendum A proposed law or state constitutional amendment presented to the voters by the state legislature.

regressive tax A tax that is assessed on everyone at the same rate and, therefore, impacts the poor more than it impacts the wealthy. The sales tax is regressive.

reserved powers Under the Tenth Amendment, powers not granted to the federal government or denied to the states that are reserved for the states or the people.

revenue sharing A program (1972–1986) that distributed federal funds to the states and municipalities with no restrictions on how the money could be spent.

reverse discrimination Programs such as affirmative action that help racial minorities and/or women and that actually discriminate against white males on the basis of race and/or gender.

revolving door The practice of government officials becoming lobbyists for the industries or companies they were responsible for regulating while they were public servants.

rider An amendment that is completely unrelated to the subject of a bill.

right-of-rebuttal rule A rule that says that a person attacked on radio or television must be given a reasonable opportunity to respond.

rule making The process by which federal agencies adopt regulations. It includes public notice, hearings, and written comments.

rule of four A rule that says that four of the nine Supreme Court justices must agree in conference to hear a case before it is put on the docket.

select committee A temporary committee of Congress set up for a specific purpose that is outside the scope of the standing committees. Also known as a special committee.

senatorial courtesy The right of a senior senator from the president's party to approve a nominee to a federal district court in his or her state.

separation of powers A key concept in the Constitution in which power in the federal government is divided between the legislative, executive, and judicial branches. It is closely tied to the concept of checks and balances.

shield laws State laws that provide journalists limited protection against revealing their sources.

soft money Money used by national, state, or local party organizations that is not regulated by the Federal Election Commission.

sound bite A very brief excerpt from a political speech aired on television or radio. The amount of time in a sound bite has decreased over the years.

Southern strategy A strategy adopted by the Republicans under Nixon, in which Republicans challenged traditional Democratic control in the southern states based on the premise that voters in the region are fundamentally conservative.

special committee *See* select committee.

splinter parties Third political parties that break off from either the Democrats or Republicans. Historically, splinter parties are the strongest third parties in terms of the popular and electoral vote.

split-ticket voting Voting for a candidate from one party for one office and from another party for another office. A person might vote for a Democrat for president but a Republican for governor; the opposite of straight-ticket voting.

spoils system A 19th-century system in which federal jobs were granted to political supporters.

stagflation A combination of high inflation and high unemployment. The United States experienced stagflation in the 1970s.

standard operating procedures Rules and procedures that are intended to make a bureaucracy run efficiently.

standing committee A permanent committee of Congress that deals with legislation and oversight in a broad policy area. For example, the Senate Foreign Relations Committee is a standing committee.

stare decisis The emphasis that courts give to precedent or previous decisions on the same issue. *Stare decisis* literally means "Let the decision stand."

straight-ticket voting Voting only for candidates from one political party; the opposite of split-ticket voting.

superdelegates Democratic political leaders who are appointed delegates to the national convention and are not bound by the primary results.

supply-side economics An economic philosophy associated with the Reagan Administration, in which taxes are cut and government regulation is reduced to give businesses the incentive to expand production. The emphasis is on business rather than the consumer.

Supremacy Clause The provision in Article VI of the Constitution that states the Constitution, federal laws, and treaties are the supreme law of the land.

Three-Fifths Compromise A compromise in which slaves were counted as three-fifths of a person for purposes of representation and taxation. An important recognition of slavery in the Constitution, which helped fully resolve the controversy over representation.

trial balloon A story presented to the media to gauge the public reaction to a policy or program under consideration.

trustee An elected official who takes the views of constituents into account but casts a vote based on his or her best judgment and/or conscience.

unemployment rate The percentage of the civilian labor force that is out of work.

unicameral legislature A one-house legislature. Congress under the Articles of Confederation was unicameral.

unitary system A political system in which all power is derived from the central government.

value-added tax A tax on products at each stage in their development. It is considered a national sales tax.

veto The president's power to reject a bill passed by Congress, provided for in Article I, Section 7 of the Constitution. Congress has the ability to override a presidential veto by a two-thirds vote of both the House of Representatives and the Senate.

voter turnout The total number of votes cast for the highest office on the ballot. It's usually expressed in terms of a percentage of the voting-age population that actually voted.

War Powers Act (1973) An act that limited the power of the president to commit U.S. military forces. Under the act, the president must inform Congress before troops are committed and must get congressional approval for a deployment of longer than 60 days.

warrantless search A search that does not require a warrant (for example, the person is placed under arrest and evidence related to the alleged crime is in plain sight at the time of the arrest).

whip A party leader in Congress who makes sure the party members are present for important votes.

whistleblower An employee who reports waste, fraud, or other illegal activities by a government agency or business.

white primary A Democratic primary in the South in which only whites could vote. This was a technique used to disenfranchise African Americans.

winner-take-all primary A presidential primary in which the candidate who gets the most votes wins all the delegates from that state. The Democratic Party does not hold winner-take-all primaries, but the Republican Party does.

workfare Inclusion of work requirements for individuals on welfare. A slogan of the welfare reform movement was "move people from welfare to workfare."

writ of certiorari A formal document issued by the Supreme Court to a lower court indicating that it will hear a case.

writ of habeas corpus A court order directing authorities to show cause for why a person under detention should not be released.

yellow journalism In the late 19th century, newspapers that relied on sensational reporting to boost circulation and to shape public opinion. Coverage of the events leading up to the Spanish-American War (1898) is an example.

The Constitution of the United States of America

Preamble

We the People of the United States, in Order to form a more perfect Union, establish Justice, insure domestic Tranquility, provide for the common defence, promote the general Welfare, and Secure the Blessings of Liberty to ourselves and our Posterity, do ordain and establish this Constitution for the United States of America.

Article I

Section 1

All legislative Powers herein granted shall be vested in a Congress of the United States, which shall consist of a Senate and House of Representatives.

Section 2

The House of Representatives shall be composed of Members chosen every second Year by the People of the several States, and the Electors in each State shall have the Qualifications requisite for Electors of the most numerous Branch of the State Legislature.[1]

No Person shall be a Representative who shall not have attained to the Age of twenty five Years, and been seven Years a Citizen of the United States, and who shall not, when elected, be an Inhabitant of that State in which he shall be chosen.

Representatives and direct Taxes[2] shall be apportioned among the several States which may be included within this Union, according to their respective Numbers, which shall be determined by adding to the whole Number of free Persons, including those bound to Service for a Term of Years. and excluding Indians not taxed, three fifths of all other Persons.[3] The actual Enumeration shall be made within three Years after the first Meeting of Congress of the United States, and within every subsequent Term of ten Years, in such Manner as they shall by Law direct. The Number of Representatives shall not exceed one for every thirty Thousand, but each State shall have at Least one Representative; and until such enumeration shall be made, the State of New Hampshire shall be entitled to chuse three, Massachusetts eight, Rhode-Island and Providence Plantations one, Connecticut five, New-York six, New Jersey four, Pennsylvania eight, Delaware one, Maryland six, Virginia ten, North Carolina five, South Carolina five, and Georgia three.

When vacancies happen in the Representation from any State, the Executive Authority thereof shall issue Writs of Election to fill such Vacancies.

The House of Representatives shall chuse their Speaker and other Officers; and shall have the sole Power of Impeachment.

Section 3

The Senate of the United States shall be composed of two Senators from each State, chosen by the Legislature thereof[4] for six Years; and each Senator shall have one Vote.

Immediately after they shall be assembled in Consequence of the first Election, they shall be divided as equally as may be into three Classes. The Seats of Senators of the first Class shall be vacated at the Expiration of the second Year, of the second Class at the Expiration of the fourth Year, and of the third Class at the Expiration of the sixth

Year, so that one third may be chosen every second Year; and if Vacancies happen by Resignation, or otherwise, during the Recess of the Legislature of any State, the Executive thereof may make temporary Appointments until the next Meeting of the Legislature, which shall then fill such Vacancies.[5]

No Person shall be a Senator who shall not have attained to the Age of thirty Years, and been nine Years a Citizen of the United States, and who shall not, when elected, be an Inhabitant of that State for which he shall be chosen.

The Vice President of the United States shall be President of the Senate, but shall have no Vote, unless they be equally divided.

The Senate shall chuse their other Officers, and also a President pro tempore, in the Absence of the Vice President, or when he shall exercise the Office of President of the United States.

The Senate shall have the sole Power to try all Impeachments. When sitting for that Purpose, they shall be on Oath or Affirmation. When the President of the United States is tried, the Chief Justice shall preside: And no Person shall be convicted without the Concurrence of two thirds of the Members present.

Judgment in Cases of Impeachment shall not extend further than to removal from Office, and disqualification to hold and enjoy any Office of honor, Trust or Profit under the United States: but the Party convicted shall nevertheless be liable and subject to Indictment, Trial, Judgment and Punishment, according to Law.

Section 4

The Times, Places and Manner of holding Elections for Senators and Representatives, shall be prescribed in each State by the Legislature thereof; but the Congress may at any time by Law make or alter such Regulations, except as to the Places of chusing Senators.

The Congress shall assemble at least once in every Year, and such Meeting shall be on the first Monday in December, unless they shall by Law appoint a different Day.[6]

Section 5

Each House shall be the Judge of the Elections, Returns and Qualifications of its own Members, and a Majority of each shall constitute a Quorum to do Business; but a smaller Number may adjourn from day to day, and may be authorized to compel the Attendance of absent Members, in such Manner, and under such Penalties as each House may provide.

Each House may determine the Rules of its Proceedings, punish its Members for disorderly Behaviour, and, with the Concurrence of two thirds, expel a Member.

Each House shall keep a Journal of its Proceedings, and from time to time publish the same, excepting such Parts as may in their Judgment require Secrecy; and the Yeas and Nays of the Members of either House on any question shall, at the Desire of one fifth of those Present, be entered on the Journal.

Neither House, during the Session of Congress, shall, without the Consent of the other, adjourn for more than three days, nor to any other Place than that in which the two Houses shall be sitting.

Section 6

The Senators and Representatives shall receive a Compensation for their Services, to be ascertained by Law, and paid out of the Treasury of the United States.[7] They shall in all Cases, except Treason, Felony and Breach of the Peace, be privileged from Arrest during their Attendance at the Session of their respective Houses, and in going to and returning from the same; and for any Speech or Debate in either House, they shall not be questioned in any other Place.

No Senator or Representative shall, during the Time for which he was elected, be appointed to any civil Office under the Authority of the United States, which shall have been created, or the Emoluments whereof shall have been encreased during such time; and no Person holding any Office under the United States, shall be a Member of either House during his Continuance in Office.

Section 7

All Bills for raising Revenue shall originate in the House of Representatives; but the Senate may propose or concur with Amendments as on other Bills.

Every Bill which shall have passed the House of Representatives and the Senate shall, before it becomes a Law, be presented to the President of the United States: If he approve he shall sign it, but if not he shall return it, with his Objections to that House in which it shall have originated, who shall enter the Objections at large on their Journal, and proceed to reconsider it. If after such Reconsideration two thirds of that House shall agree to pass the Bill, it shall be sent, together with the Objections, to the other House, by which it shall likewise be reconsidered, and if approved by two thirds of that House, it shall become a Law. But in all such Cases the Votes of both Houses shall be determined by yeas and Nays, and the Names of the Persons voting for and against the Bill shall be entered on the Journal of each House respectively. If any Bill shall not be returned by the President within ten Days (Sundays excepted) after it shall have been presented to him, the Same shall be a Law, in like Manner as if he had signed it, unless the Congress by their Adjournment prevent its Return, in which Case it shall not be a Law.

Every Order, Resolution, or Vote to which the Concurrence of the Senate and the House of Representatives may be necessary (except on a question of Adjournment) shall be presented to the President of the United States; and before the Same shall take Effect, shall be approved by him, or being disapproved by him, shall be repassed by two thirds of the Senate and House of Representatives, according to the Rules and Limitations prescribed in the Case of a Bill.

Section 8

The Congress shall have Power To lay and collect Taxes, Duties, Imposts and Excises, to pay the Debts and provide for the common Defence and general Welfare of the United States; but all Duties, Imposts and Excises shall be uniform throughout the United States;

To borrow Money on the credit of the United States;

To regulate Commerce with foreign Nations, and among the several States, and with the Indian Tribes;

To establish an uniform Rule of Naturalization, and uniform Laws on the subject of Bankruptcies throughout the United States;

To coin Money, regulate the Value thereof, and of foreign Coin, and fix the Standard of Weights and Measures;

To provide for the Punishment of counterfeiting the Securities and current Coin of the United States;

To establish Post Offices and post Roads;

To promote the Progress of Science and useful Arts, by securing for limited Times to Authors and Inventors the exclusive Right to their respective Writings and Discoveries;

To constitute Tribunals inferior to the supreme Court;

To define and punish Piracies and Felonies committed on the high Seas, and Offences against the Law of Nations;

To declare War, grant Letters of Marque and Reprisal, and make Rules concerning Captures on Land and Water;

To raise and support Armies, but no Appropriation of Money to that Use shall be for a longer Term than two Years;

To provide and maintain a Navy;

To make Rules for the Government and Regulation of the land and naval Forces;

To provide for calling forth the Militia to execute the Laws of the Union, suppress Insurrections and repel Invasions;

To provide for organizing, arming, and disciplining, the Militia, and for governing such Part of them as may be employed in the Service of the United States, reserving to the States respectively, the Appointment of the Officers, and the Authority of training the Militia according to the discipline prescribed by Congress;

To exercise exclusive Legislation in all Cases whatsoever, over such District (not exceeding ten Miles square) as may, by Cession of particular States, and the Acceptance of Congress, become the Seat of the Government of the United States, and to exercise like Authority over all Places purchased by the Consent of the Legislature of the State in which the Same shall be, for the Erection of Forts, Magazines, Arsenals, dock-Yards, and other needful buildings;—And

To make all Laws which shall be necessary and proper for carrying into Execution the foregoing Powers, and all other Powers vested by this Constitution in the Government of the United States, or in any Department or Officer thereof.[8]

Section 9

The Migration or Importation of such Persons as any of the States now existing shall think proper to admit, shall not be prohibited by the Congress prior to the Year one thousand eight hundred and eight, but a Tax or duty may be imposed on such Importation, not exceeding ten dollars for such Person.[9]

The Privilege of the Writ of Habeas Corpus shall not be suspended, unless when in Cases of Rebellion or Invasion the public Safety may require it.

No Bill of Attainder or ex post facto Law shall be passed.

No Capitation, or other direct, Tax shall be laid, unless in Proportion to the Census or enumeration herein before directed to be taken.[10]

No Tax or Duty shall be laid on Articles exported from any State.

No Preference shall be given by any Regulation of Commerce or Revenue to the Ports of one State over those of another; nor shall Vessels bound to, or from, one State, be obliged to enter, clear, or pay Duties in another.

No Money shall be drawn from the Treasury, but in Consequence of Appropriations made by Law; and a regular Statement and Account of the Receipts and Expenditures of all public Money shall be published from time to time.

No Title of Nobility shall be granted by the United States: And no Person holding any Office of Profit or Trust under them, shall, without the Consent of Congress, accept of any present, Emolument, Office, or Title, of any kind whatever, from any King, Prince, or foreign State.

Restrictions on the States

Section 10

No State shall enter into any Treaty, Alliance, or Confederation; grant Letters of Marque and Reprisal; coin Money; emit Bills of Credit; make any Thing but gold and silver Coin a Tender in Payment of Debts; pass any Bill of Attainder, ex post facto Law, or Law impairing the Obligation of Contracts, or grant any Title of Nobility.

No State shall, without the Consent of the Congress, lay any Imposts or Duties on Imports or Exports, except what may be absolutely necessary for executing it's inspection Laws: and the net Produce of all Duties and Imposts, laid by any State on Imports or Exports, shall be for the Use of the Treasury of the United States; and all such Laws shall be subject to the Revision and Controul of the Congress.

No State shall, without the Consent of Congress, lay any Duty of Tonnage, keep Troops, or Ships of War in time of Peace, enter into any Agreement or Compact with another State, or with a foreign Power, or engage in War, unless actually invaded, or in such imminent Danger as will not admit of delay.

Article II

Section 1

The executive Power shall be vested in a President of the United States of America. He shall hold his Office during the Term of four Years, and, together with the Vice President, chosen for the same Term, be elected, as follows:

Each State shall appoint, in such Manner as the Legislature thereof may direct, a Number of Electors, equal to the whole Number of Senators and Representatives to which the State may be entitled in Congress: but no Senator or Representative, or Person holding an Office of Trust or Profit under the United States, shall be appointed an Elector.

The Electors shall meet in their respective States, and vote by Ballot for two Persons, of whom one at least shall not be an Inhabitant of the same State with themselves. And they shall make a List of all the Persons voted for, and of the Number of Votes for each; which List they shall sign and certify, and transmit sealed to the Seat of the Government of the United States, directed to the President of the Senate. The President of the Senate shall, in the Presence of the Senate and House of Representatives, open all the Certificates, and the Votes shall then be counted. The Person having the greatest Number of Votes shall be the President, if such Number be a Majority of the whole Number of Electors appointed; and if there be more than one who have such Majority, and have an equal Number of Votes, then the House of Representatives shall immediately chuse by Ballot one of them for President; and if no Person have a Majority, then from the five highest on the List the said House shall in like Manner chuse the President. But in chusing the President, the Votes shall be taken by States, the Representation from each State having one Vote; A quorum for this Purpose shall consist of a Member or Members from two thirds of the States, and a Majority of all the States shall be necessary to a Choice. In every Case, after the Choice of the President, the Person having the greatest Number of Votes of the Electors shall be the Vice President. But if there should remain two or more who have equal Votes, the Senate shall chuse from them by Ballot the Vice President.[11]

The Congress may determine the Time of chusing the Electors, and the Day on which they shall give their Votes; which Day shall be the same throughout the United States.

No Person except a natural born Citizen, or a Citizen of the United States, at the time of the Adoption of this Constitution, shall be eligible to the Office of President; neither shall any Person be eligible to that Office who shall not have attained to the Age of thirty five Years, and been fourteen Years a Resident within the United States.

In the Case of the Removal of the President from Office, or of his Death, Resignation, or Inability to discharge the Powers and Duties of the said Office, the Same shall devolve on the Vice President, and the Congress may by Law provide for the Case of Removal, Death, Resignation or Inability, both of the President and Vice President, declaring what Officer shall then act as President, and such Officer shall act accordingly, until the Disability be removed, or a President shall be elected.[12]

The President shall, at stated Times, receive for his Services, a Compensation, which shall neither be increased nor diminished during the Period for which he shall have been elected, and he shall not receive within that Period any other Emolument from the United States, or any of them.

Before he enter on the Execution of his Office, he shall take the following Oath or Affirmation:—"I do solemnly swear (or affirm) that I will faithfully execute the Office of President of the United States, and will to the best of my Ability, preserve, protect and defend the Constitution of the United States."

Section 2

The President shall be Commander in Chief of the Army and Navy of the United States, and of the Militia of the several States, when called into the actual Service of the United States; he may require the Opinion, in writing, of the principal Officer in each of the executive Departments, upon any Subject relating to the Duties of their respective Offices, and he shall have Power to grant Reprieves and Pardons for Offences against the United States, except in Cases of Impeachment.

He shall have Power, by and with the Advice and Consent of the Senate, to make Treaties, provided two thirds of the Senators present concur; and he shall nominate, and by and with the Advice and Consent of the Senate, shall appoint Ambassadors, other public Ministers and Consuls, Judges of the supreme Court, and all other Officers of the United States, whose Appointments are not herein otherwise provided for, and which shall be established by Law: but the Congress may by Law vest the Appointment of such inferior Officers, as they think proper, in the President alone, in the Courts of Law, or in the Heads of Departments.

The President shall have Power to fill up all Vacancies that may happen during the Recess of the Senate, by granting Commissions which shall expire at the End of their next Session.

Section 3

He shall from time to time give to the Congress Information of the State of the Union, and recommend to their Consideration such Measures as he shall judge necessary and expedient; he may, on extraordinary Occasions, convene both Houses, or either of them, and in Case of Disagreement between them, with Respect to the Time of Adjournment, he may adjourn them to such Time as he shall think proper; he shall receive Ambassadors and other public Ministers; he shall take Care that the Laws be faithfully executed, and shall Commission all the Officers of the United States.

Section 4

The President, Vice President and all civil Officers of the United States, shall be removed from Office on Impeachment for, and Conviction of, Treason, Bribery, and other high Crimes and Misdemeanors.

Article III

Section 1

The judicial Power of the United States shall be vested in one supreme Court, and in such inferior Courts as the Congress may from time to time ordain and establish. The Judges, both of the supreme Court and inferior Courts, shall hold their Offices during good Behaviour, and shall, at stated Times, receive for their Services a Compensation, which shall not be diminished during their Continuance in Office.

Section 2

The judicial Power shall extend to all Cases, in Law and Equity, arising under this Constitution, the Laws of the United States, and Treaties made, or which shall be made, under their Authority;—to all Cases affecting Ambassadors, other public Ministers and Consuls;—to all Cases of admiralty and maritime Jurisdiction;—to Controversies to which the United States shall be a Party;—to Controversies between two or more States;—between a State and Citizens of another State,[13]—between Citizens of different States,—between Citizens of the same State claiming Lands under Grants of different States, and between a State, or the Citizens thereof, and foreign States, Citizens or Subjects.

In all Cases affecting Ambassadors, other public Ministers and Consuls, and those in which a State shall be Party, the supreme Court shall have original Jurisdiction. In all other Cases before mentioned, the supreme Court shall have appellate Jurisdiction, both as to Law and Fact, with such Exceptions, and under such Regulations as the Congress shall make.

The Trial of all Crimes, except in Cases of Impeachment, shall be by Jury; and such Trial shall be held in the State where the said Crimes shall have been committed; but when not committed within any State, the Trial shall be at such Place or Places as the Congress may by Law have directed.

Section 3

Treason against the United States, shall consist only in levying War against them, or in adhering to their Enemies, giving them Aid and Comfort. No Person shall be convicted of Treason unless on the Testimony of two Witnesses to the same overt Act, or on Confession in open Court.

The Congress shall have Power to declare the Punishment of Treason, but no Attainder of Treason shall work Corruption of Blood, or Forfeiture except during the Life of the Person attainted.

Article IV

Section 1

Full Faith and Credit shall be given in each State to the public Acts, Records, and judicial Proceedings of every other State. And the Congress may by general Laws prescribe the Manner in which such Acts, Records and Proceedings shall be proved, and the Effect thereof.

Section 2

The Citizens of each State shall be entitled to all Privileges and Immunities of Citizens in the several States.[14]

A Person charged in any State with Treason, Felony, or other Crime, who shall flee from Justice, and be found in another State, shall on Demand of the executive Authority of the State from which he fled, be delivered up, to be removed to the State having Jurisdiction of the Crime.

No Person held to Service or Labour in one State, under the Laws thereof, escaping into another, shall, in Consequence of any Law or Regulation therein, be discharged from such Service or Labour, but shall be delivered up on Claim of the Party to whom such Service or Labour may be due.[15]

Section 3

New States may be admitted by the Congress into this Union; but no new State shall be formed or erected within the Jurisdiction of any other State; nor shall any State be formed by the Junction of two or more States, or Parts of States, without the Consent of the Legislatures of the States concerned as well as of the Congress.

The Congress shall have Power to dispose of and make all needful Rules and Regulations respecting the Territory or other Property belonging to the United States; and nothing in this Constitution shall be so construed as to Prejudice any Claims of the United States or of any particular State.

Section 4

The United States shall guarantee to every State in this Union a Republican Form of Government, and shall protect each of them against Invasion; and on Application of the Legislature, or of the Executive (when the Legislature cannot be convened), against domestic Violence.

Article V

The Congress, whenever two thirds of both Houses shall deem it necessary, shall propose Amendments to this Constitution, or, on the Application of the Legislatures of two thirds of the several States, shall call a Convention for proposing Amendments, which, in either Case, shall be valid to all Intents and Purposes, as Part of this Constitution, when ratified by the Legislatures of three fourths of the several States, or by Conventions in three fourths thereof, as the one or the other Mode of Ratification may be proposed by the Congress; Provided that no Amendment which may be made prior to the Year One thousand eight hundred and eight shall in any Manner affect the first and fourth Clauses in the Ninth Section of the first Article; and that no State, without its Consent, shall be deprived of its equal Suffrage in the Senate.

Article VI

All Debts contracted and Engagements entered into, before the Adoption of this Constitution, shall be as valid against the United States under this Constitution, as under the Confederation.

This Constitution, and the Laws of the United States which shall be made in Pursuance thereof; and all Treaties made, or which shall be made, under the Authority of the United States, shall be the supreme Law of the Land; and the Judges in every State shall be bound thereby, any Thing in the Constitution or Laws of any State to the Contrary notwithstanding.

The Senators and Representatives before mentioned, and the Members of the several State Legislatures, and all executive and judicial Officers, both of the United States and of the several States, shall be bound by Oath or Affirmation, to support this Constitution; but no religious Test shall ever be required as a Qualification to any Office or public Trust under the United States.

Article VII

The Ratification of the Conventions of nine States, shall be sufficient for the Establishment of this Constitution between the States so ratifying the Same.

The Word, "the," being interlined between the seventh and eighth Lines of the first Page, the Word "Thirty" being partly written on an Erazure in the fifteenth Line of the first Page, The Words "is tried" being interlined between the thirty second and thirty third Lines of the first Page and the Word "the" being interlined between the forty third and forty fourth Lines of the second Page.

Attest William Jackson Secretary

Done in Convention by the Unanimous Consent of the States present the Seventeenth Day of September in the Year of our Lord one thousand seven hundred and Eighty seven and of the Independence of the United States of America the Twelfth In witness whereof We have hereunto subscribed our Names,

G°. Washington
Presidt and deputy from Virginia

Delaware
Geo: Read
Gunning Bedford jun
John Dickinson
Richard Bassett
Jaco: Broom

Maryland
James McHenry
Dan of St Thos. Jenifer
Danl. Carroll

Virginia
John Blair
James Madison Jr.

North Carolina
Wm. Blount
Richd. Dobbs Spaight
Hu Williamson

South Carolina
J. Rutledge
Charles Cotesworth Pinckney
Charles Pinckney
Pierce Butler

Georgia
William Few
Abr Baldwin

New Hampshire
John Langdon
Nicholas Gilman

Massachusetts
Nathaniel Gorham
Rufus King

Connecticut
Wm. Saml. Johnson
Roger Sherman

New York
Alexander Hamilton

New Jersey
Wil: Livingston
David Brearley
Wm. Paterson
Jona: Dayton

Pennsylvania
B Franklin
Thomas Mifflin
Robt. Morris
Geo. Clymer
Thos. FitzSimons
Jared Ingersoll
James Wilson
Gouv. Morris

Amendments to the Constitution[16]

The Preamble to the Bill of Rights[17]

Congress of the United States
begun and held at the City of New-York, on
Wednesday the fourth of March, one thousand seven hundred and eighty nine.

THE Conventions of a number of the States, having at the time of their adopting the Constitution, expressed a desire, in order to prevent misconstruction or abuse of its powers, that further declaratory and restrictive clauses should be added: And as extending the ground of public confidence in the Government, will best ensure the beneficent ends of its institution.

RESOLVED by the Senate and House of Representatives of the United States of America, in Congress assembled, two thirds of both Houses concurring, that the following Articles be proposed to the Legislatures of the several States, as amendments to the Constitution of the United States, all, or any of which Articles, when ratified by three fourths of the said Legislatures, to be valid to all intents and purposes, as part of the said Constitution; viz.

ARTICLES in addition to, and Amendment of the Constitution of the United States of America, proposed by Congress, and ratified by the Legislatures of the several States, pursuant to the fifth Article of the original Constitution.

Amendment I

Congress shall make no law respecting an establishment of religion, or prohibiting the free exercise thereof; or abridging the freedom of speech, or of the press; or the right of the people peaceably to assemble, and to petition the Government for a redress of grievances.

Amendment II

A well regulated Militia, being necessary to the security of a free State, the right of the people to keep and bear Arms, shall not be infringed.

Amendment III

No Soldier shall, in time of peace be quartered in any house, without the consent of the Owner, nor in time of war, but in a manner to be prescribed by law.

Amendment IV

The right of the people to be secure in their persons, houses, papers, and effects, against unreasonable searches and seizures, shall not be violated, and no Warrants shall issue, but upon probable cause, supported by Oath or affirmation, and particularly describing the place to be searched, and the persons or things to be seized.

Amendment V

No person shall be held to answer for a capital, or otherwise infamous crime, unless on a presentment or indictment of a Grand Jury, except in cases arising in the land or naval forces, or in the Militia, when in actual service in time of War or public danger; nor shall any person be subject for the same offence to be twice put in jeopardy of life or limb; nor shall be compelled in any criminal case to be a witness against himself, nor be deprived of life, liberty, or property, without due process of law; nor shall private property be taken for public use, without just compensation.

Amendment VI

In all criminal prosecutions, the accused shall enjoy the right to a speedy and public trial, by an impartial jury of the State and district wherein the crime shall have been committed, which district shall have been previously ascertained by law, and to be informed of the nature and cause of the accusation; to be confronted with the witnesses against him; to have compulsory process for obtaining witnesses in his favor, and to have the Assistance of Counsel for his defense.

Amendment VII

In Suits at common law, where the value in controversy shall exceed twenty dollars, the right of trial by jury shall be preserved, and no fact tried by a jury, shall be otherwise re-examined in any Court of the United States, than according to the rules of common law.

Amendment VIII

Excessive bail shall not be required, nor excessive fines imposed, nor cruel and unusual punishments inflicted.

Amendment IX

The enumeration in the Constitution, of certain rights, shall not be construed to deny or disparate others retained by the people.[18]

Amendment X

The powers not delegated to the United States by the Constitution, nor prohibited by it to the States, are reserved to the States respectively, or to the people.[19]

Amendment XI[20]

Passed by Congress March 4, 1794. Ratified February 7, 1795.

The Judicial power of the United States shall not be construed to extend to any suit in law or equity, commenced or prosecuted against one of the United States by Citizens of another State, or by Citizens or Subjects of any Foreign State.

Amendment XII[21]

Passed by Congress December 9, 1803. Ratified June 15, 1804.

The Electors shall meet in their respective states and vote by ballot for President and Vice-President, one of whom, at least, shall not be an inhabitant of the same state with themselves; they shall name in their ballots the person voted for as President, and in district ballots the person voted for as Vice-President, and they shall make distinct lists of all persons voted for as President, and of all persons voted for as Vice-President, and of the number of votes for each, which lists they shall sign and certify, and transmit sealed to the seat of the government of the United States, directed to the President of the Senate;—The President of the Senate shall, in the presence of the Senate and House of Representatives, open all the certificates and the votes shall then be counted;—The person having the greatest number of votes for President, shall be the President, if such number be a majority of the whole number of Electors appointed; and if no person have such majority, then from the persons having the highest numbers not exceeding three on the list of those voted for as President, the House of Representatives shall choose immediately, by ballot, the President. But in choosing the President, the votes shall be taken by states, the representation from each state having one vote; a quorum for this purpose shall consist of a member or members from two-thirds of the states, and a majority of all the states shall be necessary to a choice. And if the House of Representatives shall not choose a President whenever the right of choice shall devolve upon them, before the fourth day of March next following, then the Vice-President shall act as President, as in case of the death or other constitutional disability of the President.[22]— The person having the greatest number of votes as Vice-President, shall be the Vice-President, if such number be a majority of the whole number of Electors appointed, and if no person have a majority, then from the two highest numbers on the list, the Senate shall choose the Vice-President; a quorum for the purpose shall consist of two-thirds of the whole number of Senators, and a majority of the whole number shall be necessary to a choice. But no person constitutionally ineligible to the office of President shall be eligible to that of Vice-President of the United States.

Amendment XIII[23]

Passed by Congress January 31, 1865. Ratified December 6, 1865.

Section 1

Neither slavery nor involuntary servitude, except as a punishment for crime whereof the party shall have been duly convicted, shall exist within the United States, or any place subject to their jurisdiction.

Section 2

Congress shall have power to enforce this article by appropriate legislation.

Amendment XIV

Passed by Congress June 13, 1866. Ratified July 9, 1868.

Section 1[24]

All persons born or naturalized in the United States, and subject to the jurisdiction thereof, are citizens of the United States and of the State wherein they reside. No State shall make or enforce any law which shall abridge the privileges or immunities of citizens of the United States; nor shall any State deprive any person of life, liberty, or property, without due process of law; nor deny to any person within its jurisdiction the equal protection of the laws.

Section 2[25]

Representatives shall be apportioned among the several States according to their respective numbers, counting the whole number of persons in each State, excluding Indians not taxed. But when the right to vote at any election for the choice of electors for President and Vice-President of the United States, Representatives in Congress, the Executive and Judicial officers of a State, or the members of the Legislature thereof, is denied to any of the male inhabitants of such State, being twenty-one years of age[26], and citizens of the United States, or in any way abridged except for participation in rebellion, or other crime, the basis of representation therein shall be reduced in the proportion which the number of such male citizens shall bear to the whole number of male citizens twenty-one years of age in such State.[27]

Section 3

No person shall be a Senator or Representative in Congress, or elector of President and Vice-President, or hold any office, civil or military, under the United States, or under any State, who, having previously taken an oath, as a member of Congress, or as an officer of the United States, or as a member of any State legislature, or as an executive or judicial officer of any State, to support the Constitution of the United States, shall have engaged in insurrection or rebellion against the same, or given aid or comfort to the enemies thereof. But Congress may by a vote of two-thirds of each House, remove such disability.

Section 4

The validity of the public debt of the United States, authorized by law, including debts incurred for payment of pensions and bounties for services in suppressing insurrection or rebellion, shall not be questioned. But neither the United States nor any State shall assume or pay any debt or obligation incurred in aid of insurrection or rebellion against the United States, or any claim for the loss or emancipation of any slave; but all such debts, obligations and claims shall be held illegal and void.

Section 5

The Congress shall have the power to enforce, by appropriate legislation, the provisions of this article.

Amendment XV

Passed by Congress February 26, 1869. Ratified February 3, 1870.

Section 1

The right of citizens of the United States to vote shall not be denied or abridged by the United States or by any State on account of race, color, or previous condition of servitude—

Section 2

The Congress shall have the power to enforce this article by appropriate legislation.

Amendment XVI[28]

Passed by Congress July 2, 1909. Ratified February 3, 1913.

The Congress shall have power to lay and collect taxes on incomes, from whatever source derived, without apportionment among the several States, and without regard to any census or enumeration.

Amendment XVII[29]

Passed by Congress May 13, 1912. Ratified April 8, 1913.

The Senate of the United States shall be composed of two Senators from each State, elected by the people thereof, for six years; and each Senator shall have one vote. The electors in each State shall have the qualifications requisite for electors of the most numerous branch of the State legislatures.

When vacancies happen in the representation of any State in the Senate, the executive authority of such State shall issue writs of election to fill such vacancies: *Provided,* That the legislature of any State may empower the executive thereof to make temporary appointments until the people fill the vacancies by election as the legislature may direct.

This amendment shall not be so construed as to affect the election or term of any Senator chosen before it becomes valid as part of the Constitution.

Amendment XVIII[30]

Passed by Congress December 18, 1917. Ratified January 16, 1919.

Section 1

After one year from the ratification of this article the manufacture, sale, or transportation of intoxicating liquors within, the importation thereof into, or the exportation thereof from the United States and all territory subject to the jurisdiction thereof for beverage purposes is hereby prohibited.

Section 2

The Congress and the several States shall have concurrent power to enforce this article by appropriate legislation.

Section 3

This article shall be inoperative unless it shall have been ratified as an amendment to the Constitution by the legislatures of the several States, as provided in the Constitution, within seven years from the date of the submission hereof to the States by the Congress.

Amendment XIX

Passed by Congress June 4, 1919. Ratified August 18, 1920.

The right of citizens of the United States to vote shall not be denied or abridged by the United States or any State on account of sex.

Congress shall have the power to enforce this article by appropriate legislation.

Amendment XX

Passed by Congress March 2, 1932. Ratified January 23, 1933.

Section 1

The terms of the President and Vice President shall end at noon on the 20th day of January, and the terms of Senators and Representatives at noon on the 3d day of January, of the years in which such terms would have ended if this article had not been ratified; and the terms of their successors shall then begin.

Section 2[31]

The Congress shall assemble at least once in every year, and such meeting shall begin at noon on the 3d day of January, unless they shall by law appoint a different day.

Section 3[32]

If, at the time fixed for the beginning of the term of the President, the President elect shall have died, the Vice President shall become President. If a President shall not have been chosen before the time fixed for the beginning of his term, or if the President elect shall have failed to qualify, then the Vice President elect shall act as President until a President shall have qualified; and the Congress may by law provide for the case wherein neither a President elect nor a Vice President shall have qualified, declaring who shall then act as President, or the manner in which one who is to act shall be selected, and such person shall act accordingly until a President or Vice President shall have qualified.

Section 4

The Congress may by law provide for the case of the death of any of the persons from whom the House of Representatives may choose a President whenever the right of choice shall have devolved upon them, and for the case of the death of any of the persons from whom the Senate may choose a Vice President whenever the right of choice shall have devolved upon them.

Section 5

Sections 1 and 2 shall take effect on the 15th day of October following the ratification of this article.

Section 6

This article shall be inoperative unless it shall have been ratified as an amendment to the Constitution by the legislatures of three-fourths of the several States within seven years from the date of its submission.

Amendment XXI

Passed by Congress February 20, 1933. Ratified December 5, 1933.

Section 1

The eighteenth article of amendment to the Constitution of the United States is hereby repealed.

Section 2

The transportation or importation into any State, Territory, or Possession of the United States for delivery or use therein of intoxicating liquors, in violation of the laws thereof, is hereby prohibited.

Section 3

This article shall be inoperative unless it shall have been ratified as an amendment to the Constitution by conventions in the several States, as provided in the Constitution, within seven years from the date of the submission hereof to the States by Congress.

Amendment XXII

Passed by Congress March 21, 1947. Ratified February 27, 1951.

Section 1

No person shall be elected to the office of the President more than twice, and no person who has held the office of President, or acted as President, for more than two years of a term to which some other person was elected President shall be elected to the office of President more than once. But this Article shall not apply to any person holding the office of President when this article was proposed by the Congress, and shall not prevent any person who may be holding the office of President, or acting as President, during the term within which this Article becomes operative from holding the office of President or acting as President during the remainder of such term.[33]

Section 2

This article shall be inoperative unless it shall have been ratified as an amendment to the Constitution by the legislatures oft three-fourths of the several States within seven years from the date of its submission to the States by the Congress.

Amendment XXIII

Passed by Congress June 16, 1960. Ratified March 29, 1961.

Section 1

The District constituting the seat of Government of the United States shall appoint in such manner as the Congress may direct:

A number of electors of President and Vice President equal to the whole number of Senators and Representatives in Congress to which the District would be entitled if it were a State, but in no event more than the least populous State; they shall be in addition to those appointed by the States, but they shall be considered, for the purposes of the election of President and Vice President, to be electors appointed by a State; and they shall meet in the District and perform such duties as provided by the twelfth article of amendment.

Section 2

The Congress shall have the power to enforce this article by appropriate legislation.

Amendment XXIV

Passed by Congress August 27, 1962. Ratified January 23, 1964.

Section 1

The right of citizens of the United States to vote in any primary or other election for President or Vice President, for electors for President or Vice President, or for Senator or Representative in Congress, shall not be denied or abridged by the United States or any State by reason of failure to pay poll tax or other tax.

Section 2

The Congress shall have the power to enforce this article by appropriate legislation.

Amendment XXV[34]

Passed by Congress July 6, 1965. Ratified February 10, 1967.

Section 1

In the case of the removal of the President from office or of his death or resignation, the Vice President shall become President.

Section 2

Whenever there is a vacancy in the office of the Vice President, the President shall nominate a Vice President who shall take office upon confirmation by a majority vote of both Houses of Congress.[35]

Section 3

Whenever the President transmits to the President pro tempore of the Senate and the Speaker of the House of Representatives his written declaration that he is unable to discharge the powers and duties of his office, and until he transmits to them a written declaration to the contrary, such powers and duties shall be discharged by the Vice President as Acting President.

Section 4

Whenever the Vice President and a majority of either the principal officers of the executive departments or of such other body as Congress may by law provide, transmit to the President pro tempore of the Senate and the Speaker of the House of Representatives their written declaration that the President is unable to discharge the powers and duties of his office, the Vice President shall immediately assume the powers and duties of the office as Acting President.

Thereafter, when the President transmits to the President pro tempore of the Senate and the Speaker of the House of Representatives his written declaration that no inability exists, he shall resume the powers and duties of his office unless the Vice President and a majority of either the principal officers of the executive department or of such other body as Congress may by law provide, transmit within four days to the President pro tempore of the Senate and the Speaker of the House of Representatives their written declaration that the President is unable to discharge the powers and duties of his office. Thereupon Congress shall decide the issue, assembling within forty-eight hours for that purpose if not in session. If the Congress, within twenty-one days after receipt of the latter written declaration, or, if Congress is not in session, within twenty-one days after Congress is required to assemble, determines by two-thirds vote of both Houses that the President is unable to discharge the powers and duties of his office, the Vice President shall continue to discharge the same as Acting President; otherwise, the President shall resume the powers and duties of his office.

Amendment XXVI

Passed by Congress March 23, 1971. Ratified July 1, 1971.

Section 1[36]

The right of citizens of the United States, who are eighteen years of age or older, to vote shall not be denied or abridged by the United States or by any State on account of age.

Section 2

The Congress shall have power to enforce this article by appropriate legislation.

Amendment XXVII[37]

Originally proposed September 25, 1789. Ratified May 7, 1992.

No law, varying the compensation for the services of Senators and Representatives, shall take effect, until an election of representatives shall have intervened.

Endnotes

[1]The term *elector* as used here means voter.

[2]These words were affected by the Sixteenth Amendment, which gave Congress the power to impose income taxes.

[3]This is the so-called Three-Fifths Compromise; the phrase *all other Persons* means slaves. The language was affected by Section 2 of the Fourteenth Amendment.

[4]Direct election of senators by the voters in each state is provided for in the Seventeenth Amendment.

[5]The method of filling vacancies in the Senate was changed by the Seventeenth Amendment.

[6]Section 2 of the Twentieth Amendment changed the date to noon on January 3.

[7]Compensation to members of Congress is affected by the terms of the Twenty-seventh Amendment.

[8]This is also known as the elastic clause because it expands the power of the Congress; it is the source of Congress's implied powers.

[9]Allowing the slave trade to continue for 20 years was one of the major compromises at the Constitutional Convention; Congress did outlaw the slave trade in 1808.

[10]This clause was modified by the Sixteenth Amendment, which established the federal income tax.

[11]This provision is superseded by the language in the Twelfth Amendment. The amendment grew out of the election of 1800 when Thomas Jefferson and his running mate, Aaron Burr, tied in the Electoral College.

[12]This provision was modified by the Twenty-fifth Amendment.

[13]This language was modified by the Eleventh Amendment.

[14]The Courts have recognized exceptions to privileges and immunities (for example, state universities can charge higher tuition for out-of-state residents).

[15]This provision for the return of runaway slaves that escaped to a non-slave state was effectively made null and void by the adoption of the Thirteenth Amendment, which abolished slavery.

[16]Only the Thirteenth, Fourteenth, Fifteenth, and Sixteenth amendments had numbers assigned to them at the time of ratification. For the sake of familiarity, all the amendments are given the appropriate roman numeral.

[17]The first ten amendments to the Constitution, known as the Bill of Rights, were ratified December 15, 1791.

[18]A constitutionally protected right of privacy was found by the Supreme Court through the Ninth Amendment in the landmark abortion case *Roe v. Wade* (1973).

[19]The protection given the states in the Tenth Amendment was insisted on during the debate over ratification by the Antifederalists. Those who advocate states rights emphasize the Tenth Amendment over the necessary and proper clause.

[20]Article III, Section 2, of the Constitution was modified by the Eleventh Amendment.

[21]A portion of Article II, Section 1, of the Constitution was superseded by the Twelfth Amendment.

[22]This sentence is superseded by Section 3 of the Twentieth Amendment (1933).

[23]A portion of Article IV, Section 2, of the Constitution was superseded by the Thirteenth Amendment.

[24]Section 1 of the Fourteenth Amendment overturned the decision in the Dred Scott case with respect to African Americans. The Supreme Court ruled in the late 19th century that the citizenship provisions did not apply to Native Americans; citizenship was granted to Native Americans by an act of Congress.

[25]Article I, Section 2, of the Constitution was modified by Section 2 of the Fourteenth Amendment.

[26]The voting age was lowered to 18 years of age by Section 1 of the Twenty-sixth Amendment.

[27]This section not only eliminated the language of the Three-Fifths Compromise but implicitly established universal male suffrage and assumed that African Americans had the right to vote.

[28]Article I, Section 9, of the Constitution was modified by the Sixteenth Amendment.

[29]Article I, Section 3, of the Constitution was modified by the Seventeenth Amendment.

[30]This is the first amendment to include a time limit for ratification. It was repealed by the Twenty-first Amendment.

[31]Article I, Section 4, of the Constitution was modified by Section 2 of the Twentieth Amendment.

[32]A portion of the Twelfth Amendment was superseded by Section 3 of the Twentieth Amendment.

[33]The term limit was established by custom by George Washington. The amendment was obviously a response to the four terms that Franklin Roosevelt was elected to. By its own language, the amendment did not apply in part to Harry Truman.

[34]Article II, Section 1, of the Constitution was affected by the Twenty-fifth Amendment.

[35]When Lyndon Johnson became president following the assassination of John Kennedy, there was no vice president until January 1965 when Hubert Humphrey took the oath of office following the 1964 presidential election.

[36]Amendment XIV, Section 2, of the Constitution was modified by Section 1 of the Twenty-sixth Amendment.

[37]The Twenty-seventh Amendment was one of the 12 amendments proposed by the First Congress in 1789. It took over 200 years to get the approval of the required number of states for ratification.

Important U.S. Supreme Court Cases

Case	Issue	Summary of Decision
Abington Township School District v. Schempp (1963)	Establishment Clause	Held unconstitutional a state law requiring the school day to begin with reading a biblical passage and reciting the Lord's Prayer.
Adarand Constructors v. Peña (1995)	Affirmative action	Affirmative-action programs that give preference to minorities must respond to specific past instances of discrimination and not simply historical discrimination. A limit on affirmative action.
Agostini v. Felton (1997)	Establishment Clause	Held constitutional a program that sends public-school teachers to students in parochial schools in order to provide remedial education services.
Bethel School District v. Fraser (1986)	Freedom of speech	School officials can punish a student for statements made in a speech at school.
Barron v. Mayor of Baltimore (1833)	Incorporation doctrine	The Bill of Rights only applied to actions by the federal government, not the states.
Boumediene v. Bush (2008)	War on terror, habeas corpus	The Court held that the Military Commissions Act of 2006 was an unconstitutional suspension of the writ of habeas corpus.
Bowers v. Hardwick (1986)	Gay rights	Consensual homosexual acts performed in a person's home are not protected under the constitutional right to privacy.
Brown v. Board of Education of Topeka (1954)	De jure segregation	The "separate but equal" doctrine as it applies to public education is unconstitutional; separate schools are inherently unequal.
Buckley v. Valeo (1976)	Freedom of speech	Upheld the limits on individual contributions to political campaigns in federal election provided for in the 1974 amendments to the Federal Election Campaign Act, but declared unconstitutional the limits on expenditures as well as limits on what an individual could contribute to his or her own campaign.
Bush v. Gore (2000)	Vote counting	The Court stopped the vote recount in Florida, effectively giving the state's electoral votes and the presidential election to George W. Bush.
California Democratic Party v. Jones (2000)	Freedom of association	Struck down the Democratic Party's rule establishing a blanket primary in the state.
Chaplinsky v. New Hampshire (1942)	Freedom of speech	"Fighting words" that are likely to provoke a hostile response are not protected under the First Amendment.
The Civil Rights Cases (1883)	Fourteenth Amendment	Held unconstitutional the Civil Rights Act of 1875, which prohibited discrimination on the basis of race in places of public accommodations such as hotels, public transportation, and restaurants; Fourteenth Amendment offered protection against state action based on race, not private action. The Civil Rights Act of 1964 addressed discrimination in public accommodations. See Heart of Atlanta Motel v. United States (1964).
Clinton v. City of New York (1998)	Article II	Declared the Line-Item Veto Act unconstitutional because it granted the president authority not provided for in the Constitution. Such an extension of presidential power requires a constitutional amendment.

Case	Issue	Summary of Decision
Craig v. Boren (1976)	Fourteenth Amendment	To be valid, classifications based on gender must serve an important government objective and must be related to those objectives. This is known as heightened scrutiny.
Cruzan v. Director, Missouri Department of Health (1990)	Right to privacy	Although the Supreme Court ruled that parents of a comatose patient could not remove life support, the decision recognized that competent individuals could refuse medical treatment and have the right to die.
District of Columbia v. Heller (2008)	Second Amendment	The Court held that the Second Amendment did, indeed, cover an individual's right to bear arms. In this context, the Court struck down the District of Columbia's strict gun control ordinance.
Dred Scott v. Sandford (1857)	Slavery, property rights	African Americans were not citizens of the United States, and Scott had no right to sue. The Missouri Compromise was unconstitutional. Slaves were property and protected as such under the Constitution.
Employment Division of Oregon v. Smith (1991)	Free Exercise Clause	The prohibition against the use of illegal drugs in religious ceremonies is not a violation of the Free Exercise Clause of the First Amendment. Religious observance is not a reason for a person not complying with a valid law.
Engel v. Vitale (1962)	Establishment Clause	Requiring the recitation of a nonsectarian, government-sponsored prayer in the public school violates the principle of the separation of church and state. Ban on prayer in the public schools.
Escobedo v. Illinois (1964)	Sixth Amendment	Statements made by a murder suspect were thrown out because the police prevented him from meeting with his attorney and he was not told about his right to remain silent.
Fletcher v. Peck (1810)	Article III	Established that the Supreme Court can declare a state law unconstitutional.
Furman v. Georgia (1972)	Eighth Amendment	The arbitrary application of the death penalty constituted cruel and unusual punishment. The decision led to a moratorium on the death penalty until state legislatures rewrote their capital punishment statutes. See Gregg v. Georgia (1976).
Gibbons v. Ogden (1824)	Commerce Clause, Supremacy Clause	The decision expanded the Commerce Clause to include almost any interstate business activity.
Gideon v. Wainwright (1963)	Sixth Amendment	The right to counsel is fundamental to a fair trial. The state must provide an attorney to poor defendants charged with a felony. The Sixth Amendment applies to the states through the Fourteenth Amendment.
Gitlow v. New York (1925)	Freedom of speech	The First Amendment freedom-of-speech protection is incorporated/applied to the states through the Fourteenth Amendment. This is known as the incorporation doctrine.
Gonzales v. Carhart (2007)	Right to privacy	The Court upheld the recently enacted federal law prohibiting late-term abortions (sometimes referred to as "partial-birth abortions").
Gregg v. Georgia (1976)	Eighth Amendment	Upheld the death sentence of a person convicted of a double murder, pointing out that capital punishment per se is not unconstitutional.
Griffin v. County School Board of Prince Edward County (1955), known as Brown II	De jure segregation	Desegregation plans were to be developed by local school boards with oversight by federal district courts. Desegregation was to proceed with "all deliberate speed."

Case	Issue	Summary of Decision
Griswold v. Connecticut (1965)	Right to privacy	Struck down a state law that made it a crime to provide contraceptive information to married couples on the basis of a constitutionally protected right to privacy.
Grutter v. Bollinger (2003)	Affirmative action	The Court upheld the University of Michigan Law School's affirmative-action policy that gives a limited preference to minority applicants. The value of a diverse student body was noted.
Guinn v. United States (1915)	Fifteenth Amendment	Declared unconstitutional the grandfather clause, which exempted people—or the legal descendants of such people who were able to vote before the Fifteenth Amendment was adopted—from literacy tests or similar voter qualifications.
Hamdan v. Rumsfeld (2006)	War on terror	The type of military commissions for the trial of terror suspects violate the Uniform Code of Military Justice and the Geneva Convention. The decision led Congress to pass the Military Commissions Act of 2006.
Hamdi v. Rumsfeld (2004)	War on terror	A U.S. citizen can be detained as an "enemy combatant" but can still challenge the basis for his or her detention.
Heart of Atlanta Motel v. United States (1964)	Civil Rights Act of 1964	Congress has the power to prohibit discrimination in private businesses based on its authority to regulate interstate commerce.
Lawrence v. Texas (2003)	Gay rights	The Court overturned its decision in Bowers v. Hardwick and struck down state sodomy laws that criminalized homosexual behavior.
Lemon v. Kurtzman (1971)	Establishment Clause	When a law or state action involves religion, it must have a secular purpose. It cannot advance or inhibit religion, or excessively entangle the government with religion. This became known as the Lemon Test.
McCulloch v. Maryland (1819)	Necessary and Proper Clause, Supremacy Clause	Upheld the constitutionality of the First Bank of the United States under the Necessary and Proper Clause, and denied the state the right to tax the bank, noting that "the power to tax is the power to destroy."
Mapp v. Ohio (1961)	Fourth Amendment	Evidence that is seized illegally cannot be used as evidence in court. The exclusionary rule is applied to the states.
Marbury v. Madison (1801)	Article III	The decision established the principle of judicial review. The Supreme Court has the power to declare a law passed by Congress unconstitutional.
Miller v. California (1973)	Freedom of speech, freedom of the press	Outlines a test to define obscene materials that are not protected under the First Amendment. Community standards were included, as was LAPS, which says that a work is obscene if it has no literary, artistic, political, or scientific value.
Miranda v. Arizona (1966)	Fifth Amendment	Prior to questioning by the police, a person in custody must be informed of the following: his or her constitutional right to remain silent, that anything said can be used against him or her, that he or she has a right to have an attorney present during questioning, and that he or she has the right to have an attorney appointed if he or she cannot afford one. This became known as the Miranda warning.
Near v. Minnesota (1931)	Freedom of the press	States cannot ban offensive publications. First Amendment freedom-of-the-press protections apply to the states.

Case	Issue	Summary of Decision
New Jersey v. T.L.O. (1985)	Fourth Amendment	School officials can search a student suspected of violating school policy. School administrators have greater latitude in conducting a search than police or similar authorities in order to maintain an environment where learning can take place.
The New York Times Co. v. Sullivan (1964)	Freedom of the press	Public figures are bound by a higher standard in libel cases than ordinary citizens; they have to show not only that what was printed was false, but also that the media knew it was false and published it anyway, showing complete disregard for the truth.
The New York Times Co. v. United States (1971)	Freedom of the press	The Supreme Court refused to prevent the publication of The Pentagon Papers, a classified documentary history of U.S. involvement in Vietnam, on national security grounds. The issue in the case was prior restraint.
Nix v. Williams (1984)	Fourth Amendment	Questionable evidence can be used at trial if it can be shown that it would have been "inevitably discovered" by legal means. This is the inevitable discovery exception to the exclusionary rule.
Planned Parenthood of Southeastern Pennsylvania v. Casey (1992)	Right to privacy	States can regulate abortion as long as an "undue burden" is not placed on women. A 24-hour waiting period, counseling on alternatives to abortion, and parental consent for minors were constitutional restrictions on the right to an abortion.
Plessy v. Ferguson (1896)	Fourteenth Amendment	Segregation by race is constitutional provided the facilities are equal. This is known as the "separate but equal" doctrine.
Puerto Rico v. Branstad (1987)	Extradition	The federal courts have the power to force a state to comply with an extradition request from another state.
R.A.V. v. City of St. Paul (1992)	Freedom of speech	The Court held that a local ordinance that made it a crime to place symbols such as a burning cross or a Nazi swastika on public or private property violated the First Amendment.
Rasul v. Bush (2004)	War on terror, habeas corpus	Noncitizens detained at the Guantánamo Bay Naval Base have a right to file a habeas corpus petition to challenge their detention.
Regents of the University of California v. Bakke (1978)	Affirmative action	Setting up a rigid quota system for admission to medical school is prohibited, but race can be taken into account in the admissions process because the goal of a diverse student body is valid. The case dealt with the issue of reverse discrimination.
Reno v. ACLU (1997)	Freedom of speech	Ruled unconstitutional the attempt to control the content of the Internet through the Communications Decency Act. The provisions of the statute regarding "indecent transmission" and "patently offensive displays" violate the First Amendment.
Roe v. Wade (1973)	Right to privacy	Women have an absolute right to an abortion in the first trimester of pregnancy based on a constitutionally protected right to privacy. The state can impose restrictions in the second and third trimesters.
Romer v. Evans (1996)	Fourteenth Amendment	Ruled unconstitutional an amendment to the Colorado state constitution that voided existing local ordinances protecting gay and lesbian rights and prohibiting the adoption of such ordinances in the future.
Roper v. Simmons (2005)	Eighth Amendment	The Court held that the death penalty when applied to an individual who committed a capital offense before they were 18 was "cruel and unusual punishment."

Case	Issue	Summary of Decision
Rostker v. Goldberg (1980)	Fifth Amendment	Ruled constitutional the law that required only males to register for the draft. The exclusion of women was justified under the heightened scrutiny test because the military needs to have flexibility in the use of its troops.
Roth v. United States (1957)	Freedom of speech, freedom of the press	Obscenity is not protected under the First Amendment. The decision recognized the validity of community standards in a test to determine if materials were obscene.
Schenck v. United States (1919)	Freedom of speech	Freedom of speech is not absolute. The decision established the clear-and-present-danger test as a constitutional restriction of free speech; you cannot yell "Fire!" in a crowded theater.
Shaw v. Reno (1993)	Fourteenth Amendment	The Supreme Court determined that race cannot be the predominant factor in drawing congressional district lines just to ensure the election of an African-American representative. The oddly shaped district in North Carolina was a racial gerrymander.
Smith v. Allwright (1944)	Fifteenth Amendment	The white primary was declared unconstitutional because it effectively disenfranchised African Americans.
South Dakota v. Dole (1987)	Federalism	Upheld a statute that required states to raise their minimum drinking age to 21 years of age or risk losing a portion of their federal highway funds.
Swann v. Charlotte-Mecklenburg County Board of Education (1971)	Fourteenth Amendment	Remedies for past racial discrimination in public education include racial quotas for both teachers and students, redrawing school district lines, and busing.
Sweatt v. Painter (1950)	Fourteenth Amendment	Found that the "separate but equal" doctrine could not be applied to professional schools—in this case, separate law schools for African Americans and whites in Texas.
Texas v. Johnson (1989)	Freedom of speech	The burning of the American flag is symbolic speech and is protected under the First Amendment.
Tinker v. Des Moines Independent Community School District (1969)	Freedom of speech	The wearing of armbands by students to protest the war in Vietnam is protected speech and cannot be prohibited by school officials. Students do not give up their constitutional rights at the schoolhouse door.
Toyota Motor Manufacturing, Kentucky, Inc. v. Williams (2002)	Americans with Disabilities Act	The law covers impairments that affect a person's life, not whether he can perform a particular job. Limits the scope of the Americans with Disabilities Act.
United States v. Leon (1984)	Fourth Amendment	Evidence obtained through a faulty search warrant can be admitted if the authorities acted in "good faith" in getting the warrant. This ruling established the "good faith" exception to the exclusionary rule.
United States v. Lopez (1995)	Federalism, Commerce Clause	Congress does not have the power to prohibit guns in an area around a school under the Commerce Clause. Gun regulation, in this sense, is a function of the states or local governments.
United States v. Virginia (1996)	Fourteenth Amendment	The state of Virginia violated the Equal Protection Clause regarding women by maintaining the all-male Virginia Military Institute.
U.S. Term Limits, Inc. v. Thornton (1995)	Federalism	The states cannot impose term limits on members of Congress.
Vacco v. Quill (1997)	Right to privacy, Fourteenth Amendment	Upheld a state law that banned physician-assisted suicide.

Case	Issue	Summary of Decision
Webster v. Reproductive Health Services (1989)	Right to privacy	The states may prohibit abortions in public hospitals and clinics and by public employees. This decision limited abortion rights.
Westberry v. Sanders (1964)	Fourteenth Amendment	Struck down an apportionment system that allowed for congressional districts that varied significantly in size.
Williams v. North Carolina (1945)	Full Faith and Credit Clause	A state does not have to accept a divorce secured in another state if the parties to the divorce did not establish genuine residency in that state.

Case	Issue	Summary of Decision
Schenck v. United States (1919)	Freedom of speech	Freedom of speech is not absolute. The decision established the clear-and-present-danger test as a constitutional restriction of free speech; you cannot yell "fire" in a crowded theater.
Shaw v. Reno (1993)	Fourteenth Amendment	The Supreme Court determined that race cannot be the predominant factor in drawing congressional district lines just to ensure the election of an African-American representative. The oddly shaped district in North Carolina was a racial gerrymander.
Smith v. Allwright (1944)	Fifteenth Amendment	The white primary was declared unconstitutional because it effectively disenfranchised African Americans.
South Dakota v. Dole (1987)	Federalism	Upheld a statute that required states to raise their minimum drinking age to 21 years of age or risk losing a portion of their federal highway funds.
Swann v. Charlotte-Mecklenburg County Board of Education (1971)	Fourteenth Amendment	Remedies for past racial discrimination in public education include racial quotas for both teachers and students, redrawing school district lines, and busing.
Sweatt v. Painter (1950)	Fourteenth Amendment	Found that the "separate but equal" doctrine could not be applied to professional schools—in this case, separate law schools for African Americans and whites in Texas.
Texas v. Johnson (1989)	Freedom of speech	The burning of the American flag is symbolic speech and is protected under the First Amendment.
Tinker v. Des Moines Independent Community School District (1969)	Freedom of speech	The wearing of armbands by students to protest the war in Vietnam is protected speech and cannot be prohibited by school officials. Students do not give up their constitutional rights at the schoolhouse door.
Toyota Motor Manufacturing, Kentucky Inc. v. Williams (2002)	Americans with Disabilities Act	The law covers impairments that affect a person's life, not whether he can perform a particular job. Limits the scope of the Americans with Disabilities Act.
United States v. Leon (1984)	Fourth Amendment	Evidence obtained through a faulty search warrant can be admitted if the authorities acted in "good faith" in getting the warrant. The ruling established the "good faith" exception to the exclusionary rule.
United States v. Lopez (1995)	Federalism; Commerce Clause	Congress does not have the power to prohibit guns in an area around a school under the Commerce Clause. Gun regulation in this sense is a function of the states or local governments.
United States v. Virginia (1996)	Fourteenth Amendment	The state of Virginia violated the Equal Protection Clause regarding women by maintaining the all-male Virginia Military Institute.
U.S. Term Limits Inc. v. Thornton (1995)	Federalism	The states cannot impose term limits on members of Congress.
Vacco v. Quill (1997)	Right to privacy; Fourteenth Amendment	Upheld a state law that banned physician-assisted suicide.

The Constitution

http://memory.loc.gov/const/mdbquery.html Provides keyword/phrase searchable access to the Declaration of Independence, *The Federalist Papers,* and the Constitution. It also provides access to the Articles of Confederation and documents from the Continental Congress and Constitutional Convention from the Library of Congress.

www.archives.gov/exhibits/charters/constitution.html Provides the text of the Constitution with those sections amended or superseded in hypertext with links to appropriate amendments. The site also provides access to biographies of delegates to the Constitutional Convention and an essay by the National Archives and Records Administration on the Convention debates and ratification.

www.constitutioncenter.org This is the Web site of the National Constitution Center, which was established by Congress through the Constitution Heritage Act of 1988. Includes information on how the Constitution works, articles on constitutional issues, and aids to further research on constitutional topics.

www.gpoaccess.gov/constitution/browse.html Contains the text of the Constitution with extensive analysis and interpretation. Prepared by the Congressional Research Service of the Library of Congress.

Federalism

www.cas.sc.edu/poli/courses/scgov/History_of_Federalism.htm An overview of the history of federalism in the United States from the founding of the country through the 20th century, with links to relevant Web sites and documents.

www.cfda.gov The Catalog of Federal Domestic Assistance Web site describes federal funding programs available to individuals and private organizations, as well as to states and local governments. It provides detailed information about the grant process, including granting agencies, applicable laws and regulations, and application requirements.

www.loc.gov/rr/news/stategov/stategov.html The Library of Congress site on state and local governments provides access to Web sites of various intergovernmental lobbying groups, as well as sources on state and local government information.

Congress

http://thomas.loc.gov A service of the Library of Congress, Thomas (named for Thomas Jefferson) provides access to current and recent legislation, directories of the House and Senate, a detailed explanation of the legislative process, and a wide range of other Web sites devoted to Congress (such as the General Accountability Office and the Congressional Budget Office).

www.gpoaccess.gov/congress/index.html The Government Printing Office (GPO) provides access to essentially all congressional publications, bills, committee prints, and hearings, as well as the *Congressional Record.*

www.house.gov This is the official Web site for the U.S. House of Representatives. It provides access to all House Web sites, including individual members and the leadership, various House organizations, and pertinent publications. The rules of the House are available here, as is an extensive list of reports on Congress prepared by the Congressional Research Service.

www.senate.gov This is the official Web site for the U.S. Senate. It contains the daily schedule of the Senate, statements from the Senate leadership, a bill search feature, and information on the history of the Senate. The Senate rules are also accessible, as are the various Senate committees.

The President

www.lib.lsu.edu/gov/index.html The Louisiana State University Libraries Federal Agency Directory provides access to more than 850 executive-branch Web sites.

www.thepresidency.org The Web site of the Center for the Study of the Presidency and Congress provides access to reports prepared by the center and other publications on the presidency, as well as links to relevant Web sites, including all presidential libraries.

www.whitehouse.gov This site provides presidential speeches, documents, radio addresses, policy statements, and White House press releases, as well as links to the Executive Office of the President and cabinet department Web sites.

The Bureaucracy

www.gpoaccess.gov/fr The *Federal Register* is a daily publication of rules, proposed rules, and notices of federal agencies, as well as such presidential documents as executive orders. This is an extremely helpful source to use to follow the rule-making process.

www.gpoaccess.gov/gmanual Allows you to search recent and latest edition of *The United States Government Manual,* which provides descriptions of the functions of federal government departments, agencies, boards, and commissions.

www.usa.gov Provides extensive access to all aspects of the federal government, including agencies, laws and regulations, and statistical data.

The Judiciary

www.fjc.gov The Web site of the Federal Judicial Center provides access to reports, manuals, and other studies on the federal courts, as well as biographies of federal judges, histories of individual courts, and important legislation.

www.supremecourtus.gov The official Web site of the U.S. Supreme Court provides information on the operation of the Court, including rules and guides to filing and arguing cases, press releases, and recent decisions of the Court.

www.uscourts.gov The Web site of the U.S. Courts provides information about the federal court system, as well as various reports about the federal judiciary and statistical data. It also provides links to the Web sites of all individual federal courts.

Public Opinion

www.ciser.cornell.edu/info/polls.shtml The Cornell Institute for Social and Economic Research at Cornell University provides access to important national, regional/state, and multinational opinion survey Web sites. Each listing contains a brief description of the data.

www.electionstudies.org American National Election Studies is based on surveys of the electorate conducted every two years since 1952. The Web site provides public opinion data on such policy questions as social welfare, the role of the government, military spending, foreign policy, abortion, school prayer, and the economy.

www.ropercenter.uconn.edu The Roper Center has an extensive collection of domestic and international public opinion data. It also contains presidential approval ratings from a variety of sources and bibliographic information on articles on public opinion.

Mass Media

www.c-span.org Provides coverage of current news as well as broader policy questions such as business/economy, politics, social policy, justice, and international relations with links to live C-SPAN television and radio programming.

www.people-press.org The Web site of the Pew Research Center for People & the Press provides information about the public's attitude toward the news media, how closely the public follows major stories, and attitudes toward the traditional media and the Internet.

www.refdesk.com A directory of print and electronic media Web sites; coverage includes state, national, and international links (by country).

Political Parties

www.dnc.org The Web site of the Democratic National Committee (DNC). The site contains information on issues, press releases, and the most recent Democratic Party Platform. It also provides links to state party organizations and local Democratic groups.

www.gop.org The Web site of the Republican National Committee (RNC). Very similar to the DNC's site in scope. Provides access to information on the leadership of the RNC, state party organizations, issue statements, and affiliated Republican groups.

www.politics1.com Provides access to the Directory of U.S. Political Parties, which covers everything from the Democratic National Committee to the Workers-USA Party. For the two major parties, the site provides links to such organizations as Democratic Legislative Campaign Committee and leading elected officials of both parties in Congress.

Voting and Elections

www.electionstudies.org The American National Election Studies site provides survey data on the social and religious character of the electorate, partisanship and evaluation of political parties, political involvement and participation (voter turnout, campaign contribution), voter choice, and candidate evaluations.

www.fec.gov The Federal Election Commission Web site provides extensive information on recent election results, historical data on voter registration and turnout, electorate demographics, how the Electoral College works, voting administration, campaign finance reports and data (political action committees and party fundraising).

www.lwv.org The League of Women Voters Web site has voter information on various election-related issues such as campaign finance reform, voter participation, and election administration reform. This site helps you to find out who is running for office and candidate positions on the local, state, and national level. You can also register to vote on the site.

Interest Groups

http://clerk.house.gov The Clerk of the House Web site includes text and background on the Lobbying Disclosure Act of 1995 and information on registering as a lobbyist, including required forms. Similar information on the Senate is provided at www.senate.gov.

www.ipl.org The Internet Public Library provides access to more than 2,000 sites for professional and trade associations, cultural and arts organizations, political parties, and advocacy groups. You can search the site by keyword or browse broad headings such as business and economy, education, law, government, and politics. Entries contain a brief description of the association or group.

www.opensecrets.org The Web site of the Center for Responsive Politics allows you to identify lobbying firms and clients, and to determine how much companies and interest groups spend on lobbying. The information comes from semiannual reports filed by lobbyists with the secretary of the Senate and the clerk of the House.

Civil Liberties

http://topics.law.cornell.edu/wex/First_amendment Provides a summary of First Amendment issues, as well as links to historical First Amendment cases. It also includes recent decisions of the Supreme Court and U.S. courts of appeals, as well as links to other helpful First Amendment Web sites.

www.aclu.org The Web site of the American Civil Liberties Union provides coverage of a wide range of civil liberties and civil rights issues, including criminal justice, religious freedom, free speech, student rights, and police practices. It also provides access to the cases in which the ACLU has made statements or filed amicus briefs.

Civil Rights

www.besthistorysites.net/USHistory_CivilRights.shtml Links to sites on the civil rights movement, most of which deal with African Americans, but some of which cover Hispanics and women.

www.eeoc.gov The Web site of the U.S. Equal Employment Opportunity Commission (EEOC) provides access to laws, regulations, and policy relating to job discrimination (including the Americans with Disabilities Act). It also includes news and press releases, and instructions on how to file an action with the EEOC.

www.usccr.gov The U.S. Commission on Civil Rights Web site provides access to news releases, publications, and reports of the commission. It also provides information on how to file a complaint based on a civil rights violation and links to the Web sites of civil rights offices of federal, state, and local agencies, as well as nongovernmental civil rights organizations.

Public Policy

www.aei.org The Web site of the American Enterprise Institute, a conservative think tank that does research in a broad range of areas including economic policy, foreign and defense policy, health policy, and public opinion.

www.brookings.edu The Web site of the Brookings Institution, a liberal think tank that does research on the economy, foreign policy, and governmental affairs. This site provides short papers on a variety of policy issues known as *policy briefs,* which are accessible online.

www.fedstats.gov A source of statistical data in a variety of federal policy areas, this site can be searched by federal agency (for example, the Social Security Administration) and by subject (income, energy, and labor, for example). Search results provide a link to the Web site of the agency you're looking for and key statistics from that agency.

Economic Policy

www.cbo.gov The Web site of the Congressional Budget Office includes the current budget, economic projections, historical budget data, and current status of discretionary spending. It provides access to publications, and links to other relevant Web sites such as the Senate and House budget committees.

www.federalreserve.gov The Federal Reserve Board Web site contains press releases, statements, and testimony before Congress; minutes and transcripts of the Federal Open Market Committee; information on the Federal Reserve System; and statistical data, surveys, and reports by the Federal Reserve Board.

www.whitehouse.gov/omb The Office of Management and Budget Web site provides access to the most recent Budget of the United States Government, historical tables on the budget since 1940, news releases, and testimony regarding OMB comments on bills before Congress.

Foreign Policy

www.cia.gov The Central Intelligence Agency Web site provides access to press releases, statements, speeches, and testimony of agency personnel. It includes the CIA's World Factbook (which has country profiles).

www.defenselink.mil This is the official Web site of the Department of Defense, with press releases, news summaries, and speeches. It links to a wide variety of Department of Defense Web sites, including the Office of the Secretary of Defense, the Joint Chiefs of Staff, and the individual services.

www.state.gov The State Department Web site provides access to press releases, speeches by personnel (including the secretary of state), and a wide variety of international issues ranging from terrorism to war crimes. The site also is a source on the history of U.S. foreign policy and documents relating to U.S. foreign policy.